# On the
# Heavenly Spheres

Helena Avelar and Luis Ribeiro

ISBN-10: 0-86690-609-6
ISBN-13: 978-0-86690-609-8

Cover Design: Jack Cipolla

Published by:
American Federation of Astrologers, Inc.
6535 S. Rural Road
Tempe, AZ 85283

www.astrologers.com

Printed in the United States of America

Astrology is alive. It is whole, functional and independent.

It has been present in the human spirit from the first civilizations

when Man began his long search for meaning

It has spanned eras and cultures,

yet always remains perfectly current and relevant.


It is clear, clean, and objective knowledge: containing nothing nebulous.

Just as it must be clear for one to view the stars at night,

so too thought must be clear for one to master astrological interpretation.

# Dedication

To the students of the Academy,
who have been a constant source of improvement and inspiration to us.

# Contents

# Illustrations, Diagrams and Tables

## Chapter VII, The Houses

## Chapter VIII, The Aspects

# *Foreword*

With the vast array of astrological titles available to the reading public, to the casual observer, it might seem altogether superfluous to produce yet another. Certainly, it is a point of view with which I would have sympathy if it were not for the fact that it is a very long time indeed since a book such as this has been published—in any language.

In recent years, an increasing number of books have focused on the astrological system as encompassed by what is commonly termed "the tradition." However, no author of whom I am aware has committed the personal resources necessary to produce a work of this breadth and depth. Such dedication can be found only in those who truly love this art, and that love can be found only in those who have, by sheer hard work, discovered the glorious beauty which is astrology. Once glimpsed, there is no turning back: we must have more, see more, understand more, and is, in my opinion, the driving force behind this book.

It is my view that astrology is a divine art, a gift, to be exalted by the practitioner. Gratitude for this gift is expressed through what the artist gives of himself or herself, which ought always to be at least equal to that received. Using this kind of accountancy, it is clear from the contribution contained within these pages that the authors have obtained a very great deal from astrology.

Having gained so much, they share that with whomever will give attention to their work. How fortunate you are, dear reader, for I know how much is required in order to produce such a work of scholarship. But this is no mere copy, no simple translation from the Latin or the English of the ancient authorities. We have here a full exposition of that system and its methods which have demanded so much assiduous and conscientious study from the authors, which can be achieved only from deep understanding of and respect for the beloved art.

Rarely do I find much to recommend a modern work of astrology, very few offering much of substance and veracity. However, in this one case, I would advise that it be kept close to those ancient reference works on the shelf, used as a companion to those illuminating texts. For those who do not possess any such books, use this one as the foundation of your astrological library (very few more will be necessary)—it will serve you well for many years to come.

*Sue Ward*

# Introduction

This book on astrology is a product of our experience during many years. It is, first, the fruit of our activity as astrological teachers. It was born as a response to our students, who sought out textbooks capable of supplying the basics of astrological knowledge in a solid, structured, and practical manner. It is also the product of our research, which has given us an ever deepening understanding of the essence of astrology. This growing understanding translates within our practice into practical results with greater precision. Finally, it is a product of our contact with the reality of astrology not only in our native Portugal, but also throughout Europe and America.

Given the growing interest in traditional astrology, whether from researchers on the forefront, or from students, there was a great need for a book that explained astrology as it is, and that was written in a current vernacular and in a consistent and organized manner. Thus, this compendium emerges out of that need and is anchored by three fundamental concepts: a practical approach, an instructional structure, and the clear definition of astrological ideas.

This is a practical book, specifically directed at those who wish to learn and practice astrology effectively and substantively. It is targeted at those who seek to forge a path to learning from the wealth of astrological information currently available. Beginners will find within this book all of the fundamental basics of the art, appropriately organized and explained. Advanced students and practitioners will find a source of reference that allows them to organize all the information they need. Researchers will find in this work a guide for the study of astrological documentation.

This book is also a study guide, written as an aid to the student of astrology searching for information, and in a manner that will foster a well-grounded practice. It outlines the rules of astrology in an instructive manner and in clear and current language, thereby allowing the student to gradually acquire a complete and practical understanding. It avoids both metaphysical and overly simplistic explanations.

It is, above all, a book of astrology. It presents astrology per se, i.e., the hard nucleus of the art. It explains the astrological system through its philosophical principles, *without having to resort to concepts external to astrology*. It offers a definitive structure that sustains and provides roots for this knowledge, bridging the traditional with the current times. This book has collected the fundamentals of astrology that have been handed down by authors such as Ali ben Ragel, Abraham Ibn Ezra, Claudius Ptolemy, and William Lilly, to name only a few. In the tradition of these authors, we bring the essence of the art to today's students.

## The Astrological Tradition

In this book we often refer to the astrological tradition—a term often invoked, but rarely understood. We begin therefore, by clarifying it. When we refer to traditional astrology we are referring to the wealth of astrological knowledge practiced from the Hellenistic era to the end of the 17th century. This knowledge is a direct inheritance of the Babylonian, Greek, Arabic, and Medieval European civilizations. Its practice, which knew periods of great splendor, gradually weakened and nearly became extinct for almost two centuries (from the end of the 17th to the mid 19th centuries). Its recovery began in the 1980s, with the English republication of the book *Christian Astrology* (1602-1681), and the translation of various works from the Hellenistic and Medieval periods.

These sources gave students and contemporary practitioners the impression that the ancient astrological practice was far more complex and rich than the current one. This discovery spurred a wave of studies and translations of ancient works that slowly began to reveal the practice of astrology in all its splendor: an academic discipline of great richness and depth, capable of generating interpretations of exceptional precision in any area of human experience.

Those who pursued these studies employed the term "traditional astrology" in order to differentiate it from contemporary astrology (reconstructed upon an incomplete foundation at the end of the 19th century and which since then has already produced a myriad of divergent approaches).

Since traditional astrology emerged from this scenario of multiple lineages, some have confused it as just another approach among the many that currently exist. However, the term "traditional astrology" does not refer to just another type of astrology, but to astrology itself. Traditional astrology takes astrological practice back to its roots and returns to it its former greatness and dignity.

On our astrological journey, we studied and practiced the modern versions of astrology in their psychological and esoteric aspects. Nonetheless, it was in the traditional that we found a complete and effective system that allowed us to attain what we most sought: the essence of astrology.

**Astrology Today**

The recovery of tradition is of great significance in the current times, given that astrology has become a fad which has become widely integrated into popular culture. To consult an astrologer or to study astrology has become common practice that few find strange. This integration has helped to dust off a subject that was previously looked upon with suspicion and fear; but it has also brought with it some serious disadvantages, among them the popularization that leads to the cheapening of its quality to the lowest common denominator. As a result, anyone can freely opine on astrology, no matter how ignorant or silly that opinion, since few have sufficient knowledge to detect (and fewer yet, to counter-argue) the inconsistencies. Astrology has become a free zone for every type of opportunism and speculation. In truth, much of what today is called astrology—and accepted as such by most students—is nothing more than a collage of unconnected ideas, vaguely supported by astrological symbolism. The disinformation is so widespread that many practitioners think, in good faith, that they are working effectively, without the understanding that what they have been taught is confused, incomplete, and devoid of solid foundations. In fact, many of the current astrological systems extensively identify themselves with therapeutic and psychological approaches (often in surprisingly amateurish and irresponsible ways) and relegate the actual astrology to a secondary role.

Today, despite the vast array of available information, it is almost impossible to obtain reliable information about real astrology. The excess of information has generated an ill-defined collection of approaches and practices, where the actual astrology emerges as a mere and ever-rarefied add-on. In summary, there are more and more astrologers, and less and less astrology. Popular astrological practice has become increasingly simplistic from a technical perspective, and increasingly complicated at a conceptual level. The rules and astrological fundamentals have been reduced to generalized prescriptions, and the interpretations are immersed in an increasingly confused cloud of spiritualities, psychologies, and disparate metaphysical systems.

It is essential that astrology preserve its cohesion and depth. To misrepresent astrological knowledge is to mutilate our cultural legacy. Personally, we will not consent to that loss, nor will we passively accept that mutilation. This book is our contribution toward preserving and maintaining the dignity of astrology. It consists of a work that is instructional, organized, and overreaching in scope in order to provide students with an adequate learning method. This is a crucial step, because only those who learn appropriately can practice correctly. This is, therefore, a work dedicated to those who honor astrology and practice it correctly, whether from a technical or ethical perspective. It is through them that the cultural legacy of astrology is handed down and kept alive, whether for the current generation or for those yet to come.

## Learning Astrology

To those who want to learn astrology, it is important that the first steps be solid, because they will trace the path for future studies. For this reason, the student should have a clear idea of the nature and specificity of the subject he or she seeks to study. The student should know its history, its philosophy, and its principles. It is therefore vital that we first clarify some important points.

First, we need to reiterate what should be obvious: astrology is studied. It has laws, rules, and postulates that define it as a consistent and functional body of knowledge. These rules need to be learned by the student, both theoretically and in their practical application. It is a vast, rich, and solid body of ideas that require dedication and time to be duly assimilated.

It is equally important to recognize astrology as a specific field of study. Its goal is the correlation between celestial movements and terrestrial events. In order to attain this goal, it has specific rules (as previously mentioned) at its disposal, as well as its own techniques and tools. It is from the correct application of these rules, laws, and concepts that we derive the astrological interpretation. The student should know these rules and techniques well in order to distinguish what is and is not astrology.

Another concept is that astrology is autonomous. It does not have to rely on other areas of study to define itself nor to demonstrate its functionality. It is cohesive and self-sufficient.

Finally, it is important to understand that astrology has practical applications. It is true that astrology has a deep and very rich philosophical and metaphysical structure, but this is not limited to its theory, nor exclusively to the symbolic realm. It is a live body of knowledge, capable of being applied and tested. In its widest sense, astrology is a language, a description of reality. It generates objective descriptions applicable to the most diverse areas of life and capable of addressing all types of topics, from the most mundane to the most transcendent.

With these things in mind, we now turn to the astrology.

*Helena Avelar*
*Luis Ribeiro*

*Chapter I*
# Astrology

The world is in a constant state of change. Some changes are natural and expected, because everything on Earth is born, matures, and dies. Other changes are sudden and unexpected, reminding us that we live in an imperfect world where chaos and pain can arise at any moment. Only the immense heavens persist immutably in our eyes and, consequently, become symbols of perpetual perfection. Nevertheless, it is still possible to perceive motion even within the immutable heavens: the rising and setting of the Sun, the phases of the Moon, the movement of the planets. As the macro is a measure of the micro, the motion of the heavens produces effects on Earth—the tides, the passage of the seasons, the changes in climate.

Understanding this heavenly motion and its effects upon earthly events has always been a goal for man. For centuries, dedicated sky-watchers scrutinized the skies in search of patterns and cycles. Night after night, they studied the subtleties of planetary motion with attentive eyes. Equal attention was given to terrestrial events in an attempt to find correlations in them. In time, this effort produced fruits and allowed for the deduction of the laws that link stellar motion to worldly events. Thus, mankind discovered the key to astrology.

Many hours have been dedicated to the study and cataloguing of these laws, many scholars have dedicated their lives to the study of this knowledge, and many civilizations have contributed to its development. This endeavor has always been colored by a profound sense of reverence at the grandiosity of celestial order. In this way, astrological thought became the cornerstone that explained the universe and its meaning. This knowledge deepened and grew, producing a set of consistent principles and techniques possessing great precision and efficacy. These structures make up the astrological system that has reached us via the tradition.

## The Heavens in Motion

The Sun, Moon, and planets are the only bodies we see moving in the heavens. Each night, their movements change the appearance of the sky. Every day the Sun sets at a place different from the night before, and every night, the Moon waxes or wanes and the planets shift ever so slightly. Because of this mobility, which contrasts with the apparent stillness of the stars, these bodies become grand icons of change. It is these moveable pieces that make the astrological system a dynamic one. Incidentally, this system was conceived of in order to predict and interpret those very same movements.

In addition to their motion in relation to the fixed stars, the planets also participate in the grand rotation that "drags" the firmament—along with all its stars—from sunrise to sunset to sunrise again in the space of a day. In order to study the movement of the planets in relation to the sky, we use a system of celestial coordinates: the zodiac and its twelve divisions, the signs. The movement in relation to the horizon is measured by a system of terrestrial coordinates: the astrological houses, which divide the sky into segments projected from the horizon. Thus, the movements of the planets are measured and qualified in accordance with their position within these two coordinate systems. In other words, we measure the position of the planets in their houses and signs. Each sign and house has its own specific meaning, which is combined with the meaning of the planet in order to generate the nexus of an astrological interpretation. These meanings can then be applied in the description of any type of event—personal or collective. In this manner, astrology constitutes a system that describes terrestrial reality by means of celestial movements.

## Prediction

A natural outgrowth of this system is the concept of prediction. If it is possible to interpret celestial motion to describe the present, then logically, it is also possible to foresee future celestial movements and from these to describe a future reality. In a similar manner, it is equally possible to know the past movements of celestial bodies and, as a consequence, to describe the past reality. Astrology thus describes the reality of the present, past, and future by means of the movements of the celestial bodies and their relationship to Earth. Applied initially to natural phenomena, and then later to political and individual events, prediction has always been a chief goal of astrology.

## The Branches of Astrology

Astrological knowledge has become specialized into various branches that are defined by subject. There are four principal branches: mundane astrology, natal astrology, horary astrology, and electional astrology.

As the name implies, mundane astrology studies the mundane world. This branch examines subjects such as civilizations, human trends, politics, economics, wars, social movements, etc.—essentially, all of the phenomena affecting humanity as a collective. On the other hand, this branch of astrology is also concerned with natural phenomena, such as earthquakes, storms, and droughts, and is also known as natural astrology.

Technically, mundane astrology interprets the charts produced by annual ingresses (the beginning of the four seasons of the year), the charts of eclipses, and other relevant celestial phenomena (for example, comets), as well as the charts of nations and their governments.

Natal astrology concerns itself with nativities, or birth charts. Its subject of study is the human being: behavior, capacities and challenges, social relationships, and destiny. The principal tool of natal astrology is the natal chart, or the astrological chart for the moment of birth of the individual.

Horary astrology is the most divinatory of all the branches, because it purports to give answers to specific questions by interpreting the chart for the moment the question was formulated. Because of the pivotal importance it gives to the astrological moment—that is, to the question's hour—it is called *horary*. This branch concerns itself with all types of questions: jobs and promotions, buying and selling of goods and property, the future of relationships, legal questions, the whereabouts of lost objects and people, etc. Its primary tool is the astrological chart erected for the moment when the question was posed to the astrologer. The astrologer then applies specific interpretative techniques to answer the question.

Astrological elections are used to select, or elect, the astrological moment most appropriate to initiate an action. They allow for the selection of the right moment to, for example, begin construction of a building, launch a business, send a message, or schedule a wedding. Whereas mundane, natal, and horary charts are interpreted in order to understand the condition of a nation, individual, or question, in an election we try to construct the appropriate chart for the desired result.

There are also specialties in astrology that combine the tools of different branches. With the goal of understanding, diagnosing, and curing illness, medical astrology is the most representative of these specializations. This specialty relies on horary and natal techniques in order to diagnose a patient, on electional astrology to determine the best moment to initiate or administer a treatment, and more pointedly, on mundane in order to understand the larger social context of a particular disease.

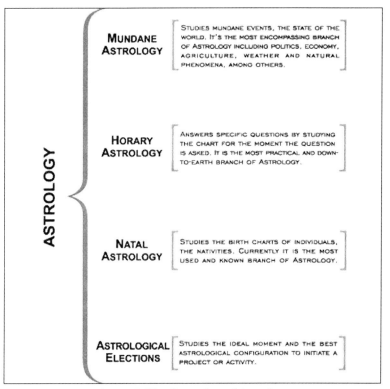

**Figure 1, The Branches of Astrology**

The rules of astrology are common to all of the branches. The difference in interpretation comes from the context that is applied to the significations of the planets, houses, and signs. Additionally, each branch also contains its own set of techniques that are particular to its study.

## Astrological Types

It is important to understand the difference between an astrological branch and an astrological type. As discussed above, the astrological branches are distinguished by their particular focus, whereas an astrological type results from the integration of a philosophy or creed into the practice of astrology. Thus, instead of one astrology, there is a proliferation of multiple variations of astrology, some more coherent and valid than others. We therefore have, for example, psychological, humanistic, holistic, karmic, esoteric, and experiential astrologies.

In most cases, the differences are more apparent than real. In reality, despite their beguiling names, many of these variants are very similar, diverging only in the name and the personal creed of each astrologer; the techniques and methods employed are usually the same. Additionally, the majority of these approaches limit their study to natal astrology and make few incursions into the other branches. Many of these variants appeal to a supposed esoteric or spiritual understanding of the natal chart, alleging that traditional astrology is purely materialistic. This, of course, is absurd, as those who study the tradition can readily attest. Astrology rests upon metaphysical principles that encompass all facets of the life of the human being, including, naturally, spirituality.

From another perspective, there exist approaches that are considered astrological in content, but which diverge considerably in technical terms from the nucleus of traditional astrology. Among these we find the cosmobiology school developed by German astrologer Reinhold Ebertin (1901-1988), whose technical principles are for the most part different from those of traditional astrology and use the mathematical relationships between planets (for example, distance proportions) as a basis for interpretation. Also of note are Uranian astrology, created by German astrologer Alfred Witte (1878-1941), which uses eight hypothetical planets, and the Huber method, created by the Swiss couple Louise (b. 1924) and Bruno Huber (1930-1999). The latter is more similar to traditional practice but relies on its own interpretative techniques (geometric figures, colors, etc,).

## Brief History of Astrology

The presentation of a compete history of astrology and its development falls beyond the scope of this book. What we present here is a very abridged version that highlights the principal moments, but which nevertheless leaves out some important references. Our objective is to give the student a general notion of the history of this discipline.

Astrology is one of the oldest forms of knowledge. Its origins are lost in time but are attested to as far back as the birth of human civilization. The observation and study of the movements of the stars emerged at a time when the lives of humans were tied to the cycles in nature. The observation of the seasons of the year and the phases of the Moon is ancient, and the regularity of these cycles is an orienting marker for humans. The significance of this knowledge was such that early on a symbolic and transcendent importance was attributed to it. The interpretative, symbolic, and metaphysical slant of these observations became the basis of astrology, while the mathematical vein appeared later to give rise to the study of astronomy. Until the 17th century these two aspects of celestial knowledge were inseparable.

### Origins of Astrology

The oldest vestiges of celestial observation go back to pre-history to myths involving known constellations, some as old as 30000 BCE. However, astrology as we know it today only began to develop after man set down roots, its origins being intimately connected with the development of agriculture (Neolithic period ca. 6th millennium BCE). The need to understand nature's cycles was essential for growing crops. In the near east, we encounter the earliest civilizations adoring the heavens and the stars and building megalithic structures in alignment with astronomical configurations or divine advice.

### Mesopotamic Period

The oldest divinatory observations involved not only the stars and planets but also other celestial factors such as rainbows, the flight of birds, or the appearance of clouds. But an astrology similar to what we might recognize today began to develop in Mesopotamia around the 2nd millennium BCE. One of the oldest and most extensive documents from this period is known as the *Enuma Anu Enlil* and consists of a compilation of astrological observations and their corresponding omens. We also know that by this time, Egypt was already assigning astrological significance to constellations, thereby timing their solar calendar. Thus, by the time of the old Babylonian period, astrology had become as important as other older divinatory methods and began to be expressed in the form of celestial omens. However, the astrological charts as we know them today did not yet exist.

The planets are the oldest factors used in astrology. By the 2nd millennium, they were already a part of the Babylonian astral religion and the characteristics of their tutelary deities were already more or less established and attributed to them, although some alterations did occur as astrology migrated westward into Greece. In contrast, the houses and the aspects did not yet exist, and calculations and interpretations followed different rules from what we use today. It was during the 1st millennium BCE that more refined observational methods and astronomical calculations began to come into use. This evolution led to the development of the zodiac and, with it, the attribution of planetary rulerships to signs.

All of the religious tapestry of this time was favorable to the development of astrology. In fact, astrology was practiced by priests who emphasized its magical, religious, and sacred aspects. Astrology was, above all, used for the study and prediction of collective events. Personal predictions were relatively rare and, in general, reserved for kings and other important figures.

Astrological development reached its pinnacle during the Persian occupation (ca. middle of 6th century BCE). During this period, the calendar was perfected and diaries of eclipses and other astronomical phenomena were compiled. The architecture of these civilizations also considered celestial phenomena: temples and palaces were oriented with stellar alignments, and large construction projects were only begun when celestial conditions were considered favorable.

## Greek or Hellenistic Period

Around 700 BCE, the expansion of trade routes and the increase of contact between the populations of the Mediterranean led to the transmission of religious and philosophical thought. Astrology captured the interest of the Greek civilization, and was further developed, transforming it into a structured discipline with scholastic standing. Very important figures such as Pythagoras ca. 571 BCE-ca.497 BCE) brought a wealth of knowledge from the Middle East that would be refined over the centuries. The geometrical theories and the great philosophies that underpin western astrology appeared. Renowned Greek thinkers such as Plato c. 428 BCE-347 BCE) and Aristotle (384 BCE-322 BCE) developed astronomy and astrology with the creation of physical and metaphysical models of the universe.

The earliest evidence for the calculation of the Ascendant dates to about 200 BCE, an innovation that permitted the precise calculation of the astrological houses. This increased mathematical precision led to the implementation of new concepts. The astrological chart, with all its components, was born. Simultaneously, natal astrology also emerged and individual birth charts gradually became more popular.

In the early centuries CE, new thinkers and noteworthy astrologers began to appear. Many manuals and treatises were written at this time. Of these scholars, Claudius Ptolemy (ca. 100-ca. 178) stands out; he compiled a large part of the astrological knowledge of the time in his work *Tetrabiblos*. Later, this work became one of the great foundations of Medieval astrology (Arabic and European).

With the slow disintegration of the Roman Empire and the adoption of Christianity as the official religion (in 313 by decree of the Emperor Constantine), the practice of astrology suffered its first decline. The Christian religion generated a strong anti-pagan current, and astrology began to fall into disfavor. The hostility toward astrology (and other disciplines such as mathematics, philosophy, and medicine) on the part of the Christian religion, seriously curbed its formal study. The situation was aggravated by the social and political uprisings that swept the Roman Empire during the following 100 years, culminating in its fall in the mid 6th century CE, when Europe entered the Dark Ages.

## Medieval Period

After 632 CE, the Arabs became one of the great world powers, occupying the Middle East, northern Africa, and southern Europe (the Iberian Peninsula). Blessed by an immense interest in all advanced learning, the Arabs sought to collect Greek, Babylonian, and Persian knowledge in order to preserve and develop architecture, medicine, philosophy, and astrology/astronomy. It is thanks to the scholars of this period that much of western astrological thought has been preserved. Around 700 CE, several celebrated thinkers whose astrological works would influence and model western astrological thought began to appear in the Arabic world. The Iberian peninsula (particularly the Al-Andalus) was at that time one of the principal scholastic centers of the world. Arabic astrologers provided continuity with Greek astrology, deepening its mathematical precision and expanding certain branches, notably horary.

With the Christian Reconquest[1] and the Crusades in the 11th century, a phase of intellectual exchange was initiated that would foster development and innovation of astrological thought in the Christian world. An appreciation for the western tradition was renewed as many Arabic and Greek works were translated. During this time, astrologers achieved important roles in society, acting as advisors to kings and nobles. Nonetheless, tension with the Catholic Church continued, making astrology a risky profession. Astrology was primarily used as a means for diagnosing health problems. It also had a prominent role in political consulting.

## The Renaissance

The 15th and 16th centuries initiated an important change in attitude: the Renaissance. The concept of the individual was expanded and the world was perceived in a different manner. The sciences and the arts were reenergized and astrology underwent some transformations. The classical techniques were questioned and some of the main principles were modified. The growing political discontentment with the Arabs (represented by the Ottoman empire), and the resurgence of Greek ideas, led to the adoption of Ptolemy's treatise as western astrology's primary source. Yet Ptolemy did not mention several significant traditional factors, and proposed a form of astrology that was divergent from that of his contemporaries. Thus, several traditional elements understood to be "Arabic innovations" were progressively discarded from the tradition. These changes created a schism between the Medieval astrologers and those of the Renaissance, engendering instability in astrological practice.

During this time the antagonism between astrology and the Catholic Church reached its apex. The Church condemned astrological judgments (a.k.a. judicial astrology) because of its political implications and because of the power it conferred to astrologers, notwithstanding the fact that many clerics were steeped in astrological knowledge. The "official" practice of astrology in Christian kingdoms was restricted to less controversial matters, namely medicine and weather forecasting. In Protestant countries, astrology was more easily tolerated; its flowering in northern Europe after the 15th century was particularly notable.

## Decline of Astrology

At the end of the 16th century, the development of the Age of Reason and the scientific approach provoked an irreparable crisis in astrology. The scientific reasoning of the age declared astrology to be a superstition, and it was considered obsolete. The final severing between astrology and astronomy occurred in 1650. The practice of astrology still had some impetus in the 17th century, but thereafter entered into a rapid decline, having, by the start of the 18th century, almost completely disappeared. In 1770, the University of Salamanca ceased teaching astrology, and the subject definitively left academic circles. Ironically, and in the context of the times, the loss of academic support constituted the collapse of the only protection keeping astrology from falling into superstition and mediocrity.

In an attempt to keep the practice of astrology alive, some astrologers sought to reconcile astrology's symbolic and metaphysical ideas with the mechanistic vision of scientific rationalism. However, their efforts produced more problems than benefits. In the hope of attaining acceptance from the prevailing views, they oversimplified the astrological system, impoverishing it in quality and function. The attempt to explain astrology scientifically led to the distortion of its fundamental principles. Astrology was relegated to popular entertainment and was increasingly ridiculed in popular almanacs at the end of the 18th century. Without adequate support or practice, the millennial astrological tradition was forgotten.

## Revival

In the second half of the 19th century, a revival of Oriental spirituality occurred. Many esoteric concepts and branches of thought were studied and recovered, and astrology was among them. The authors of this age de-

---

[1]Christian Reconquest: a period of approximately 800 years in the Middle Ages in which several kingdoms of the Iberian Peninsula (present-day Portugal and Spain) strived to retake the land from Muslim dominion.

sired not only to become restorers but also reformers of the astrological tradition. Most notable was Theosophist Alan Leo, who, to avoid being charged with violating British laws against fortune-telling, innovated the practice of character analysis from the chart.

Notwithstanding most good intentions, their work left something to be desired as it attempted to reconstruct astrology on the basis of a model that was already abbreviated and devoid of any profound knowledge of the tradition. It was upon this fragile and incomplete foundation that modern astrology found its footing. It centers almost entirely around natal astrology and discounts the tradition's predictive inflection. In addition, the modern approach lacks a philosophical structure and offers an impoverished oversimplification of interpretative techniques.

This inadequate situation gave rise to several problems. On the one hand, it allowed personal opinions—even the most ineffectual and uninformed ones—to assume an authoritative voice. As a consequence of this proliferation, astrology propagated into numerous currents and approaches, many of which lack much substance. On the other hand, it led serious practitioners to dedicate themselves to other disciplines in an attempt to compensate for the shortcomings of their astrological practice, thereby perpetuating its convoluted state.

## Modern Approach

By the 20th century, with the emergence of psychology and the increasing interest in personal growth, psychological and humanistic astrology were born, centering astrology around the human being. This marriage of astrology, psychology, and the social sciences led to the appearance of ideological movements that called for astrology's use as a tool for self-growth. The psychological language was then adapted to astrology and the concept of astrology as an adjunct to psychological counseling emerged. This astrology revolved around a sort of simplified form of psychoanalysis based upon astrological symbolism, rather than upon astrological interpretation itself.

This point of view influenced every avenue of astrological development of the 20th century. Natal astrology, which examines the individual horoscope, became the most practiced form of astrology, relegating the other branches, such as mundane and horary, to near extinction. Parallel to this, astrology was separated from the embarrassing legacy of prediction in such a way that its predictive function, an essential nucleus of astrology, became a taboo subject that was replaced by generalized forecasts.

Understandably, the increase in astrological popularization led to the emergence of simplified variations. Sun-sign astrology and magazine horoscopes are obvious products of the simplification of a once more highly complex system. In the 1960s and 1970s, a pro-spiritual culture emerged, an outgrowth of the 19th century importation of oriental philosophies into Europe and America. It was at this time that themes such as reincarnation, karma, and meditation become a part of the common vernacular. In astrology, this influx of new ideas was translated to karmic, spiritual, and esoteric approaches, varying greatly in quality. Some were serious studies, while others involved the fastening of personal beliefs to the astrological system. Meanwhile, the spiritual and metaphysical foundations of astrology remained largely ignored by the majority of its practitioners.

In technical terms, the 20th century brought to astrology the ease of calculation provided by computers. Although this is a blessing to the serious practitioner of the art, it brings with it some inconveniences because it allows those with insufficient knowledge of astrology to "professionally" cast and interpret charts.

Currently, we also bear witness to the appearance of numerous astrological techniques, some of them mere mathematical variations with little or no practical use. The thinking seems to be "what is new is good," as new techniques and approaches are invented every year. One finds, in addition to the inclusion of the trans-Saturnian planets (Uranus, Neptune and Pluto), the indiscriminate use of copious asteroids and plane-toids, leading to ever more elaborate and unnecessary interpretations.

As a reaction to the lack of objectivity in modern astrology, the 1990s brought a movement toward a more classical and traditional orientation. This was encouraged by the translation and publication of ancient texts. A comparison between the millennial practical tradition and the current one brings with it the understanding of how far contemporary astrology has strayed from its roots. And, the rediscovery of tradition resulted in a resurgence of the forgotten branches of horary and mundane astrology. Currently, astrology has begun a slow return to its origins from where it is hoped it will reemerge as an intact, solid, and functional body of knowledge. It is up to its current students and practitioners to continue to restore and venerate the astrological tradition.

# Chapter II
# The Universe According to Astrology

## Models and Perspectives

In order to understand astrology one first must understand the cosmology upon which it rests. Without this knowledge, it is not possible to obtain a real understanding of its foundation, its dynamics, or the metaphysics of astrology. The most important thing to consider is the fact that this model describes the Universe according to parameters that are astrological, which differ substantially from contemporary scientific models.

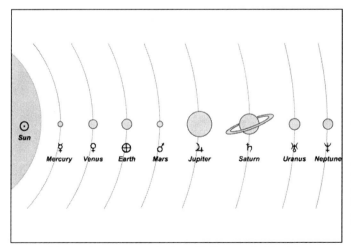

**Figure 1. Astronomical or Heliocentric Model: the Celestial Bodies Orbit Around the Sun**

When we currently speak of stars and planets, the image that most frequently comes to mind is that of the solar system with the Sun at the center and the eight known planets (as well as Earth) orbiting around it. Figure 1 depicts the image of the solar system as if observed from a point in space outside of it. Viewed this way, it is easy to forget that we reside inside the solar system and that it is from within that we see the planets and stars.[2] This representation expresses the objective reality of the solar system and emphasizes the concrete and physical reality of the planets. Albeit correct, this perspective does not express a viewpoint that is appropriate for astrology.

---

[2]This manner of viewing the solar system from the "exterior" is so rooted in our society that many forget that the planets are visible from the earth; one only needs to observe the night sky.

## The Astrological Reality

In astrology, the observational point of view is Earth. All astrological knowledge is constructed as a function of the reality observable from our planet. Thus, the planets are represented as they are seen by a terrestrial observer. To the observer, the planets appear to move around the Earth and not around the Sun. As such, it is understood that in terms of symbolism and interpretation, astrology considers the Earth as its center (geocentric perspective), not the Sun (heliocentric perspective). It is not a matter of choosing one of the models over the other, but of understanding that both represent the same reality but from different perspectives: the heliocentric model displays the solar system in its entirety, while the geocentric model displays the sky as it is seen from Earth. The key, then, is to select a model that is appropriate to the objective at hand. When the objective is the study of astrology, which observes the stars from a terrestrial perspective, a geocentric model should be adopted.[3]

## The Celestial Spheres Model

The astrological universe is remarkably well pictured in the Ptolemaic model (also known as the celestial spheres model), from which were taken the majority of the significations and behaviors of the astrological planets. In this model, the Earth is situated at the center of the universe—the point of greatest materiality. Around it, the seven planetary spheres (including the Sun and Moon), as well as the sphere of the fixed stars and of the zodiac, are grouped into concentric circles.

In addition to the spheres, says the tradition, we also find there the divine kingdoms, which transcend astrology itself and constitute a topic of theological study.

The ninth sphere, the one most distant from Earth, is called *The Primum Mobile*. It is called this because it is from this sphere that the primary motion is generated; this is the motion that causes the rotation of the heavens from east to west in the course of 24 hours.[4] *Primary motion* is the most powerful and important of all the celestial movements: it carries the stars, the Sun, the Moon and the planets around Earth. In this way, it marks the passage of the days and ascribes to the planets their power to act because it establishes when they rise, culminate, and set. It is also within this celestial sphere that the zodiac, the basis of astrological interpretation, is represented.

Just below this, we find the eighth sphere, that of the fixed stars, which constitute the starry background that is observed in the night sky. This sphere, also called the *firmament*, represents the immutable sky of the constellations and stars in all its majesty and symbolism.

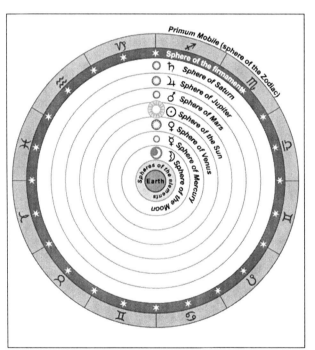

**Figure 2. Ptolemaic Model: the Celestial Bodies Depicted as They Are Seen from Earth**

---

[3]As is common knowledge, some astrologers work with the heliocentric model. This is an experimental technique that diverges from the Tradition and which will not be employed in this book.

[4]Although this apparent motion is in reality caused by the rotation of the Earth, from the perception of a terrestrial observer, it is the stars that appear to move, while the Earth (the horizon) remains still.

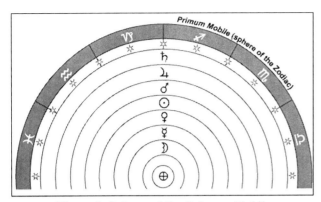

**Figure 3. Sphere of the *Primum Mobile***

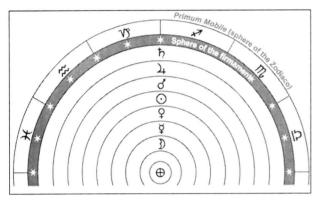

**Figure 4. Sphere of the Fixed Stars,
Also Called Firmament**

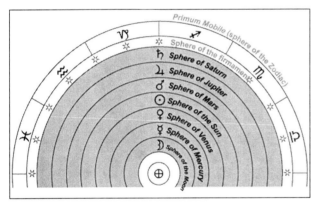

**Figure 5. Spheres of the Planets**

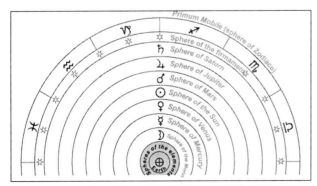

**Figure 6. The Earth and the Spheres of the Elements**

Next we find the seven planetary spheres, which contain the seven planets visible to the naked eye. The sequence is ordered according to the apparent speed of each planet. Thus, Saturn, the slowest body, occupies the seventh and most distant sphere (also known as "the seventh heaven"). Jupiter's sphere is next, then that of Mars, that of the Sun (which occupies the center of the sequence), then that of Venus, that of Mercury, and lastly, that of the Moon, the swiftest of the visible celestial bodies.

At the center, encircled by all the other spheres is Earth, differentiated by four layers that correspond to the four elements: fire, earth, air, and water. To the earth element, the heaviest, corresponds the solid part of the planet: the islands, continents, mountains, etc. Water obviously corresponds to the oceans, rivers and lakes. Above the earth and water hovers the air, which corresponds to the atmosphere and the winds. According to the tradition, these elements would have been encircled by a fiery sphere from which phenomenona, such as falling stars, comets, and the aurora borealis, would have originated (today we might establish a parallel between the fiery zone and the uppermost layer of the terrestrial atmosphere where one can observe friction and where cosmic radiation strikes).

According to the tradition, the celestial spheres are composed of a spiritual substance and, therefore, they are perfect and immutable. Only the elemental sphere, also called the sublunar world (because it is below the lunar sphere), is subject to changes due to its material nature. We know today that the heavens are not immutable nor perfect and are composed of the same substance as Earth. Nonetheless, for a terrestrial observer, this is how the celestial sphere is perceived: perfect, immutable and grand.

From an astrological point of view, these presuppositions continue in place: everything terrestrial is subject to change and will eventually encounter deterioration and decay. These changes, however, do not occur randomly but according to a rhythm dictated by the movement of the planets. As they move, the planets act upon the four terrestrial elements, changing them in different ways, and consequently causing changes on Earth and on everything it contains, including human beings. *This is the fundamental principle of astrology: there exists a correla-*

*tion between celestial movements and the events on Earth that permits us to interpret and foresee these changes.*

Thus, in order to understand how the planets and stars are related to the changes on Earth, it is necessary to identify the correlations of each planet, sign, and star with the four elements—that is, with the terrestrial world. This is the basis of astrological study.

## The World of the Elements

Now that we have a general view of the astrological universe, we'll take up the matter of the elements, the forces on Earth upon which the planets act.

### Primary Qualities

The elements, the building blocks of the universe, are in turn composed of four fundamental principles, the *primary qualities*. These are: hot, cold, dry, and moist. These qualities represent the dynamic basis of all behavior pertaining to substances: energy, density, resistance, and malleability. They explain the essence of the elements and, consequently, of matter and of the material world.

As they combine with each other, the primary qualities define the four elements. The qualities also define the essence of the various astrological factors, namely of the planets and signs. Hot and cold imprint dynamism onto the whole system, the reason they are called active qualities. These are associated with the concept of *energy*: hot represents what is active, energetic, radiant, centrifugal, luminous, light and subtle.

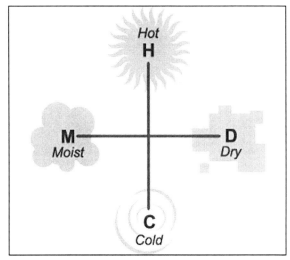

**Figure 7. The Primary Qualities**

Cold represents what is static, absorbent, centripetal, dark, heavy and dense. The hot quality corresponds to the masculine, which is expansive and dynamic; cold corresponds to the feminine, which is contracting and static. The masculine principle represents activity, dynamism, exteriorization and expansion, while the feminine corresponds with receptivity, contemplation, internalization and contraction.

Everything in the universe is subject to opposing forces, which manifest as polarities such as light-dark, expansion-contraction, movement-immobility, activity-passivity, etc. The interaction between hot and cold generates two new poles: moist and dry. The moist quality corresponds with a fluid interaction. It is generated from the quality of cold, since the increase in coldness has humidity as a natural consequence (for example, the coldness of night leads to the condensation of dew). It represents adaptability, malleability, plasticity, smoothness, and, as a consequence, those things that are easily molded, slippery, soft, and smooth. It has no form in

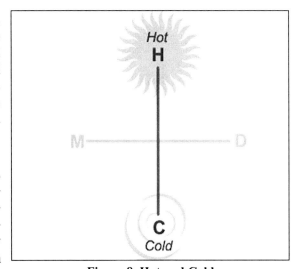

**Figure 8. Hot and Cold**

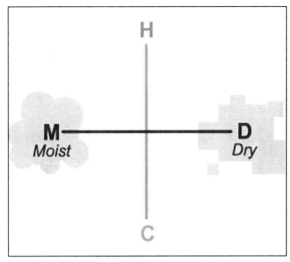

**Figure 9. Moist and Dry**

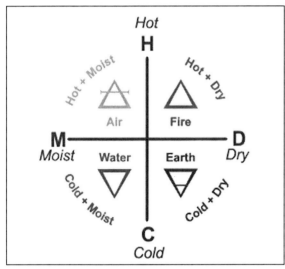

**Figure 10. The Formation of the Elements**

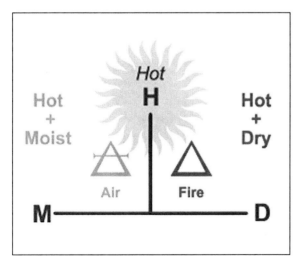

**Figure 11. Fire and Air**

itself, but represents the principles of cohesion and form.

The quality of dry corresponds with a tense interaction. It is generated from the quality hot, since the increase in heat has dryness as a consequence (as may be verified when anything is left to dry out in the Sun). It represents resistance, hardness, rigidity, and, therefore, those things that are abrasive, breakable, and cold. Its principle property is the maintenance of form: containing, giving structure, and crystallizing. Because they are generated from the active qualities, moist and dry are called passive qualities. They are connected to the concept of *form* (for example, clay is malleable when it is moistened but hardens when dried in an oven).

### Formation of the Elements

Each element is composed of two primary qualities: an active one and a passive one.

The fire element is generated from the union of hot and dry. It is characterized by an expansive, radiant action (hot) that imposes itself naturally without molding itself to the external environment (dry). From the union of hot and moist we get air, equally dynamic (hot) but adaptable (moist); it is characterized by changeable, adaptable, and dispersive activity.

Because they share the hot quality, fire and air are both masculine, dynamic, and extroverted. They are characterized by a strong centrifugal impulse (exteriorizing).

On the other hand, the connection between cold and dry generates the element earth, contracted, inert (cold), hard and non-molding (dry). From the union of cold and moist emerges water, which is characterized by receptivity and density (cold), but which is extremely malleable (moist).

Because they are both cold, earth and water are feminine elements, reflexive and introverted; they have a receptive and centripetal motion.

We can also group the elements according to their passive, or secondary, qualities.

Thus, fire and earth share the dry quality, which gives them a tense, resistant and non-molding expression. Fire resists by imposing its radiance; it consumes and burns what it touches, but also illuminates and energizes, transmitting its heat to everything. Similarly, earth resists through its persistence, its permanence. It possesses a sort of immovability that creates obstacles and blocks, but that also structures and gives cohesion and stability. Air and water share the moist quality and are therefore malleable, changeable, and adaptable. While air expresses this malleability in an active manner, expanding itself freely in any direction, water expresses it in a more retracted manner: it molds itself, absorbs influences, infiltrates itself, and dissolves structures.

The four elements are spread out over spheres according to their subtly and density. Earth is the densest element; therefore, it occupies the center of the sublunar worlds, comprising the continents. On account of its gravity (weight), it represents everything that tends toward static permanence (a rock, for example). It maintains fixed and structured forms, crystallizes and turns substances hard, giving them permanence, durability, and stability. Those things characterized by earth are dark, of dull colors, and rough, heavy, and very solid.

Water occupies the subsequent sphere since it is less dense than earth. It represents the oceans and all watery bodies on Earth. Notwithstanding the fact that it is a dense element (cold), the moist quality gives water great plasticity and adaptability. Water turns the densest materials pliable and has adhesive properties, which makes it an aggregating element, preventing objects from becoming dry and brittle. Those things characterized by water tend toward dark colors, can have reflective properties or appear to play with color (like water itself), have limited flexibility, and are lighter than those things represented by the earth element.

The air corresponds to the third sublunar sphere, representing the terrestrial atmosphere. It has lightness and the capacity to penetrate as its characteristics and is connected with great mobility and plasticity. As with water, it has a unifying role, but in a more subtle manner, so it is associated with transportation (for example, smells and sounds are transported through the air).

Those things characterized by the air are scintillating, clear, smooth, and light, displaying great agility and flexibility.

Fire, the most subtle element, occupies the outermost sphere of the sublunar worlds. Because it is extremely

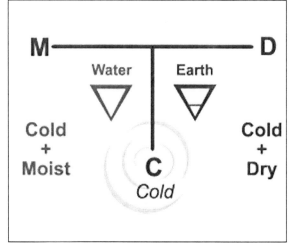

**Figure 12. Water and Earth**

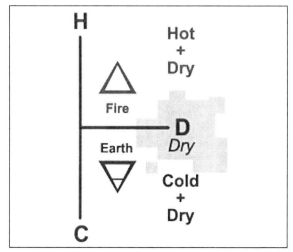

**Figure 13. The Dry Elements: Fire and Earth**

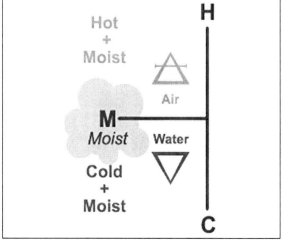

**Figure 14. The Moist Elements: Air and Water**

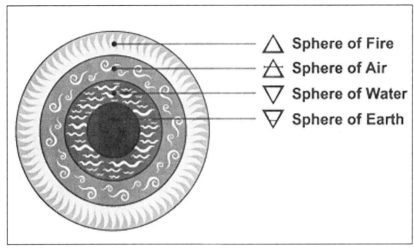

△ **Sphere of Fire**

△ **Sphere of Air**

▽ **Sphere of Water**

▽ **Sphere of Earth**

**Figure 15. The Spheres of the Elements**

rarefied, its presence is primarily detected through its qualities of luminosity, heat and "electricity." This element allows the various energy exchanges between various forms. It acts on matter by causing the creation and transformation of the varied substances, and on living beings, conferring vitality and promoting growth. Those things characterized by fire are luminous, brilliant, of radiant colors, and very alive. They are also light, but display some harshness and resistance.

Everything that exists on Earth is associated with one of the elements or with a mixture of elements (to be precise, we may state that fire, earth, air, and water are present in everything, albeit in different proportions). On the other hand, each sign and each planet is associated with a particular element. The movements and celestial configurations can therefore be interpreted from the perspective of the movement and combination of elements. We may thus recognize the elements as the bridge between terrestrial events and celestial reality. Their dynamic interrelationships, manifested via the movements of the planets and stars, give us insights into terrestrial events (for example, mundane events, the climate, human behavior, diseases, etc).

## The Temperaments

We also find the four elements in the human being as manifested through the four temperaments: choleric, sanguine, melancholic, and phlegmatic, associated respectively with fire, air, earth and water.

**Figure 16. The Temperaments, 16th Century Illustration**

The temperaments define what the ancients called the *complexion* of each individual: the set of their physical and behavioral traits, as well as their psychological and metabolic predispositions. Thus, to each temperament is associated a group of behavioral patterns, a specific physical structure, and a humor, which is its physiological counterpart. Each human being exhibits a predominant temperament, but the remaining three will also be present in the constitution, albeit in smaller proportions. This system of temperaments constitutes a type of ancient psychology that allows us to make complex and subtle assessments of the motivations, behaviors, and dynamics of each individual. This evaluation is extremely useful not only in natal astrology but also in medical astrology.

### Choleric

The choleric temperament unites the qualities of hot and dry and is associated with the fire element. It manifests as enthusiasm, energy, and rapid actions. It produces resolute, courageous, and ambitious personalities, always ready for action, enterprising and enthusiastic, and never capitulating to obstacles. If rightly moderated, it gives the native a spirit of leadership and strong will. Although enthusiasm isn't easily lost, the choleric tends to change his or her mind frequently and to start several projects throughout life. The focus of interest is on action and conquest, rarely letting details deter the intent. The choleric can sometimes be precipitated and inconstant. Due to a lack of patience, this temperament is not given to study or investigation.

In emotional terms, the choleric is not very emotional and "dryness" may cause him or her to be rigid and insensitive. Impatience makes this individual lack grace in expression to the point of rudeness and hostility. The choleric reacts with great intensity to threats or external challenges, being capable of aggression or even violence. In extreme cases, the combined lack of sensitivity and easily expressed rage can result in cruelty.

If the choleric temperament has traces of melancholic, the personality tends to be more moderated in its actions. In this combination the dry quality predominates, which indicates a tendency to retain ire, giving rise to mistrust and bad temper. Nevertheless, this combination of temperaments produces greater constancy, curiosity, and a capacity for study because the coldness of the melancholic moderates the heat of the choleric.

The presence of the phlegmatic temperament cools the constant activity and the impulsive reactions of the choleric because it involves a mixture of complimentary primary qualities (hot and dry on the one hand, and cold and humid on the other). However, it provides a greater emotional contrast, generating all manner of temperamental attitudes.

If the secondary temperament is sanguine, there will be greater lightness and sociability, which attenuates the choleric expression. There is more sensibility and adaptability (the humid moderates the harshness of the dry), but because both share the hot quality, it produces a certain agitation and inconstancy.

In physiognomic terms, the body of a choleric tends to be slim, muscular, and hairy. The frame is average or short. The skin is coarse, hot, and shiny, of a yellowish or reddish tone. These traits may be modified by other temperaments.

In the medical/physiological realm, the choleric temperament is associated with the humor known as *yellow bile* (the term bilious is often synonymous with choleric). According to the ancient medical system, this humor, which is centered in the gall bladder, would have been used to process the remaining humors; it confers movement and action and heats up the body.

### Sanguine

The sanguine temperament combines the qualities of hot and moist and is associated with the air element. As in the choleric type, it produces a dynamic and active personality, but the moist quality makes the native more versatile and adaptable. The sanguine is characterized by a vivacious, spontaneous, and enthusiastic personality that is very communicative and sociable. Interests comprise a great many topics, and when properly tempered, it produces curious, studious, and inquiring individuals.

In emotional terms the saguine is very sensitive and cries easily, a way to shed worries and anxieties. For this reason the individual does not harbor anger and is naturally happy and friendly. Extreme fluidity can lead to dispersion, a lack of concentration, and a notorious lack of perseverance. Other negative aspects are a lack of organization and discipline, as this temperament can be very unsettled and restless. Immense sociability may also degenerate into superficiality and futility.

If melancholic traces are found, the dynamic nature and changeability of the sanguine acquire more structure and consistency. The vivacity and joy of this temperament become contained and the individual becomes more serious and conservative. It is a very balanced combination due to the contrasting primary qualities present (hot and moist with cold and dry) and is particularly suited to the pursuit of study and investigation.

When the secondary temperament is phlegmatic, you get a sort of dissolution of the sanguine temperament; the presence of cold makes the individual less exuberant and happy, more self-oriented yet still changeable and adaptable due to the moist quality. When combined with the choleric traits, a predominance of hot results and the temperament becomes more intense and bellicose and loses some of its natural flexibility. Nevertheless, the dryness confers greater determination and perseverance to the actions of the sanguine.

In physiognomic terms, the sanguine temperament tends to be meaty and full, but not fat. The frame is robust, of medium height or tall. The skin is smooth, hot and moist to the touch, with a white or rosy hue.

In medical terms, the sanguine temperament is associated (as its Latin name indicates) with the *blood*. Conveyed through the arteries and veins, this humor has, as its function, the elimination and transport of substances through the body.

*Melancholic*

The melancholic temperament combines the qualities of cold and dry and is associated with the earth element. It has a reflective and focused personality. The native can be very reserved and moderated in his or her manifestations, and is sometimes underestimated, seeming to be less interested in things than is actually true. The focus of attention is objective reality, which gives the individual a sense of firmness and security. He or she tends to deal better with facts than with ideas, and is generally resourceful and a good investigator, displaying a great deal of patience and perseverance.

In emotional terms, the individual is not very demonstrative and, as with the choleric, is rigid in sensibilities. Nonetheless, the cold quality makes these people especially susceptible, with a tendency toward melancholy, pessimism, and when emotionally unbalanced, toward depression. Due to the dry quality, they have difficulty crying and may retain their anger for a long time, to the point of resentment. The rigidity of this temperament makes one obstinate, distrustful, and anti-social, which can lead to loneliness. Generally critical and a perfectionist, this individual in extreme cases is capable of being intolerant and cold-hearted.

When combined with the sanguine temperament the melancholic becomes more sociable, bold, and joyful, exhibiting a temperament that is less pessimistic and defensive. This combination is considered very measured as it combines opposite qualities. If it exhibits a choleric undertone, it acquires greater vitality, sociability, and determination. Nonetheless, the predominance of the dry quality confers onto it a solitary and individualistic attitude. In its fusion with the phlegmatic temperament, the predominance of the cold quality is emphasized, which reinforces the tendency toward reserve and withdrawal. This produces behavior similar to that of the pure melancholic type, albeit a bit more flexible and adaptable.

In physiognomic terms, the body of the melancholic has a medium frame and a slim constitution. The skin is coarse and cold to the touch, generally of a yellowish or dull color, with sparse hair that tends to be dark.

The melancholic temperament is associated with the humor known as *black bile*. Its function is the retention of substances in the body, bestowing consistency to the muscle tissues and liquids, solidifying the bones, and strengthening memory and sobriety. Its containing organ is the spleen.

*Phlegmatic*

The temperament of the phlegmatic combines the qualities of cold and moist and is associated with the water element. It produces a sensitive and reserved personality with a powerful emotional drive. Like the melancholic, this type is introverted, but the presence of the moist quality confers plasticity and adaptability. The native has a powerful emotional drive, making decisions that help maintain security and emotional well-being. By favoring emotional reasoning, these people can be very subjective and inconstant ("what is good today because it makes me feel safe, may be bad tomorrow because it makes me feel poorly") to the point of incongruence. They are interested in what they feel and in what promotes security, and they delight in new people and new situations, but can easily adopt a passive and slightly lazy attitude. Generally speaking, the melancholic has a timid and serene temperament.

While emotion and feelings are the basis of behavior, these are seldom openly expressed. Although sensitive and sympathetic, the phlegmatic avoids commitments and is not terribly expressive. He or she tends to assume conciliatory roles and is excessively patient. When emotionally disturbed, this temperament can become reclusive and apathetic. Due to its excessive malleability, laziness and indolence can become larger flaws. Only with difficulty, does the individual display courage and determination in his or her actions. At its worse, emotional self-centeredness manifests as greed, cowardice, deceit, and emotional manipulation.

When combined with the choleric temperament, the phlegmatic gains greater agility and daring. The general expression tends to be more tempered due to the opposing qualities of each. The union with the sanguine type adds the hot quality, which gives it greater joy and vitality, minimizing the more static aspects of the phlegmatic type. The predominance of the moist quality reinforces the flexibility and elasticity of the personality. The combination with the melancholic temperament gives emphasis to the cold, enhancing the introverted characteristics. Nonetheless, the addition of the dry quality confers greater solidity and perseverance to the native.

In physiognomic terms, the phlegmatic tends to have a medium to short frame, with a meaty, flaccid body that can easily put on weight. The skin is soft and cold to the touch, generally pallid or white in color and with little hair.

This temperament is associated with the *phlegm* humor, which is responsible for the maintenance of the body's temperature and its lubrication. In modern terms, it corresponds to mucus and lymph.

**Practical Application**

The temperaments constitute the key to interpreting a natal chart. Each planet or sign has affinities with each of the four temperaments, which serve as the basis for defining its characteristics. The combination of a planet's temperament with the temperament of the sign where it is posited makes up the core of astrological interpretation. In natal astrology, it is possible to determine the temperament (or combination of temperaments) of each individual. This global temperament describes the core characteristics that condition all the behaviors, motivations, and personal dynamics of the individual. The manifestation of the details shown in the chart is always underscored by the predominant temperament. For example, an astrological marker of aggression will have a different expression in the chart of a choleric temperament (which reinforces an aggressive tendency) than it will in the chart of a phlegmatic (which will weaken it). Temperament is, therefore, a type of background upon which the personality will manifest.

The calculations for determining the individual temperament are somewhat complex, as they take into account the relative weight of the four primary qualities in the chart. In the scoring, one considers the primary qualities of the Ascendant and the Moon (as well as the planetary configurations associated with it), to which is added the temperament of the solar sign. This assessment will be covered in greater detail in an Appendix.

*Chapter III*
# The Astrological Chart

The horoscope or astrological chart is the principal working tool of an astrologer. It is a diagram containing a representation of the position of the planets in the sky as well as the degree of the Ascendant and of the various astrological houses. The term *horoscope* means "the observation of the hour"; that is, the observation of the configurations in the sky at a specific moment in time. Originally, the term referred solely to the rising sign with terms like "map," "figure," or "chart" being used to refer to the astrological diagram. Currently, the term horoscope also arises as a synonym of the astrological chart.

To calculate an astrological chart it is necessary to know the exact date, hour and location of the event represented in it (the birth of a human being, a question, an event, etc.). It is on the basis of these spatial and temporal coordinates that we calculate the positions of the planets in signs (in relation to the zodiac) and in the houses (in relation to the horizon). It is then simply a matter of consulting tables of planetary positions, ephemerides, and tables of houses. After making a few adjustments, we obtain the necessary data necessary to construct the chart.

The calculation of a chart or astrological figure requires, above all, rigor. To do this, one must certify that all the data obtained are as accurate as possible. Generally, the hour is the most problematic because it is normally considered superfluous information. For this reason, it isn't always recorded, and when it exists, it is usually approximated. The hour is, nevertheless, the principal element required for the construction of a horoscope. Without it, it is not possible to calculate the Ascendant and derived angles, the house cusps, nor the exact position of the Moon. In truth, without the time there is no horoscope in the real sense of the term (since *horoscope* means "to observe the hour." In such cases, one can only obtain approximate positions for the planets in the signs, which are insufficient for an effective astrological study. For this reason, the student should always determine the hour with the greatest precision possible.

> Basic instructions for the calculation of an astrological chart are found in Appendix 7, Astrological Chart Calculations

In the case of natal charts, one should try to obtain the birth hour from a family member, preferably one present at the moment of birth and whose recollection is trustworthy. Birth certificates will generally provide a reasonably approximate time, although one should count on some rounding. In any case, one should be careful with errors, delays in registering birth times, poor transcriptions, etc. It is worthwhile, if possible, to compare the data of the official records with those of the family member's recollection.

In case of doubt, an approximate hour is better than none, although it should not be considered a definitive time. From a probable birth time, it is possible, through rectification techniques, to search for a more proximate time. This, however, is only viable if the margin of error is not greater than 30 minutes.

When dealing with the charts of celebrities, one can never be too careful. In these cases, it is always necessary to obtain the source of the data; that is, the exact origin of the date and hour of birth. Unfortunately, many professional astrologers neglect this convention and circulate charts without sources to the point where there are often in circulation charts of the same person with different birth times and even dates. Sometimes "invented" hours or Ascendants appear, simply derived from the supposed intuition of the astrologer. These data should be regarded as hypothetical and of little astrological value until a reliable source (human or documented) confirms such conclusions. Recall that the role of the astrologer is not to guess signs or Ascendants, but rather to interpret, as correctly as possible, the horoscopes constructed from reliable data.

Only in the case where the hour is unknown should one resort to a partial calculation where only the approximate sign positions of the planets can be known. In any event, it is always preferable to calculate a chart without a birth time than to invent an Ascendant. When the hour is unknown, it is advisable to calculate the planetary positions for noon and obtain the average planetary positions for that day. Again we repeat that any interpretation based upon these data is very incomplete and will only give a general idea of the behavior of the individual (or of the dynamics of an event). The individual particularities, in all of their complexity and depth, can only be identified in a comprehensive astrological chart.

## The Representation of the Astrological Chart

There are several ways to draw a horoscope or figure. The most common design, which is used in this book, consists of three concentric circles:

- The first and outermost circle depicts the 12 signs of the zodiac and contains a ruler representing the 360 degrees.
- The second circle is also divided into 12 parts, but these are unequal divisions. It represents the 12 houses and is further subdivided into two circles, and the outermost of the two depicts the degrees and minutes where the house begins, i.e., the house cusp. The interior and wider circle contains a representation of the planetary positions with its glyph, degree, sign, and minute.
- The third and innermost circle can either depict the title of the horoscope or the lines corresponding to the aspects (the angles that each planet makes to one another).

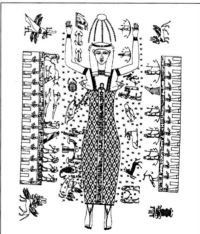

### The Horoscope Through History

The first known horoscopes consisted of simple lists where the planets' sign positions were indicated; there were no diagrams. Later, we find some representations of astrological charts in tombs and buildings in the form of reliefs or paintings, which simultaneously fulfilled an informative, decorative, and sacred function.

In the Greco-Roman period, simple diagrams appear with the positions of the planets in the signs and houses. Generally, these charts had

**Figure 2. Egyptian Horoscope**

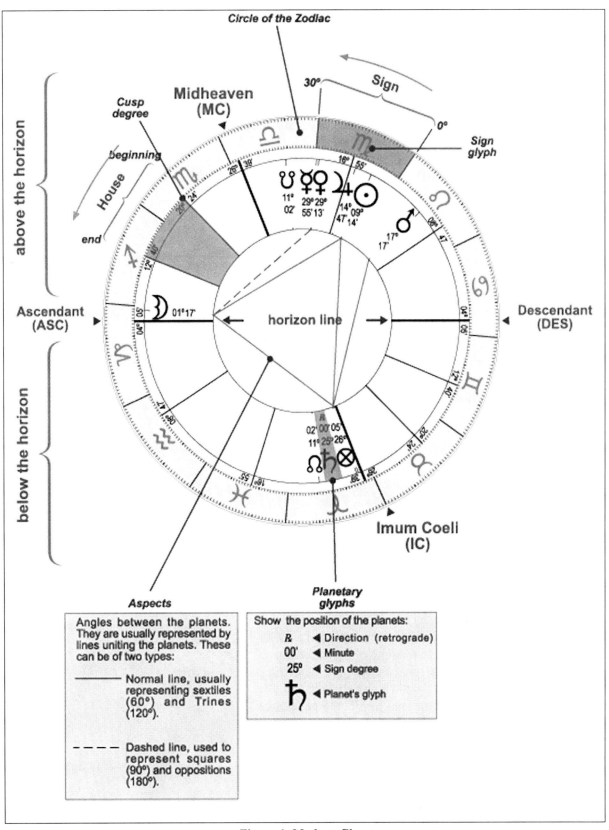

**Figure 1. Modern Chart**

a square format and were divided into 12 areas representing the 12 houses. Inside each area we find a symbol (or name) of the planet and its respective sign position, with the degree and minute of its location.

The square style continued into the 17th century with only slight aesthetic variations reflecting the period and culture. The choice of a square format is due, on the one hand, to its ease of drawing, and on the other hand, to the fact that its interpretation was based upon the four angles (or principal houses) which form, in these charts, a central "cross." Here are some examples:

In some charts the houses occupied the whole square, while in others (generally in the more recent charts) a central square was left blank so that the author could write in the title and data of the astrological chart.

To read a square chart, first identify the 12 houses and next observe the positions of the planets. If the planet is in the sign of a particular house, it is generally drawn on the cusp of that house. If it is in the next sign, it is placed in parallel to the next house (which begins with that sign). In the majority of the diagrams, the degrees and minutes of each house and planet are indicated. (See Figure 7 on page 24.)

In other versions, dotted lines are drawn to separate planets located in different signs but in the same house. In some texts, the authors take artistic liberties, introducing much variety and imagination in their designs.

Currently, there is a preference shown for the circular astrological chart, which in the majority of cases also includes a wheel with the zodiac. This sophistication is due no doubt to technological advances that exempt the student from the arduous task of drawing the figure by hand; if this were not the case, the square chart would still be in use as it is easier to draw. In fact, if we observe the horoscopes of the beginning of the 20th century, we find that they are very simple, consisting simply of a circle divided into 12 parts (houses) within which is noted the positions of each house, and inside, the position of the planets by sign.

Later, the central space of the wheel begins to be used to depict the angular relationships between the planets, known as aspects. This is the type of chart most used today.

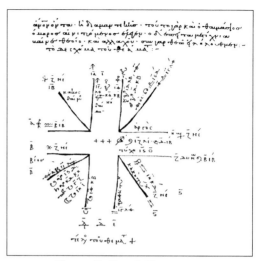

**Figure 3. Greek Horoscope**

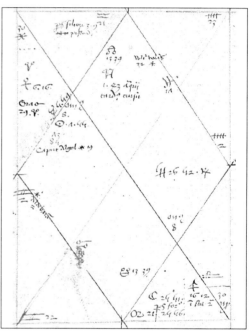

**Figure 4. Medieval Horoscope**

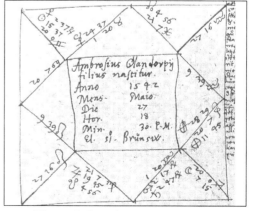

**Figure 5. Renaissance Horoscope**

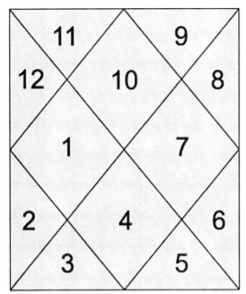
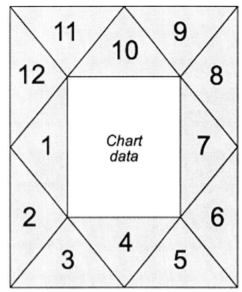

**Figure 6. The Houses in Square Charts**

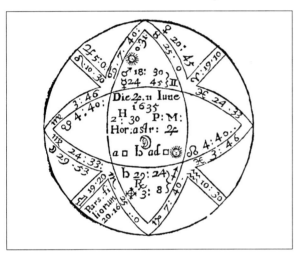

**Figure 8. A "Circular" Square Chart**

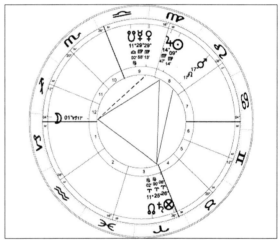

**Figure 10. Circular Chart with Aspects**

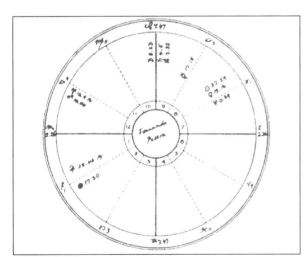

**Figure 9. Circular Chart,
Beginning of 20th Century**

From this idea emerged many variations whose differences are based solely upon aesthetic preferences. Despite the variations, they all convey the same information.

Of all the options available today, what is most important is that the diagram present the astrological information in a clear, complete, and unequivocal manner. A diagram with these characteristics is, in reality, the first step to a quality astrological delineation.

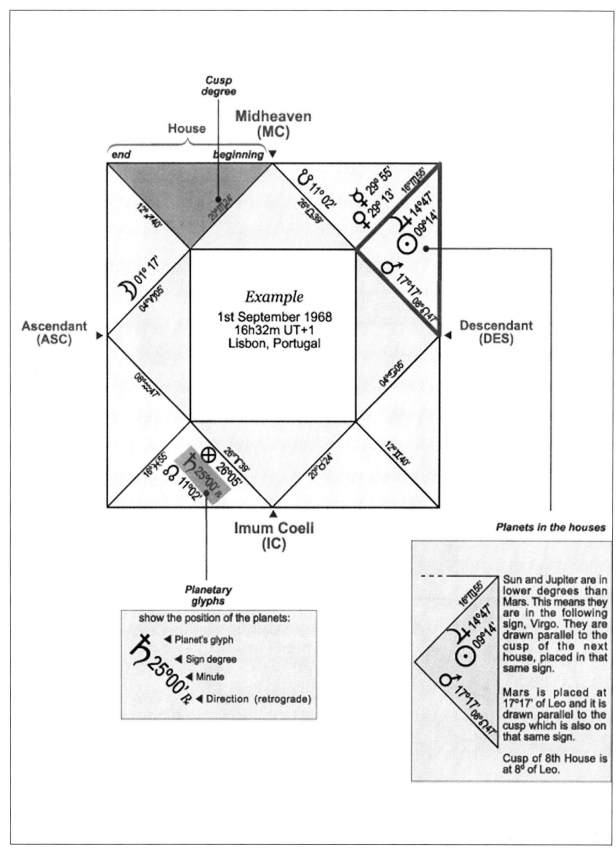

**Figure 7. How to Read a Square Chart**

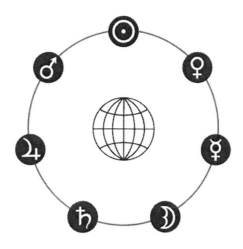

*Chapter IV*
# *The Planets*

The planets are the foundation of astrology because it is through their motion, expression, and interaction that it is possible to make astrological interpretations. To the terrestrial observer, the planets first appear as luminous points similar to stars. However, the planets change position over time, while the stars always maintain their relative positions.[5] In fact, the word "planet" comes from the Greek word πλανητος, which means "errant" or "wanderer." Because of their erratic movement relative to the immutable stars (the celestial sphere), the planets stand for what is mutable in the sky. They are therefore, the principal instruments for measuring and qualifying those celestial changes, as well as their counterparts in the mundane world.

## Planetary Symbols

In astrology, each planet is represented by a symbol or glyph. These symbols represent some of the attributes of the planet or the deity associated with it. The origin of the current symbols is Greco-Roman, and although they have undergone changes over time, their basic symbolism has survived. (See Appendix I for a brief reference to the more ancient planetary symbols.)

☽      The Moon is perhaps the most recognizable and simple of all the glyphs. It is the lunar crescent.

☉      The Sun is represented by a circle with a point in the center, symbolizing origin and the creative force.

♂      Mars is represented by a circle from which an arrow emerges. Although it has changed over time, the arrow has been a constant feature.

♀      Venus is represented by circle atop a cross. Some authors say it depicts the mirror of Venus.

☿      The symbol for Mercury is similar to that of Venus except that it has a crescent at the top. It is inspired by the caduceus (a staff with two intertwined serpents) of the Greek god Hermes (whom the Romans called Mercury).

♃      The glyph for Jupiter, which looks like the number 4, is in reality a variation of the letter Z for Zeus, the Greek name of this deity.

---

[5]Although the relative position of the stars is not immutable, their motion is too slow to be detected in terms of individual, or even civilization life-spans.

♄     The symbol for Saturn is composed of a semi-circle capped by a cross. It may possibly represent a scythe, symbol of the deity associated with the planet.

## Planetary Hierarchy

In order to understand the nature and function of each planet, it is necessary to study its position in the celestial scheme introduced in Chapter II. The first thing to keep in mind is the order in which the planets are distributed. This is known as the Chaldean order[6] and it distributes the planets from the most distant sphere to the nearest in order of its apparent motion. Thus, the slowest planet, Saturn, starts the sequence, followed by Jupiter, Mars, the Sun, Venus, Mercury and the Moon.

### The Luminaries and the Planets

First, we need to distinguish between *luminaries* and *planets*.[7] The luminaries, or lights, are the Sun and the Moon. Due to their luminosity, they are considered the king and queen of the heavens. The Sun/Moon pair make up a basic model, structured in terms of polarities, for the classification of the planets: masculine/feminine, diurnal/nocturnal, etc.

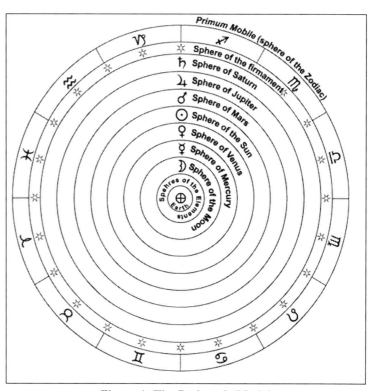

**Figure 1. The Ptolemaic Model and the Chaldean Order**

The Sun is the most important star. According to the Chaldean order, it is located in the center of the sequence of the planetary spheres and is considered the symbolic center of the heavens. The Moon is his consort, the queen of the heavens. The remaining planets constitute the royal retinue, the court of the luminaries. This distinction of the two luminaries from the five planets is fundamental in the astrological system.

### Superior and Inferior Planets

The Sun, as the center of the planetary sequence, also influences the manner in which the planets are grouped. Mars, Jupiter and Saturn, which are above the solar sphere and therefore have a motion slower than the star-king, are called superior planets. Since they move more slowly, their effects are considered more enduring and prolonged (particularly those of Jupiter and Saturn). Those situated in the sphere below that of the Sun—Venus, Mercury, and the Moon—are called inferior planets. As these planets move more quickly, their effects are more transitory; but their action is more dynamic. It should be noted that the inferior and superior classification has nothing to do with good or bad qualities, but rather with their positioning below (inferior) or above (superior) the solar celestial sphere.

---

[6]The name of this sequence comes from the Chaldeans, a people originating in the Middle East in the region currently occupied by Kuwait and southern Iraq. The Chaldeans are among the oldest civilizations to practice astrology.

[7]Sometimes, the luminaries are designated "planets" simply because it is more convenient to do so. There is no problem in this designation as long as one realizes that the Sun is in reality a star, and the Moon a natural satellite of the Earth.

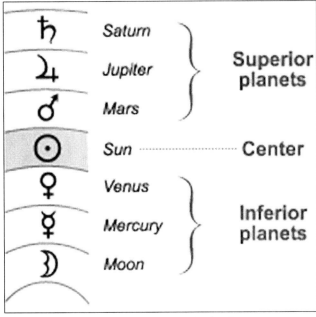

**Figure 2. Superior and Inferior Planets**

### The Modern Planets

Uranus, Neptune and Pluto, the trans-Saturnian, or modern, planets are not visible with the naked eye, so they do not belong in the scheme of traditional astrology. Since the objective of this book is to provide the student with the foundations of traditional astrology, the three modern planets will not be included in the central body of this work. (The integration of these three planets in the astrological system is covered in Appendix 2, The Modern Planets.)

## The Nature of the Planets

The nature of each planet derives from various astronomical characteristics determined by direct observation. These are: movement, appearance, luminosity, and most important, the position in the celestial scheme.

### The Temperaments

In astrological theory, each planet is characterized by two primary qualities that synthesize its essential nature and that are attributed to it according to its position in the celestial spheres.

The **Sun**, due to its heat and radiance, has a hot and dry nature. Nevertheless, its action is considered moderate, because without its heat and light, life would not be possible. Its luminosity varies depending upon the season, which also contributes to its moderation. However, when a planet is too close to the Sun, the star-king loses his temperate nature and becomes exceedingly hot and dry. Then it is said that this planet is combust.

The **Moon** is characterized principally by the moist quality, due to its association with the oscillating motion of liquids. Second, it has coldness as a quality because it complements the Sun, which is hot. However, since the amount of light reflected by the Moon is oscillating, it is said that she becomes relatively hotter when she is waxing (and therefore more luminous), and relatively colder when she is in a waning phase (thus, darker).

**Saturn**, the most distant visible planet has an excessively cold and dry quality.

**Mars**, on the other hand, has an excessively hot and dry quality, due to its proximity to the sphere of the Sun.

**Jupiter**, lying in between these two extremes (the coldness of Saturn and the heat of Mars), has a temperate and fertile nature; it is moderately hot and moist.

**Venus** has the same temperate nature as Jupiter. It is hot because it is close to the sun's sphere, and moist because it is situated in the inferior celestial spheres, thus closer to the Moon. Some authors nevertheless attribute a cold quality to it because it is a feminine planet. In any event, it is its moist quality that is important; as to its temperature (hot or cold), the most relevant aspect is its moderation.

**Mercury** has an ambiguous nature. It may be dry, because it is never far from the Sun, but it is also moist because it is near the lunar sphere. Thus, the qualities of this planet tend to change according to the circumstances in which it finds itself. Notwithstanding this, some authors say that Mercury's own nature—that is, when it is alone and does not interact with other planets—tends to be dry.

Three other important concepts that describe the natures of the planets are derived from classifying the planets through their qualities: the existence of the malefics and benefics, masculine and feminine planets, and diurnal and nocturnal planets.

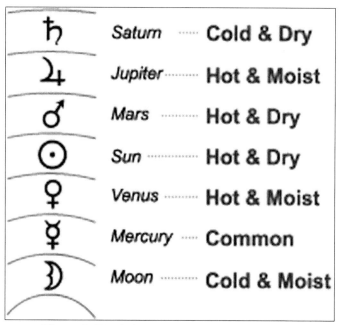

Figure 3. The Primary Qualities of the Planets

### Malefic and Benefic Planets

The terms "malefic" and "benefic" may be the most misunderstood in modern astrology. The confusion arises by equating, in a simplistic and judgmental manner, the term benefic with good and the term malefic with bad. Due to the current insistence on what is politically correct, and to a lack of astrological knowledge, these terms are frowned upon in current astrological vocabulary. First, it is important to recall that the origin of astrological symbolism comes from an essentially agricultural context, not from a judgment about individual morality. Thus, the terms malefic and benefic are essentially functional. If a planet brings benefits and has an expression that is naturally constructive, it is considered benefic. If a planet represents effort, deprivation, and restriction, and has a naturally destructive expression, it is considered malefic.

With regard to the nature of the planets, the terms benefic and malefic arise in connection with the primary qualities. Hot and moist are favorable to life and growth, as they produce fertile environments. The contrary qualities, cold and dry, are antagonistic to life, as they produce wild and sterile environments. To understand this symbolism, one need only ob-

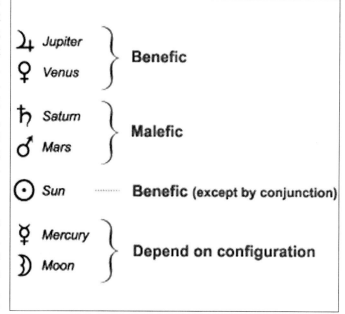

Figure 4. Benefic and Malefic Planets

serve the growth of plants, which develop better in warm, humid environments. Thus, Jupiter and Venus, which have the qualities hot and moist in moderate quantities, are considered benefic planets—favorable to life, growth and prosperity. Saturn is excessively cold (and dry), while Mars is excessively hot (and dry). Because of this, they are considered contrary to life, representing the principles of destruction and decline, which is why they are considered malefics. In agricultural terms, Saturn symbolizes frost, which gives rise to "cold burns," while Mars is the searing heat that weakens the plants and the drought that kills them. In the human body, the cold of Saturn represents, for example, a state of hypothermia, while the excessive heat of Mars may be associated with feverish states.

Since Saturn is the slowest moving planet, its effects are more prolonged, so it is known as the great, or greater, malefic. Mars is faster, so its effects are not as long lasting; therefore, it is called the minor, or lesser, malefic. Of the benefics, Jupiter moves more slowly and thus is called the greater, or greater, benefic, while Venus, moving more quickly, is known as the minor, or lesser, benefic.

The Sun is generally considered a benefic because it is the giver of life and light. Nevertheless, if it is too close to another planet, it is considered malefic since its heat "burns" and its light "blinds." The Moon and Mercury, due to their variable natures, alternate between benefic and malefic. As usual, the classification of Mercury depends upon its combination with other planets. When it is located near benefics, it assumes their benefic traits; when near malefics, it acquires a malefic expression. The Moon tends to be benefic when it is waxing, since it carries more light and heat, and is relatively more malefic when it is waning, since it loses light and heat.

There are still a few important points to consider with regard to this classification. First, it is important to emphasize that the benefic and malefic role of a planet depends greatly upon the context of its interpretation. If the destruction of something is beneficial (the destruction of a disease, for example), then a malefic planet becomes favorable. In addition, we should also recall that in this chapter we're only discussing the basic nature of the planets. This may be altered by various circumstances (namely, their position by sign and house) whereby a malefic planet may have a benefic effect and vice-versa. Lastly, we need to consider that all excesses are destructive and, therefore, malefic. For example, although heat and humidity are generally beneficial to life, their excess favors the growth of fungus and promotes rotting; thus, under certain circumstances, they may be considered malefic. Again, it all depends upon context.

## Gender: Masculine and Feminine

Just as previously stated, everything in the manifest universe can be classified into two genders: feminine and masculine. The classification "masculine" refers to an extroverted and active expression, while the term "feminine" refers to an introverted and receptive expression. However, in the case of the planets, it is their effect (or manifestation) that is classified, not the planet as an entity. We might consider that the planets are essentially neutral, being capable of manifesting either feminine or masculine qualities. Nevertheless, in their effects, certain polarities may predominate.

Again, it is the primary qualities that are at the basis of this classification. Thus, the essentially humid planets, such as the Moon and Venus, have a predominantly feminine expression and are given the feminine gender. The essentially hot or dry planets, such as the Sun, Jupiter, Mars, and Saturn, tend toward the masculine. Again, Mercury is considered neutral, and capable of expressing both tendencies, depending upon the circumstances.

When a planet is positioned in a feminine sign, its expression will be "feminine," more reserved and discrete; when situated in a masculine sign, it acquires a "masculine" expression, more direct and visible. In general terms, a planet is considered to be more comfortable and stable when it finds itself in a sign of its same polarity (masculine planets in masculine signs, and feminine planets in feminine signs). In the inverse situation (masculine planets in feminine signs, and feminine planets in mascu-

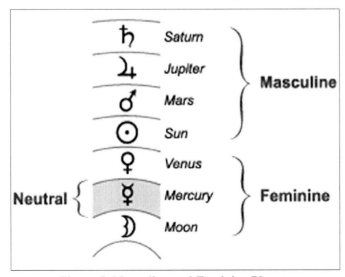

**Figure 5. Masculine and Feminine Planets**

line signs) the expression of the planet occurs less easily because it is assuming a role contrary to its natural expression.

## Sect: Diurnal and Nocturnal

This classification arises from the basic division between day, dominated by the Sun, and night, governed by the Moon. Diurnal sect contains the planets that have an affinity with the day. Their expression is facilitated by the heat and dryness of the day, which equates to a more extroverted, active, and visible expression. The nocturnal sect includes the planets whose expression is enhanced by the humidity and cold of the night, and is characterized by a more introverted, reflective, and discrete expression.

The diurnal planets are the Sun, Jupiter, and Saturn, and the nocturnal planets are the Moon, Venus, and Mars. The classifications of the Sun as diurnal and the Moon as nocturnal are self-evident because the former defines the actual day, and the latter is the celestial body that illuminates the night. Jupiter, as a masculine and hot planet, has an expansive and active expression when diurnal, while Venus, a feminine and moist planet, has a more natural expression when nocturnal. Saturn and Mars are special cases because their classification does not come from an affinity between sect and essential nature, as is the case with the others. Since we're dealing with planets that are considered malefics, a different criteria is used: instead of emphasizing its nature, we seek to moderate it. For this reason, it is associated with the sect that compensates for its excesses and makes its expression more constructive. Thus, Saturn is integrated into the diurnal sect so that its extreme cold is mitigated and its destructive expression tempered by the heat of the day. The "paralyzing" and covert actions of this planet are compensated for by the activity and visibility of daytime. On the other hand, Mars, an extremely hot and dry planet, has its expression moderated by the cold and humidity of nighttime. The abruptness and sharpness belonging to Mars, are in this way compensated for by the reflective and intro-

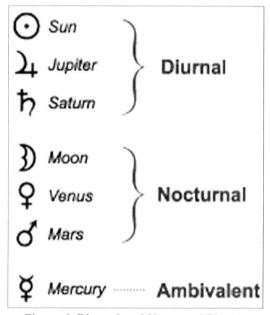

**Figure 6. Diurnal and Nocturnal Planets**

verted nature of the night. Mercury, being a neutral planet, can have both a nocturnal or diurnal expression, depending upon its position by sign and its relation to the Sun.

## Sect Implications in Planetary Expression

Similar to gender, the nocturnal and diurnal condition of a planet affects its expression. A diurnal planet will have a stronger and more stable expression when it is located in the diurnal hemisphere, while the inverse occurs with a nocturnal planet.

The Sun is the most important factor since it marks the separation between day and night. Obviously, when it is located above the horizon, the horoscope is classified as diurnal, and when it is below the horizon, the horoscope is nocturnal. Jupiter and Saturn are diurnal if they are above the horizon in a diurnal horoscope, and below the horizon in a nocturnal horoscope, or expressed in another way, when they are on the same side of the horizon as the Sun.

The Moon, Venus, and Mars are considered nocturnally positioned when they are below the horizon in a diurnal horoscope—that is, when they are on the side of the horizon opposite the Sun.

The condition of Mercury (neutral planet) depends upon its position by sign and other factors.

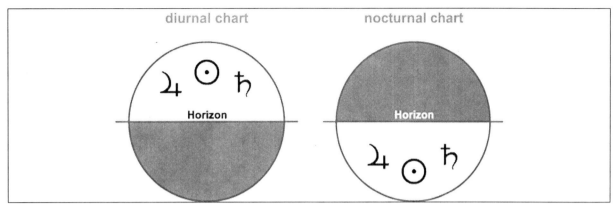

**Figure 7. Diurnal Planets in a Diurnal Condition**

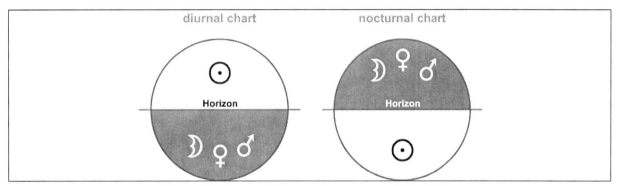

**Figure 8. Nocturnal Planets in a Nocturnal Condition**

## Characteristics of the Seven Planets

The characteristics and qualities of a planet are derived from a combination of the various facets of its nature. Thus, a planet is first described by its temperament (primary qualities), gender, sect, and malevolence or benevolence. To these basic characteristics are added others of a mytho-symbolic nature. Many of the practical expressions of the planet (for example, Venus, goddess of love, and Mercury, messenger of the gods), as well as some characteristics of astronomical content (color, brilliance, velocity, cycle, etc.) are included. The nature of the planet thus results from a combination of all of these descriptive levels. Below is a description of the natures of each of the seven traditional planets:

### Saturn ♄

Saturn is a diurnal, masculine planet, dry and cold. It is associated with the earth element and the melancholic temperament.

Saturn is the most distant and slowest of the five traditional planets. Its distance makes it a symbol of cold, austerity, and hardness. In this respect, Saturn represents isolation, distance, and limitation, but also responsibility and seriousness. Its pale brilliance represents night and darkness, all that is black, sinister and obscure, and by extension, fear, the occult, and evil. Seen another way, it also represents deep thought, making it a symbol of memory, reflection, and strategy. The slow motion of Saturn makes it a representative of time, maturity, old age, decline, and finally, death. Thus, Saturn becomes a planet of antiquity, whether as the wise and respected sage, or as the decrepit and senile old man. It is also a symbol of containment, frugality, structure, hard work, and austere actions that demand order. Its actions always imply responsibility and duty.

Saturn is the greater malefic, and because its nature is cold and dry, it is contrary to life, which is hot and moist. It is considered a malefic because it limits, concludes, and causes decline. In its dignified expression, it signifies depth, severity, and rigor. It represents reserve, thriftiness, strategy, and patience. In a more debilitated expression, Saturn represents miserliness, pettiness, fear, jealousy, and malicious actions. It also symbolizes stubbornness, mistrust, and pretense.

## Jupiter ♃

Jupiter is a diurnal, masculine planet, moderately hot and moist. It is associated with the air element and the sanguine temperament.

Jupiter is one of the most brilliant planets in the sky, only surpassed by the brightness of Venus. Its radiant and luminous expression, in combination with its slowness and distance from Earth, make it a symbol of harmony, well-being, and kindness. In many mythologies, Jupiter is associated with the heavenly king. Its tempered nature, its role as mediator between the extremes of cold and heat (Saturn and Mars), and its clear radiance make Jupiter a symbol of the intermediary and legislator—he who promotes temperance. Jupiter thus symbolizes moderation, justice, religion, law, and magnanimous actions. Because it is a slow-moving planet, Jupiter is one of the *Chronocrators,* or Markers of Time, as is Saturn. Their conjunction cycles represent important changes in societies and civilizations.

This planet is known as the greater benefic because its moderately hot and moist nature is beneficial to life. This fact makes Jupiter the representative of abundance, growth, and balance. In its dignified expression, Jupiter represents modesty, sobriety, and justice. It expresses magnanimity, loyalty, and daring. It is a symbol of the aspiration to high ideals reached through honorable and just means. Honor, nobility, and religiosity belong to its nature. It also represents indulgence, generosity, and charity, and its actions are direct and moderate. Jupiter's debilitated expression gives rise to extravagance, obstinacy, fraudulent actions, and hypercritical religiosity. It can be pompous, boastful of knowledge and status it doesn't possess, and express itself in a rude manner. It can represent ignorance and carelessness.

## Mars ♂

Mars is a nocturnal and masculine planet, excessively hot and dry. It is associated with the fire element and the choleric temperament.

Mars is the swiftest of the superior planets and has a characteristic reddish-orange color. Due to its nature, Mars is a planet of action and courage, and its actions imply combat, struggle, challenge, and competition. It is thus associated with fire and war. This planet is known as the lesser malefic because its excessive nature makes it incompatible with life. Mars is thus representative of violence, conflict, aggression, and destruction.

When dignified, it is defiant, daring, confident, and unflappable; it puts victory above all else and often risks itself. It is combative, valiant, and a lover of war and bellicose things. It does not submit itself freely to anyone or anything, and likes to announce its actions. When debilitated, Mars expresses itself through boasting and immodesty. It goes from being combative to becoming a bully, getting involved in confrontations, disrespect, and violence. In extreme cases, it is turbulent, precipitous, and careless; shows no respect for others; and can be ungrateful, covetous, and greedy.

## Sun ☉

The Sun, the lord of the day, is masculine and its nature is moderately hot and dry.

The Sun is the king of the stars, the greatest luminary. It is the giver of light, heat, and life, a symbol of radiance, power, and force. It represents the creative principle and is a symbol of the divine. It is also a symbol of sight since its light enlightens, revealing the truth. It represents dignity, nobility, and authority figures in general, and the father figure in particular.

Its element is fire. But the fire of the Sun is moderate: it illuminates and warms, in contrast with the fire symbolized by Mars, which destroys. Due to its qualities of moderation and light, the Sun represents vital energy and spirit, the principle underlying all things. However, if the Sun is too close, it becomes excessive: its light blinds and its heat consumes.

When dignified, the Sun represents fidelity, promises kept, and the ability to govern. It symbolizes prudence, good judgment, majesty, and status, and the search for fame, honor, and riches. It also indicates sumptuousness and magnificence. If debilitated, the Sun indicates arrogant, prideful, and disdainful behavior, when its nobility is false and its discernment weakened. Its manifestations are restless, disorderly, dominating, and inconsequential, and there is an underlying feeling of personal entitlement.

## Venus ♀

Venus is a nocturnal feminine planet. Its nature is moderately hot and moist (cold and moist, according to some authors). It is associated with the elements of air and water, and the sanguine and phlegmatic temperaments.

Like Jupiter, its tempered nature leads to fertility and growth. Venus is the most luminous planet in the sky, representing beauty, grace, softness, and delicacy; it is known as the lesser benefic. Venus symbolizes the principle of love, both conceptually and in the carnal sense of the term. Friendship, accord, fraternity, and sympathy are all under its jurisdiction, as is passion, sensuality, sexuality, dating, and marriage. Another aspect of Venus' expression is the playful side of life: games, entertainment, and indulgences and pleasures of all types. In its negative aspect, it represents the distortion of all those facets. Thus, it equally indicates luxury, licentiousness, superficiality, and vanity.

When dignified, Venus suggests peace and serenity. All actions are realized in good faith, without malice or distrust. Its expression is pleasant, composed and joyful, although not given to work or effort, and little attention is given to intellectual questions, disputes, or discussions. It symbolizes love, play, and artistic matters (particularly with regard to music). In a debilitated state, Venus represents laziness, extravagance, unruliness, and bad company. It equally symbolizes greed, jealousy, infidelity, and licentiousness.

## Mercury ☿

Mercury is a neutral planet. Its nature varies, assuming the traits of the position where it is located and of the planets it contacts. Some authors state that it has a dry nature when it is isolated and does not interact with other planets.

Due to its variability, Mercury represents the principles of communication and contact. It is the messenger of the gods. Mercury symbolizes all forms of communication, transportation, commerce, and trade, as well as language, writing, and education. It also represents the intellect, which is responsible for these activities.

When in a dignified condition, Mercury represents the subtle and strategic intellect, debate, eloquence, discrimination, and cultural refinement. It leads to the investigation of mysteries and knowledge in a perceptive and shrewd manner, and represents the ability and desire to learn, and a love of travel and desire to see other places. Mercury also represents curiosity, ingenuity, and commerce.

When debilitated, its actions are frenetic and argumentative, leading to discord. It represents a disorganized mind, and can indicate a teller of tall tales or an easily deceived fool. In the extreme, it represents deception, malice, shallow conversation, lies, and boasting. Another aspect of a debilitated Mercury is provocation, mockery, and derision.

## Moon ☽

The lady of the night is feminine and of a cold, moist nature.

The Moon is queen of the celestial bodies, the lesser luminary. Its symbolism is intimately connected with the Sun, its consort and counterpart. Like the star-king, the Moon is a symbol of life, representing organic life, biological forms, and matter (as a counterpart to the solar vitality). The Moon represents the cyclical process of birth, growth, and decay, which the Sun nourishes with its vital energy. This symbolism of the Moon is directly related to the Moon's phases: the New Moon is associated with birth, the waxing phase to growth, the Full Moon to fullness, and the waning phase to decline. Due to its apparent fluctuations, the Moon indicates change, variability, and inconstancy.

The light reflected from the Moon makes it a symbol of mirrors and of the soul. Due to its moistness, the Moon is also a symbol of the feminine. All female figures are under its jurisdiction: mother, wife, queen, etc. The public and the masses are also represented by this celestial body. It represents the average person, as well as the populace.

When dignified, it indicates kindness, love of liberty, novelty, and the propensity for change. It suggests adaptability and the capacity to learn any task. The Moon's actions are oriented toward the present, but have a hesitant and tentative quality to them. When debilitated, it represents the drifter and inactive or lazy people, and also the drunk or the lunatic who lacks status or ambition. In the extreme, the Moon depicts inertia and passivity.

## Rulerships and Associations of the Planets

In addition to its essential nature, the planets are also associated with other aspects of daily life, namely colors, tastes, minerals, and places. These attributions have an affinity with the nature of the planet. For example, Saturn, a cold and dry planet (therefore, sterile and unfavorable to life), appears naturally associated with freezes, winter, cemeteries, and graves. The visible characteristics of the planet also contribute to these associations. For example, Venus the most luminous planet, is associated with bright colors, while Mars, being of a reddish hue, appears naturally associated with red and derived tones.

> Important Note: all of the associations presented here refer to the basic nature of the planet. They may be modified by the position of the planet in a house or sign.

It is important to note that this type of association is not applicable to all branches of astrology. Many of them should be used within the context of specific techniques, namely in the description of objects, places, and people (horary astrology), in the determination of diseases (medical astrology), in the description of individuals (natal or horary astrology), and in the localization of events (mundane astrology).

## Colors

The association of planets with colors is especially relevant in the description of objects, clothes, animal furs, and others, and is particularly useful in horary astrology. For example, an item of clothing signified by the Moon will have light colors, varying between white and blue-green.

Saturn ♄     Black or black mixed with yellow, dark green, leaden gray.

Jupiter ♃     Light colors, yellowish or brownish white, bright or glittering colors, solemn colors: blue, purple, burgundy red.

| | |
|---|---|
| Mars ♂ | Red, yellow, bright fiery colors, saffron. |
| Sun ☉ | Bright yellow, golden, orange, scarlet, purple, solar colors in general. |
| Venus ♀ | Pure white, pastel and milky colors, luminous and light tones (some authors mention green). |
| Mercury ☿ | Complex colors, multicolored patterns, mixtures, bluish gray, some metallic tones. |
| Moon ☽ | Light blue, white, pale green, silver. |

## Odors and Flavors

The planets can function as descriptive aids, in particular for places and foods. They are also used for the selection of medical treatments and talismans.

| | |
|---|---|
| Saturn ♄ | Astringent and unpleasant odors, acetic and offensive odors, bad smells; bitter, sour, or aggressively unpleasant flavors. |
| Jupiter ♃ | Sweet smelling things and any pleasant and moderate odor; sweet and bittersweet flavors. |
| Mars ♂ | Aggressive and spicy odors; bitter and strong flavors that burn the tongue |
| Sun ☉ | Pungent odors; flavors that are rich, bittersweet, strongly aromatic, or spicy but nice and moderate. |
| Venus ♀ | Odors that incite to pleasure and lust; flavors that are tasty, sweet, fatty, moist or delicious. |
| Mercury ☿ | Composite odors, subtle but penetrating; mixed and complex flavors. |
| Moon ☽ | Fresh, wet, and mild odors; salty, bland, or slightly bitter flavors. |

## Places

The places associated with the planets are particularly useful in horary astrology to find objects, animals, or missing persons.

| | |
|---|---|
| Saturn ♄ | Deserts, dark places, caves, holes, mountains, graveyards, ruins, coal mines, wells, and dirty and bad smelling places. |
| Jupiter ♃ | Places of worship, buildings with a religious function, courts of law, and clean and tidy places. |
| Mars ♂ | Blacksmith shops, furnaces, chimneys, brick and pottery ovens, places where fuel is burned, and slaughter houses. |
| Sun ☉ | Royal courts, palaces, grandiose showrooms (theaters, opera houses, salons), and majestic buildings. |
| Venus ♀ | Gardens, fountains, wedding suites, pretty chambers, dance schools, and places of pleasure and amusement. |
| Mercury ☿ | Places of commerce, shops, markets, schools, libraries, public spaces, and casinos. |
| Moon ☽ | Fountains, streams, springs, ports, docks, rivers, lakes, aquariums, fish pounds, swimming pools, bath houses, roads, and desert places. |

## Minerals

The mineral associations can provide information about the material from which a lost object is made, and be useful in the production of talismans. There are many variations of this table. The one presented here is the more common.

| | |
|---|---|
| Saturn ♄ | Metals: lead, loadstone, scum from other metals, debris; any impure of bad quality material. Gems and minerals: sapphire, onyx, jet and other black stones, stones that are hard to polish |

or have sad colors (grey, black).

| | |
|---|---|
| Jupiter ♃ | Metal: tin. Gems and minerals: amethyst, sapphire, emerald, marble, and stones that are easy to cut. |
| Mars ♂ | Metals: iron and antimony. Gems and minerals: hematite (loadstone), jasper (especially blood stone), arsenic, and sulphur. |
| Sun ☉ | Metal: gold. Gems and minerals: jacinth, diamond, carbuncle, chrysolite (olivine), and ruby. |
| Venus ♀ | Metals: copper and brass. Gems and minerals: coralline, coral, alabaster, lapis lazuli, beryllium, and chrysolite (olivine). |
| Mercury ☿ | Metal: mercury. Gems and minerals: topaz, silex, and all stones of diverse colors. |
| Moon ☽ | Metal: silver. Gems and minerals: selenite, moonstone, rock crystal, and all soft stones. |

## Physical Appearance

These associations of the planets are used particularly to describe the physical appearance of individuals. They have practical applications in natal, horary, and medical astrology.

| | |
|---|---|
| Saturn ♄ | Dry and lean figure, slightly bent, medium stature, pale completion, and dark hair and eyes. |
| Jupiter ♃ | Pleasant figure, upright stature, pinkish completion, oval and full face, fair hair, light eyes, and strong thighs. |
| Mars ♂ | Strong body, medium stature, reddish completion, round face, coarse hair of a fair color (tending toward red), and light piercing eyes. |
| Sun ☉ | Large and strong body, ruddy skin, big round eyes, and generally light hair with a tendency to baldness. |
| Venus ♀ | Medium body, light but not pale skin, dark and beautiful eyes, and abundant (usually light colored) hair. |
| Mercury ☿ | Tall and slim figure, dark skin and hair, big forehead, thin lips and nose, and long harms and hands. |
| Moon ☽ | Full figure, round face, light skin, abundant hair, and short and fleshy hands. |

## Professions

These associations indicate vocation and skills, as well as describing people.

| | |
|---|---|
| Saturn ♄ | Professions associated with the earth are given to Saturn: those who work toil it, such as farmers and gardeners; those who work below it, such as miners; those who work with minerals such as stonemasons, brick makers, coal merchants, potters, those who work with tin, asphalt layers; and construction professions. |
| | Saturn rules religious professions that imply isolation, such as monks, or auxiliary church personnel, such as sextons. It indicates activities associated with old age, such as retirement. Saturn is also connected with pastoral professions and, in general, professions that deal with livestock, stables and stable hands, and hide tanners. Another type of Saturn profession is associated with debris and its cleaning, such as plumbers, chimney-sweepers, sanitation workers, and in general, professions considered of a low social status. For this reason, it also rules beggars and those who work odd jobs. Saturn is also connected with those who deal with death and cadavers, such as grave diggers and morticians. |
| Jupiter ♃ | Jupiter rules professions associated with the law and with politics, such as judges, senators, chancellors, lawyers, and law professors; religious professions such as clerics, bishops, |

priests, vicars; and professions associated with advanced education, such as graduate, university and college students.

Mars ♂   Because it is associated with war, Mars represents conquerors, generals, captains, commanders, military people in general, armorers, police officers, and bailiffs. Mars also represents physicians, surgeons, and pharmacists, as well as professions associated with fire, such as alchemists (chemists), metalworkers, and firefighters. It also rules professions that rely on metal or cutting tools, or those who work directly with metals, such as blacksmiths, tanners, barbers, tailors, carpenters, cobblers, watchmakers, butchers, bakers, and cooks. Other professions under this planet are dyers, athletes, and movers. In its negative aspect, Mars symbolizes all tyrants and oppressors, usurpers, executioners, and thieves.

Sun ☉   Kings, princes, emperors, dukes, marquises, counts, and nobles, and those in administrative, high-status, and power positions, such as magistrates, butlers, and courtesans.

Venus ♀   Since it is associated with pleasure, Venus represents musicians, singers, and game players. In the arts and crafts, silk and fabric traders, embroiderers, dressmakers, painters, jewelers, designers, decorators, and all professions connected with aesthetics and beauty are associated with Venus.

Mercury ☿   Mercury is associated with authors, philosophers, mathematicians, astrologers, merchants, secretaries, clerks, poets, orators, ambassadors, teachers, printers, money traders, accountants, lawyers, salespeople, transporters, messengers, delivery personnel, and letter carriers, as well as thieves, liars, and swindlers.

Moon ☽   The Moon rules seafarers, sailors, fishing personnel, producers and sellers of alcoholic beverages, bartenders, delivery workers and messengers, carriage drivers, taxi drivers, hunters, millers, housekeepers, midwives, and nurses.

## Meteorology

These planetary associations govern weather forecasting (natural astrology) as its goal. It is important to note that this branch of astrology follows very specific rules regarding the planets and the chart as a whole.

Saturn ♄   Cloudy skies, thick dark clouds, cold weather, and eastern winds.

Jupiter ♃   Serene, good weather, and northern winds.

Mars ♂   Reddish clouds, thunder and lightning, pestilential airs (dry and hot), and western winds.

Sun ☉   Weather according to the season of the year, and eastern winds.

Venus ♀   Good weather in summer, rain or snow in winter, and southern winds.

Mercury ☿   Windy and turbulent weather, and sometimes rain and storms.

Moon ☽   Weather according the planet it contacts, thus reinforcing the planet's nature.

## Planetary Periods

In the tradition, each planet rules specific periods of time, known as planetary periods. These periods are divided into maximum, greater, middle and lesser years. In practice, these values are used every time it is necessary to calculate the duration of an event. The maximum years are used with events on a historic scale (for example, the foundation of a dynasty), while the remaining periods refer to more human time scales. The lesser and maximum years are obtained from the geocentric periods of the planets (zodiacal and/or synodic cycles). The greater years result from the total number of degrees corresponding to the Egyptian terms of the planet (in the case of the Sun and the Moon, they are symbolic numbers). The middle years result from the average of the lesser and greater years. The following listing shows the planetary periods:

| Planet | Lesser | Middle | Greater | Maximum |
|---|---|---|---|---|
| ♄ Saturn | 30 | 43,5 | 57 | 256 |
| ♃ Jupiter | 12 | 45,5 | 79 | 246 |
| ♂ Mars | 15 | 40,5 | 66 | 284 |
| ☉ Sun | 19 | 69,5 | 120 | 1461 |
| ♀ Venus | 8 | 45 | 82 | 1151 |
| ☿ Mercury | 20 | 48 | 76 | 461 |
| ☽ Moon | 25 | 66,5 | 108 | 520 |

**The Ages of Man**

The planets are also associated with different phases of human life. Every stage of life is generically under the rulership of a planet which bestows upon it its attributes and characteristics. The first years of life, marked by rapid changes and by a total dependency upon the parents, are under the dominion of the Moon. Infancy, whereupon the development of communication and of the rational faculties are experienced, is under the rulership of Mercury. The hormonal changes of adolescence and the development of social skills are dependent upon Venus. Youth, a phase when the young adult seeks to conquer a place in society is governed by the Sun. Maturity, the stage for the consolidation of strength and of the capacity to act, is associated with Mars. The pinnacle of life, a stage of reflection and of the attainment of honors and or recognition is under the jurisdiction of Jupiter. Finally, old age, marked by natural decline and by the limitations of age, is attributed to Saturn.

| Planet | Years | Ages | Phase of Life |
|---|---|---|---|
| ☽ Moon | 4 | 0 - 4 | The Baby |
| ☿ Mercury | 10 | 4 - 14 | Infancy |
| ♀ Venus | 8 | 14 - 22 | Adolescence |
| ☉ Sun | 19 | 22 - 41 | Youth |
| ♂ Mars | 15 | 41 - 56 | Maturity |
| ♃ Jupiter | 12 | 56 - 68 | Pinnacle of life |
| ♄ Saturn | 30 | 68 – 98 | Old age |

After 98 years, the cycle repeats.

**The Phases of Gestation**

The tradition associates the nine months of fetal gestation with the planets according to the Chaldean order. The first month is attributed to Saturn and corresponds to the initial phase when pregnancy may or may not proceed. The second month is under the jurisdiction of Jupiter, a benefic and fertile planet that stimulates growth and the multiplication of cells. Mars is next, ruler of the third month, which energizes gestation with its heat and activity. The fourth month, governed by the Sun, corresponds to the phase when spirit directly influences matter, bestowing upon it the human form. In the fifth month, from the nature of Venus the organs are completed and sensibility increases. Next is Mercury's month, the sixth month when the ability for movement increases. In the seventh month, under the auspices of the Moon, the baby completes its form and the use of its organs. If it is born during this phase, it may now survive on its own. Saturn returns to rule over the eighth month, cooling down and firming up the form; it is considered less promising for there to be a birth during this phase than in the previous one due to the excessively cold nature of this planet. Finally, the cycle completes itself in the ninth month, ruled by Jupiter, whose abundance and fertility protects the baby and favors birth. The following listing shows the phases of gestation and their planetary rulers:

| Planet | Month | |
|---|---|---|
| ♄ Saturn | 1st | Beginning, fixation |
| ♃ Jupiter | 2nd | Multiplication |
| ♂ Mars | 3rd | Activity, heat |
| ☉ Sun | 4th | Human form, Spirit |
| ♀ Venus | 5th | Sensitivity |
| ☿ Mercury | 6th | Movement |
| ☽ Moon | 7th | Vitality, completion of form |
| ♄ Saturn | 8th | Consolidation, hardening |
| ♃ Jupiter | 9th | Birth |

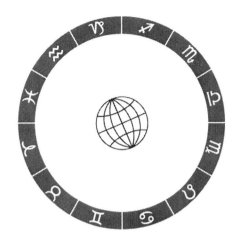

## Chapter V
# The Zodiac and the Signs

The word zodiac comes from the Greek Ζῶον, which means life or animal. The zodiac is, therefore, the band of life, or the band of animals, because many of the constellation images found along this band depict the figures of animals (ram, bull, lion, etc.).

The zodiac is generated from the apparent movement of the sun around the Earth during the course of the year. (In reality it is the Earth, that in its translation movement, circles the sun; but this is not what is visible by a terrestrial observer.) This apparent motion, traces a line, known as the ecliptic, around the Earth, and it is along this line that the Moon and the planets move through space.

Because the apparent trajectory of the planets does not coincide exactly with the ecliptic, a band of about 16° in width (8° above and below the ecliptic) was defined to encompass the total area where the visible planets move. It is this band that is called the zodiac.

This band and its divisions, the signs, are the principal point of reference in astrology. In it are measured the movement of the planets, as well as the variations in their qualities and effects as they cross the different signs.

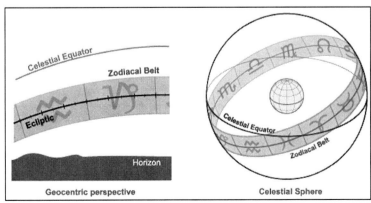

**Figure 1. The Zodiac**

### The Zodiac and the Signs

The variations in light and heat caused by the motion of the Sun throughout the year produce the four seasons: spring, summer, autumn, and winter. Therefore, both the seasons as well as the zodiac arise from the motion of the Sun and are intimately connected to it. In fact, the zodiac was originally conceived of as a calendrical device in order to "measure" the seasons. In this way, the zodiac is divided into four distinct areas, each one corresponding to a season of the year. The points of division are on the spring equinox, the summer solstice, the autumn equinox, and the winter solstice; that is, the points where the Sun finds itself at the start of each season.

The zero point of the ecliptic (and of all celestial references) is the spring equinox, also known as the **vernal point**. This equinox marks the point at which days and nights are of equal length. From that point on, the days gradually increase in length, while the nights become shorter. The weather becomes warmer, and heat joins the accumulated humidity of winter, producing fertility and growth. It is a time of agitation, of great "simmering" in the natural world. Springtime is a hot and humid season, associated with the air element and the Sanguine temperament. Its symbol is a germinating seed.

Maximum daylight is reached during the summer solstice. The Sun reaches its highest altitude in the sky and the weather continues to become warm, drying the humidity of springtime. It is a time for the maturation of fruits because of hotter days. Summertime is a hot and dry season, associated with the fire element and the choleric temperament. Its symbol is a germinated seed.

During the autumn equinox, the days and nights again have the same length. After this point, the height of the Sun in the sky gradually begins to decrease. The weather remains dry, but temperature and hours of daylight decrease. It is a season for harvest and for preparing for the harsh times of winter. The autumn is a cold and dry phase, associated with the earth element and with the melancholic temperament. The symbol of autumn is a fully grown plant that has begun to dry out:

The shortest day (and the longest night) is reached at the winter solstice, producing a sea-

**Figure 2. The Four Seasons**

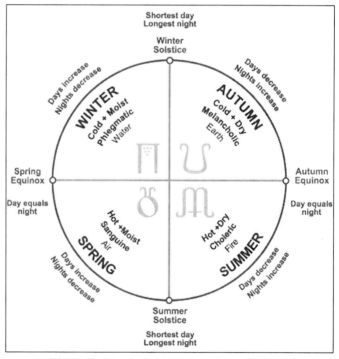

**Figure 3. The Qualities of the Four Seasons**

son of cold and sparse daylight since the Sun is at its lowest altitude in the sky. During this phase, the rains are abundant and nature is relatively static, awaiting the spring. The winter is a cold and moist season, associated with the water element and the phlegmatic temperament. The symbol for winter represents warehoused foods:

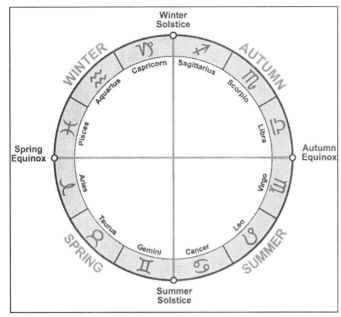

**Figure 4. The Twelve Signs**

Each of the four seasons is divided into three parts corresponding to the beginning, middle, and ending phases. By dividing the zodiac into four seasons, and each season into three parts, we get 12 segments that correspond to the 12 signs. The first three signs signal the spring: Aries, which marks the beginning of the season; Taurus, which corresponds to its culmination; and Gemini, which signals its end.

The sequence repeats itself in the other seasons throughout the year. The signs for the summer are Cancer, Leo, and Virgo; signs of autumn are Libra, Scorpio, and Sagittarius; and those of winter are Capricorn, Aquarius and Pisces. Although it is subordinate to the temperament of the season to which it belongs (and which defines it in general terms), each sign presents its own temperament and mode of action.

## The Images and Symbols of the Signs

Some signs are symbolized by an animal image, such as the Ram (Aries), the Bull (Taurus), the Crab (Cancer), the Lion (Leo), and the Fish (Pisces). Others are symbolized by human figures, such as the Twins (Gemini), the Virgin (Virgo), Libra (a young woman holding Scales), and Aquarius, also called the Water-bearer (a youth that pours water from a jug). There are also signs that are represented by mythological figures: Capricorn, an animal that is half goat and half fish, and Sagittarius, a centaur, half man, half horse (some versions substitute the centaur for an archer on horseback. These images have their origin in very ancient attributions that have come down to us through Greco-Roman mythology. Nevertheless, the signs are far older than these civilizations, their origins lost in time. The signs are represented by symbols that are stylized images of the figures that give them their names.

In the symbols of Aries and Taurus can be seen the heads of their respective animals: ♈, ♉

The symbol for Gemini is the Roman numeral 2, referring to the two twins: ♊

The symbol for Cancer evokes the pincers of the animal: ♋

That of Leo looks to derive from a stylization of the head and mane of the lion: ♌

Note: The signs and their symbolism are directly related to the seasons of the year in the northern hemisphere because it was here that all the civilizations that contributed to the construction of the western astrological system arose and flourished. Despite this, practice has shown that the system is perfectly applicable to horoscopes for the southern hemisphere, maintaining the same symbolism.

Virgo is represented by a stylized letter M: ♍

In Libra we see the two plates and fulcrum of the scales: ♎

That of Scorpio is a stylization of the animal with its respective stinger: ♏

Sagittarius is symbolized by an arrow, referring to the arrow (*sagitta* in Latin) of the archer: ♐

Capricorn by a stylization of the mythical creature (half goat, half fish): ♑

The symbol of Aquarius is the flowing water poured out by the water-bearer: ♒

Pisces is symbolized by two stylized fish, united by a cord: ♓

The manner of representing the signs has changed considerably over the ages. Currently, there are many artistic variations, but the basic design of the symbols is always the same (see Appendix 1, The Astrological Symbols). Following are the symbols of the signs that should be memorized:

♈ Aries
♉ Taurus
♊ Gemini
♋ Cancer
♌ Leo
♍ Virgo
♎ Libra
♏ Scorpio
♐ Sagittarius
♑ Capricorn
♒ Aquarius
♓ Pisces

The signs divide the zodiacal circle into twelve equal 30-degree parts. In other words, the circumference of the zodiac (360 degrees) is divided into 12 segments of 30 degrees, the signs. Each sign begins at zero degrees and zero minutes and ends at 29 degrees and 59 minutes (the 30th degree of a sign corresponds to the zero degree of the next sign). In zodiacal notation we use degrees and minutes of arc: the degrees are represented by the symbol ° and the minutes by ′. When noting a planet's position in the zodiac, we say that a planet is in a certain degree and minute of a sign. This manner of locating a planet is known as **zodiacal longitude**.

For example, if the Moon is located at 12 degrees and 40 minutes of Sagittarius, it is written as shown in Figure 6.

The position of a planet in a sign changes over time. For an accurate astrological interpretation it is necessary to know, with precision, not only its sign but also the degree and minute in which a planet is located at a given moment in time. For example, in the horoscope of the poet Florbela Espanca, Saturn is located at 03° and 28′ of Scorpio, which is written as shown in Figure 7.

In summary:
- The zodiac is created by the apparent motion of the Sun around the Earth.
- It is the segment of the sky where the Sun, the Moon, and the planets move.
- It is divided into four seasons, which are in turn divided into three parts (a beginning, middle and end); thus creating the 12 signs (four seasons of

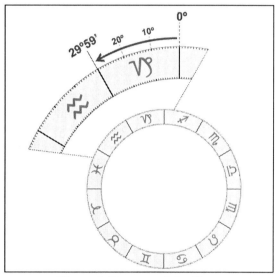

**Figure 5. Degrees of the Signs**

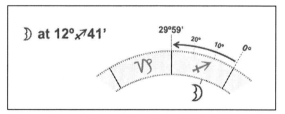

**Figure 6. The Planets in the Zodiac**

**Figure 7. Zodiacal Notation of a Planet's Position**

three signs each).
* This division is based upon the equinoxes and solstices (the start of the seasons of the year).
* Each sign is a segment of 30° of the zodiac (which totals 360°, a circumference).
* The position of the various astrological elements in the signs is called zodiacal longitude and is expressed in degrees and minutes of a sign.

## The Nature of the Signs

Each sign represents a particular group of qualities as defined by the season of the year to which it belongs, as well as its position in the zodiacal sequence. This positioning bestows upon it a specific temperament, which is the basis for its nature. Therefore, as with the planets, the signs may be classified in various ways: according to the phase of their season (beginning, middle, or end), that is, according to their **mode**; according to their primary qualities, that is, **element** and **temperament**; according to their gender, **masculine** or **feminine**; according to their sect, **nocturnal** and **diurnal**; and according to the planet under which they are governed, their **ruling planet**.

### The Modes

The signs that begin the seasons are called moveable or cardinal since they "move" or "drive" the characteristics of the season. The signs of the middle of the season are called fixed or solid, since they establish or "fix" the characteristics of that time of year. The final signs are called common, double-bodied or by-corporeal, or mutable, because they represent the time when the seasons change. At this time, the climate shares in the characteristics of two seasons, the one ending and the one that draws near. Thus, these three types—moveable, fixed, and common—represent the mode of action of the sign.

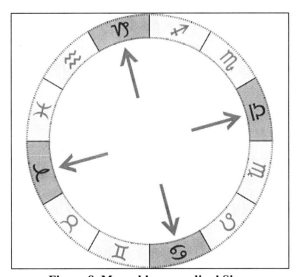

**Figure 8. Moveable or cardinal Signs**

The moveable signs that begin the seasons, are characterized by a strong drive for action, a love of movement and agitation. They represent unexpected and objective actions, but which end as quickly as they began. The moveable signs are Aries, Cancer, Libra and Capricorn.

If the moveable mode describes:
* the behavior of a person, it indicates impulsivity, impatience, difficulty respecting limits, resources and people; propensity for action, transitioning easily from ideas to actions;
* an object, it will be light, dynamic, possibly sharp, its function tied to action;
* an event, suggests dynamism but also a tendency to change quickly;
* a period of time, it indicates rapidity, immediacy.

The fixed signs, which signal the middle of the season, are characterized by stability and durability; to them is attributed a certain conservatism and inertia. They represent cautious, defensive, but also persistent and consistent actions. The fixed signs are Taurus, Leo, Scorpion, and Aquarius.

If the fixed mode describes:
* the behavior of a person, it indicates a strong drive for security, continuous actions, defense and self-control, but also stubbornness, reactions that are slow, cautious, defensive and very controlled; rigidity and difficulty giving in;

- an object, it will be heavy; solid, not easily moved, its function tied to maintenance and conservation;
- an event, it indicates that which has a long-lasting impact; or
- a period of time, it suggests a long wait.

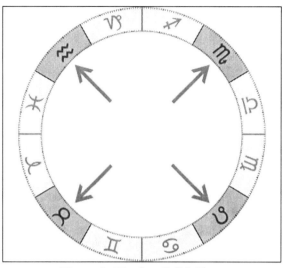

**Figure 9. Fixed or Solid Signs**

The common or double-bodied signs, which mark the end of the season and, consequently, a change in climate, are characteristically ambivalent and variable. Since they indicate a transitional phase, they present characteristics from both the previous two modes: they vacillate between rapid impulses (characteristic of the moveable mode) and the tendency toward inertia (typical of the fixed mode). They are characterized by the multiplicity of action, by diversity of responses, and by a certain adaptability. The common or double-bodied signs are Gemini, Virgo, Sagittarius, and Pisces.

If the common or double-bodied mode describes:
- the behavior of a person, it indicates vitality, curiosity and the capacity to adapt, also present is a certain inconsistency and scattering;
- an object, it indicates everyday, common (of little value) items, and those with more than one function;
- an event, it suggests simultaneous actions, or those with multiple impacts; or
- a period of time, it will be of average duration: not as long as the fixed nor as immediate as the cardinal.

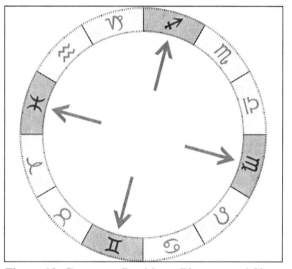

**Figure 10. Common, Double or Bi-corporeal Signs**

### The Temperaments of the Signs

Besides mode, each sign is associated with an element and its respective temperament. The attribution of the elements to the signs always follows the same order: fire, earth, air and water. To the first sign is given fire, to the next earth, then, air, then water, and so on. Thus, the first sign, Aries, belongs to the fire element; followed by Taurus, tied to earth, Gemini to the air, Cancer to water and so on. The distribution obtained is summarized in Figure 11.

There are three signs for each element, and each of these groups is called a **triplicity**. The fire triplicity is made up of Aries, Leo and Sagittarius; the air triplicity by Gemini, Libra, and Aquarius; the earth triplicity, by Taurus, Virgo, and Capricorn; and the water triplicity by Cancer, Scorpion, and Pisces.

The signs that belong to a masculine element (fire and air) are also classified as masculine and diurnal, while those of a feminine element (earth and water) are classified as feminine and nocturnal. As was previously mentioned, in the zodiacal sequence the masculine and diurnal signs alternate with the feminine and nocturnal ones. The masculine and diurnal signs are naturally expressive and expansive, and positively project their natures. Their core is action and movement.

| Sign | | Element | |
|---|---|---|---|
| ♈ | Aries | △ | Fire |
| ♉ | Taurus | ▽ | Earth |
| ♊ | Gemini | △ | Air |
| ♋ | Cancer | ▽ | Water |
| ♌ | Leo | △ | Fire |
| ♍ | Virgo | ▽ | Earth |
| ♎ | Libra | △ | Air |
| ♏ | Scorpio | ▽ | Water |
| ♐ | Sagittarius | △ | Fire |
| ♑ | Capricorn | ▽ | Earth |
| ♒ | Aquarius | △ | Air |
| ♓ | Pisces | ▽ | Water |

**Figure 11. Elements of the Signs**

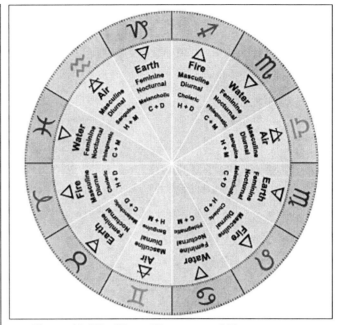

**Figure 12. The Signs, Elements and Temperaments**

The **fire** signs carry the choleric temperament, acquiring a positive, triumphant, and naturally radiant expression. They are characterized by impetuosity, daring, aggressiveness, and the tendency to dominate.

The **air** signs carry the sanguine temperament, more fluid and restless than the one before; they have a dynamic expression that is sociable and relational. Its core is the intellect, communication, and curiosity.

The feminine and nocturnal signs are naturally reserved and contemplative. Of an introverted nature, they express themselves in a more guarded and defensive manner. Their core is security and preservation.

The **earth** signs carry the melancholic temperament, which gives them a great focus on practical and functional action. They are of a constructive nature, appreciate solidity and express themselves in an organized and pragmatic manner.

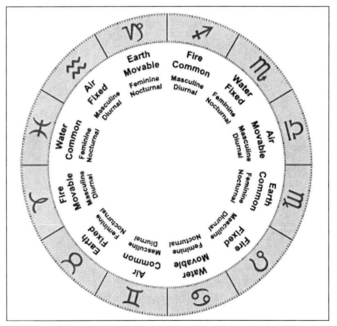

**Figure 13. The Nature of the Signs**

The **water** signs carry the phlegmatic temperament, more unstable and wavering then the melancholic, but susceptible to sudden changes. Its core is emotionality, comfort and security.

It is from the combination of temperament and mode that the basic characteristics of a sign are defined, that is, the fundamental nature of the sign is characterized by: gender and sect (which in the signs are intimately connected), by the primary qualities (from which are derived element and temperament) and by mode.

## The Planetary Rulers

Each sign is also under the dominion of a planet, which is called its ruler. This planet acts as a sort of master key to the sign and contributes greatly to its characterization. The rulers of the signs are:

| Sign | | Planetary Ruler | |
|------|------|------|------|
| ♈ | Aries | ♂ | Mars |
| ♉ | Taurus | ♀ | Venus |
| ♊ | Gemini | ☿ | Mercury |
| ♋ | Cancer | ☽ | Moon |
| ♌ | Leo | ☉ | Sun |
| ♍ | Virgo | ☿ | Mercury |
| ♎ | Libra | ♀ | Venus |
| ♏ | Scorpio | ♂ | Mars |
| ♐ | Sagittarius | ♃ | Jupiter |
| ♑ | Capricorn | ♄ | Saturn |
| ♒ | Aquarius | ♄ | Saturn |
| ♓ | Pisces | ♃ | Jupiter |

Thus, the signs ruled by Mars (Aries and Scorpio) display the martial traits of conquest, wounding and aggression; those ruled by Venus (Taurus and Libra) display calm, peaceful, and comforting, etc. traits. Obviously, these planetary shades must be contextualized by the nature of each sign. Thus, the aggressive tenor of Mars manifests itself in a more extroverted manner in Aries (masculine, fire and cardinal) than it does in Scorpio (feminine, water, fixed), where it manifests as defensive attitudes. The topic of planetary rulers is of prime importance in astrological interpretation and will be covered more thoroughly in subsequent chapters. When the tenor of a planet is combined with the core characteristics, we obtain the nature of the sign.

## The Nature of the Signs

**Aries:** Masculine, diurnal, of fire, choleric (hot and dry), cardinal or moveable, ruled by Mars. The combination of fire and cardinality creates a very rapid and dynamic expression with great brilliance and energy. The ruler, Mars, gives it a courageous nature which may exaggerate its tendencies to the point of aggression.

**Taurus:** Feminine, nocturnal, of earth, melancholic (cold and dry), fixed or solid, ruled by Venus. This sign, which combines the earth element with the fixed mode, displays a conservative, stable, tenacious nature, but also inertia with a tendency toward stubbornness. Its ruler Venus, gives it a touch of grace and tolerance.

**Gemini:** Masculine, diurnal, of air, sanguine (hot and moist), mutable, bi-corporeal or common, ruled by Mercury. The mutable air of this sign represents movement and swiftness, with traces of instability and dispersion. To this is added the dynamism, versatility, and vivacity of the ruler, Mercury, intensifying its variability and bustle.

**Cancer:** Feminine, nocturnal, of water, phlegmatic (cold and moist), cardinal or moveable, ruled by the Moon. The combination of cardinality and water produces a dynamic but little externalized expression, which results in sentimental and defensive behaviors. The rulership of the Moon adds a vacillating, alternating nature with cyclical variations.

**Lion:** Masculine, diurnal, of fire, choleric (hot and dry), fixed or solid, ruled by the Sun. Because it's fixed and fiery, this sign has a positive expression, characterized by constancy and solidity, which can be imposing. The Sun as ruler, gives it a powerful, radiant and grandiose aspect.

**Virgo**: Feminine, nocturnal, of earth, melancholic (cold and dry), mutable, bi-corporeal or common, ruled by Mercury. The mutable earth of this sign combines the characteristics of concreteness and versatility, producing multifaceted efficiency. Mercury, the ruler, adds swiftness and a certain lightness.

**Libra**: Masculine, diurnal, of air, sanguine (hot and moist), cardinal or moveable, ruled by Venus. The air element combined with the cardinal mode produces in this sign a fluid and dynamic expression. Venus endows it with softness, a touch of beauty, and artistic expression.

**Scorpio**: Feminine, nocturnal, of water, phlegmatic (cold and moist), fixed or solid, ruled by Mars. This sign combines the emotiveness and sensitivity of the water element to the stability and stubbornness of the fixed mode, producing a defensive and persevering expression of which the emotions occupy a central focus. Mars, the ruler, contributes with its bellicose nature.

**Sagittarius**: Masculine, diurnal, of fire, choleric (hot and dry), mutable, bi- corporeal or common, ruled by Jupiter. The mutable fire produces a multifaceted expression, positive but directed toward various simultaneous objectives. The nature of Jupiter, the ruler, adds a sense of justice and temperance, which somewhat stabilizes the combination.

**Capricorn**: Feminine, nocturnal, of earth, melancholic (cold and dry), cardinal or moveable, ruled by Saturn. This cardinal sign of the earth combines action with a constructive impulse, which produces an essentially pragmatic nature. Saturn endows it with deliberation and persistence, producing a resistant, rigorous, disciplined, but conservative expression.

**Aquarius**: Masculine, diurnal, of air, sanguine (hot and moist), fixed or solid, ruled by Saturn. The fixed air associates the fluid and dynamic characteristics with constancy and perseverance, giving rise to an expression that is distant, individualistic, and with a great tendency toward abstraction.

**Pisces**: Feminine, nocturnal, of water, phlegmatic (cold and moist) mutable, bi-corporeal, or common, ruled by Jupiter. This sign of mutable water combines sensibility and variability, which produces a multiplicity of expressions and sentiments. Jupiter associates its temperance with this dynamism, producing idealism and moderation.

The nature of the sign defines everything that it represents: behaviors, objects, places and regions, spatial directions, the parts of the body, etc. For example, the sign Gemini, represents a multifaceted (mutable), curious and communicative behavior (air element); but also indicates a mountainous terrain with hills or gaming and entertainment places; in the human body it represents the arms and hands.

### Additional Characteristics

The nature of the sign can also be complimented by a set of other secondary attributes. These secondary characteristics enrich the description of the sign and are applied when a more detailed or specific description of a person, action, or tendency shown by the sign is needed. Thus, the signs are also:

- Bestial (referring to beast, animal) or quadruped: Aries, Taurus, Leo, Sagittarius and Capricorn.
- Human: Gemini, Virgo, Libra, Aquarius and the first half of Sagittarius.
- Fierce or Feral: Leo

This classification is associated with the **images**, animal or human, that make up the signs; in terms of interpretation, they refer to subtle behavioral traces. The quadruped signs impart a behavior similar to the animal that symbolizes it, in that it has an abrupt physical expression. The human signs (those represented by human figures) describe a more social behavior and with a greater propensity for communication and the use of the mind. The sign Leo is characterized as fierce since it is represented by a wild animal, thereby one attributes more assertive and pointed characteristics to it.

- Fertile: Cancer, Scorpio, and Pisces
- Barren: Gemini, Leo, Virgo
- Moderately Fertile: Taurus, Libra, Sagittarius
- Moderately Barren: Aries, Capricorn, Aquarius

This classification is used when one desires to obtain a number or a quantity. For example, in the study of a chart to determine the probable number of children or siblings. As is apparent, the fertile signs correspond to many, the barren signs to none (or in some cases, one) and the remaining to few (only one or two).

- Of strong voice: Aries, Leo, and Sagittarius
- Of middle voice: Virgo, Capricorn, and Aquarius
- Mute: Cancer, Scorpio, and Pisces

This classification characterizes the power of the individual's oratory and is generally applied to the ascending sign and to the sign placement of Mercury, due to its connection with speech/communication. The signs of strong voice easily project their voice, those of middle voice have an average voice, and the mute signs tend to be shut down in their vocal expression.

- Bitter: Aries, Leo, and Sagittarius
- Sweet: Gemini, Libra, and Aquarius
- Salty: Cancer, Scorpio, Pisces
- Sour: Taurus, Virgo, Capricorn

This classification is useful in the descriptions of foods, medications, and other elements of a medical nature.

These are the attributes more frequently used in the astrological practice. It is important to keep in mind that these attributes must be integrated into an appropriate interpretative context. Understandably, it makes no sense to include attributes such as "bitter" or "fertile" in the description of a behavior. Similarly, in the description of an object, the use of attributes such as "impulsive" or "emotional" are equally absurd.

- Long Ascension or oblique: Capricorn, Aquarius, Pisces, Aries, Taurus, and Gemini
- Short Ascension or straight: Cancer, Leo, Virgo, Libra, Scorpio, and Sagittarius.

This classification refers to the **time** that each sign takes to rise over the horizon. Due to the inclination of the Earth's axis, the signs do not all take the same time to rise. The exact use of this division will be covered in a subsequent chapter.

## Interpretation of the Signs

The signs are like divisions in a board game. They are only relevant in an interpretation when there is something placed in them. Thus, a sign colors with its qualities any planet (or other astrological point of the horoscope) that is located in it. The expression of that planet or factor is then molded by the sign and acquires a set of traits that condition its manifestation. The planets possess their own natures, but their movement through the signs alters the manifestation of that nature. *It is from the combination of the natures of the five planets and the luminaries with the twelve basic qualities of the signs that all diversity of expression in nature are derived. This expression may be translated into various forms: human behavior, climatic variations, worldly events, etc.*

## Interpretation of Planets in Signs

To determine the effects of planets in signs, one must combine the nature of the planet with the sign in which it finds itself. The planet will have its own expression and natural signification altered by the characteristics of the sign. The result will be more or less fluid, depending upon the agreement between the natures of the planet and the sign.

Never forget that the focus of the interpretation is always centered on the planet. The planet indicates what is in play (for example, Mars indicates action, combat, etc.); the sign refers to the traits by which it expresses itself (for example, Taurus indicates a solid and slow expression, while Cancer represents an expression that is emotional and variable).

In astrology, what is important is understanding, not memorization. It is critical to possess a solid understanding of the nature of each planet and sign in order to understand the result of any planet-sign combination. The student who internalizes this understanding will be able to handle any combination without having to depend upon "cookbook" descriptions or descriptive tables.

Let's take the Moon as an example: its signification includes, among other things, the moods, emotional tones, and sensibilities of the individual. If it is positioned in Leo, these moods will acquire the characteristics of this sign. We have then a fiery sign, hot and dry, with a dynamic expression, positive and enthusiastic; a masculine and diurnal sign, therefore, extroverted; a fixed sign, possessing confident and lasting action. In this manner, the moods and emotions represented by the Moon in Leo will be enthusiastic, positive (fire/choleric), not passing without notice (masculine and diurnal). Their expression will be firm, possibly often being stubborn (fixed). The expression of the planet is more joyful and extroverted, but less receptive since the natural sensibility of the Moon is diminished in a hot and dry sign, which contradicts the cold and moist (phlegmatic) facet of the luminary. Also, the natural plasticity of the Moon will be more restrained because of the fixed Leo nature.

If we consider another fire sign, such as Aries, we discover that the traits of enthusiasm, affirmation, and extroversion are common. Nonetheless, a Moon in Aries portrays a greater restlessness and propensity for activity, since it is a moveable sign. Similarly, a Moon in Sagittarius, a mutable, fire sign, acquires a more adaptable, multifaceted and dispersed expression.

It is also important to note the impact of the ruling planet of the signs (of which we will speak in more detail ahead): in this case, the Sun, ruler of Leo, Mars, ruler of Aries, and Jupiter, ruler of Sagittarius. The Moon in Leo will portray distinctly positive traits (Sun), in Aries, more bellicose and sharp ones (Mars), and in Sagittarius, an "advocating" (Jupiter) motivation. We may also consider the secondary attributes of the signs. Leo is a fierce sign, which indicates a more intense and domineering emotional expression than in the other fire signs. On the other hand, Leo, Aries and Sagittarius are bestial signs, which implies more abrupt attitudes with a greater negative social impact. Of the fire signs, Sagittarius has a double aspect, since it is depicted by a figure that is half man and half animal, which makes it swing between abruptness and sociability. Notwithstanding, the fluctuations are softened by Sagittarius also being an autumn (calmer) sign and having Jupiter (planet of moderation) as its ruler.

If we consider, by contrast, the Moon in Capricorn, the delineation will be very different. In this case, we have a cold and dry sign, of air, melancholic, feminine and nocturnal, and moveable. Here the attitudes and emotions signified by the Moon will have a more discrete and restrained expression (feminine/nocturnal), overlaid by a pragmatic and slightly suspicious and cautious (earth, melancholic) attitude, but which is very active and dynamic (moveable). Again we have a quadruped sign, making its expression a bit abrupt, as in previous examples (although moderated by the earth element and by the sobriety of the ruler, Saturn).

The same rationale should be applied to the remaining planets and signs. We repeat: *it is of no use to memorize the signification of the planets in each sign; what is truly important is to understand the astrological principles that are at the root of those significations*.

> Note: Although each planet always has a natural signification (Mars signifies action, Venus affection, Mercury understanding, etc.) what is truly important in interpretation, is the **particular signification** that each planet acquires in the chart. The position by sign gives us only the qualities through which the celestial body expresses itself; it does not indicate its function or importance in the general context of the horoscope. This information is given to us from the house position and by the rules of delineation. The interpretation by sign is only made by beginners as a practice exercise.

## Characterization and Description by Sign

The characterizations that we list below have diverse applications. For example, in a natal horoscope, they describe the behavioral traits of an individual, in a horary chart, they give a description of the person asked about; in still other horary charts, they describe the "characters" represented by the planets situated in the respective signs. Following is the expression and behavior of the signs:

| | | |
|---|---|---|
| ♈ Aries | Hot + Dry<br>Choleric<br>Movable<br>Ruled by Mars | Its behavioral expression is characterized by impulsivity and rapid response; action is at the core of its motivations. It describes an enthusiastic and passionate attitude that can also be a bit abrupt and precipitated, and often aggressive. The expression is emotive and expansive, but lacks a degree of sensibility, tact and subtly. |
| ♉ Taurus | Cold + Dry<br>Melancholic<br>Ruled by Venus | Characterizes a calm, pondered behavior with a tendency toward inertia and laziness. The attitude is pragmatic, practical, and centered on comfort and satisfaction. Not given to action, it tends to be more reactive to external stimuli than to initiate actions. It cultivates security and stability. The emotional expression is made through physical demonstrations or concrete expressions. |
| ♊ Gemini | Hot + Moist<br>Sanguine<br>Double or Common<br>Ruled by Mercury | Its behavioral expression is characterized by curiosity, a variety of interests, and the capacity to change one's attention from one topic to another. It exhibits great dynamism (especially at the intellectual or social level), but the expression tends to be dispersed, often manifesting itself with volatility and inconsistency. It tends to be more rational than emotive. |
| ♋ Cancer | Cold + Moist<br>Phlegmatic<br>Movable<br>Ruled by the Moon | Behaviorally, it exhibits a calm, receptive, and sympathetic attitude, but subject to emotional ups and downs since emotional security is at the core of its behavior. It responds easily to changes in the environment, but in a defensive or hesitant manner. |

| | | |
|---|---|---|
| ♌ Leo | Hot + Dry<br>Choleric<br>Fixed<br>Ruled by the Sun | The behavioral expression is characterized by a natural radiance which results in an affirmative and dominant attitude. Its actions are firm and consequential, although personal in perspective. A generous and warm personal expression, but simultaneously not very receptive and exhibiting some abruptness and impulsivity. |
| ♍ Virgo | Cold + Dry<br>Melancholic<br>Double or Common<br>Ruled by Mercury | The behavior represented by this sign, is distinguished by a utilitarian, practical and detailed expression. The expression is agitated, very focused on conceptual questions and practical details. The actions are precise, but tend to get lost in a multiplicity of details. The rational streak predominates, making the emotional expression appear "dry." |
| ♎ Libra | Hot + Moist<br>Sanguine<br>Movable<br>Ruled by Venus | There is great attention to social interactions, which acquire a dynamic and varied expression. It cultivates contacts, friendships and groups, tending to maintain a socially acceptable and conservative expression. It tends to express itself in a more rational than emotive manner and cultivates moderation. |
| ♏ Scorpio | Cold + Moist<br>Phlegmatic<br>Fixed<br>Ruled by Mars | It represents a contained, introverted and defensive expression. The actions are based upon security and emotional control, giving rise to distrust and caution. With a reserved expression, it avoids showing feelings and sensitivity. |
| ♐ Sagittarius | Hot + Dry<br>Choleric<br>Double or Common<br>Ruled by Jupiter | It is characterized by an active and dynamic expression, very adaptive and good-humored. The actions are expansive and expressive with a certain idealistic and self-righteous inclination. It's nature is adventurous, experimental and optimistic. |
| ♑ Capricorn | Cold + Dry<br>Melancholic<br>Movable<br>Ruled by Saturn | The behavior is firm and enterprising. The motivation is pragmatic, centered on practical and useful actions, which combine objectivity and dynamism. The emotional expression is restrained, vacillating between sobriety and reserve. |
| ♒ Aquarius | Hot + Moist<br>Sanguine<br>Fixed<br>Ruled by Saturn | A taste for concepts and ideals, to which the mind adheres in a persevering and often stubborn manner. It cultivates its own manner of acting, distancing itself from anything that is of a general mindset. Not very emotional, it tends to be more theoretical than practical. |
| ♓ Pisces | Cold + Moist<br>Phlegmatic<br>Double or Common<br>Ruled by Jupiter | Calm, receptive, and sentimental behavior, of a plastic and adaptive nature; sometimes fickle, since the actions are based upon sentiments and the sensibilities of the moment. At ease attitude to the point of dispersal and disregard. |

In other astrological contexts, as in mundane or horary, a planet may represent actions or animated objects. In these cases, the attributes listed above will represent the characteristics of that action or object. Let us take the Moon once more as an example. Generally, an action represented by the Moon would be fast (given that the Moon is the fastest planet), of great visibility (it is a luminary), with a strong emotional element (it symbolizes the emotional nature), but short-lived (it has a changeable nature). If it is positioned in Leo, it also represents an action that is enthusiastic and intense (fire), but controlled or restricted (fixed). In Capricorn, it signifies an action that is faster and more sudden (cardinal) but also discrete, orderly, and objective (earth). If we refer to an object, the Moon may represent (along with many other things) a glass or cup (receptivity). If positioned in Leo, the cup will be eye-catching and shiny (fire), possibly golden (Sun), but with a heavy appearance (fixed), whose function will be to adorn or to symbolize status. A Moon in Capricorn will represent a cup of a darker more plain material (earth), of little worth or old (Saturn), of easy use (cardinal or moveable), and with a practical function (earth).

> Note: The behaviors indicated by the sign must always be combined with the planet that occupies it. For example, the enthusiastic behavior represented by Cancer will be expressed differently by Saturn—more cautious and reserved—or by Mars—more assertive and dynamic.

## Rulerships and Sign Associations

The sign position can also give more complex associations, such as a spatial direction (east, north, west, south) or describe locations, such as the part of a house, a territory, a nation, etc. For example, a plane in Leo indicates, in terms of the interior of a house, a fireplace or a place where fire is present, while Capricorn represents places near the ground and doorsteps. Just as with the planets, the signs are associated with various aspects of daily life. Each sign rules (or is associated with) the parts of the body, places, colors, plants, animals, etc. For this book, we've selected the associations with the most practical application; the remaining associations may be easily found in the majority of sources referenced.

### Body Parts

Particularly used in medical astrology, these associations determine the place in the body subject to illness and also to determine birthmarks and blemishes in physical descriptions.

| | | |
|---|---|---|
| ♈ Aries | | Head, face and ears |
| ♉ Taurus | | Neck and throat |
| ♊ Gemini | | Arms, hands, shoulders and shoulder blades |
| ♋ Cancer | | Breast, bosom, ribs, stomach and spleen |
| ♌ Leo | | Heart, back, spinal column |
| ♍ Virgo | | Belly, intestines e diaphragm |
| ♎ Libra | | Bellybutton, kidneys, bladder, urinary system (purification of blood) |
| ♏ Scorpio | | Genitals and anus |
| ♐ Sagittarius | | Thighs, buttocks and muscles in general |
| ♑ Capricorn | | Knees (and black bile) |
| ♒ Aquarius | | Legs and ankles (circulatory system) |
| ♓ Pisces | | Feet (and phlegm) |

### Physical Appearance

These are particularly used to describe physical characteristics of people. They have practical applications primarily in natal, horary and medical astrology. Following is a list of physiognomic traits of the signs, which are relative to the rising sign and not to the Sun sign. In addition, they may be modified by planets located in the first house or which aspect the Ascendant (in this case, the planets add additional characteristics to this basic structure).

| | | |
|---|---|---|
| ♈ Aries | | Dry body, medium-tall height, strong bones and limbs, wide shoulders, long face and neck, dark complexion, thick eyebrows. |
| ♉ Taurus | | Short and full stature, large shoulders, wide forehead, big eyes and mouth. Dark hair, large hands. |
| ♊ Gemini | | Straight tall body, long arms but short hands and feet. Dark hair, sanguine complexion, although darker. |
| ♋ Cancer | | Short stature, larger upper body, pale complexion, dark hair, small eyes. |
| ♌ Leo | | Above average stature, full body, large shoulders but narrow chest. Big round head, light curly hair, Tanned skin, big goggle eyes. |
| ♍ Virgo | | Medium height, medium body, thin and harmonious with a tendency to have short limbs. Dark complexion and hair. |
| ♎ Libra | | Tall and thin body, harmonious and straight. Round face, fair complexion with pinkish skin and soft light hair. |
| ♏ Scorpio | | Strong robust body, hairy, stocky and compact, with slightly bowed legs. Dark complexion and coarse hair. Long face and short neck. |
| ♐ Sagittarius | | Above average height, robust body, harmonious limbs. Pleasant face, long but full. Tanned complexion and light hair. |
| ♑ Capricorn | | Dry body, medium to short stature, long neck, narrow chest, dark hair, long and lean face, narrow chin. |
| ♒ Aquarius | | Stocky body, large, fleshy or strong, well proportioned and not too tall. Long face, light sanguine complexion. |
| ♓ Pisces | | Short stature, fleshy body, not very harmonious, a little curved, pale complexion and large face. |

## Spatial Directions

These are used in horary astrology to find lost animals or people, thereby giving a general indication of the direction they may have taken.

| | |
|---|---|
| ♈ Aries | East |
| ♉ Taurus | South by East |
| ♊ Gemini | West by South |
| ♋ Cancer | North |
| ♌ Leo | East by North |
| ♍ Virgo | South by West |
| ♎ Libra | West |
| ♏ Scorpio | North by East |
| ♐ Sagittarius | East by South |
| ♑ Capricorn | South |
| ♒ Aquarius | West by North |
| ♓ Pisces | North by West |

## Locations

Locations are used in horary astrology to find missing objects, animals or people. In this context the signs describe the location.

| | |
|---|---|
| ♈ Aries | Outside: pastures and stables for small animals; recently ploughed lands or where bricks or lime have recently been burned; ploughed or undulating fields. In the home: roofs, ceilings, and plaster. |
| ♉ Taurus | Outside: horse stables, isolated pastures, level lands or recently trimmed lands, where corn or wheat is planted. In the home: basements and low rooms. |
| ♊ Gemini | Outside: elevations and mountains, barns, corn silos, high places. In the home: walls and plaster, wood-lined walls, game rooms. Safes and chests. |
| ♋ Cancer | Outside: the sea, large navigable rivers, springs, streams, wells, swampy lands, and banks, dykes. In the home: basements, laundry rooms and cisterns. |
| ♌ Leo | Outside: forests, woods, places that are deserted, steep, rocky, inaccessible, or frequented by wild animals. Palaces, castles, forts and parks. In the home: near chimneys or fireplaces. |
| ♍ Virgo | Outside: corn fields, mounts of straw, barley or wheat, barns, places where malt or dairy is stored or manufactured. In the home: the office, places with books and bookcases. |
| ♎ Libra | Outside: mountaintops, slopes, place of fresh air, sandy or gravel-filled lands, falconry and hunting grounds, sawmills, cooperages, places near windmills, barns, isolated agricultural storage. In the home: upper rooms, attics, chambers and rooms within rooms. |
| ♏ Scorpio | Outside: swampy and muddy lands, quicksand, places used by crawling animals, gardens, orchards, wineries, tanks and ruined houses near water. In the Home: kitchen, pantries and laundry rooms. |
| ♐ Sagittarius | Outside: hills, the highest places around, stables for horses or cattle. In the home: upper rooms near fire. |
| ♑ Capricorn | Outside: uncultivated lands with sharp shrubs, stacked dirt and manure. sheep pastures, cattle enclosures, wood or ship storage. *In the Home:* low dark places, near the ground or doorsteps. |
| ♒ Aquarius | Outside: elevated or non-level places, newly excavated grounds, quarries or other places where minerals are extracted, wineries, and places near springs and fountains. In the home: roofs, eaves and high places. |
| ♓ Pisces | Outside: watery lands or with springs, lakes, and rivers rich in animals and birds, water mills, motes. In the home: wells and places near water, water pumps, or reservoirs. |

## Countries or Regions

These rulerships are primarily used in mundane astrology to determine the location of events. Just as in the case of the planets, one should remember that these associations are very ancient and that they do not always coincide with the current boundaries of nations. Additionally, there are occasional differences between the various sources. In natal and horary astrology, these correspondences help to assess the affinity between individuals and places, and they are particularly useful in situations involving travel and business.

| | |
|---|---|
| ♈ Aries | Germany, Poland, Upper Burgundy superior, France, England, Denmark, Silesia superior, Judea, Palestine, Syria, Sinai, Arabia, and parts of Persia and Austria. |
| ♉ Taurus | Greater Poland, northern Sweden, Russia, Ireland, Switzerland, Lorraine, Campania, Persia (mainly current Iraq), Cyprus, Parthia, Medes, Cyclades Islands, Lydia and Ionia. |

| | |
|---|---|
| ♊ Gemini | Egypt, Phoenicia, Scotland, Flanders (Brabant), Sardinia, Lombardi, west and south-west England and the Azores Islands. |
| ♋ Cancer | Scotland, Zeeland, Norway, Russia, Holland and part of Flanders, Britannia, Kingdom of Granada (South of Spain), Armenia, Numidia, Ethiopia, Algeria, Tunisia. |
| ♌ Leo | Bohemia, Alps, South Gaulle, Italy (Apulia), Sicily, Ithaca (part of Greece), Chaldea, Phoenicia, Damascus, the Red Sea and part of Turkey. |
| ♍ Virgo | Greece, Southwest France, Croatia, Mesopotamia (particularly Assyria), Athens. |
| ♎ Libra | Upper Austria, Duchy of Savoy, Alsace, Livonia, African coast of the Red Sea (particularly Ethiopia). |
| ♏ Scorpio | Norway, Western Sweden, North of Bavaria, Scotland, Cappadocia (Turkey), Mauritania, Morocco, Libya, Syria, Judea. |
| ♐ Sagittarius | Spain (and Iberian Peninsula in general) Arabia, Hungary, Tuscany, Gaulle, Malta, Moravia, Slavonia, Dalmatia. |
| ♑ Capricorn | Portugal, Thrace, Macedonia, Albania, Bulgaria, Bavaria, Lithuania, Styria, Saxony (southeast), Thuringia, Orkney Islands, India. |
| ♒ Aquarius | Aragon (part of Spain), Ethiopia, parts of Bohemia and Bavaria, Russia, Sweden (middle), Croatia. |
| ♓ Pisces | Portugal, Galicia, Calabria, part of Turkey, Ireland, Normandy, northern Egypt. |

## *Cities*

These attributions are similar to those of countries and regions. Many of them may originate with the foundation of the cities, with the sign indicated corresponding to the city's Ascendant. Sometimes, several signs are attributed to the same city.

| | |
|---|---|
| ♈ Aries | Naples, Florence, Genoa, Capua, Ferrara, Ancona, Verona, Utrecht, Krakow, Marseille, Augusta, Padua, Bergamo, Babylon, Zaragoza, Tortosa, Valladolid, Cuidad Rodrigo, Logreno, Najara. |
| ♉ Taurus | Bologna, Salerno, Parma, Toro, Girona, Burgos, Novohrad, Trento, Mantua, Sena, Constatinople, Troy, Narbonne, Girona, Carlstad, Nantes, Liepsig, Palermo, Badajoz, Astorga, Huelva, Alcântara, Elvas, Almeida, Castelo Branco, Nisa, Portalegre, Moura. |
| ♊ Gemini | Tireno, London, Leuven, Bruges, Sena, Turim, Viterbo, Nuremberg, Hasford, Mont, Bamberg, Cesena, Trento, Siguença, Talavera dela Reina, Cordova, Madrid, Monviedro, Ecija, Maguncia, Azores islands. |
| ♋ Cancer | Babylon, Constantinople, Carthage, Venice, Milan, Genoa, Pisa, Mantua, Ferrara, Cantabria, Amesterdam, York, Magdburg, Wittenberg, Saint Luca, Cadis, Tunes, Albares, Granada, Barcelona, Santiago de Compostela, Zaragoza, Logrosa, Burgos, Victoria, Najara, Navarrete, Algarve, Lisbon, Beja, Setubal, Santarem, Leiria, Ourem. |
| ♌ Leo | Meca, Damascus, Rome, Syracuse, Cremona, Ulm, Mantua, Ravenna, Palermo, Prague, Lintz, Bristol, La Pulla, Leon, Murcia, Madrid, Braga. |
| ♍ Virgo | Athens, Jerusalem, Corinth, Pavia, Rhodes, Paris, Lyons, Basel, Ferrara, Heidelburg, Tolosa, Las Algeziras, Medina del Rio Seco, Toledo, Ávila, Lerida. |
| ♎ Libra | Frankfurt, Vienna, Urbino, Piedmont, Piacenza, Arles, Friburg, Teba, Parma, Sesa, Salamanca, Burgos, Salerno, Almeria, Lisbon, Viana, Almeida, Gouveia, Coimbra. |
| ♏ Scorpio | Catalonia, Valencia, Urbino, Forum Julii, Vienna, Messina, Ghent, Frankfurt (Oder), Ferrara, Patavia, Genoa, Valencia, Lugia, Tangier, Morocco, Burgos, Malaga, Murcia, Pedroso, Tudela, Braga. |

| ♐ Sagittarius | Buda, Narbonne, Nuremberg, Rotenberg, Ludemburg, Cullen, Stargard, Tuscany, Jerusalem, Avignon, Toledo, Calahorra, Jaen, Medina Celi, Malta, Faro, Serpa, Moura, Évora. |
| ♑ Capricorn: | Hassia, Oxford, Cleves, Brandenburg, Ghent, Ingolstad, Constantinople, Savoy, Carmona, Tortosa, Osma, Soria, Olmedo, Salamanca, Constância, Ferrara and Verona, Castro Marim, Tavira, Loule, Alcoutim. |
| ♒ Aquarius | Hamburg, Bremen, Montsferat, Trento, Ingolstadt, Jerusalem, Urbino, Zamora, Palencia, Palencia, Medina del Campo, Seville, Carmona. |
| ♓ Pisces | Alexandria, Rhemes, Wormes, Ratisbon, Compostela, Padua, Sevilha, Orense, Ecija, Oporto, Faro. |

## The Movement of the Planets in the Signs

The motion of the planets in the zodiac follows the order of the signs. Thus, the planets move from Aries to Taurus, then to Gemini, etc.

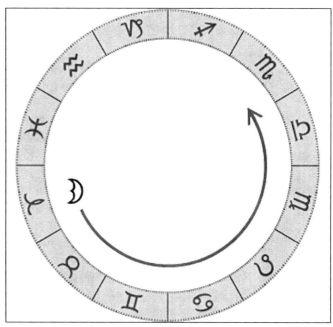

Figure 14. The Movement of the Planets in the Signs

On its normal path, a planet increases the number of degrees it traverses in a sign until it leaves it, transiting into the succeeding sign.

Mercury and Venus, in contrast to the other planets, are never very distant from the Sun. This happens because (from a heliocentric perspective) their orbits are inside that of the Earth. Therefore, for a terrestrial observer, Mercury, whose orbit is closest to the Sun, is never more than 28° (approximately a sign away) from the Sun's zodiacal position. Venus, which has a wider orbit, is never more than 48° (approximately a sign and a half) away. This maximum distance is known as **elongation**.

Along their trajectory, Mercury and Venus make two conjunctions to the Sun; once on the side opposite to the Earth (called a **superior conjunction**), the other when they are between the Earth and the Sun (**inferior conjunction**). In the superior conjunction, the planet is on the other side of the Sun, moving therefore above the Sun (thus, the term superior), while in the inferior conjunction, the planet passes between the Earth and the Sun, below it. In an astrological chart, the inferior conjunction always corresponds to the retrograde motion of the planet (which will be explained later).

### Velocity

The progression of the planets along the signs happens at different speeds. The fastest body, the Moon, moves at an average rate of 13° per

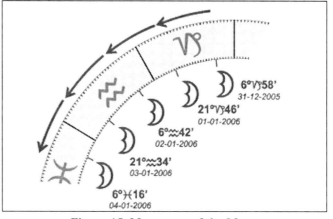

Figure 15. Movement of the Moon

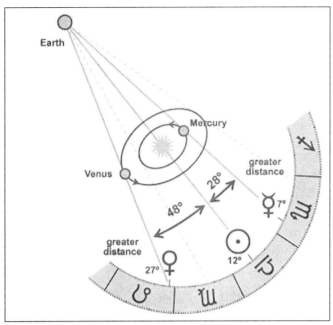

**Figure 16. Maximum Distance of Mercury and
Venus to the Sun, Projected in the Zodiac**

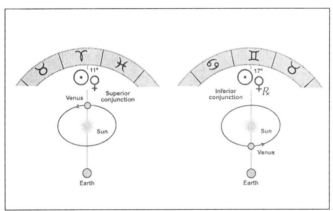

**Figure 17. Inferior and Superior Conjunction of Venus**

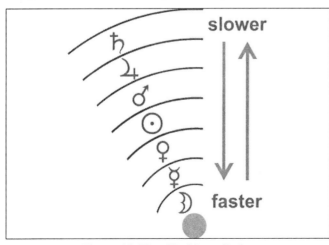

**Figure 18. The Chaldean Order
and the Speeds of the Planets**

day, advancing about 1° every two hours and covering a complete sign in about two and a half days. Saturn, the slowest of the traditional planets, advances on average 2° a day and takes about two and a half years to cross a sign. These different speeds are represented on the model of the planetary spheres by the Chaldean order—Saturn, Jupiter, Mars, the Sun, Venus, Mercury, and the Moon.

Each planet has a specific cycle measured by the amount of time it takes it to complete a revolution around the zodiac. The Moon takes about 27.5 days to return to the same place in the zodiac; Mercury, Venus and the Sun take about 1 year (since they are never far apart); Mars, about 2 years; Jupiter, about 12 years; and Saturn, approximately 29 years.

Nevertheless, along its course, the apparent speed of the planet varies due to its proximity or distance in relation to Earth. These are the average daily speeds of the planets:

| Planet | Average Daily Speed |
|---|---|
| ♄ Saturn | 00°02′01″ |
| ♃ Jupiter | 00°04′59″ |
| ♂ Mars | 00°31′27″ |
| ☉ Sun | 00°59′08″ |
| ♀ Venus | 00°59′08″ |
| ☿ Mercury | 00°59′08″ |
| ☽ Moon | 13°10′36″ |

Although the Sun, Venus, and Mercury have identical average speeds, Mercury reaches a maximum speed of little more than 2°10′ per day. Venus is less, with a maximum of 1°16′, and the Sun with 1°01′.

Note: the apparent daily velocity of the Moon fluctuates between 11°41′ and 15°23′; the Sun ranges between a minimum of 57°10′ and a maximum of 1°01′10″. For the remaining planets, the maximum daily motions are approximately 47′ for Mars, 14′ for Jupiter, and 07′ for Saturn.

In the case where the daily motion of the planet is shorter than the one presented in the table, it is said that the planet is slow; when greater than the average, the planet is said to be fast. A fast planet is considered to have a swifter and more effective action, and a slow planet has a more protracted action.[8]

## Retrogradation

Planetary movement normally occurs in the order of the zodiac signs, (Aries, Taurus, Gemini, etc.). This is called **direct motion**. At certain times along its celestial course, however, the planet slows down its motion until it apparently stops, reverses its course, and begins to move in a direction opposite to the order of the signs. This phenomenon is known as **retrograde motion (or retrogradation)** and it occurs periodically during the zodiacal cycle of the planet. Thus, a planet is said to be retrograde when its apparent motion in the celestial dome is contrary to the zodiacal signs (Gemini, Taurus, Aries, etc). This apparent reversal occurs when Earth passes the slower planets that are outside of its orbit. A similar phenomenon occurs when a car passes another moving in the same direction but at a slower speed. The passengers in the faster car perceive the slower car to be moving backwards.

In the case of the planets on the inside of Earth's orbit, Mercury and Venus, retrogradation occurs when these bodies (moving within their own orbits around the Sun) come close to Earth, passing between it and the Sun (see Figure 30). Retrograde motion is an apparent phenomenon caused by the observer's change in perspective as Earth circles around the Sun. In reality, a planet never stops its movement around the Sun; it is a purely geocentric phenomenon.

In a table or in a horoscope, a retrograde planet is indicated by this symbol—℞—located next to the planet.

The Sun and Moon are never retrograde. In the case of the Sun, it is the Earth that orbits around it, such that the apparent motion is continuous. The Moon has its orbit directly around the Earth, which makes retrogradation impossible.

### *The Effects of a Retrograde Planet*

Direct motion is what a planet normally assumes while on its course and is considered nor-

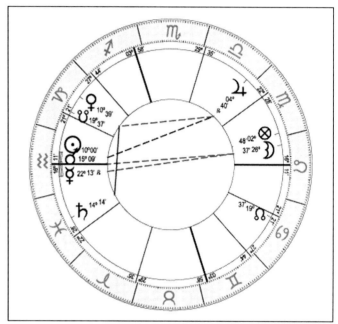

**Figure 19. Retrogradation of Mars**

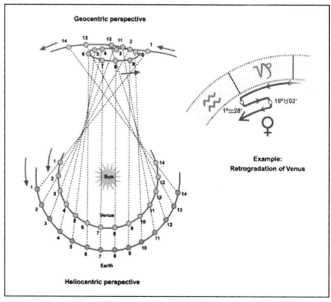

**Figure 20. Retrogradation of Venus**

---

[8]Some authors consider that a slow planet is debilitated since its movement is similar to that of Saturn, the slowest and most malefic of the traditional planets.

mal, since it does not interfere in its expression. Retrograde motion, because it makes the planet appear to move backward, is considered an interference in its normal functioning. Thus, a retrograde planet is considered debilitated because its expression is challenged. Its actions are discontinuous and given to sudden changes. It can signify reversals, delays, and the canceling of plans.

*The Stations*

The change in direction from direct motion to retrograde motion does not occur suddenly. The planet slows down gradually until it appears to stand completely still. It then begins to slowly move in the opposite direction, increasing in speed until it reaches its normal speed. We call this stopping point **the station**, and the planet that appears stopped is **stationary**.

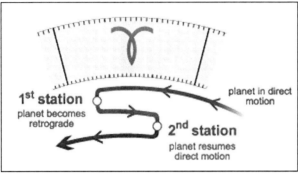

**Figure 21. The Stations**

At the transition from direct to retrograde and back to direct, the planet makes two stations. The **first station** occurs when a planet, in direct motion, gradually diminishes its speed until it stations, to then begin its apparent retrograde motion. The second station occurs when, during retrograde motion, the planet slows down, stations, and then resumes its direct motion. In practice, a planet in the first station is considered more debilitated than a planet in the second station, since after the last one the planet resumes direct motion (considered normal).

**The Latitude of the Planets**

As was stated at the start of this chapter, the celestial position of the planets does not always coincide exactly with the ecliptic. With the exception of the Sun, which traces the ecliptic with its apparent path, the Moon and the planets may be located a bit above or below the ecliptic. This occurs because of the existence of differences between the orbits of the Earth and of the other planets. This divergence is expressed in terms of another celestial coordinate, **latitude**. When a planet is above the ecliptic, that is, in the north, it is said to have northern latitude; when it is located below, in the southern part, it is said to have southern latitude.

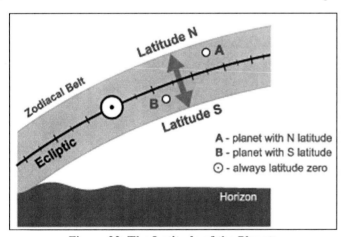

**Figure 22. The Latitude of the Planets**

Latitude is also expressed in degrees and minutes of arc, and ranges between 0° and 90°. In practice, it is represented by a number of degrees and minutes and the notation N if the latitude is north, and S if it is south. For example, 5°N23′ indicates a planet with a north latitude of 5 degrees and 23 minutes.

The zodiac is defined as a band of 16° (8° above and 8° below the ecliptic, which is the central line), such that it may accommodate the variations in latitude that the planets exhibit over time. The latitude of each planet has a varying range of maximum and minimum distance. Of the traditional planets, Venus has the greatest variation in latitude, since its maximum latitude reaches close to 9°.[9]

---

[9]Of the modern planets, Pluto exhibits the greatest variation in latitude, almost 18° (which puts it outside the traditional limits of the zodiac during most of its orbit); Uranus and Neptune exhibit maximums between 1° and 2°, respectively.

In contrast to zodiacal longitude, the latitude of the planets does not get represented directly in the horoscope. It is generally located in adjacent tables.

In practice, the latitude is not used in the basic body of the interpretative system; it is merely applied interpretatively on a case by case basis when one makes more specific studies of the planets (for example, as an aid to physical description). As a general rule, the closer a planet is to the ecliptic, the stronger and more stable its effects. Traditionally, a planet with a north latitude is preferred to one with a south latitude since for an observer in the northern hemisphere it has greater visibility (it appears higher in the sky and stays longer above the horizon).[10] Nonetheless, as was stated earlier, the application of these rules is very secondary, being eclipsed by other interpretative elements of greater significance.

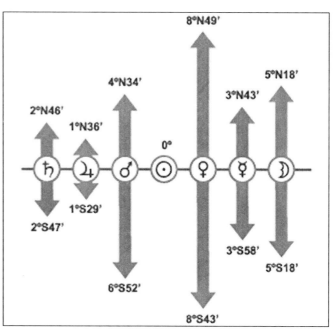

**Figure 23. The Range of Latitude of the Planets**

## The Cycles of the Planets

The motion of the planets in the zodiac is cyclical in nature because every planet repeats its own apparent motion around the Earth in regular periods of time. These cycles are important in order to understand the dynamic of the planet as well as a part of its symbolism. The planets have two cycles or major periods: a zodiacal cycle, also called sidereal, and a synodic cycle.

### Zodiacal or Sidereal Cycle

This is the period of time that it takes for a planet to complete a revolution around the Earth, or a revolution around the zodiac. The duration of the zodiacal cycle depends upon the speed of the planet.[11]

| Planet | Zodiacal Cycle |
| --- | --- |
| ♄ Saturn | 29y 5m 13d |
| ♃ Jupiter | 11y 10m 18d |
| ♂ Mars | 1y 10m 22d |
| ☉ Sun | 1y |
| ♀ Venus | 1y (aprox.) |
| ☿ Mercury | 1y (aprox.) |
| ☽ Moon | 27.5d |

---

[10]In principle these rules should be inverted for the southern hemisphere, for obvious reasons. However, there are no conclusive studies attesting to this.

[11]Due to their periods of retrograde motion, Mercury and Venus have an oscillating zodiacal cycle. Nonetheless, because of their proximity to the Sun, the values are always close to 365 days, that is, a year.

*Synodic Cycle*

The synodic cycle corresponds to the period of time that it takes a planet to return to its starting point in relation to the Sun. In practice, it consists of the period between two successive conjunctions of a planet to the Sun. The difference between this cycle and the previous one resides in the fact that it accounts for—aside from the speed of the planets—the speed of the Sun.

| Planet | Synodic Cycle |
|---|---|
| ♄ Saturn | 1y 13d |
| ♃ Jupiter | 1y 34d |
| ♂ Mars | 2y 50d |
| ♀ Venus | 1y 34d |
| ☿ Mercury | 219d |
| ☽ Moon | 29.5d |

In the case of planets that move faster than the Sun, when the planet returns to the same point in the zodiac, the Sun has already moved and it is necessary that the planet travel a bit more to reach it. As for the slower planets, it is the Sun that reaches them.

## The *Auge* of the Planets

This is a traditional concept that comes up in the context of the model of the celestial spheres and does not have a direct application to the astronomical heliocentric model. It is frequently mentioned by traditional authors, which is why we've decided to include it here even though its importance in astrological interpretation is extremely small.

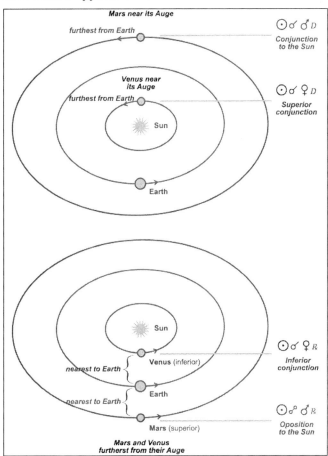

During their travel around the Sun, planets may be closer or farther from Earth. The phase of greatest distance is known as **auge.** When a planet gets close to this point, it is said to "ascend to its *auge*" and is considered to be advantaged; when it gets far from this point, it is said to "descend from its *auge*" and is considered to be disadvantaged.

In an astrological chart we can determine this situation by observing the conjunctions of the planets with the Sun. The superior planets (Saturn, Jupiter and Mars) reach their *auge* close to the conjunction with the Sun; they are said to ascend to their *auge* when the Sun gets close to them, and to descend from their *auge* when the Sun moves away from them. The inferior planets (Venus and Mercury) are at their *auge* during the superior conjunctions of the Sun (that is in direct motion), finding themselves farthest from *auge* when they are in inferior conjunction (during retrograde motion). The Moon is close to its *auge* when its speed is slower, and far from it when it is faster.

**Figure 24. The *Auge* of the Planets (Apogee and Perigee)**

We may equate *auge* to the planet's apogee and its opposite point, perigee.[12] Although these concepts are generally applied to the Moon, in a geocentric perspective, they may be applied to the remaining planets.

### The Zodiac in Astronomy and History

The zodiac is a very ancient celestial structure that was probably defined by Mesopotamian civilizations. Its representation may be found in almost all of the classical civilizations. The 12 divisions probably derived from the seasons of the year and lunar movement since the Sun and Moon encounter each other 12 times in a year at the New Moon. This gave birth to the 12 calendar months and, as a consequence, to the 12 divisions in the sky along the path of the Sun.[13]

At an earlier time, these divisions marked by stars and the signs of the zodiac would have corresponded to groups of stars: the zodiacal constellations. This zodiac, based upon constellations, is known as the **sidereal zodiac.**

With the passage of time, astrologers/astronomers noted that the beginning of the seasons and the signs were not in sync and that this discrepancy increased with time. Thus the phenomenon known as the **precession of the equinoxes** was discovered. This motion causes the dislocation of the vernal point (the point where the Sun is located on the spring equinox) in relation to the background stars. In this manner, the vernal point crosses all the constellations of the zodiac in a period of 25,920 years (changing a sign every 2,160 years). This motion occurs in the inverse order of the constellations (that is, the equinox moves from the constellation of Aries to Pisces, then to Aquarius, etc.) and is caused by the cyclical wobble of the Earth's axis.

In order to avoid this distancing and to definitively associate the zodiac with the seasons, the sidereal zodiac was replaced by the tropical

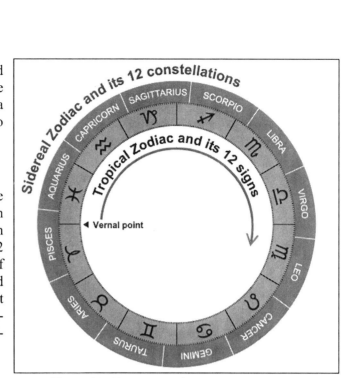

**Figure 25. Sidereal Zodiac, Tropical Zodiacal**

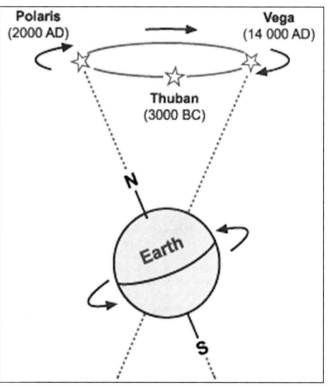

**Figure 26. The Precession of the Equinoxes and Earth's Axis**

---

[12]The term apogee comes from a Greek term that means "far from the Earth" in the same way that perigee means "close to the Earth" in Greek. The same is applied to the planets in relation to the Sun: aphellium means "far from the Sun" and perihellium means "close to the Sun."

[13]It should be noted that sometimes there are 13 lunations in a solar year, which causes a discrepancy between the solar and lunar calendars.

zodiac, wherein the signs are divisions of the four seasons of the year. This is the zodiac used by the western tradition (and whose structure was covered in this chapter). We do not know when this change was made. Its great promoter was, without a doubt, Claudius Ptolemy (c.100-c.178), but the concept may be far older than this author. Because both zodiacs were almost the same at the time of Ptolemy (beginning of the Christian era), it is extremely difficult to determine which of the two zodiacs was used by the astrologers of the time. Nevertheless, almost all post-Ptolemaic western authors use the tropical zodiac. The great exception is Hindu astrology, which evolved separately from the western tradition after the Greek period and still uses the sidereal zodiac.

## Constellation Versus Sign

Thus, in the western astrological tradition, when we speak of the **signs** we are not referring to constellations. The names coincide because the symbolism of the signs was extrapolated to a great extent from the constellations. When someone says that he or she was born in the sign of Capricorn (referring to his or her Sun-sign), you'll perhaps be surprised to discover that from an astronomical perspective, the Sun is in fact in the constellation of Sagittarius. The actual current discrepancy between both zodiacs is 24° and it is known as an *ayanamsa* (a Sanskrit term).

> Despite the fact that astrologers have known of this difference for at least 2,000 years, many students and (even worse) some astrology professionals, not knowing this fact, (or purposely ignoring it for simplicity), insist upon referring to the signs as constellations, thus, perpetuating the confusion.

This point does not invalidate astrology, as is often argued; it merely indicates a reference that is different from that used in astronomy. Seasons and signs are the references used in the tropical zodiac, and the groups of stars (constellations) are those of the sidereal zodiac.

## The Astrological Ages

Another phenomenon associated with the precession of the equinoxes is the sequence of astrological ages. Since the vernal point takes 2,160 years to cross a constellation, it is said that during that period that particular constellation rules over and determines worldly topics. This is the case of the famous Age of Aquarius, into which we are all heading, according to some, or in which we are currently living, according to others.

On the basis of the most common computations, the vernal point is found at this moment at roughly 6° Pisces and is slowly progressing (1° every 72 years) into the constellation of Aquarius. If this calculation is correct, we should enter the Age of Aquarius in 432 years. Since the boundaries of constellations are highly disputed, these calculations are left to the imagination and creativity of the various authors.

> The Ages are often used by modern mystical/esoteric systems to explain the evolution of humanity throughout history and to justify apparent alterations in human behavior. Although interesting, this theory is not mentioned in any significant manner in the traditional sources, nor is any practical application attributed to it by the tradition (as far as we know). There is no evidence for the astrological interpretation of the precession of the equinoxes prior to 1870. It is therefore a relatively recent concept. In contrast, the traditional system does frequently, and in a more practical manner, employ other types of cycles, particularly in the areas of mundane astrology.

## Chapter VI
# *The Essential Dignities*

### The System of Essential Dignities and Debilities

We've now seen how the planets express their natures and how that expression is colored by the characteristics of the signs in which they find themselves. We will now further develop that concept.

When placed in the same sign, planets exhibit common qualities given to them by that sign. Nevertheless, some planets have a greater ease of expression in particular signs than they do in others. It all depends upon the comfort level the planet has in that zodiacal position. Thus, there are areas in the zodiac where the expression of a planet is naturally strong and stable, while in others the same planet experiences difficulties. These areas are defined by the natural order of the zodiac and the celestial spheres.

When a planet finds itself in a segment of the zodiac in which its nature is reinforced, it is said to be dignified; when it finds itself in an area where its expression is challenged, it is said to be debilitated. These states of dignity and debility are known as **essential** because they reinforce or challenge the manifestation of the planet's essence. When dignified, the planet acquires greater *status* in the horoscope and becomes, to a greater or lesser degree, lord of its own actions. When debilitated, the planet loses power and becomes conditioned by the remaining planets.

In the system of essential dignities, there are five dignified states and two debilitated states.

### The Major Dignities
The major dignities are domicile, or rulership, and exaltation. When a planet has dignity, it acquires power and its expression is more marked. Opposing these dignities are the debilities of detriment and fall. If a planet has debility, its expression is weak and irregular. Because of their importance and the power they bestow on planets, dignities (and corresponding debilities) are designated major, fundamental, and complete.

### *Domicile or Rulership*
The most important dignity is that of domicile, or rulership. Each sign has a ruling planet that acts as king or lord of that "territory." **The ruler is the key through which the characteristics of the sign are expressed.**

Thus, in addition to the primary qualities (elements, modes, and gender), the signs are characterized by their ruling planet. As we've seen, the signs ruled by Saturn have a structured and austere expression due to the nature of its ruler; the signs ruled by Jupiter share a posture that is enthusiastic and adaptable; those of Mars have a bellicose and assertive manner; the sign ruled by the Sun is radiant; those of Venus express themselves in a gentle and harmonious manner; those of Mercury are multifaceted; and the sign of the Moon has a changeable and flowing expression.

When the ruling planet is in the sign that it rules, it is said to be dignified. As with a king who is ruling his land, the planet expresses its best nature in the most stable and productive manner. For example, if Venus is posited in one of its ruling signs, Taurus or Libra, its expression will be gentle and pleasant, whether in terms of the sensual and practical aspects of the earth (Taurus) or in the social and communicative aspects of air (Libra).

> Important: In the ancient sources, the sign that a planet rules is also called "the house of the planet"; often, the terms **domicile** and **house** are used interchangeably. In classical works, there are frequent references to the sign of Cancer as "the house of the Moon," or to Capricorn or Aquarius as the "house of Saturn." To avoid confusion between the astrological houses and the signs (in the domicile sense) we will not use "house" to refer to signs in this book. The reader should nonetheless be aware of this use of terminology when consulting the traditional authors.

*How Rulership is Assigned*

The assignment of rulership is based upon a combination of two distinct factors: the seasonal characteristics of the sign and its order in the celestial spheres (the Chaldean order). Let's see how these two factors interact.

As was stated, the zodiac is based upon the four seasons of the year. The signs Cancer and Leo mark the height of summer. Since they correspond to the times of greatest daylight, they have the two lights as rulers: the Sun and the Moon. The Sun—the masculine light and lord of the day—rules Leo, a masculine and diurnal sign. The Moon—the feminine light and lady of the night—rules Cancer, a feminine and nocturnal sign. Saturn, the most distant and darkest planet—rules the two winter signs, Capricorn and Aquarius. Because it is a symbol of scarcity, Saturn belongs to the rulership scheme opposite the two lights, symbols of abundance and life. The remaining planets are distributed throughout the signs according to their positions in the celestial spheres, the Chaldean order. Jupiter, the planet that succeeds Saturn in the order of the spheres, rules the two adjacent signs, Sagittarius and Pisces. Mars rules the next two signs,

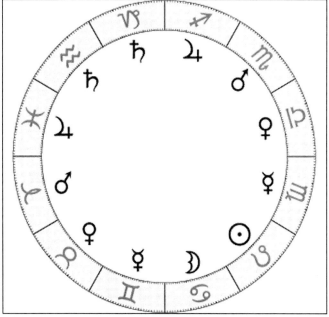

**Figure 1. Planetary Rulers**

Aries and Scorpio. Venus rules Taurus and Libra, and Mercury rules Gemini and Virgo. *Contrary to what is often stated, the rulerships are not assigned on the basis of affinities between signs and planets.*

You'll note that in this scheme Venus and Mercury retain, in relation to the lights, the same maximum distance that they attain relative to the Sun. Since Mercury is never more than one sign from the Sun, it is given rulership over the signs next to the two lights (Sun and Moon). Venus rules the next two signs since its maximum distance from the Sun never exceeds two signs.

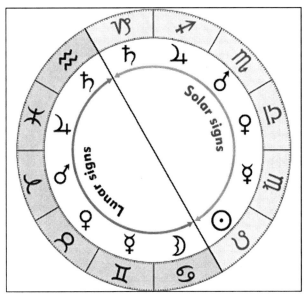

**Figure 2. Solar and Lunar Signs**

We can then see that the rulership scheme projects onto the zodiac the perfection of the celestial spheres. The perfect distribution of the planetary rulers generates several symmetrical relationship arrangements among the planets that are crucial for an understanding of astrological foundations. This distribution divides the zodiac into lunar signs (from Aquarius to Cancer) and solar signs (from Leo to Capricorn).

Each planet is also assigned a diurnal rulership for a masculine sign and a nocturnal rulership for a feminine sign. Thus, each planet has an extroverted expression (diurnal, masculine) and an introverted expression (nocturnal, feminine). For example, Venus has a nocturnal rulership in Taurus, a feminine and nocturnal sign, and a diurnal rulership in Libra, a masculine and diurnal sign.

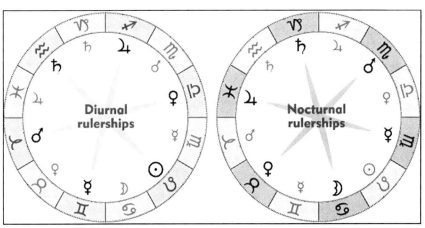

**Figure 3. Diurnal and Nocturnal Rulerships**

The lights do not possess this duplicity because they define the concept of day and night.

*Joy by Sign*

In some rulerships, the nature of the planet is tempered by the nature of the actual sign; when this happens we say that the planet is in its joy. Jupiter, a masculine and diurnal planet, has its joy in Sagittarius, a sign equally masculine and diurnal. Venus, a feminine and nocturnal planet, has its joy in Taurus, which shares the same nature. Mercury, which is essentially dry, has its joy in the cold and dry sign Virgo.

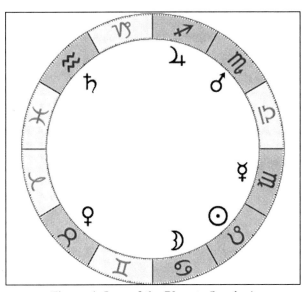

**Figure 4. Joys of the Planets (by sign)**

This moderating action manifests both by reinforcement (the cases above) as well as by contraposition (the case

> Note: the joy by sign should not be confused with the joy by house.

of malefic planets). Mars, which is nocturnal, is more constructive in Scorpio, also a nocturnal sign, but whose cold and moist qualities temper the excessively hot and dry qualities of the planet. Saturn (diurnal) is more balanced in the sign Aquarius, where its excessively cold and dry nature is tempered by the hot and moist qualities of the sign.

*Exile or Detriment*

When a planet is in the sign opposite its rulership it is said to be in exile or detriment. This is the state opposite to that of domicile. In this situation the expression of the planet is debilitated. Its performance becomes insecure and indirect. Because it has difficulty expressing itself, its nature is weakened and distorted. When in detriment, the natural qualities of the planets transform themselves into their corresponding defects (the distortion of these qualities). Thus, the sobriety and caution of Saturn become melancholy and meanness; the generosity and optimism of Jupiter become squandering and disregard; the courage and assertiveness of Mars manifest as cowardice and aggression; the natural authority of the Sun becomes arrogance; the sensuality and sociability of Venus inclines toward luxury and frivolity; the curiosity and ingenuity of Mercury expresses itself as intrigue and fraud; and the adaptability of the Moon slips into inertia and laziness.

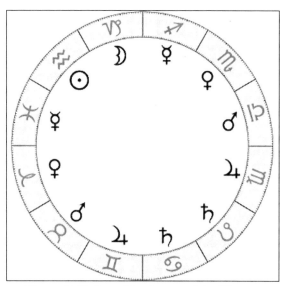

**Figure 5. Exile or Detriment of the Planets**

If the planet in detriment represents an object, it suggests something in a bad condition, not valuable, and possibly broken. Some authors use the terms exile or envy to designate this debility.

*Exaltation*

In some cases the ruler of a sign may have a planet that is second-in-command that shares with it the governing functions of the "realm." The name exaltation is given to this second state of dignity. The term exaltation comes from the Latin *exalto* and means to raise up, elevate, and honor. We may compare exaltation to the role of prime minister: a dignitary with many honors and power but whose action continues to be dependent upon the approval of the king. An exalted planet finds itself in a state of great power. We may even say that it expresses its na-

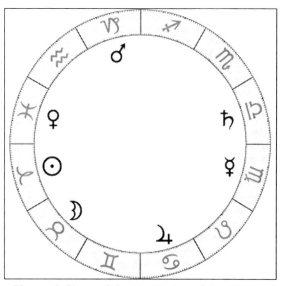

**Figure 6. Signs of the Exaltation of the Planets**

ture with a greater intensity than it has in its rulership state. However, the expression of an exalted planet is more inconstant, going through highs and lows. Each planet is exaltated in only one sign.

In an astrological interpretation we might consider that an exalted planet simultaneously indicates value and exuberance. If the planet represents an individual, it suggests someone respected and well-intentioned but with a tendency toward exaggeration and even arrogance. An object represented by an exalted planet will be in good condition, but may seem more valuable than it actually is. Some authors use the term **honor** to refer to this dignity.

*Fall*

Corresponding to the exaltation is a debility known as fall, which occurs in the opposite sign. Just as in the case of detriment, a planet in fall has difficulties expressing its nature. In fall, that difficulty is characterized by instability in its expression. The planet becomes "clumsy," its action is inadequate, inappropriate. Some authors refer to this debility as **depression** or **shame**.

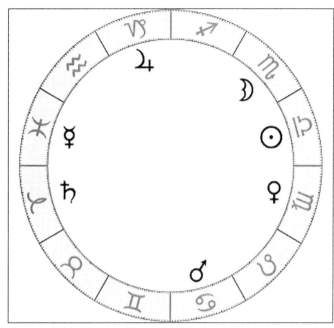

**Figure 7. Signs of Fall of the Planets**

*How Exaltation and Fall Are Assigned*

The explanation of exaltation also has an "agricultural" logic as its basis. It is tied to the degree of fertility of the planet and to its affinity with a particular season of the year.

The **Sun** is exaltated in Aries because spring begins[14] when it enters this sign, and the days begin to get longer and warmer. Its hot and dry nature is identical to that of Aries and its ruler Mars. Its fall occurs in Libra, a sign that signals the diminishing of light and the beginning of autumn.

The **Moon** is exalted in Taurus, a feminine spring sign, adjacent to Aries, the sign of the Sun's exaltation. As queen of the heavens, she remains positioned next to her king. Furthermore, if the Sun were in Aries, the Moon when leaving its rays, would be visible for the first time in Taurus. Scorpio, opposite Taurus, is its sign of fall.

**Saturn** is exaltated in Libra, the sign opposite the exaltation of the Sun. Libra signals the start of autumn, a season when temperatures become colder and the days decrease in length. It is thus the ideal sign for exaltation of the coldest planet, Saturn. By the same logic, its fall is in Aries, the first sign of spring.

**Jupiter**, planet of fertility and abundance, is exaltated in Cancer, a sign of summer and of the ripening of the crops. Its fall is in Capricorn.

**Mars**, is exaltated in Capricorn, where its extreme heat is tempered by the cold of winter. Its fall is in Cancer.

**Venus**, a feminine and moist planet, is exalted in Pisces, a sign of humidity that makes way for the fertility of Spring. Its fall is in Virgo, a sign that marks the passage into autumn and the predominance of dryness.

**Mercury**, of a dry nature, is exaltated in Virgo, a cold and dry sign (which it also rules), and in its fall in Pisces, a cold and moist sign.

*The Degrees of Exaltation*

Tradtional authors also assign specific degrees of exaltation to the exaltation of the planets. Thus, the Sun has its exaltation at 19 Aries, the Moon at 3 Taurus, Jupiter at 15 Cancer, Mercury at 15 Virgo, Saturn at 21 Libra, Mars at 28 Capricorn, and Venus at 27 Pisces. Fall occurs in the same degree of the opposite sign. In practice, however, the exaltation is considered in the full width of the sign. These degrees appear to indicate the points of greater strength. Some researchers believe them to be symbolic positions, what remains of an astronomical system of great importance to the ancients.

---

[14]Recall that astrological logic has the northern hemisphere in mind. In the southern hemisphere the ingress of the Sun into Aries corresponds to the Autumn.

## Secondary Dignities

Rulership, exaltation, detriment, and fall are the major dignities (also called "complete") of the astrological system. It is possible to perform a basic interpretation of a horoscope relying solely on the scoring of these four factors.

However, the system of dignities is more complex. In addition to rulership and exaltation, there are three other levels of dignity: triplicity, term, and face. These additional dignities, apart from having specific technical applications, allow for a better evaluation of the potential expression of every planet in the various degrees of the zodiac. By using the whole system, we can understand how in some horoscopes, apparently debilitated planets can have an expression more consistent with their natures. One might additionally say that, in contrast to rulership and exaltation, the triplicities, terms, and faces don't have a complimentary debility. For this reason, they are also designated incomplete dignities.

### Triplicities

The triplicities are dignities assigned according to the element of each sign. Three planets are assigned to each element: one called diurnal, another nocturnal, and a third called participating or common (mixed). These three planets are common to the signs belonging to each element.

For the fire element, the Sun is the diurnal triplicity, the nocturnal triplicity is Jupiter, and Saturn is the participating triplicity.

The air element has Saturn for the diurnal triplicity, Mercury for the nocturnal triplicity, and Jupiter for participating triplicity.

For the earth element, the diurnal triplicity is Venus, the nocturnal is the Moon, and the participating is Mars.

Water also has Venus as the diurnal triplicity, Mars has the nocturnal triplicity and the Moon is participating.

As can be seen, the assignment of the triplicities to each element follows the sect of the planets: diurnal planets are attributed to the diurnal sect, and nocturnal planets to the nocturnal sect.

| Element | | Diurnal Triplicity | Nocturnal Triplicity | Participant Triplicity |
|---------|------|--------------------|----------------------|------------------------|
| Fire | ♈ ♌ ♐ | ☉ | ♃ | ♄ |
| Air | ♊ ♎ ♒ | ♄ | ☿ | ♃ |
| Earth | ♉ ♍ ♑ | ♀ | ☽ | ♂ |
| Water | ♋ ♏ ♓ | ♀ | ♂ | ☽ |

In practice, a planet in its triplicity is literally among family since it finds itself in the element of its own sect. It is not in its realm (as in rulership), nor is it the prime minister (as in exaltation), but it is a part of the royal family and therefore enjoys some power. A planet in its own triplicity is among friends.

Some authors state that in a diurnal chart the diurnal triplicity is the strongest and that the nocturnal will have more impact in a nocturnal chart. The participating triplicity will always have a moderate strength. In any event, a planet posited in a sign in which it possesses triplicity is in a state of dignity, independent of whether the chart is diurnal or nocturnal.

The rulers of the triplicities are generally considered in sequence, receiving the label of first, second, and third triplicity. This sequence depends upon whether the chart is diurnal or nocturnal. (Recall that in diurnal charts, the Sun is above the horizon, and in nocturnal charts it is below the horizon.) In diurnal charts we give

| **Figure 8. Diurnal Sequence of Triplicities** | | |
| --- | --- | --- |
| Element | *First Triplicity* | *Second Triplicity* | *Third Triplicity* |
| Fire | ☉ | ♃ | ♄ |
| Air | ♄ | ☿ | ♃ |
| Earth | ♀ | ☽ | ♂ |
| Water | ♀ | ♂ | ☽ |

| **Figure 9. Nocturnal Sequence Triplicities** | | |
| --- | --- | --- |
| Element | *First Triplicity* | *Second Triplicity* | *Third Triplicity* |
| Fire | ♃ | ☉ | ♄ |
| Air | ☿ | ♄ | ♃ |
| Earth | ☽ | ♀ | ♂ |
| Water | ♂ | ♀ | ☽ |

### Variations in the Assignment of Triplicities

The group of triplicities that we present in this book is the most common among traditional astrologers, and is known as The Dorothean Triplicities, not because this author created them, but because he is the oldest source to reference them.

During the Renaissance there was a large reformation of astrological theory on the basis of Ptolemaic teachings. Consequently, the Dorothean triplicities were gradually substituted by versions based upon Ptolemy's works. Ptolemy changed the participating planets in the fire element, substituting Saturn for Mars, and in earth, substituting Mars for Saturn. He also altered the triplicities for water, giving the sequence as: Venus, Moon, Mars.

One of the currently most popularized versions is from the English school, of which well-known authors such as William Lilly are the most representative. This lineage uses only the diurnal triplicities in diurnal charts, and the nocturnal triplicities in nocturnal charts. The sequences are the same as those in Dorotheus, but the participating planet is abandoned. The only exception occurs in water, where Mars (nocturnal ruler for water in Dorotheus) is considered simultaneous ruler of the diurnal and nocturnal triplicities.

precedence to the diurnal triplicity, followed by the nocturnal and the participating; in nocturnal charts, the precedence is given to the nocturnal triplicity, followed by the diurnal and the participating.

In very specific interpretative techniques (see Appendix 4, Additional Considerations Concerning the Houses), the triplicities indicate temporal sequences. It is in these cases that the diurnal and nocturnal sequences become more relevant because the order of the planets is decisive.

*Terms*

The terms are divisions of the signs into five unequal divisions. To each part (or term) is assigned the rulership of one of the five traditional planets: Jupiter, Venus, Mars, Saturn. The Sun and Moon do not rule terms.

The greatest peculiarity about the terms is irregularity. Each division consists of unequal parts of the same sign, and each sign is divided in different ways. In addition, the sequence of the rulers also differs from sign to sign; that is, no two signs are the same with respect to their terms. For example, in Aries the first division has 6°; the second has 6°; the third has 8°; and the fourth and fifth each have 5°. In the following sign, Taurus, the respective divisions have 8°, 6°, 8°, 5°, and 3°. Also, the sequence of planets is completely different in these signs. In Aries, the first term belongs to Jupiter, the second to Venus, the third to Mercury, the fourth to Mars, and the last to Saturn. While to Taurus, the sequence of term rulerships is: Venus, Jupiter, Mercury, Saturn and Mars.

The logic for these divisions has been lost in time. The most ancient authors, namely Ptolemy, suggest that the distribution depends upon the degree of dignity that each planet has in a sign, giving priority sometimes to rulership, sometimes to exaltation, sometimes to triplicity. Mars and Saturn, because they are malefics, tend to rule over the last two terms, while the benefics, Jupiter and Venus, are given the initial terms.

The terms most frequently used in this book are the Egyptian Terms. This sequence appears in the works of most ancient authors and has been most consistent throughout time.

The term of a planet can be compared to its "fiefdom" within a sign. A planet in its own term is in its own private territory, even if the sign where it is located is not particularly favorable to it. It can therefore act according to its own rules (literally, "on its own terms"). The term also has an effect on the quality of expression of the planets. For example, a planet in the terms of Saturn, will have a more reserved expression, while a planet in the terms of Jupiter will have a more jovial expression. Some authors use the words "limits," "boundaries," or "ends" to refer to this dignity.

*Faces*

The faces[15] or decanates are regular 10° divisions of a sign, and because each sign has 30°, there are three faces in each sign. To each face is assigned a ruling planet according to the Chaldean order. Assigned to the first face of Aries is Mars, the planet that rules Aries, followed by the face of the Sun and of Venus. The following planet in the Chaldean order is Mercury, the planet assigned to the first face of Taurus, followed by the Moon and Saturn. Jupiter, the next planet in the sequence, is assigned to the first face of Gemini, followed by Mars and the Sun. The Chaldean order continues through the zodiac.

The faces are relatively weaker dignities because they only slightly reinforce the nature of the planet. Apart from being a part of the scoring system of essential dignities and debilities, they are applied in specific interpretative systems, where they serve to detail behavioral differences of the signs. From this perspective they are used in detailed interpretations of the Ascendant and the Sun.

There are other types of dignities that arise from divisions of the zodiac that are even smaller or from the attribution of qualities to particular degrees. Since these dignities do not have such a widespread application, we will not discuss them in this chapter. Some of these systems are referred to in Appendix 3, Minor Dignities.

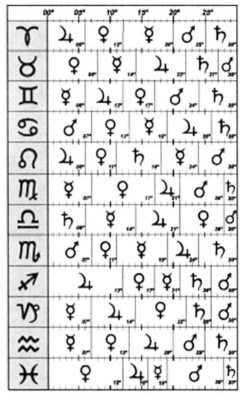

**Figure 10. Egyptian Terms**

### Variations on the Assignment of the Terms

There are other variations on the terms that are worth mentioning. The most important is the table of Ptolemaic terms. This version of the terms is suggested by Ptolemy in his work *Tetrabiblos.* It is also mentioned in Medieval sources, but its use seems to have been very sporadic. During the Renaissance, Ptolemy's work became more prevalent and his table was popularized. Nevertheless, various versions of his table were circulated with significant variations (many of them mere scribal errors). Two versions of this table are currently in use (see Appendix 3, Minor Dignities). Ptolemy refers to an additional table which he designates as the Chaldean terms, but which is not presented in any other contemporary work. There are no known examples of its use.

---

[15]This designation derives from phase, referring to a stage in time, and not, as might be supposed, to face, in the sense of facial appearance.

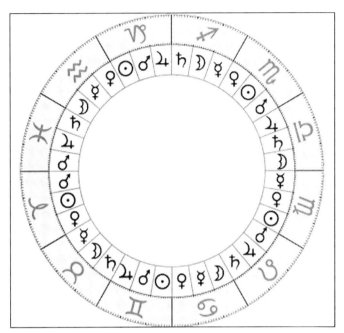

**Figure 11. The Faces**

| | Figure 12. Essential Dignities and Debilities | |
|---|---|---|
| | Rulership or Domicile | +5 |
| | Exaltation | +4 |
| **Digities:** | Triplicity | +3 |
| | Term | +2 |
| | Face | +1 |
| | | |
| **Debilities:** | Fall | -4 |
| | Exile or Detriment | -5 |

## Variations on the Assignment of the Faces

With respect to the western astrological tradition, there are no known variations on the assignment of faces to the planets. Nevertheless, a variant based upon the Hindu astrological decanate system, which is very different from the western faces, is currently being widely published. In the Hindu system, the distribution of the planets is based upon the elements and the sign rulerships. The first decanate of a sign is assigned to the ruler of that sign, the second to the ruler of the subsequent sign of the same element, and the third to the last sign of the same element. For example, for Capricorn, the first decanate corresponds to Saturn (ruler of Capricorn), the second to Venus (ruler of Taurus, the next earth sign), the third to Mercury (ruler of Virgo, the remaining earth sign).

Although interesting, this system is a part of another tradition and should not be mixed with the system of the western tradition. Its insertion into western astrology is a consequence of the great trend of eastern importations of the end of the 19th century and was made by authors who did not know the fundamental rules of astrology.

Other decanate systems based upon mixtures or derivations of the traditional or the Hindu are often referenced in the astrological literature, but their validity and origin are questionable and will not be treated in this work.

## Dispositors and Rulers

### The Dispositor

The ruler of a sign is similar to a king: he has dominion over everything that is found in his kingdom (the sign it rules). This applies not only to planets situated in that sign, but also to the house cusps, Parts, etc. It is said that the ruling planet disposits (or rules) those other planets or astrological factors. The concept of dispositor is of primary importance in astrological interpretation. On the one hand, it adds a coloring of its nature to all of the planets and elements of the horoscope that find themselves in its sign. For example, if Venus, a planet naturally agreeable and sociable, is in Capricorn, its expression will become more reserved because Saturn is its dispositor.

On the other hand, the dispositor regulates the expression of the planet it disposits, confirming or contradicting its characteristics. In interpretation, it indicates the motivations underlying the expression of the planet. For example, considering Venus in Capricorn once more, its expression is further modified by the conditions of Saturn in the horoscope. If Saturn is strong, the reserve it bestows upon Venus will manifest with moderation and elegance; if it is weak it could indicate defensiveness and trepidation.

In summary, the dispositor bestows upon the planet that it disposits its own state or condition in the horoscope, adding to the action of the disposited planet its own capabilities (if it is dignified) or difficulties (if debilitated). Returning to the previous example, if Venus in Capricorn is disposited by a dignified Saturn (for example, positioned in Aquarius, the sign of its rulership), the expression of Venus will be enabled by the positive condition of Saturn. The motivations underlying the emotional expression of Venus will be sober (since Saturn is dispositor), but that sobriety is socially acceptable and integrated such that it will not engender great problems.

If, on the other hand, the same Venus in Capricorn is disposited by a debilitated Saturn (for example, in Cancer, the sign of its detriment), the reserve of Venus will be colored by the emotional fears and difficulties characteristic of Saturn in that position, generating defensiveness and trepidation, which are motivated by the debilitated condition of the dispositor. In comparison, if the debility of Saturn results from being posited in Aries (the sign of its fall), the motivations that it bestows upon Venus will be of a different nature. Instead of exhibiting a tinge of shyness (Cancer), Venus will flaunt the dry and abrupt characteristics of Saturn in Aries. We can thus see that the nature of the difficulties varies in accordance with the type of debility of the dispositor.

In some cases the dispositor is found in the same sign of the planet that it disposits. This then becomes its own dispositor, creating a type of "crossed" disposition. In such a case it is said that the two planets are in **mutual disposition**. For example, Venus in Capricorn will be in mutual disposition with Saturn if Saturn is in Taurus or Libra (signs of Venus). When this happens, the planets reinforce each other mutually even if their natures are not particularly compatible.

If we apply the system of dispositions to all the planets of a horoscope, we find that in some cases the chain of dispositions ends in one sole planet. This planet is designated the **final dispositor** and has great predominance in the chart. For example, consider a horoscope with the following planetary positions: Saturn in Sagittarius, Jupiter in Cancer, Mars in Aquarius, Sun in Libra, Venus and Mercury in Virgo, Moon in Gemini. If we follow the dispositions of the planets, Mercury is the final dispositor; that is, Mars in Aquarius is disposited by Saturn, which in Sagittarius is disposited by Jupiter; Jupiter in Cancer has the Moon as its dispositor, and since the Moon is in Gemini, it is disposited by Mercury in Virgo. Placed in its own sign of rulership (Virgo) Mercury has no dispositor. There are two planets missing: the Sun and Venus. Since the Sun is in Libra, it is disposited by Venus in Virgo, which brings us once more to Mercury. In practice, all the motivations in this horoscope would be colored by the analytic capabilities of Mercury in Virgo.

> Note: not all horoscopes have a final dispositor or mutual dispositions; some have other patterns of disposition, which are not as relevant and which are not detailed here.

Although it is usually applied to the ruler, the concept of disposition is also valid for other essential dignities: exaltation, triplicity, term, and face. The disposition will have more or less power according to the degree of dignity that the planet has in that area of the zodiac. Exaltation can serve as a second ruler, dispositing (by exaltation) the planets that are located there. The triplicity rulers are used in more specialized interpretations, providing indications about the different facets of a planet. Disposition by term is applied in only very specific cases, while the disposition by face is practically ignored since it is a weak dignity.

The planetary dignities and debilities are a system for assessing the capacity of expression of the planets. A dignified planet has its expression facilitated, and the same happens in relation to everything that the planet signifies in the horoscope. When it is in its own **rulership,** the planet has all its capabilities and expresses itself easily and with stability. In its **exaltation** it manifests with identical ease but with greater exuberance and less stability, and tends to suffer fluctuations. When it is in its own **triplicity**, the planet is comfortable and has a fluid expression. In its own **term**, it has a stable and secure behavior, although not as obvious as in the other cases. A planet in **face** is relatively well, although its power is greatly limited.

A debilitated planet manifests some difficulties and these extend themselves to everything that the planet signifies in the horoscope. When in **detriment**, the manifestation of the planet is difficult and laborious, with a tendency to deviate from its natural inclination. In **fall**, one feels, above all else, the instability, which translates into irregular, out of sync, and disproportionate manifestations.

Another of the functions of the system of dignities is to determine the ruling planets. These rule (that is, dominate) whatever planet finds itself in the signs where they hold power. For this reason, the system of dignities therefore reveals "the powers game" underlying the planets in the horoscope.

## Interpretation of Dignities and Debilities of the Planets in Nativities

Before explaining the system of scoring of the dignities and debilities, it is important to bring to light some fundamental considerations. These concern common mistakes in the first attempts at interpreting natal charts. For example, beginners frequently state that a debilitated Mercury indicates a stupid person, or that a debilitated Venus indicates someone lacking the capacity to love. This statement is based on profoundly incorrect presuppositions. The first statement presupposes that a debilitated planet does not work and that it indicates a bad person. In truth, the debilitated planet indicates difficulties in the area to which it is assigned (the house where it is positioned and also the houses it rules). These difficulties can only be understood when a planet is contextualized into the general dynamics of the horoscope.

There are other factors besides the essential dignities that can minimize this difficulty. In the life of a human being, these difficulties manifest as poorly executed or planned actions, or as confrontations with people and situations that are hard to deal with. The individual, however, can learn to manage all of these situations. The same can be said about erroneous conclusions related to dignified planets: it is incorrect to consider that they indicate, by themselves, exceptional qualities and good people.

The other incorrect presupposition is to attribute the cause of all manner of ills to a sole planet. Because of this, it is, at the very minimum, naive to evaluate the characteristics of the personality on the basis of a planetary position. The excessive use of the general signification of a planet also contributes to this mistake. For example, Mercury = mind, Venus = love, etc., without taking into account its specific signification in a particular horoscope.

## Scoring of Dignities and Debilities

### The Scoring System

The evaluation of essential dignities and debilities of the planets is made by a point system. A planet in rulership is awarded 5 points; a planet in exaltation, 4 points; in triplicity, 3 points; in term, 2 points; and in face, 1 point. As to the debilities, detriment corresponds to -5 points and fall to -4.

To score a particular planet, determine if the planet is found in any of its dignities, and if so, give it the re-

29°♏09′
- ♂ 5 (rulership) + 3 (triplicity) = **8 points**
- ♀ 3 (triplicity) + 1 (face) = 4 points
- ☽ 3 points (triplicity)
- ♄ 2 points (term)

**Figure 13. Scoring of Essential Dignities and Debilities**

spective number of points. The same procedure is followed for the debilities, giving them the corresponding negative points. The final score, negative or positive, for each planet shows the degree of dignity or debility of that planet. For example, Mercury at 16 Cancer is in its own term and face. It therefore receives 2 points for term and 1 for face, for a total of 3 points. Since Mercury has no debility in this sign, no points are subtracted. Another example: Jupiter at 4 Gemini is in its own participating triplicity and in its own face, for a total of 4 points. However, Jupiter is also in its detriment in this sign, so it loses 5 points. The final result is 1 negative point.

If the final score for the planet is positive, the planet is dignified. The more positive points the planet accumulates, the greater its dignity. A planet in rulership or exaltation that also has dignity by triplicity, term, or face reinforces its power.[16] The same occurs when a planet accumulates triplicity with term or face because the nature of the planet is reinforced. Planets that apparently are neutral in a horoscope can reveal themselves to be stronger than they appear. Thus, a planet with a positive score is considered in good condition. With a score above 4 points, it is considered strong. Above 5 points, it is considered very strong.

> Note that the state of debility is always given by detriment and fall, which are opposite the major dignities (rulership and exaltation); the dignities that mitigate that condition are always the minors (triplicity, term, or face), not having sufficient power to negate the debilitated state.

A planet with a negative score is considered debilitated. Although the debility may be attenuated by minor dignities, the planet will continue to have difficulties in its expression.

A planet with a negative score is thus considered in poor condition. With a score lower than 4 negative points, it is said to be clearly debilitated.

In some situations, debility is overcome by dignity, which results in a planet with some strength. Because they are opposites, rulership and exaltation cannot coexist with their respective debilities (detriment and fall). Nonetheless, there can exist overlaps between the debilities and other dignities: a planet in detriment or fall can at the same time be in triplicity, term, or face. In this case, the secondary dignities will mitigate the debilitated state of the planet in detriment or fall, and in specific instances they can even recover the dignity. For example, consider Venus at 12° Virgo. In this position Venus is in the sign opposite its own exaltation (Pisces), and thus in fall. The score of a planet in fall is -4. However, Venus has triplicity in Virgo and at 12° it is also in its own term and face. It thus gains 3 points for the triplicity, 2 for term, and 1 for face, and a total of 6 points. If we subtract the 4 negative points, there are still 2 positive points. Thus, an apparently debilitated planet can, if the minor dignities are counted, have some dignity. In practice, whatever Venus represents in the horoscope would not be greatly affected by the debility.

In other cases, the dignities and debilities cancel each other out, leaving the planet with a score of 0 points. In these cases, we consider that the planet is slightly weakened. For example, Venus at 8 Scorpio is in detriment, giving it 5 negative points; nonetheless, because it is in a water sign, it has diurnal triplicity, which gives it 3 points, and in this degree of Scorpio it is in its term, which adds 2 more points to it. The sum of the 5 negative points with 5 positive points is zero. We can then consider that the initial debility of the planet is attenuated by the minor dignities. There is still difficulty in expression, but it is not as noticeable.

There is one special case. When a planet has absolutely no dignity in its position, it is called **peregrine**. The term peregrine means "in passing." The planet has nothing of itself in that area of the zodiac, and therefore is subject to the "lords" that govern there and has little freedom of action. It is also considered a type of debility, which is aggravated in the case where it is added to detriment and fall.

---

[16]Ptolemy states that a planet which adds its major dignity with one or more minor dignities is in "its carriage" (in its victory chariot), or "elevated in its throne". A planet in these conditions is in a powerfully dignified state.

The **Sun** is peregrine in all of Taurus; in the first and second thirds of Gemini; all of Cancer; the second and third thirds of Virgo; all of Libra (where it is also debilitated by fall); the first and third thirds of Scorpio; the first and second thirds of Capricorn; all of Aquarius (where it is debilitated by detriment); and all of Pisces.

The **Moon** is peregrine in the signs Aries, Gemini, and Leo; in the second and third thirds of Libra; the first and third thirds of Sagittarius; and the first and second thirds of Aquarius.

Note: some authors designate a planet without dignity or debility in its position as peregrine. However, the majority seem to concur in attributing the peregrine designation to a planet without dignity, independently of whether or not it is debilitated. The actual term seems to point to this conclusion, since it suggests the idea of a wanderer, without ties or responsibilities.

**Mercury** is peregrine in Aries from 0° to 12° and from 20° to 29°; in Taurus from 14° to 29°; in the first and second thirds of Cancer; in Leo from 0° to 17° and from 24° to 29°; in Scorpio from 0° to 11° and from 19° to 29 °; in Sagittarius from 10° to 17° and from 21° to 29° (in this sign it is also in detriment); in Capricorn from 8° to 29°; and in Pisces from 0° to 16° and from 19° to 29° (in this sign it is also in detriment and fall).

**Venus** is peregrine in Aries from 0° to 16° and from 12° to 20° (in this sign it is also in detriment); in Gemini from 0° to 12° and from 17° to 29°; in Leo from 0° to 6° and from 11° to 29°; in Sagittarius from 0° to 12° and from 17° to 29°; and in Aquarius from 13° to 29°.

**Mars** is peregrine in Gemini from 0° to 10° and from 24° to 29°; in Leo in the first and second thirds; in Libra from 0° to 28° (in this sign it is also in detriment); in Sagittarius from 0° to 26°; and in Aquarius from 0°to 20° and from 25°to 29°.

**Jupiter** is peregrine in Taurus from 0° to 14° and from 22° to 29°; in Virgo from 0° to 17° and from 21° to 29° (where it is also in detriment), in Scorpio from 0° to 19° and from 24° to 29°; and in Capricorn from 14° to 29° (where it adds to the debility by fall).

**Saturn** is peregrine in the first and second thirds of Taurus; in Cancer from 0° to 26° (where it adds to detriment); in Virgo from 0° to 28°; in Scorpio from 0° to 24°; and in Pisces from 10° to 27°.

## Variants on the Scoring System

The system of scoring that we presented is the most current, particularly since the end of the Middle Ages. However, some Arabic authors such as Ali Ben Ragel and Al-Biruni, gave more importance to term than to triplicity. In that system of scoring (apparently older) term received 3 points and triplicity 2. In the medieval astrological literature there also exist references to other systems, but these appear not to have had a practical relevant expression.

## Example Scoring of the Essential Dignities

This example uses the horoscope of German philosopher Friedrich Nietzsche to score the dignities and debilities of the planets. We start by noting the zodiacal position of each planet and, using the table of essential dignities, assign the respective scores.

**Saturn** is at 0° Aquarius 46′. In this position it receives 5 points for rulership and 3 more for the diurnal triplicity ruler of this air sign. It has no debilities. Saturn, therefore, has 8 total points.

**Jupiter** is at 26° Pisces 02′. It also has rulership, therefore receives 5 points; but it has no other dignity, therefore we do not add any more points. Since it also has no debility, no points are subtracted from it. It totals 5 points.

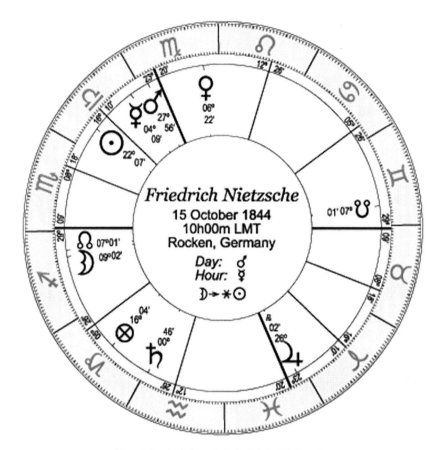

**Chart 1. Nativity of Friedrich Nietzsche**

**Mars** is at 27° Virgo 56′. Because it is in an earth sign, it receives 3 points for participating triplicity; it also has 2 points for being in its own terms. Since it has no debilities, it accumulates a total of 5 points. The **Sun** is located in Libra, at 22°07′. In this sign the Sun has no dignity at all. Since it is in fall, it receives 4 negative points. It has a total of -4 points. **Venus** is at 6° Virgo 22′. It receives 3 points for diurnal triplicity for being in an earth sign, but 4 points are subtracted for being in the sign of its fall. Its final score is -1 point. **Mercury** is at 4° Libra 09′. In this air sign it receives 3 points for nocturnal triplicity. It has no more dignities nor debilities, making a total of 3 points. The **Moon** is at 9° Sagittarius 02′. In this zodiacal position the Moon has no dignity or debility at all; it thus receives 0 points.

Comparing the results, we can see that Saturn is the most dignified planet with a total of 8 points, followed by Jupiter and Mars, both with 5 points, and Mercury with 3 points of dignity. All these planets are dignified, therefore everything that they signify in the chart will have a stable and constructive expression.

On the other hand, the Sun and Venus have negative scores, finding themselves debilitated. Those things they signify in the chart will have a more difficult and laborious expression. The Moon has 0 points, it is therefore not dignified; in these cases we consider that the planet is slightly debilitated. The Moon in Sagittarius and the Sun in Libra are peregrine, where the latter adds the condition of peregrine to that of fall.

With this scoring system we can determine with ease the operational state of the planets. Although these scoring systems serve to measure the quality of a planet's expression, they are only one factor in delineation, they should not be interpreted by themselves. The dignity or debility of a planet only makes sense in the context of the entire horoscope.

The scoring system serves only to aid the astrologer in the evaluation of dignity and debility. It gives us an approximate notion of the effective power of the planets and should not be applied in a rigid manner. One must remember that this *quantitative* method is an aid to interpretation, which is *qualitative*.

In practice, there is no point wasting time on overly detailed comparisons of the scores of planets. The idea is to have a notion of its relative strength and apply that information to the (properly contextualized) interpretation of the planet.

**Almuten**

The word *almuten* is a corruption of an Arabic term that means "the victorious" or "the winner." In astrology the *almuten* is considered to be the planet that possesses the most dignity in a particular point in the horoscope. As an example, consider Mercury at 4° Libra 09′ in Nietzsche's horoscope. Through the table of essential dignities we'll see which planets have dignity in this degree of the zodiac. Since the sign is Libra, with Venus as its ruler, Mercury receives 5 points. In Libra, the exaltation belongs to Saturn, so it gets 4 points, and since Libra is an air sign, Saturn also has diurnal triplicity, so it gets 3 more points. In the table we can see that the fourth degree of Libra is also the term of this planet, so it receives 2 more points. Saturn, therefore, scores a total of 9 points. The remaining triplicities of the air element belong to Mercury (nocturnal) and Jupiter (participating) therefore both acquire 3 points in this position. Now consider face: consulting the table, the first 10° of Libra are under the dominion of the Moon, so 1 point is added.

04°♎09′
- ♀ 5 points (rulership)
- ♄ 4 (exaltation) + 3 (triplicity) + 2 (term) = **9 points**
- ♃ 3 points (triplicity)
- ☿ 3 points (triplicity)
- 1 point (face)

**Figure 14. Scoring of Planets at 4° Libra 09′**

Saturn is clearly the planet with the highest score in that degree; we therefore conclude that Saturn is the *almuten* of Mercury in this horoscope. This means that in the interpretation of Mercury we must add a Saturnine tone (containment, reserve, and depth of thought) to the more leisurely and social expression of Mercury in Libra.

> Note that in this calculation we did not figure the debilities (Libra is the detriment of Mars and the fall of the Sun). The calculation of *almuten* seeks to determine the planet with the most dignity in a degree (that is, the planet that has "command" of that point), so the debilities do not need to be considered.

The calculation of *almuten* is also used to determine which planet has the most power over nonplanetary points in the horoscope—for example, the Ascendant. Let's look again at the example of Nietzsche, who has the Ascendant at 29° Scorpio 09′. The ruler is Mars, who therefore receives 5 points. Since we are dealing with a water sign, Mars also has nocturnal triplicity, adding 3 more points. The total is 8 points. Venus also has triplicity (diurnal) in water signs, so it receives 3 points, to which we also add 1 more point since it also has face in the last 10° of Scorpio. The sum total being 4 points. The Moon gets 3 points for being participating triplicity and Saturn gets 2, because this degree of Scorpio is in its term. See Figure 15.

29°♏09′
- ♂ 5 (rulership) + 3 (triplicity) = **8 points**
- ♀ 3 (triplicity) + 1 (face) = 4 points
- ☽ 3 points (triplicity)
- ♄ 2 points (term)

**Figure 15. Scoring of Planets at 29° Scorpio 09′**

We conclude then that Mars is the *almuten* of the Ascendant. Since Mars is already the ruler, this conclusion confirms its power over that point of the horoscope. As can be seen, *almuten* always corresponds to the rulership or exaltation of the respective sign, thus corroborating the power of one of the major dignities.

A*lmuten* indicates the most powerful planet in a particular point in the horoscope. We can also use the calculation of *almuten* to determine the planet that has dominion over a group of points in the chart (planets, houses, etc.), which synthesizes their combined qualities. These points are not selected by chance, but because of their joint significance in a particular area of study. For example, in a natal chart, *almuten* of the Moon and Mercury gives indications about the type of mental structure that characterizes the individual (obviously the information given by *almuten* should be considered along with other interpretative factors).

| | Saturn | Jupiter | Mars | Sun | Venus | Mercury | Moon |
|---|---|---|---|---|---|---|---|
| Moon | 3 | 5+3+2 | | 3 | | 1 | |
| Mercury | 4+3+2 | 3 | | | 5 | 3 | 1 |
| Total: | 12 | 13 | 0 | 3 | 5 | 4 | 1 |

**Figure 16. Calculation of the Moon-Mercury Almuten**

| | Ruler | Exalt. | Triplicities | Egiptian Terms | | | | | Faces | | | Exile | Fall |
|---|---|---|---|---|---|---|---|---|---|---|---|---|---|
| | (sign) | (sign) | (sign) | 05° | 10° | 15° | 20° | 25° | 10° | 20° | | (sign) | (sign) |
| ♈ | ♂ | ☉ | ☉ D, ♃ N, ♄ P | ♃ | ♀ | ☿ | ♂ | ♄ | ♂ | ☉ | ♀ | ♀ | ♄ |
| ♉ | ♀ J | ☽ | ♀ D, ☽ N, ♂ P | ♀ | ☿ | ♃ | ♄ | ♂ | ☿ | ☽ | ♄ | ♂ | |
| ♊ | ☿ | | ♄ D, ☿ N, ♃ P | ☿ | ♃ | ♀ | ♂ | ♄ | ♃ | ♂ | ☉ | ♃ | |
| ♋ | ☽ J | ♃ | ♀ D, ♂ N, ☽ P | ♂ | ♀ | ☿ | ♃ | ♄ | ♀ | ☿ | ☽ | ♄ | ♂ |
| ♌ | ☉ J | | ☉ D, ♃ N, ♄ P | ♃ | ♀ | ♄ | ☿ | ♂ | ♄ | ♃ | ♂ | ♄ | |
| ♍ | ☿ J | ☿ | ♀ D, ☽ N, ♂ P | ☿ | ♀ | ♃ | ♂ | ♄ | ☉ | ♀ | ☿ | ♃ | ♀ |
| ♎ | ♀ | ♄ | ♄ D, ☿ N, ♃ P | ♄ | ☿ | ♃ | ♀ | ♂ | ☽ | ♄ | ♃ | ♂ | ☉ |
| ♏ | ♂ J | | ♀ D, ♂ N, ☽ P | ♂ | ♀ | ☿ | ♃ | ♄ | ♂ | ☉ | ♀ | ♀ | ☽ |
| ♐ | ♃ J | | ☉ D, ♃ N, ♄ P | ♃ | ♀ | ☿ | ♄ | ♂ | ☿ | ☽ | ♄ | ☿ | |
| ♑ | ♄ | ♂ | ♀ D, ☽ N, ♂ P | ☿ | ♃ | ♀ | ♄ | ♂ | ♃ | ♂ | ☉ | ☽ | ♃ |
| ♒ | ♄ J | | ♄ D, ☿ N, ♃ P | ☿ | ♀ | ♃ | ♂ | ♄ | ♀ | ☿ | ☽ | ☉ | |
| ♓ | ♃ | ♀ | ♀ D, ♂ N, ☽ P | ♀ | ♃ | ☿ | ♂ | ♄ | ♄ | ♃ | ♂ | ☿ | ☿ |
| | +5 | +4 | +3 (each) | +2 | | | | | +1 | | | -5 | -4 |

**Figure 17. Essential Dignities and Debilities**

As an example, let's calculate the *almuten* of the Moon and Mercury in Nietzsche's horoscope. The Moon is at 9° Sagittarius 02′. In this sign, Jupiter has rulership, nocturnal triplicity, and term, for a total of 10 points (5+3+2). Saturn simply has participating triplicity, so it receives 3 points. The Sun has diurnal triplicity, so it also receives 3 points. Mercury has face in this degree, which yields it 1 point.

Mercury is at 4° Libra 09′. Venus is ruler, so it gets 5 points. Saturn owns its exaltation, the diurnal triplicity, and term, thus garnering 9 points (4+3+2). Jupiter owns the participating triplicity, so it receives 3 points. Mercury has diurnal triplicity, which awards 3 points. The Moon has dignity by face, receiving 1 point. If we place these calculations in a table, we get the results shown in Figure 16.

Jupiter has the highest score; therefore, it is the *almuten*. However, Saturn is close (1 point less), so it is considered a co-*almuten*; that is, it adds its coloring to that of Jupiter. The significance of these two planets is also reinforced by the large difference in scores to the remaining planets. In practice, Nietzsche's mindset is thus colored by a mix of Jupiter (philosophical thought, faith, mysticism) and by Saturn (scientific thought, skepticism, critique). The result of this complex mixture is, by the way, apparent in his writing.

> Note: A second *almuten* (co-*almuten*) is only valid when *almuten* of various combined points is considered. In the case of *almuten* of a single point, only consider a co-*almuten* if two planets are equally tied in the dignity scoring.

*Almuten* is a specialized adjunct of interpretation. It is used only in particular cases when it is necessary to make very detailed delineations. It is never used indiscriminately, whether when applying the calculation to an isolated point or in the synthesis of various points in the chart. In summary, it is useless to calculate *almuten* for groups of random points, because the results will be meaningless. On the other hand, *almuten* (as, by the way, everything in astrology) is never interpreted in isolation; one must always consider the general context of the horoscope.

It is useless to state, for example, that a given planet is the *almuten* of the Ascendant, immediately drawing conclusions from this fact; one must understand in detail the dynamic of that planet and of the actual Ascendant, for the information given by *almuten* to make sense. Only when properly contextualized, can this information compliment and deepen the basic interpretation of the horoscope.

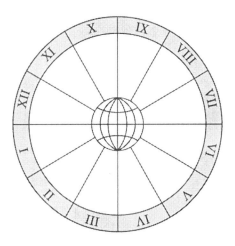

## Chapter VII
# *The Houses*

In previous chapters we discussed the celestial elements of astrology: the planets and the signs. This chapter focuses on the "terrestrial" component of astrology, the houses, which are created by dividing the sky into 12 parts. This division varies according to the location used in the chart's calculation, which makes the houses the most individualized factor in the horoscope. Without them no astrological chart exists and one can only make generic interpretations.

The astrological houses have two reference points as a basis: the **horizon** and the **meridian**. The horizon differentiates the stars that are visible (above the horizon) from the stars that are hidden (below the horizon). In the sky, the eastern and western points of the horizon are crucial because the stars rise in the east and set in the west. The east defines the Ascendant, since it is at this point that the stars rise (ascend) in the sky.

The west point defines the Descendant, where the stars descend and set.

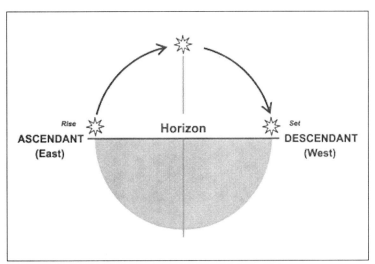

**Figure 1. The Horizon: Rise and Set**

The **meridian** represents the point where the stars culminate, where they reach the highest place in the sky along their nascent (ascendant) and setting (descendant) trajectory. On this meridian there are two points: the *Medium Coeli* (MC), where the stars culminate above the horizon and the opposite point, the *Imum Coeli* (IC), the lowest point. The Medium Coeli and the Imum Coeli make up the vertical axis of a horoscope.

Thus, the stars always rise in the east, culminate in the meridian, and descend toward west. They take an identical route in the lower hemisphere, returning to rise at the Ascendant about 24 hours later. This cycle, in which the whole sky appears to make a revolution in 24 hours, is a natural consequence of Earth's rotation. Because it is so evident, it is called the **primary motion**.

### The Hemispheres

The Ascendant and the Descendant make up the horizontal axis of a horoscope and divide the celestial sphere in two hemispheres. The part that lies above the horizon is called the **superior hemisphere**, the one below the horizon is called the **inferior hemisphere**.

The general rule is that the stars located above the horizon signify things that are public, visible, and expressed in a social environment, while the stars situated below the horizon represent more private and less visible matters.

The sky can also be divided into two hemispheres by the axis defined by the MC and IC. In this case, we get the oriental hemisphere, or Ascendant, located to the East, on the side of the Ascendant, and the occidental hemisphere, or Descendant, located to the west, on the side of the Descendant.

### The Quadrants

With these two axes, the sky is divided into four quadrants. The quadrants are numbered in the direction set by the primary motion (in clockwise direction) and have the following characteristics:

**First Quadrant**: goes from the Ascendant to the Midheaven; it is called oriental or vernal (related to spring); it is masculine, hot and moist, and it has a sanguine temperament. **It symbolizes infancy**.

**Second Quadrant**: goes from the Midheaven to the Descendant; it is called northern or estival (related to Summer); it is feminine, hot and dry, and it has a choleric temperament. **It symbolizes youth**.

**Third Quadrant**: goes from the Descendant to the IC; it is called occidental or autumnal

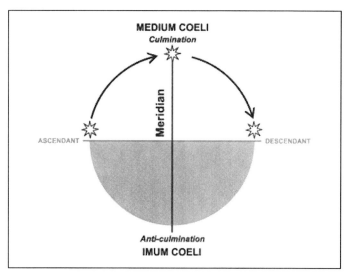

**Figure 2. The Meridian: Medium Coeli and Imum Coeli**

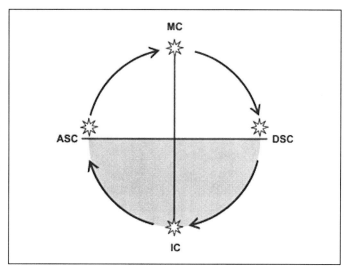

**Figure 3. Primary Motion**

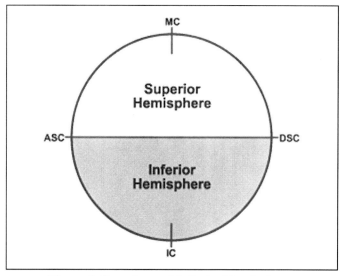

**Figure 4. Superior and Inferior Hemispheres**

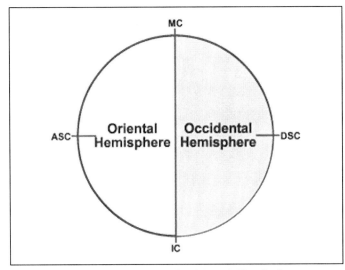

**Figure 5. Oriental and Occidental Hemispheres**

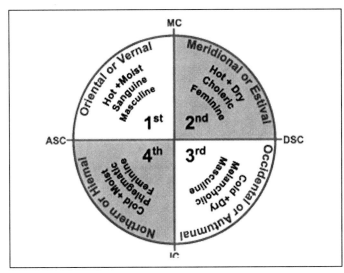

**Figure 6. The Four Quadrants**

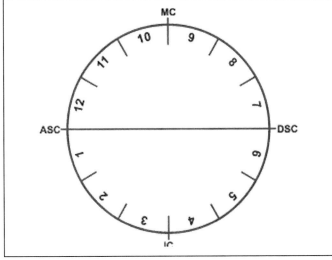

**Figure 7. The Twelve Houses**

(related to autumn); it is masculine, cold and dry, and it has a melancholic temperament. **It symbolizes maturity**.

**Fourth Quadrant**: goes from the IC to the Ascendant; it is called southern or hiemal (related to winter); it is feminine, cold and moist, and it has a phlegmatic temperament. **It symbolizes old age**.

Important: this division is very different from the divisions proposed by the contemporary astrological movement (post 19th century). The traditional classification presented here is based upon the daily motion of the planets through the houses, while the contemporary approach (omitted here because it is commonly found in various manuals) is based upon the order of the houses.

## The Twelve Houses

Each quadrant is divided into three different areas, indicating the beginning, middle, and end of the cycle of planetary ascension. Thus, we get twelve divisions known as astrological houses. Each house represents a specific area in which the signs and planets act.

The 12 houses are numbered in ascending order, or counterclockwise. Just below the horizon is the first house, or the first place to ascend; after that, the second house, or the second place to ascend; and so on. This numbering system can be confusing since beginning students often conclude that the movement of the planets in the houses proceeds in the same direction (from the first to the second, etc.). Although this seems logical, it is not what actually happens with respect to the houses. In their daily motion, the planets go from the second house to the first, where they cross the Ascendant, proceeding into the twelfth, eleventh, etc. Thus there is a difference between the movement of the planets in the zodiac (counterclockwise) and in the houses (clockwise).

To understand this apparent inconsistency, it is necessary to remember that the houses are "slices of the sky" traced across the horizon and the local meridian. The houses, therefore, are a static reference system that does not move relative to the horizon (the first house is always in the east, the tenth always above, etc.). What moves is the zodiac (along with the planets) following the primary motion from east to west and circling around all 12 houses in 24 hours.

Each house has its beginning in a degree of the zodiac known as the **cusp**. In a horoscope, the most noteworthy cusps are the Ascendant (cusp of the first house), the Midheaven (cusp of the tenth house), the Descendant (cusp of the seventh house), and the IC (cusp of the fourth house). The remaining cusps, calculated from these points, are called **intermediary cusps**. The cusp is the point of greatest expression of the house: its position in the zodiac defines the qualities of the house. For example, the cusp of the eleventh house in Aries defines the qualities of that sign (dynamism, impetuosity, etc.) for this area of life (friends, allies, etc.).

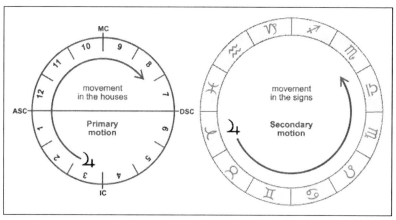

**Figure 8. The Primary and Secondary Motion**

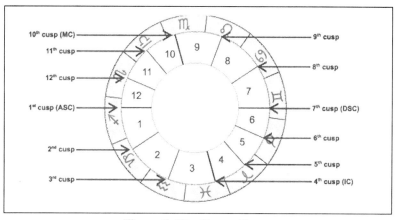

**Figure 9. The House Cusps**

Although they are equal divisions of the sky (30°), when they are projected onto the zodiac, the houses are somewhat distorted; thus, a chart may have houses with different sizes. This difference depends upon the location of the Earth for which the chart is calculated; the degrees of the Zodiac that are rising and culminating at that moment; and upon the type of mathematical division used in that calculation.

For more details on the different types of calculations, consult Appendix 4.

Note that the size of the house does not necessarily imply a greater or lesser importance; its significance depends upon the planets positioned there.

## Classification of the Houses

*Angularity*
Like the planets and signs, the astrological houses can be classified in several ways. The most important classification is angularity, which divides them into three types: **angular**, **succedent**, and **cadent**.

Houses one, four, seven, and ten are called angular houses; their cusps correspond to one of the four major angles (the Ascendant, the IC, the Descendant, and the Midheaven, respectively). Planets positioned in these houses have a very powerful expression.

The succedent houses, so-named because they succeed the angular houses, are the second (which succeeds the first), the eleventh (which succeeds the tenth), the eighth (which succeeds the seventh), and the fifth

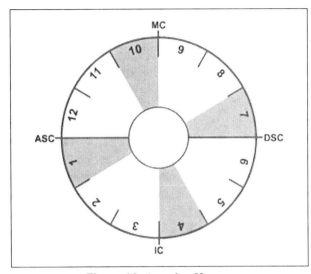

**Figure 10. Angular Houses**

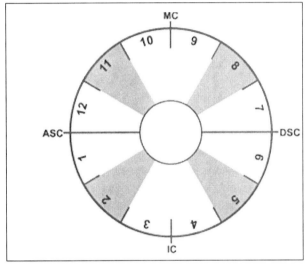

**Figure 11. Succedent Houses**

(which succeeds the fourth). Planets located in the succedent houses have a medium level of expression.

The cadent houses (from the Latin verb *cadere*, meaning to fall) are so named because planets in them "fall away" from the angles; these are the twelfth, (which falls away from the Ascendant), the ninth (which falls away from the tenth), the sixth (which falls away from the seventh), and the third (which falls away from the fourth). Planets located in these houses have little power of expression.

Angularity is directly related to the diurnal motion of the planets. The power of expression of a house increases the closer it is to an angle. Having passed this angular high point, the planet "falls" from the angle to a cadent house and loses (expends) its power. It begins to recuperate it when it passes into the adjoining succedent house, returning to its maximum power in the subsequent angular house. Note that in a chart, the planets are actually stationed in a specific position. This dynamic concept serves only to explain the various house classifications.

Aside from these more general gradations of power, we can also establish gradations of strength between the 12 houses. The strongest are evidently, the four angular houses. But of these, the first is the most powerful, followed by the tenth, seventh and fourth. Of the succedent houses, the strongest is the eleventh, followed by the fifth, second, and eighth. Of the cadents, the strongest is the ninth, followed by the third, sixth and twelfth.

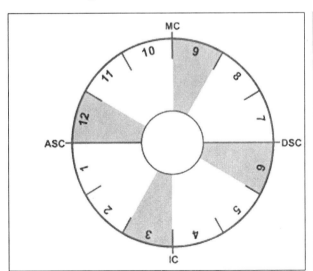

**Figure 12. Cadent Houses**

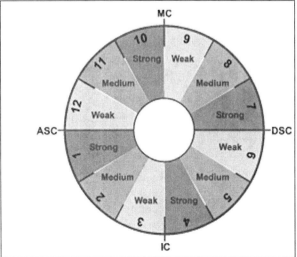

**Figure 13. The House's Power**

There are however, exceptions: although the cadent houses are as a general rule weaker than the succedents, the ninth and third houses (despite being cadent), have a greater expression than the second and eight houses (which are succedent). This exception is tied to the relationship between the houses and the Ascendant, which we will discuss below. Thus, the sequence of power of the houses is as follows: first (the most powerful), tenth, seventh, fourth, eleventh, third, second, eighth, sixth, and twelfth (the weakest). Although largely accepted, the sequence can generally vary in association with very specific interpretative methods.

*Gender*

Another form of classifying the houses concerns gender; the houses considered masculine are odd numbered (first, third, fifth, seventh, ninth, and eleventh), and those considered feminine are even numbered (second, fourth, sixth, eighth, tenth, and twelfth). This classification is not very significant in practical terms.

## The Signification of the Twelve Houses

Each house contains a very rich array of significations: it defines topics, people, actions, directions, colors, parts of the body, etc. Nevertheless, not all of these significations are applicable to all areas of astrology; some are specific to mundane astrology, others to horary, etc.

The principal significations of each house are noted in the following pages, along with the appropriate branch of astrology (when necessary). Also listed for each house are the specific associations and rulerships, such as the colors used in horary astrology, and the anatomy used in medical astrology.

**First House—Angular and Masculine**

The first house has the Ascendant as its cusp, making it the most important of the astrological chart. The Ascendant represents the principle of individuality in the chart. It marks the hour of birth and therefore the total celestial configuration of that moment or birth. It is the foundation of the astrological chart. The term "horoscope" comes from the Greek ὡροσκόπησις and means "to see the hour." For classical authors, the term horoscope is synonymous with Ascendant (thus, if in a classical text it states that the horoscope of an individual is Leo, for example, it means Leo is the rising sign and not the Sun sign).

The first house always represents the individual, whether in a birth chart or in a horary. In charts of events or collectives, it also indicates the subject in question (country, business, project, etc.) and its characteristics.

In a nativity, this is the house of life, signifying all of the conditions that surround the individual. It refers to physical appearance (stature, appearance, and form) as much as to motivations and objectives. The tastes, mannerisms, and mentality are in large part defined by the first house. In questions of health, it signifies the vitality and the general appearance. In the body, it is specifically tied to the head and the face. Thus, in a medical context, the planets in this house can represent conditions or blemishes (diseases, birthmarks, scars, etc.) in those parts of the body.

In horary astrology, the first house defines the individual that poses the question, describing that person's appearance and state of mind at the moment the question was asked. With respect to color, the position of a significator[17] in this house describes people, animals, or objects that are white, gray, or generally light in color.

In a mundane horoscope (eclipse, ingress, etc.) the Ascendant indicates the general state of the location for which the chart was constructed. It signifies the nation or kingdom, as well as its people and condition.

---

[17]The planet that represents the thing asked about.

**Second House—Succedent and Feminine**

The second house represents resources, whether they refer to an individual or to a collective. Because it is the house succeeding the Ascendant, it is considered to support the ascension of the first.

In a birth chart, the second house represents the resources and assets of the person, his or her wealth or poverty, and the way he or she manages possessions.

In horary astrology, the second house signifies the possessions of the querent and his or her moveable goods. It refers to questions about loans, profits, and losses, and in the case of duels and legal questions, it represents those who support the querent (friends and assistants).

On the matter of colors, it is associated with green (sometimes with shades of red).

In a mundane chart, it indicates the resources and economy of a people or nation, its supplies, its allies or supporters. In battle, it signifies the attacking army.

In medical astrology, the second house represents the neck, from the nape to the shoulders.

**Third House—Cadent and Masculine**

The third house represents brothers, sisters, and close relatives in general (cousins, siblings-in-law, etc.). It indicates the conditions that surround them and their relationship with the native. It is also the house of short journeys—travel to places nearby or within the same cultural context. In traditional terms the third house also represents journeys by land, as opposed to journeys by sea, which are signified by the ninth house.

The third house shares with the ninth house the topic of religion and legal knowledge, although to a lesser degree. The third house seems to be related more to the practical and mundane expression of these topics, although this distinction is not always clear in the works of ancient authors. Thought, intellect, and communication are also central topics of this house.

In horary astrology, the third house represents all types of messages (letters, conversations, etc.) as well as those who transmit them (messengers, postal carriers, telephones, internet, etc.). Within this context, rumors and gossip are also topics of this house.

Colors associated with the third house are orange, yellow, and similar tones (saffron, rust, etc.).

In a mundane chart, the third house represents means of transportation (streets, bridges, etc.), the media (newspapers, magazines etc.), and all manner of reports and official communication.

In medical astrology, the third house signifies the shoulders, arms, hands, and fingers.

**Fourth House—Angular and Feminine**

The fourth house, also known as the angle of Earth, represents the base or foundation of the horoscope. Its symbolism is very rich.

In a nativity, the fourth house symbolizes the family of origin. Generally, it represents the parents, but in particular it signifies the native's father. Along the same lines, it indicates ancestral roots or any matter pertaining to one's genealogy.

Other central topics of this house are assets and possessions. In contrast with the second house, which represents solely moveable possessions, this house is related to the immoveable possessions of the individual (houses, lands and other types of property) or the resources acquired through the family's inheritance.

In another context, it also represents the end of life and the conditions that surround it, what happens after death, and the grave.

In a horary question, it signifies all topics related to land and houses, from its purchase or leasing, to its cultivation and the treasures buried in it. It indicates the quality of the land or the house that is purchased, as well as the quality of the soil of an agricultural plot. It can also be used to determine the end of a matter.

With respect to colors, the fourth house is associated with red.

In mundane astrology, this house represents castles, forts, and buildings in general, as well as gardens, fields, forests, grazing, and crop lands. Natural resources (mineral and timber, etc.) are also a part of its symbolism. The wife of the king (the consort queen), as well as his concubines, are also indicated by this house. Similarly, it also represents his enemies or those of the government. In a more specific context, it can also represent a city and its mayor.

In medical astrology, the fourth house is associated with the thorax, chest, and lungs.

## Fifth House—Succedent and Masculine

In a natal chart, the fifth house includes the children, their condition, and their relationship to the individual. Also associated with this house are all playful activities, entertainment, pleasure, and loves and passion. Artistic expression is also included in its symbolism.

In a horary question, the fifth house signifies the matter of one's offspring, children in general, pregnancy and fertility, as well as invitations for banquets, parties, and other leisure-time activities.

In terms of colors, it represents white, black, or honey-colored things.

In mundane terms, the fifth house represents ambassadors and embassies, as well as places of entertainment (bars, stadiums, etc.). In some contexts, it represents the resources of a city, its foods, and supplies.

In medical astrology, the fifth house signifies the stomach, liver, heart, back, and sides of the body.

## Sixth house—Cadent and Feminine

In a nativity, the sixth house represents diseases and lesions, the weaknesses and tendencies of the individual toward debilitation, as well as the constitution (and humors) that originate them. It also represents the people that work for the native and his or her relationship with them (traditionally, servants and slaves; today, contracted labor and services). Obligations and daily tasks are also topics of this house.

Domestic animals and livestock (smaller than sheep) are also indicated by the sixth house. Today, we use this attribution for pets (cats, dogs, etc.).

The color associated with this house is black.

In horary astrology, the sixth house is related to questions about disease (their nature and duration), as well as employees, cattle, or pets.

In mundane astrology, the significations are the same but are instead associated with the country or region under study.

In medical astrology, the sixth house represents the lower abdomen, stomach, and intestines.

## Seventh House—Angular and Masculine

The seventh house signifies the generic "other" because this house is opposite the first (the Ascendant). In nativities, it is the house of marriage, conjugal and romantic relationships, and partnerships. The "other" may be personified by the spouse (fiancé, dating relationship, etc.), associates, and business partners, as well as opponents and the open enemies referenced by the tradition. This house defines, therefore, the dynamics of the relationships of the individual: how he or she relates to others; the type of partner; how he or she deals with confrontation; and the nature of his or her opponents (enemies).

In horary questions the symbolism is practically the same. It represents the spouse and romantic situations, enemies, or the person being asked about. In particular, it defines the opponents in a legal case, the enemy in war or in duels, the thief in cases of theft, and fugitives in general. It also indicates the doctor in questions about health, and the consulting astrologer. It also indicates the destination of a trip (the point of arrival, in opposition to the Ascendant, which represents the departure).

In terms of colors, it signifies black, dark, and green hues.

In a mundane horoscope, the seventh house represents the opponents, but in this case it is the enemies of the country, kingdom, or people, as well as wars and conflicts.

The part of the body attributed to the seventh house is located from the bellybutton to the hips.

## Eighth House—Succedent and Feminine

The eighth is the house of death and everything associated with it. In natal charts, it represents death, its nature, and all matters that involve death and loss. It, therefore, refers to wills, legacies, and inheritances. It is also associated with feelings of fear, worry, and angst, as well as with obsessions and, in general, somber and obscure states of mind. It likewise represents occult matters, ancient things, and ancestors (in a broader sense than that of the fourth). In another context, it also refers to the partner's resources, such as a dowry.

The eighth house has identical meanings in horary and mundane astrology. In legal cases, it gives indications of the supporters of the opponent, and in battle, of the resources and army of the enemy.

With respect to colors, it is associated with green and black.

The genitals and organs of excretion are the parts of the body represented by this house.

## Ninth House—Cadent and Masculine

The ninth house is associated with knowledge and matters of faith and religion, representing all manner of religious people (monks, priests, pastors, etc.) as well as temples and churches. It is often called the House of God. It is also associated with long journeys.

Additionally, the ninth house represents knowledge and education, having signification over schools, books, universities, and professors. Other topics associated with it are dreams, visions, and their interpretation, and prophecy, stories, fables, and narratives about the past. Within this context, astrology itself is signified by this house.

Journeys of long duration (in earlier times, travels by sea) and to foreign lands are other topics of this house. The "house of pilgrimages" is another name by which it is known.

In natal astrology, the ninth house indicates the attitude of the individual in relation to knowledge and learning, as well as the treatment of religion or philosophy that is most in accord with the individual's nature. More specifically, it relates to the relatives of the partner.

In horary and mundane astrology, the ninth house represents any matter associated with religion, knowledge, dreams, or travels. Specifically in horary astrology, this house indicates an individual's knowledge or the quality of such knowledge.

The  ninth house has white and green as its colors.

In medical astrology the ninth house represents the buttocks and thighs.

## Tenth House—Angular and Feminine

The tenth house is the most elevated house of the horoscope. Just as with the fourth, it too has a very rich symbolism. It is associated with temporal power, with figures of authority and with actions that have a social impact.

In a nativity, the tenth house represents the actions of the native—his or her projects or objectives in life. It signifies the vocation, career, and profession of the native, giving indications of its nature and quality. It is also representative of public life as well as of fame and social impact. In traditional terms, it indicates dignity, power, and distinction.

One particular aspect of this house is its association with the mother, in the same way that the fourth is associated with the father.

In horary astrology, in addition to the significations already mentioned for natal astrology, the ninth house additionally indicates topics having to do with power, figures of authority (governors, employers, managers, etc.), the profession of the querent, and its current state. In legal matters, it represents the judge and the verdict.

In mundane astrology, its principal representations are authority figures (kings, presidents, heads of state, dukes, princes, prefects, etc.), and in general, the current government of a nation.

It is associated with white and red.

Anatomically, the tenth house represents the knees and thighs.

## Eleventh House—Succedent and Masculine

This house is often called the "good spirit" because it is considered fortunate. In natal astrology, it represents friends and allies, those who support and help, and the type of relationship that the native has with them. It is also the house of hopes, signifying one's dreams and expectations. In some ways, it also represents faith, not necessarily in the religious sense of the word, but more as an "optimistic expectation." Confidence and social recognition are likewise topics of this house.

In horary astrology, the meanings are identical.

The colors represented are saffron and yellow hues in general.

In mundane astrology, the eleventh house represents the favored, councilors and allies of the king, and government. Within this context, it represents governing bodies such as the parliament, the state councils, and other legislators. Other mundane significations include the treasury, taxes, and finances of the country. In matters of war, it indicates the resources (army and munitions) of the head of state.

With respect to the parts of the body, it represents the legs and ankles.

### Twelfth House—Cadent and Feminine

The twelfth house is the house of prisons and limitations, frequently called the "bad spirit."

In a nativity, this house always represents situations that limit and condition the native. It is associated with sadness, lamentations, tribulations, and afflictions. It is also the house of secret (or hidden) enemies—those who we do not know are our enemies. Thus, envy, betrayal, and acts of sabotage are associated with the twelfth house. Equally important topics are illicit acts, as well as prisons, enclosures, and cases of isolation in general.

From another perspective, the twelfth house also represents the conditions prior to birth; that is, what happened to the native while in the mother's womb.

In horary astrology, this house has identical meanings.

In terms of color, the twelfth house symbolizes green.

> Important Note: The diverse significations of a house should not be related to each other because they exist on different planes. For example, the tenth house represents the career, fame, and the mother of the individual as significations. Nonetheless, it is incorrect to think that the mother has influence over the career or the fame of the individual. Similarly, siblings and short journeys have no relationship to each other, although both are signified by the third house.

Within a mundane context, this house represents the secret enemies of a country, nation, or institution. Thus, it may represent spies, saboteurs, criminals, and all manner of subversive agents. A less common signification of the twelfth (valid in any of the astrological branches) is that of large animals. In this category are included domesticated animals of a larger size (horses, camels, cattle, and the like) or wild animals in general (traditionally, "beasts").

In medical astrology, the twelfth house represents the feet.

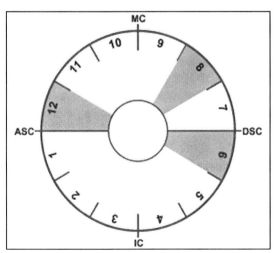

**Figure 14. Malefic Houses**

*Benefic and Malefic Houses*

As with the planets, the houses can be classified as benefic or malefic. Generally, the first, eleventh, tenth, ninth, seventh, fifth, third and second are considered benefic because they represent areas of life that favor the individual. On the other hand, there are three houses that are considered malefic because they represent more challenging and laborious facets of life: the sixth, associated with illness and servitude; the eighth, associated with death; and the twelfth, associated with limitations. In some cases, the seventh house can also acquire a malefic character because, although it represents matters that are considered benefic such as marriage and partners, it also indicates opponents, enemies, and conflicts (note that this house is opposite the Ascendant, thus, representing that which opposes it). Another house with an ambiguous signification is the fourth, which can equally represent the home and the family, a beneficial situation, and the end of life, wherein it acquires a more malefic character.

This classification derives not only from the signification of the house but from its angular position relative to the Ascendant. The twelfth, sixth, eighth and second form weak angles with the Ascendant (30° between the first and the second, and between the first and the twelfth; and 150° between the first and the sixth, and between the first and the eighth). Planets placed in these houses do not contribute to the expression of the Ascendant. Only the second house is spared this symbolism because it is adjacent to the first and because this is taken to mean that it can support it.

### Derived Houses

Besides the primary or radical significations described earlier, each house can also have more specific meanings derived from its relationship to other houses. These significations, called "derived," are obtained when, instead of taking the Ascendant as the starting point, another house is used. In this way, when we want to examine a specific topic in-depth, we use the cusp of the house that represents the matter under study as the Ascendant. The remaining houses will then derive their significations relative to this derived Ascendant in their natural order.

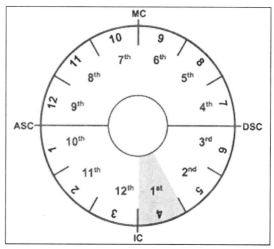

**Figure 15. House Derivation**

For example, to learn specific information about the father of an individual, the fourth house of that child's chart can be used as a starting point (the fourth house signifies the father). From this perspective, the child's fifth house then becomes the derived second house—the second house from the fourth. The child's fifth house thus acquires as a derived signification the resources (second house) of the father (fourth house). Similarly, the child's sixth house becomes the derived third house, or the siblings (third) of the father (fourth). The remaining houses follow the same logic.

Although any house studied by means of derivation becomes the Ascendant, the derived house never loses its original meaning. It is the derived house of the chart that acquires a new signification, always relative to its position in relation to the "starting" (derived Ascendant) house.

Note that the derived houses never replace the natal (or horary, mundane, etc.) houses; the derived meanings are always a complement to the indications of the natal houses. Nonetheless, there is no overlap between the natal and derived significations. For instance, in the previous example, the natal fifth house, besides signifying the children of the native, also derivatively signifies the resources of the father. Nevertheless, the father's money is not related to the children of the native. The derived interpretation serves to add depth to specific topics, but in order to avoid unnecessary confusion it should not be mixed with the natal interpretation.

### Derived House Significations

Below are listed some derived significations for the houses. Because not all the significations are useful for interpretation, the list is limited to those most important. As with everything in astrology, there is no point in memorizing this list of significations. What is important is to understand the method of derivation and to know how to use it when it is necessary.

**First house**: friends' siblings (third from the eleventh); father of the mother, that is, the maternal grandfather (fourth from the tenth); opponents' partners (seventh from the seventh); religion or travels of the children (ninth from the fifth); father's occupation, or the mother of the father—paternal grandmother (tenth from the fourth); siblings' friends (eleventh from the third).

**Second house**: friends' parents or family (fourth from the eleventh); mayor's children (fifth from the tenth); death of the partner (eighth from the seventh); travels due to illness (ninth from the sixth); children's profession or honors (tenth from the fifth); father's friends (eleventh from the fourth).

**Third house**: friends' children (fifth from the eleventh); governor's or the mother's illnesses (sixth from the tenth); partner's religion (ninth from the seventh); children's friends (eleventh from the fifth).

**Fourth house**: siblings' money and income (second from the third); the friends' illnesses (sixth from the eleventh); king's opponents (seventh from the tenth); travels related to death (ninth from the eighth); enemy's or partner's profession (the tenth from the seventh).

**Fifth house**: father's possessions (second from the fourth); siblings of the siblings, when from another father or mother (third from the third); friends' partners (seventh from the eleventh); governor's or mother's death (eighth from the tenth); partner's friends (eleventh from the seventh).

**Sixth house**: children's possessions (second from the fifth); father's siblings, that is, the paternal uncles/aunts (third from the fourth); siblings' father, when they are half siblings from a different father (fourth from the third); death of friends (eighth from the eleventh); mother's religion or travels (ninth from the tenth).

**Seventh house**: employee's assets (second from the sixth); children's siblings, when from another father (third from the fifth); father's father—paternal grandfather (fourth from the fourth); siblings' children, that is, the nieces/nephews (fifth from the third); mother's profession or the mother's mother—maternal grandmother (tenth from the tenth).

**Eighth house**: partner's or opponent's assets (second from the seventh); siblings' illnesses or employees (sixth from the third); mother's friends (eleventh from the tenth).

**Ninth house**: partner's or opponent's siblings (third from the seventh); children's children, that is, the grandchildren (fifth from the fifth); father's illnesses (sixth from the fourth); siblings' partners, that is, the siblings in-law (sevnth from the third); friends' friends (eleventh from the eleventh).

**Tenth house**: partner's father, that is, the father-in-law (fourth from the seventh); children's illnesses (sixth from the fifth); father's partners or opponents (seventh from the fourth); siblings' death (eighth from the third).

**Eleventh house**: mother's or governor's assets (second from the tenth); partner's children, that is, step-children (fifth from the seventh); employee's illnesses (sixth from the sixth); children's partners-daughters/sons-in-law (sevnth from the fifth); death of the father (eighth from the fourth); religion or travels of the siblings (ninth from the third).

**Twelfth house**: friends' assets (second from the eleventh); the mother's siblings, that is, the maternal uncles/aunts (third from the tenth); partner's illnesses (sixth from the seventh); children's death (eighth from the fifth); father's religion (ninth from the fourth); siblings' profession (tenth from the third).

To avoid excessive, or even worthless, information, this technique should be employed with moderation, good sense, and within the appropriate context. For example, in the interpretation of a natal chart, it is of little use to know that the second house signifies the children of the boss (the derived fifth house from the natal tenth), or that the eighth house represents the brother's employees (sixth derived from the natal third). Having said that, these examples can make total sense within the context of horary or mundane astrology.

## House-Sign-Planet Interaction

### Sign-House Interaction

*House Cusp Sign*

The sign on the cusp of the house characterizes the matters of that house. Through the nature of that sign—polarity, element, mode, etc.—we can evaluate the behaviors and the types of actions that characterize the expression of that house. Even if another sign with a greater number of degrees occupies the house, the principal characterization of that house is always given by the sign located on the cusp. This is because the qualities of the cusp are being evaluated, not the "quantity" of the sign within that house.

*House Ruler*

The sign on the cusp also determines another essential interpretative factor: **the ruler of the house**. This is the planet that rules the sign found on the cusp. It is called the ruler or the lord of the house. If, for example, the tenth house of a horoscope has 22° Taurus on its cusp, Venus, the planet that rules that sign, will be the ruler of the tenth house (this is the case in the chart of Agatha Christie).

Obviously, the planet that rules the cusp is not always located in the house that it rules; many times it is in an-

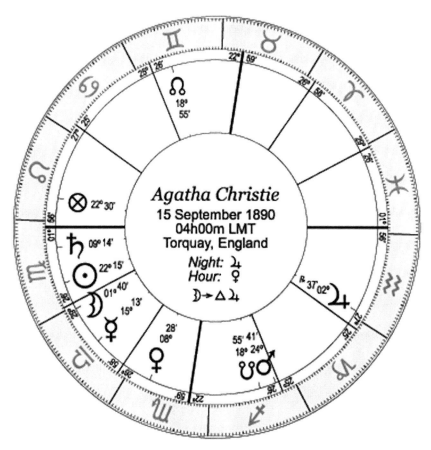

**Chart 2. Nativity of Agatha Christie**

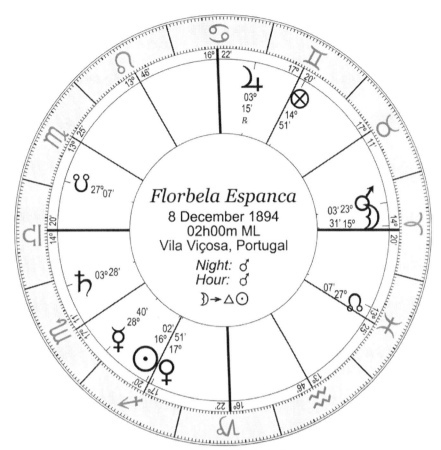

**Chart 3. Nativity of Florbela Espanca**

other house and another sign. The position in the chart of the ruling planet indicates **where** and **how** the topics signified by the house will be realized: the area of life (where), as indicated by the house, and the manner of action (how), as indicated by the sign where the ruling planet finds itself.

In the example of Agatha Christie, Venus, ruler of the tenth house, is in the third house in Scorpio. Thus, the matters of the tenth house (career) will be directed toward the area of writing and communication (third house) in a focused and tenacious manner (Scorpio, a fixed sign). We see then that the ruling planet of a house becomes the **accidental significator** of the matters of that house. In the case of Agatha Christie, Venus is the accidental significator of profession (because it rules the tenth house).

Next we will examine the chart of Florbela Espanca. The cusp of the second house is at 17° Scorpio; Mars, the ruler, is positioned in Aries in the seventh house. Here, Mars is the topical significator for resources. This configuration indicates that many of the writer's resources (second house) are tied to her partners/marriages (seventh house). Because it is dignified in Aries, Mars suggests abundance of resources, but the fiery and cardinal nature of the sign also indicates some imprudence in its management.

It is worth clarifying that in both charts the ruling planet used as an example is located in a house that it also rules. In Agatha Christie's chart, Venus also rules the third house, which has Libra on the cusp; in Florbela Espanca's chart, Mars also rules the seventh house, with Aries on the cusp. These placements, reinforce the signification of the planet.

The other essential dignities can also rule the houses of a chart. Thus, besides its ruling planet, the house also has a ruler for exaltation, three per triplicity, one for term, and one for face. Of these, the most noteworthy is the exaltation ruler, which can in particular cases acquire the status of co-regent of the house. The triplicities of the house (the three rulers of the element of the cusp's sign) are used in specialized interpretations. Term is used on a case by case basis, while the ruler for face, is generally ignored since it is considered a very weak dignity. For example, in Florbela Espanca's chart, the seventh house, whose cusp is at 14° Aries 20′ has—besides the sign's domicile ruler, Mars—an exaltation ruler: the Sun; three rulers for triplicity: Jupiter, the Sun, and Saturn (rulers of the fire triplicity); a ruler for term: Mercury; and a ruler for face: the Sun.

It is also possible to calculate an *almuten* for the house cusp. Sometimes the *almuten* is a different planet from the ruling planet, in which case it is considered a co-ruler for the matters of the house. The "normal" ruler continues to have priority in interpretation, but the *almuten* also has something to add. Note that the *almuten* (as presented in this book) is always the rulership or exaltation ruler of the sign. This fact merely reinforces the role that exaltation plays as co-ruler. Returning to the previous example, Florbela's seventh

house has the Sun as *almuten*, since it receives 8 points for simultaneously being exaltation, triplicity, and face ruler of 14° Aries 20′. Mars, ruler of the house (and sign), has only 5 points. Here, the Sun participates as co-ruler of the house, which not only contributes to the fiery nature of Florbela Espanca's relationships (Sun in Sagittarius) but to an interest in important partners or those with some social status (the Sun).

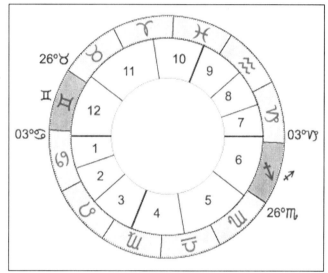

**Figure 16. Intercepted Signs**

*Intercepted Signs*

It is common to find two signs in a house: one on the cusp and one that begins farther into the house. Sometimes it happens that a house begins in one sign, extends itself into the next, and only ends in the third sign over. In such a case, the sign in the middle has its 30 degrees completely contained within the house. This phenomenon is called **interception**, whereby the sign contained within the house is the **intercepted sign**.[18]

In the case of Nietzsche, Sagittarius is intercepted in the first house (which starts at 29° Scorpio and ends at 5° Capricorn. For this reason, Jupiter, ruler of Sagittarius, becomes co-ruler of the first house, and combines with Mars (ruler of Scorpio), which is the primary ruler. Note that Scorpio, in spite of only occupying one degree of the first house, is more important than Sagittarius because it is not the number of degrees that counts, but the sign on the cusp. On the other hand, Capricorn does not have any signification in the matters of the first house, but is nonetheless the determining sign of the second house. It is important to keep in mind that co-rulership only occurs when a sign is intercepted in a house; in other cases, the qualities of the second sign are transferred to the next house.

A look at the chart makes it obvious that the interception always affects two opposite signs and houses. In the current example, if Sagittarius is intercepted in the first, Gemini—the opposite sign—is intercepted in the seventh house, opposite the first.

---

[18]In extreme cases where the latitude of the place is very elevated (very far north or very far south of the globe) larger distortions can occur; a house can contain two or even three intercepted signs.

[19]Note that the word "accidental" is not used here with the negative attributions found in common language. In an astrological context, this term means "by chance" or "a particular instance." In this context, it is used to designate a condition that changes from chart to chart, such as the location of a planet in a particular house.

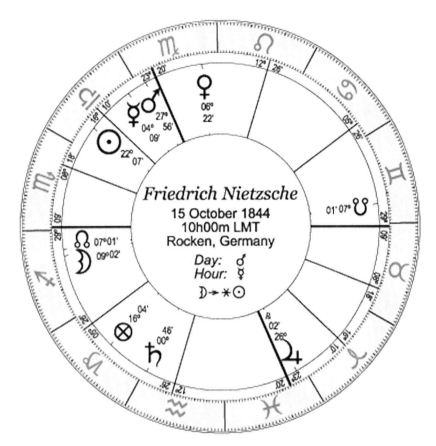

**Chart 3. Nativity of Friedrich Nietzsche**

## House-Planet Interaction

The houses are crucial in what is called **accidental rulership**[19], that is, the particular function of the planet in a given horoscope. This determination can occur in two ways:

*By Placement*: By being placed in a particular house, a planet has the area of life represented by the house as its main focus of expression. The planet will then characterize the activity of that house, determining its nature (and qualities), behaviors, people, events, etc.

*By Rulership*: By ruling one or more houses, a planet becomes designated as the significator of the matters of the house it rules, independently of the position it occupies in the astrological chart.

In the chart of Florbela Espanca, Mercury is located in the second house, so it is considered to act within the area of resources (determination by placement). On the other hand, Mercury also rules the ninth house, which makes this planet a specific significator of study, religion, and travel (determination by rulership).

This accidental determination is the master-key to delineation and astrological interpretation, since it will define with greater precision the significations of the planets. Thus, the natural (or universal) signification of the planet will be associated with its specific function in the horoscope. In the current example, we can say that Florbela Espanca's resources are related to activities of the nature of Mercury (writing, communication, language, etc.) and are also associated with matters of the ninth house, ruled by Mercury (study, etc,). This interpretation will be combined with the one given earlier, wherein the resources of the poet were related to her partners/marriages (Mars, ruler of the second, in the seventh). In an astrological interpretation, both pieces of information combine to describe the activity represented in the chart concerning her resources.

*Planets in Houses*

Before beginning the interpretation, we need to determine in which house the planet is located. Technically speaking, the planet is located in a particular house when it finds itself between the cusp of that house and the cusp of the next one. However, the great majority of authors consider that the house extends its influence up to 5° before the cusp. Thus, if a planet is within less than 5° of the next house cusp, it is considered to be active in that next house. This is known as **the 5° rule**.

We might compare a planet in this situation with a person that is on his or her doorstep but not yet home. In such a case, the person can have some say in the affairs of the house even though he or she is still on the outside. This condition is more noticeable when the planet is in the same sign as that on the cusp.

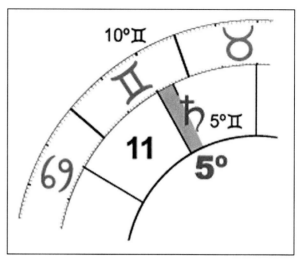

Figure 17. Five-degree Rule

Note: The 5° rule only applies to the houses, not to the signs. A planet is considered to be in a sign from 0°00′00″ to 29°59′59″ of that sign. In the case of the signs, there is no such margin of error. Signs and houses are different points of reference and have distinct rules.

The placement of a planet in a house gives two distinct pieces of information: on the one hand, it tells us in which area of life the planet acts, and on the other hand, it indicates the planet's intensity within the general context of that horoscope. In effect, its placement by house is the key to the planet's level of expression, whether intensifying or diminishing it. This means there are two situations to consider: angularity and the joys.

*Degrees of Angularity*

The degree of a planet's angularity is without a doubt the most determining factor with regard to its power of expression. A planet can have three levels of angularity: **angular**, when placed in the first, tenth, seventh, and fourth houses; **succedent**, in the eleventh, eighth, fifth and second houses; **cadent**, in the twelfth, ninth, sixth, and third.

A planet with an angular placement becomes highly distinguished in the chart's overall context, often overriding all other factors. Inversely, a cadent planet is considered very weak, making little impression on the chart's overall context. The planets in succedent houses obviously have an intensity that lies between both these extremes. There are three angular planets in Florbela Espanca's chart: Saturn in the first, and a conjunction of the Moon and Mars in the seventh. In the life of this poet, the contrast between a depressive and introverted vein (Saturn in Scorpio in the first house) and a fiery and agitated one (Moon and Mars in Aries in the seventh) are noteworthy. These factors are apparent in the behavior and life of Florbela Espanca. The other planets, although equally important, are expressed in a less obvious manner.

*The Joys*

There is another type of placement that gives a planet a special significance: **the joy.** A planet is said to be in its joy when it is placed in a house whose signification has a greater affinity with its nature. When located in this house, the planet acquires power of expression. Each planet has its joy in a single house, this being known as the "residence" or "temple" of the planet:

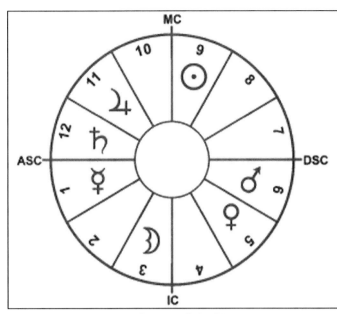

**Figure 18. Joys of the Planets**

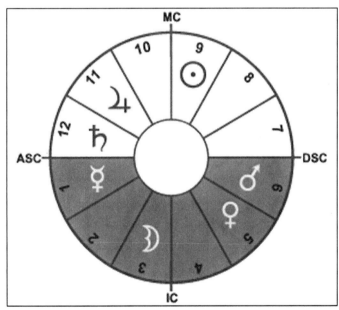

**Figure 19. Joys and Sect**

**Mercury**, significator of the mind, has its joy in the first house, of the *persona* of the individual.

**The Moon**, the fastest and most mutable planet, has its joy in the third house, since this is the house of movement, of short trips, and of communication.

**Venus**, planet of love and pleasure, expresses its joy in the fifth house of love, games, and romance.

**Mars**, planet of war and of force, has its joy in the sixth house of illnesses and servitude.

**The Sun**, lord of the heavens, source of light and life, has its joy in the ninth house, of faith, religion, and foresight.

**Jupiter**, the greater benefic, has its joy in the eleventh house of allies, friends, and hopes.

Note: Do not confuse the joys by house with those by sign mentioned in Chapter VI. The joys by sign refer to a particular state of essential dignity of the planet, while the joys by house are related to an affinity between the nature of the planet and the significations of the house where it has its joy.

**Saturn**, carrier of limitations and greater malefic, has its joy in the twelfth house of tribulations, restrictions, and imprisonments.

Thus, in traditional astrology, the fifth house, for example, may be referred to as the temple of Venus or the joy of Venus.

The system of joys also reflects the natural symmetry of the planets. Thus, the nocturnal planets (Moon, Venus and Mars) have their joys in houses below the horizon (third, fifth and sixth), while the diurnal ones (the Sun, Jupiter, and Saturn) have them above the horizon (ninth, eleventh, twelfth). This system also emphasizes the planets of the same nature, which are positioned in houses opposite each other. Thus, the Sun-Moon pair (luminaries) are placed in the ninth and third houses, respectively; the Jupiter-Venus pair (benefics) on the eleventh-fifth axis, reinforce the fortunate nature of these houses; the pair Saturn-Mars (malefics) on the twelfth-sixth axis, underlie the less pleasant aspect of these houses.

Note also that the joy placements favor the houses considered to be less powerful. There are joys in the four cadent houses (Moon in the third, Mars in the sixth, Sun in the ninth, and Saturn in the twelfth) and in two of the succedent houses (Venus in the fifth and Jupiter in the eleventh). Of the angular houses, who by them-

### The Sorrow of the Planets

Some traditional authors state that the house opposite that of the joy of a planet is the house of its sorrow. In this place the planet would be in a more incapacitated position. Although it seems to have a logical basis (since it repeats the rulership-exile and exaltation-fall pairs of the rulership system of dignities), this concept is not very functional in practical terms. For example, Jupiter, planet of fertility and abundance, would have its sorrow in the fifth house (opposite the eleventh of its joy). However, in practical terms, the placement of the planet of fertility in the house of children is very favorable. Similarly, the position of Venus in the eleventh house (where it would be in its sorrow) is traditionally interpreted as marriage for love, representing, therefore, a very happy situation.

This is an example of how pure logical deduction does not always apply in the astrological system. Note also that the oldest authors do not mention the sorrows of the planets, which suggests that it may have been a later development (probably from the late Middle Ages).

selves are considered the most powerful, only the first is the joy of a planet (Mercury).

*Integration of Essential Dignity, Angularity and Joy*

It is important to mention that the highlight given to a planet in angular condition or joy does not modify its essential condition (dignity or debility). These conditions can combine and reinforce each other, but they never negate each other. Thus, even if debilitated by zodiacal position (fall or detriment, etc.), a planet may still be highlighted in the chart by virtue of its angularity or joy. Inversely, a planet in excellent zodiacal condition (rulership or exaltation) can see its strength diminished by being in a cadent house.

Let's look first at the interaction between joy and the essential condition of the planet. In the chart of Karl Marx, for example, we find two planets in their joy: the Moon in the third and

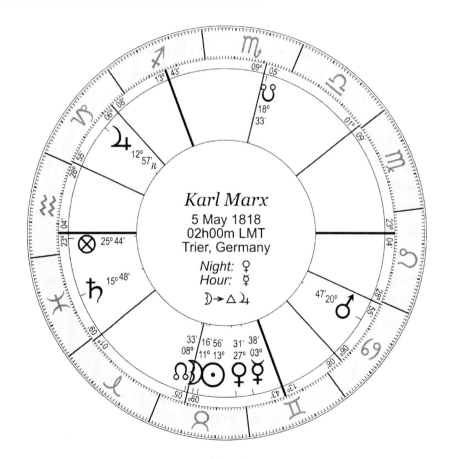

**Chart 4. Nativity of Karl Marx**

Jupiter in the eleventh. But they have very different zodiacal conditions because the Moon is exalted in Taurus and Jupiter is in fall in Capricorn. The Moon in its joy and exaltation is obviously a powerful planet in this horoscope. It represents a great capacity to materialize (Taurus) its ideas (notably through journalism and books, natural topics of the third house). Jupiter's situation is different; on the one hand, it is strengthened by being in its joy, on another, it is weakened by being in fall. These two factors, apparently contradictory, combine to contribute to their interpretation. The placement of Jupiter by joy suggests that the individual has allies (eleventh house) with great power; however, since the planet is debilitated, we can deduce that these allies, while powerful, are inconstant and promise more than they can deliver.

> In Appendix 4, Additional Considerations about the Houses, is information concerning the 12 houses. Topics such as the origins of the houses, the house systems and their problems, and other information can be found there.

A similar situation can occur with debilitated but angular planets, although an angular planet always has an apparent expression. If its essential nature is debilitated, it tends to express its more challenging side. In the chart of King Sebastian, for example, the Sun is angular (conjunct the Ascendant) but debilitated (in fall and peregrine in Aquarius). The angularity of the Sun gives this king authority and natural brilliance, but these qualities tend to become imposing and inappropriate, or even arrogant, due to the debilitated condition of the Sun (this condition is even more emphasized by the conjunction of the Sun with choleric Mars). With respect to dignified but cadent planets, the reverse situation occurs; the expression of the planet, while discreet, is stable, balanced, and of good quality.

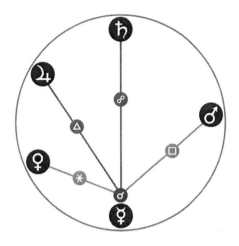

## Chapter VIII
# *Aspects*

The term "aspect" is of Latin origin (*adspectu*) and means to observe, see, look at. From an astrological context, two planets are considered to be in aspect when they "look at" one another, thereby establishing a relationship between them. The aspects between planets indicate the types of dynamic relationships formed between them and describe the actions of the planets in the horoscope.

### The Five Aspects

The aspects derive from the geometry of the actual zodiac and from the nature of the signs. Planets posited in the same signs are subject to the same qualities; for this reason, we conclude that their actions combine. In this case, its is said that the planets are in **conjunction**. Planets in signs opposite each other act contrary to one another, provoking conflict and division. They are said to be in **opposition**. When two planets are situated in signs of the same element, they are under the influence of the same primary qualities and their actions combine with ease and grace. They are said to be in **trine**. Similarly, planets in signs with different elements but of the same gender share the same temperature: hot, in the case of the masculine signs, and cold in the case of the feminine signs; they are said to be in **sextile**. Their relationship is not as flowing as with the trine, but the relationship is agreeable. Planets situated in signs whose temperatures are incompatible but who share the same mode are said to be in **square**. This aspect depicts a difficult relationship, inclining toward friction.

In astrological practice, an aspect is more narrowly defined. Instead of considering the signs

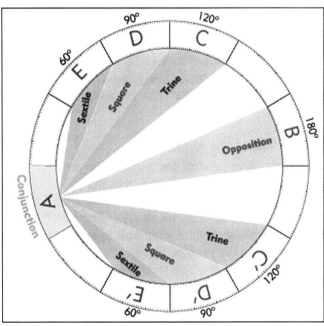

**Figure 1. Aspect Geometry**

to determine the aspectual relationship, only the angle that the signs form in the zodiac is considered. Signs in opposition are at an angle of 180°; in trine, at an angle of 120°; in square, at an angle of 90°; and in sextile, at 60°. Therefore, the relationship between signs is converted into a geometrical relationship. The planets are thus considered to be in opposition when there is an angle of 180° between them, in trine when there is 120°, etc. In this manner, the aspect is defined in practice as an angular relationship between two planets rooted in the geometrical structure of the zodiac.

Note that the angles represented by the aspects are geocentric, meaning they are measured from the center of Earth. They represent the angular relationship between two planets from the perspective of a terrestrial observer.

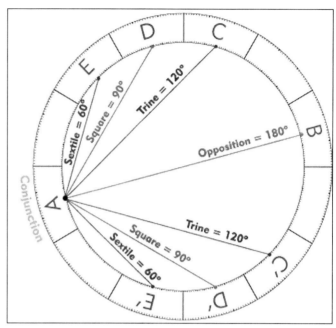

**Figure 2. Aspects as Angular Relationships Between Two Planets**

## Inconjuncts

Four signs are left out of this system: the two immediately adjacent to the starting place (at 30° distance) and the two that flank the sign opposing (at 150°), both of which are not a part of the traditional system of aspects. These signs share nothing with the starting sign—neither temperature, nor mode—and thus cannot establish a relationship with it. Traditionally it is said that these signs cannot "see" each other, meaning they cannot aspect each other. Some authors state that the angular relationships of 30° are very weak and that those of 150° do not result from a whole division of the circle and therefore should not be considered. These angular relationships of 30° and 150° are known as an inconjunct.

## Light as a Basis for Aspects

At the root of the concept that planets in aspect can "see" or "observe" one another is the light

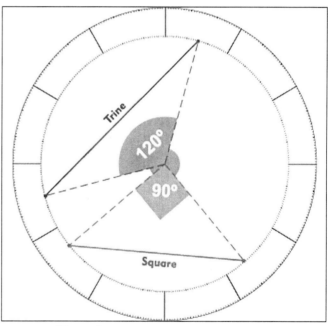

**Figure 3. Aspects as Geocentric Angles**

cast by the planets. The astrological tradition holds that the aspects of 180°, 120°, 90°, and 60° are formed because the planets involved touch each other with their light. In the case of the conjunction, the planets meet each other "physically," mixing their light together, whereas the remaining aspects form by radiating their light. In the case of the opposition, trine, square, and sextile, the planet radiates its light, which touches another planet, allowing them to see each other and form the aspect.

This concept is based upon the principles of ancient Greek optics. Ancient scholars believed that vision was possible because the eyes emitted rays; when they touched an object, these rays allowed for their visualization. We know today that what actually occurs is the exact opposite: it is the eyes that capture the light from

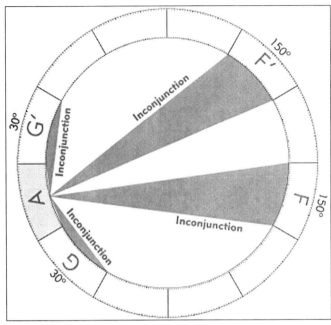

**Figure 4 – The Inconjunction. In modern astrology, these relationships are called semi-sextile (30º) and quincunx (150º). They are minor aspects (see Appendix 5.)**

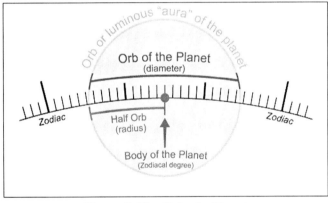

**Figure 5. The Orb of a Planet**

objects and can therefore see them. Nonetheless, the basic principle is the same, underscoring the importance of light in traditional astrology.

From this perspective, the conjunction should not be considered an aspect since it consists of the bodily interaction between planets and not their mutual visualization. In truth, one must distinguish between a bodily conjunction and the aspects so defined. To simplify things in this book, we'll refer to the conjunction as an aspect, despite the distinction.

## Orbs

In horoscopes we rarely find exact aspects. Each planet has a field of influence from which it can interact (form an aspect) with other planets. This field, known as an orb may be envisioned as an "aura" radiating around the planet. The center of this sphere or orb, is the actual degree where the planet is located—its body. The orbs are expressed as a radius, which means that the influence of the planet's orb will extend in front of and behind the planet a certain number of degrees. The orb of each planet varies according to its astrological "weight." The values are shown in Figure 6:

The orbs are generally measured in terms of radii. Some authors give orbs that are slightly different from these (for instance, 17º of radius for the Sun, and 8º for Venus), but the majority use the orbs given here.[20]

For example, the orb for the Moon has a diameter of 24º, 12º extending behind and 12º to the front of the zodiacal position of the planet. If the Moon is located at 17º of Capricorn, its orb extends from 5º to 29º of the sign. Within this range, the Moon may form conjunctions.

For the other aspects, the orb of the Moon radiates, as if it projected beams of its light into areas of the zodiac where it can form aspects. In this way, the Moon aspects by opposition anything situated between 5º and 29º of Cancer (the sign opposite Capricorn); it forms a square to any planet located at the same degrees of Aries and Libra (the signs located 90º from Capricorn); it forms a trine to any planet in the same degrees of Taurus and Virgo (signs of the same element at 120º from Capricorn); and lastly it forms a sextile with any planet or point situated at the same degrees of Pisces and Scorpio (signs at 60º of Capricorn).

Therefore, an aspect is formed when the orb of the planet with the larger aura touches the body, (the zodiacal degree) where the other planet is physically located. In the previous example, the Moon was at 17º Capricorn and Mars at 10º Virgo. We find here that the orb of the Moon, which extends from 5º to 29º of the sign, touches by trine the position of Mars. Similarly, the orb of Mars, which extends from 2º to 18º Virgo

| Figure 6. Orbs of the Planets (radius and diameter) | |
| --- | --- |
| *Planet* | *Orb Radius (diameter)* |
| Saturn | 9° (18°) |
| Jupiter | 9° (18°) |
| Mars | 8° (16°) |
| Sun | 15° (30°) |
| Venus | 7° (14°) |
| Mercury | 7° (14°) |
| Moon | 12° (24°) |

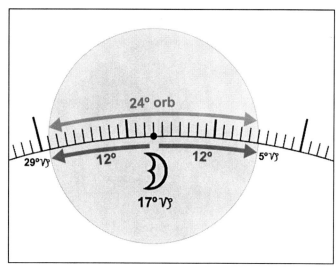

**Figure 7. Orb of the Moon**

touches, through its rays, the degree of the Moon. It is said then that the aspect between the planets is **mutual**.

### Partile and Platic Aspects

Nevertheless, this Moon-Mars aspect would not be exact. For that to occur, both planets would have to occupy the same degree in their respective signs: for instance, 10° Virgo (Mars) and 10° Capricorn (Moon). We can thus distinguish between two types of aspects: **partile** and **platic** aspects. A partile aspect occurs when the planets are located in the same degree and the aspect between them is exact. When the aspect is outside of that degree but still within the necessary orb, it is said to be a platic aspect. The closer to exact is the aspect, the more intense are its effects.

Due to the differences in orbs for the planets, often the aspects are not mutual. The orb of planet A may touch the body of planet B, but the orb of planet B may not touch the body of planet A. In such a case, we have a slightly weaker aspect. Only when both planets are within each other's orbs is the aspect especially active. For exam-

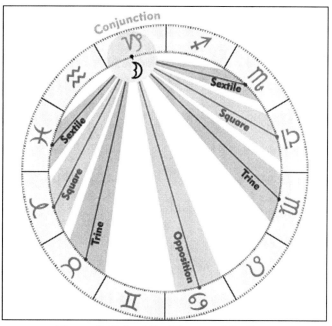

**Figure 8. Orb of the Moon and its Rays**

ple, consider the Sun at 2° Gemini and Saturn at 13° of the same sign. The orb of the Sun (with 15° of range) extends to 17° Gemini and touches the body of Saturn at 13°. However, the orb of Saturn only reaches as far as 4° Gemini, and thus does not touch the body of the Sun. We then say that Saturn is within the orb of the Sun, but the Sun is not within the orb of Saturn. There is a conjunction between the planets, but the aspect is one-sided and doesn't express itself completely. The same logic applies to oppositions, trines, squares and sextiles.

---

[20]These values come from the Sun's relationship with the planets. For instance, 15° is approximately the degree range of luminosity of the Sun and 12° is the distance that the Moon needs to have from the Sun before it is again becomes visible. The values for the planets probably result from adjustments made in accordance with the planets' relationships with the lights and their individual importance. Thus, the slower, superior planets Saturn and Jupiter, have a slightly larger orb than the faster planets, Venus and Mercury, which have smaller orbs.

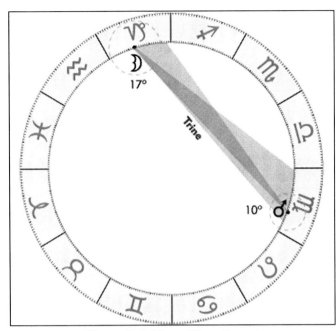

**Figure 9. A Moon-Mars Aspect**

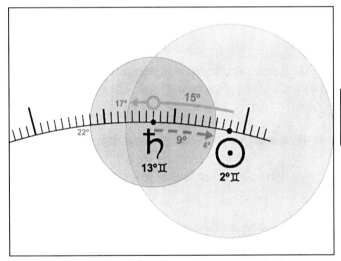

**Figure 10. Unilateral Aspect: a Sun-Saturn Conjunction**

## Out-of-Sign Aspects

Due to the range created by the orb of the planet, an aspect between signs without affinity or compatibility may occur. This happens when the planets are located at the end of one sign and their orb reaches into the next sign, or when they are located at the beginning of one sign and the orb reaches back into the previous sign. This is called an out-of-sign aspect. These are some examples (see Figure 11):

- Planet A is at 28° Leo and planet B is at 2° Virgo, forming a very tight conjunction (only 4° apart), but the aspect between two adjacent signs that do not see each other.
- Planet C at 1° Taurus forms a sextile to planet D at 29° Aquarius; it is a tight aspect (2° apart), but between signs that are naturally square one another.
- Planet E at 27° Virgo forms a square to planet F at 2° Capricorn, and despite being a tight square (5° apart), the signs involved are normally in a trine relationship to each other.

> The term partile can simply be substituted by the expression "exact" and platic by "within the orb."

- Planet G is at 27° Cancer, in opposition to planet H, at 1° Aquarius in a tight opposition (4° apart) that ties together signs that normally do not aspect each other.

The aspects can also form aspects to other components of the chart, such as the Ascendant, the Midheaven, Arabic Parts, etc. Since these factors are mathematical points and not celestial bodies, they do not have any orb. In these cases, we simply use the orb of the planet to calculate the aspect.

The conjunction and opposition are less affected by out-of-sign aspects since their effects derive mainly from the positions of the planets (corporally together or in opposite placements of the chart) rather than from the signs involved.

The validity of these aspects is often a source of debate between authors. Apparently, the more ancient authors only considered the aspect when it occurred in the appropriate sign, while later authors consider the aspect valid as long as it was within orb. There are recorded cases of aspects by degree in the ancient Greek authors.

The problem is somewhat academic. Practical experience has demonstrated that out-of-sign aspects represent circumstances that, without impeding the action of the aspect, can nevertheless disrupt its normal functioning. Thus, out-of-sign trines and sextiles display some instability, while the squares appear to be more fluid, characteristics that are not typical of these aspects. In any case, there is no existing doctrine with regard to out-of-sign aspects; their interpretation depends on their particular context.

**Variations in the Definitions of an Aspect**

Some Renaissance authors (15th and 16th centuries) use a slightly different rule for the definition of aspects. Although they also use the concept of orb, they contend that the orb is formed when one planet's half-orb touches the other planet's half-orb. There is thus a division of the orbs into halves, whose technical term is *moiety* (from the French *moitié* meaning "half"). For example (see Figure 12), consider the Moon at 14° Gemini and Mercury at 22° of the same sign. To see if there is an aspect, we take the *moiety* of the Moon's orb, or 6° (half of 12), and the *moiety* of Mercury's 3°30' (half of 7°); the result is 9°30' (6°+ 3° 30'). This is the range within which the planets may touch each other in the formation of an aspect. Since in this instance the

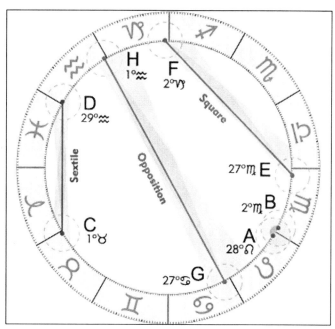

**Figure 11. Out-of-sign Aspects**

distance between both planets is 8° (a value smaller than the range) there exists an aspect since the *moieties* of the planets slightly overlap.

We can say that the Moon and Mercury are conjunct. This is a more mathematical perspective on the concept because it takes the "average" of the degrees of orb of each of the planets involved. The earlier method is more "physical." We therefore have two systems:

- The **orb-body system**, which we use in this book, considers the aspect to occur when the ray from planet A touches the body of planet B.
- The **system of moieties**, which considers the aspect to occur when half of planet A's orb touches the half of planet B's orb.

Currently, the last system is more popular among students and practitioners of traditional astrology. This happens not because this system is more logical or practical than the other, but because it is more well-known. Its popularity is credited primarily to William Lilly (the most well-known traditional author in the English language) who uses it in his significant work *Christian Astrology*.

We use the orb-body system, which is the typical system in the majority of traditional texts. Besides that, it is a system that rests on the principles of ancient optical theory: an object is only visible when the rays that it emits touch the "body" (the eyes) of the observer. In this sense, the orb-body system is more reasonable because it argues that the aspect occurs when the light from a planet touches the body of another. In the *moiety* system, it is the light from both planets that touch one another, which seems inconsistent with classical optical theory. In any event, the practical difference between both systems is

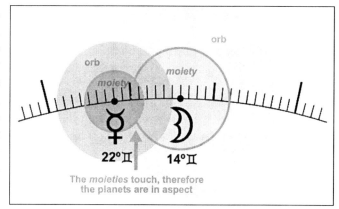

The *moieties* touch, therefore the planets are in aspect

**Figure 12. *Moieties***

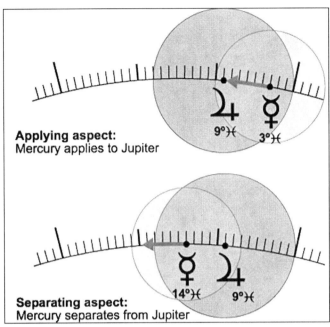

**Applying aspect:**
Mercury applies to Jupiter

**Separating aspect:**
Mercury separates from Jupiter

**Figure 13. Applying and Separating Aspects**

negligible. The orb-body system tends to be a bit more generous, allowing for slightly wider aspects.

*Aspects in Motion: Applications and Separations*

When we look at a chart, we see a fixed moment in time. The planets are "frozen" in their trajectories and for that reason the aspects appear static. However, this is only a practical convenience because nothing in nature is static. Because the planets are always in motion, the aspects constitute dynamic relationships. *The dynamism characteristic of the aspects derives from each planet's distinct speed.* An aspect is always formed by the swiftest planet because it is this planet that approaches or distances itself from the slower planet. For example, consider Mercury at 3° Pisces and Jupiter at 9° of the same sign. Mercury, being the faster planet, forms the aspect to Jupiter, which in this case is a conjunction. Because Mercury is at 3° Pisces and Jupiter at 9°, one can easily conclude that the exact aspect will only occur when Mercury physically joins Jupiter at 9° Pisces. The aspect is within the orb, but it is still forming. This aspect is then referred to as **applying**. If Mercury were at 14° Pisces and Jupiter still at 9° of the same sign, it would also be a conjunction, but Mercury would be separating from the exact aspect. This is thus called a **separating** aspect.

When planet A, the faster planet, comes into orb of the aspect with planet B, the slower planet, the aspect begins to form. In this phase, the planet is applying to the aspect with planet B. At a certain point, the planets reach the exact distance for the aspect to form and the aspect then completes itself, or *perfects*. We then have a partile or exact aspect. As soon as planet A begins to distance itself from planet B by more than 1°, the aspect begins to break up. In this phase, planet A separates itself from the aspect to planet B. The separation continues until planet A (the faster planet) leaves the orb and the aspect ends.

Recall that the relative speeds of the planets is given to us from the Chaldean order: the Moon, Mercury, Venus, the Sun, Mars, Jupiter and Saturn. The Moon is always the fastest celestial body, so it presents no problem. The Sun has a relatively constant speed or approximately 1° per day. The remaining planets, despite following the Chaldean order, often exhibit slight irregularities in their speeds (this happens when they change the direction of their motion from direct to retrograde and back again). For a more precise study it is necessary to consult planetary tables in order to determine their exact speeds (see planetary speeds in Chapter V).

Particular situations occur when one of the two planets involved in the aspect is retrograde. For instance, suppose planet A is approaching the aspect to planet B, which is retrograde and also approaching the aspect to planet A. In this case the planets are in **mutual application** because they are approaching one another. Similarly, planet A may be separating from planet B, which being retrograde, may also be separating from planet A. In this case, there is a **mutual separation**.

Applications and separations illustrate the dynamic nature of the aspects and are extremely important in determining the outcome of the actions described in the horoscope. Applying aspects describe what will happen, while separating aspects describe what has happened. This type of interpretation is particularly relevant in horary astrology and in event charts.

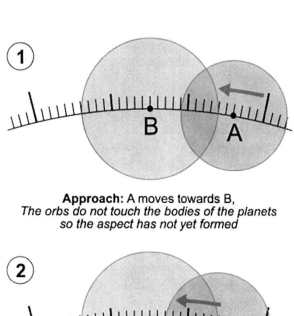

**Approach:** A moves towards B,
*The orbs do not touch the bodies of the planets
so the aspect has not yet formed*

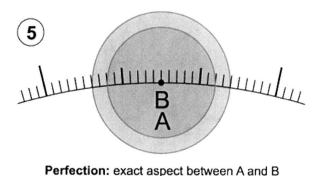

**Perfection:** exact aspect between A and B

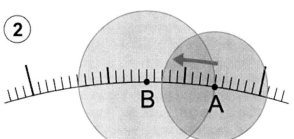

**Beginning of application:** A enters the orb of B
*The aspect forms*

**Beginning of separation:** A is 1 degree away from B

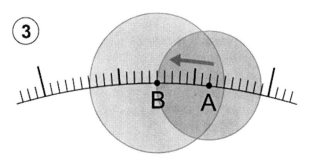

**Application:** the aspect becomes stronger as
the orb of A reaches B

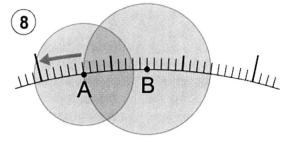

**Separation:** B exits the orb of A, the aspect weakens

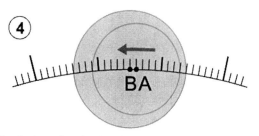

**Beginning of perfection:** A is at less than 1 degree from B

**End of separation:** A exits the orb of B; the aspect ends

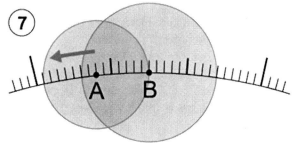

**Figure 14. The aspect's Cycle: Application, Perfection and Separation**

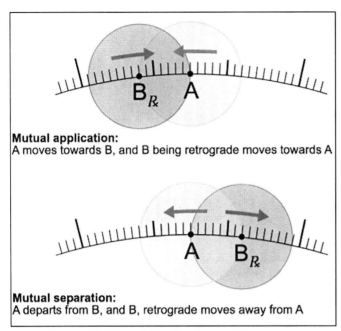

**Mutual application:**
A moves towards B, and B being retrograde moves towards A

**Mutual separation:**
A departs from B, and B, retrograde moves away from A

**Figure 15. Mutual Application and Separation**

*Specific Cases: Void of Course and Feral*

When a planet forms no aspects to other planets, it is said to be **void**, or **void of course.** In these instances, it forms only separating aspects. Since applying aspects describe future actions, or motivations (in the case of nativities), a planet in this conditions has its capacity for action diminished or impeded. It indicates a state of inaction and lack of will in the matters signified by the planet. This type of situation is particularly important with the Moon, which, because it is the fastest planet, is the one most frequently void. Besides that, the Moon is the planet that describes the most eminent actions in a horoscope. This type of analysis is particularly relevant in a horary chart or mundane chart, or in an election. In a natal chart, although the concept is equally valid and applicable, the interpretative context is different and its significance is relative.

Although apparently simple, the definition of void of course has led to some discussions between modern authors. Some say that a planet is void of course only when it doesn't form any aspects to another planet before it leaves the sign where it is posited. Thus, a planet that makes only separating aspects but that applies to an out-of-sign aspect is considered void. This would not be true in the previous definition. This difference of opinion is due to incomplete or questionable definitions from various sources because most traditional astrologers did not consider out-of-sign aspects. Thus, a planet would have to enter into the next sign to form an aspect, even when the orb would allow it to form the aspect in the previous sign.

> Note: applications and separations only occur between planets. Aspects of planets to the ASC, MC, Part of Fortune, and other points, follow different rules. See page 115.

In our opinion, this discussion is academic. The objective of the interpretation is to obtain a description of the action of the planet. The fact that a planet does not make an application reveals a lack of action. If, on the other hand, the aspect that the planet applies to is only perfected in the following sign (in effect void of course for some authors) we have an indication that some circumstance will change (change in sign) before any action can occur (the perfection of the aspect). What's most important in such questions is to describe the chart, rather than theorizing about it. This is the difference between an understanding of the chart based upon practical experience and one based strictly upon theoretical study.

When a planet is totally devoid of aspects (applying or separating) it is said to be **feral**. This condition is considered unfortunate because the planet does not share its qualities with any of the other elements of the chart. Since it has no direct interaction with other planets, its expression becomes weak, and as a consequence, the planet is highlighted in the chart. The effect of a feral planet is even more apparent if the planet is alone in its sign.

For instance, in the horoscope of Agatha Christie, Mercury is feral. In this case, mercurial qualities (communication, rationality, intellect) are highlighted, which is obvious in the life of this author of detective stories. Nonetheless, the feral condition of Mercury creates a disintegration between her notable career as a writer and her personal life, which was far more removed. The condition is more noteworthy given the fact that Mercury is the Ascendant ruler.

The dynamism of the planetary aspects, whose basis is the application and separation of the planets, produces even more complex patterns which will be discussed later in this chapter.

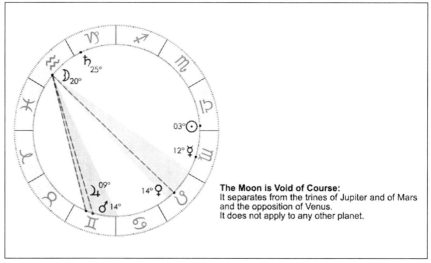

**The Moon is Void of Course:**
It separates from the trines of Jupiter and of Mars and the opposition of Venus.
It does not apply to any other planet.

**Figure 16. A Void-of-Course Planet**

### Dexter and Sinister Aspects

Of the five traditional aspects, the trine, square and sextile are considered double aspects. These aspects can occur in two directions from the starting point, one to the left and one to the right. Thus, there are actually two types of trines, squares and sextiles. Those that occur to the left of the planet, in the direction of the order of the signs, are called **sinister aspects**. Those that occur to its right, in the direction contrary to the order of the signs, are called **dexter aspects**. The word sinister, from the Latin, means "left" and does not have the negative connotations which we currently attribute to it.

To distinguish between a dexter and a sinister aspect, one must start with the faster planet, which is responsible for the formation of the aspect. If the aspect is formed in the direction contrary to the order of the signs, it is a dexter aspect. If it is formed in the direction of the order of the signs, it is a sinister aspect. Seen another way, if one looks at the faster planet from the center of the chart, all of the aspects which form to its right are dexter, while all that form to its left are sinister. For instance, consider Venus at

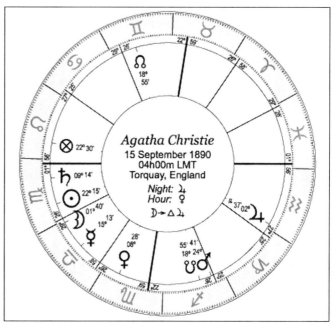

**Chart 2. Nativity of Agatha Christie**

7° Cancer, Saturn at 10° Scorpio, and Jupiter at 5° Aries. Venus is within the orb of the two slower planets, projecting a trine to Saturn and a square to Jupiter. The trine to Saturn is sinister because it is projected along the order of the signs (Cancer to Leo to Virgo to Libra and, finally, to Scorpio). The square to Jupiter is dexter because it is formed in the order contrary to the order of the signs (from Cancer to Gemini to Taurus and, finally, to Aries).

A dexter aspect is thought to be stronger than a sinister aspect because it is formed in the direction in which the signs *rise*. It is therefore considered more significant in its actions. On the other hand, the sinister aspect is milder because it is formed in the direction counter to the rising of the signs, but along the natural pace of the moving planets. Because it is milder, it allows for a greater freedom of choice in the actions it represents.

This concept is often ignored because it reveals only a very minor difference in the strength of the aspect. Although it doesn't always assume a prominent role in interpretation, it is very useful when studying an aspect in greater detail.

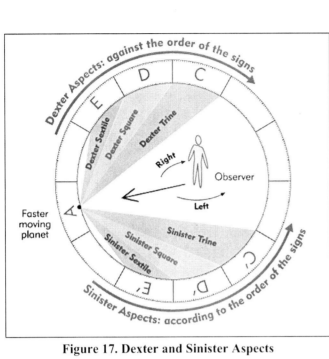

**Figure 17. Dexter and Sinister Aspects**

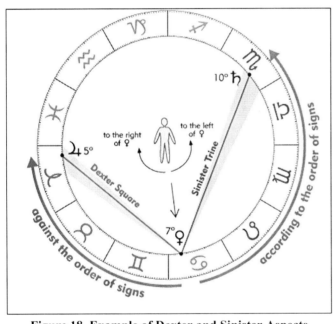

**Figure 18. Example of Dexter and Sinister Aspects**

## Aspects to Non-Planetary Points

Planets can also make aspects to non-planetary points in an astrological chart. The most important are aspects of planets to the Ascendant, Midheaven, and Part of Fortune. Since these points do not cast light (they have no physical form), they cannot have orbs nor form aspects. The planets, however, can aspect them. In contrast to interplanetary aspects, aspects between planets and points are unilateral because only one of the two (the planet) actively participates in the aspect; the other is merely aspected.

To calculate these aspects, we consider whether the point in question is within the limits of the orb of the planet (in the case of the conjunction) or within its projected rays (in the case of the trine, square, and sextile). For the four angles of the chart and the Part of Fortune, applications and separations are not considered because the movement of these points through the zodiac follows different parameters from the motion of the planets.

As to sinister and dexter aspects, the definition is the same, although in this case the active point is always the planet, independent of its speed. For example, in the Friedrich Nietzsche's horoscope, the Ascendant (29° Scorpio 09′) receives a sinister sextile from Mars (27° Virgo 56′) and a dexter trine from Jupiter (26° Pisces 02′).

In the case of the four angles, only aspects to the Ascendant and Midheaven are considered. Aspects to the other two angles can easily be deduced from these two. In reality, we are actually examining two axes which unite opposite angles: the Ascendant/Descendant and the Midheaven/Imum Coeli. Any planet that is conjunct

---

## Aspects and Sign Ascension

Some authors claim that the nature of an aspect can be partially modified by the sign in which the aspect occurs. Thus, aspects that form between signs of fast ascension (Capricorn to Gemini) are "shortened." The square acquires the properties of a sextile and the trine those of a square. Aspects that form between signs of long ascension (Cancer to Sagittarius) are "stretched": the sextile acquires the properties of the square and the square becomes like a trine. Although this concept is applied by some practitioners with good results, others contest its validity because it results from combining different frames of reference: the velocity of the sign's ascension (due to the inclination of the ecliptic), and the aspects, which are based upon the signs.

one of these points is in opposition the other; when in trine with one, it is sextile the other (and vice versa); when in square to one, it is square the other. It is therefore unnecessary to note the aspects to all of the angles; it is enough to know the aspects to one side of the axis in order to deduce those to the other.

Aspects to the house cusps should also be avoided due to the uncertainties as to the most accurate method of house calculation (see Appendix 4, Additional Considerations About the Houses). It makes no sense to consider aspects between the various angles nor between two nonplanetary points; because they do not "possess their own light," they cannot aspect each other.

## Representing Aspects in the Horoscope

### Aspect Notation

To facilitate representation, aspects have specific symbols that derive from the geometry that is associated with each. The conjunction is represented by a circle with a single line, signifying reunion. The opposition is represented by two opposing circles united by a line. The trine and the square are depicted by their geometrical correlates: a triangle and a square, respectively. The sextile is represented by a six-pointed star, a variation on the hexagon.

It is essential to a practical working knowledge of astrology to be able to read and notate the aspects. Many students place too much trust in astrological software applications, thinking that these will relieve them from tedious calculations. One should note, however, that to function properly, any program must be configured properly. In order to do this, technical knowledge of the calculation of aspects is a prerequisite. Besides, even if the application traces them correctly, the student must still know how to identify them and interpret them correctly. An aspect must always be noted, beginning with the fastest planet. This one is responsible for the formation and separation of the aspect; so it should be noted first. The notation is made using the symbols of the planets and aspects as shown below:

| Aspect | Degrees | Symbols |
|---|---|---|
| Opposition | 180° | ☍ |
| Trine | 120° | △ |
| Square | 90° | □ |
| Sextile | 60° | ✶ |
| Conjunction | 0° | ☌ |

For example, let's take a square between Venus and the Moon. Since the Moon is faster than Venus, it is the Moon that forms the square. The notation is made by writing the symbol of the Moon followed by the symbol of the aspect, and then of Venus:

$$☽ □ ♀$$

A less correct notation is used if the aspect is witten like this:

$$♀ □ ☽$$

If the aspect is applying, an "a" is added to the end. If it is separating, an "s" is added. For example:

Mars applies to a sextile of Saturn = ♂ ✶ ♄ a

Sun separates from the opposition to Jupiter = ☉ ☍ ♃ s

## A Guide for Mapping Aspects in a Chart

*Step One: Identifying the Aspects*

Start with the fastest planet, the Moon. Look at its degree and minute and note the range of its orb. This is done by subtracting and adding to its position, the value of its allowed orb (12° in the case of the Moon). Next, look for planets close to the Moon to see if there are any conjunctions. These are easy to see. Then, look in the same degrees of the opposite sign for any oppositions. Then search the chart from the opposition point to the conjunction for any possible aspects: trine (two signs after the opposition), square (the sign after the trine), and sextile (the sign after the square). After this, do the same on the other side of the chart. In this process, you must always consider the orb of the planet and select other bodies situated within that range.

Whenever an aspect is located, note whether it is applying or separating (and also if dexter or sinister). When all aspects of the Moon are noted, do the same with the next fastest planets: Mercury, Venus, the Sun, etc. (following the Chaldean order). Note that once an aspect from, for example, Venus to Jupiter is identified, it is unnecessary to record this same aspect when the aspects of Jupiter are identified. This way, the farther along one proceeds in the order of the planets, it is necessary only to note the aspects to slower planets, avoiding any duplications.

Recall once more that:

1. A conjunction occurs in the same sign and is easy to spot.

2. An opposition occurs between opposing signs, six signs away, and is also easy to detect.

3. The sign next to the opposition is inconjunct and does not create aspects.

4. The trine occurs between signs with the same element, four signs away.

5. The square occurs between signs of the same mode, three signs away.

6. The sextile occurs between signs of the same gender, two signs away.

7. The sign adjacent to that of the planet is also inconjunct and does not create aspects.

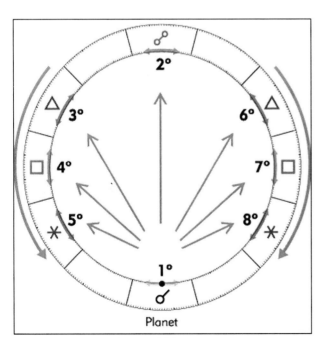

Look for out-of-sign aspects. If the planet is at the beginning or end of a sign it is likely that it may form an aspect outside of the expected signs. The student should pay special attention in these cases.

*Step Two: Mapping the Aspects*

The aspects can be represented in a chart by colored lines. This step is optional since it is a matter of visual preference. Some people do not illustrate the aspects in a chart, preferring to identify them in the moment. The ideal is to identify the aspects yourself and avoid the aspect lines in the center of the chart.

Having said that, there is no standard for illustrating the aspects, so we suggest the following:

• The tension and conflict-indicating aspects (square and opposition) should be drawn in red.

• The harmonic aspects (trine and sextile) should be drawn in blue.

**Figure 19. Identifying the Aspects**

In order to distinguish between applying and separating aspects, you can use a dashed line for the separating aspects and an uninterrupted line for the applying aspects. If color is not used, then a dashed line may be used for the opposition and square, and an uninterrupted line may be used for the trine and sextile (in this case, however, they would not distinguish applications from separations). Only aspects between planets should be drawn. Aspects to the Ascendant, Midheaven, or Part of Fortune should be listed separately. This prevents the chart from becoming overly cluttered with lines, which make its reading difficult.

As an example, King Sebastian's chart is used to calculate the planetary ranges in Chaldean order:

Start with the Moon located at 26° Leo 37′. The range of its orb will run from 14° Leo 37′ (12° before) to 8° Virgo 37′ (12° after). Then look for planets that lie within this orb or its rays. There are no planets near the Moon; therefore we start at the opposite sign, Aquarius. There are three planetary candidates to an opposition of the Moon: Mercury at 22°13′, Mars at 14°37′ and the Sun at 10°00′. The orb of the Moon reaches to 14°37′; thus, only Mercury and Mars are within the rays of the opposition. We have therefore, two oppositions: the Moon to Mercury and the Moon to Mars. Since the Moon is at 26°, it has passed the exact degrees of Mercury and the aspect is separating. Mercury is retrograde and, therefore, also separates from the Moon, a mutual separation. Since the distance between both planets is 4°24′ (26°37′ - 22°13′) and the orb of Mercury is 7°, the aspect is mutual.

The aspect to Mars is also separating (since it is even farther from the Moon than Mercury); however, the distance between them is 11°28′. This is a separating aspect very close to the limit, whereby the orb of Mars does not touch the Moon. So it is a weak aspect of little note in the chart. The remaining planets are in positions without an aspect: Venus and Saturn are in signs adjacent to the opposition, and Jupiter is totally out of orb to form any aspect.

Note the aspects this way:

☽ ☍ ☿ s

☽ ☍ ♂ s

Next is Mercury, the second fastest planet, at 22° Aquarius 13′. Its orb extends from 15°13′ to 29°13′ of the sign (7° before and after). In the same sign we find Mars and the Sun. Although the orb of Mercury does not reach these planets' positions, keep in mind that their orbs are larger. The distance from Mercury to Mars is 7°04′, slightly out of orb for Mercury (7°), but within the orb of Mars (8°). Therefore, we have a Mercury-Mars conjunction. Because Mercury is retrograde, it is moving toward Mars, while Mars in direct motion is moving toward Mercury. We have in this case a mutual application. Although Mars is not within the orb of Mercury, the difference is very close (0°04') and the planets are approaching one another, which gives the aspect great power.

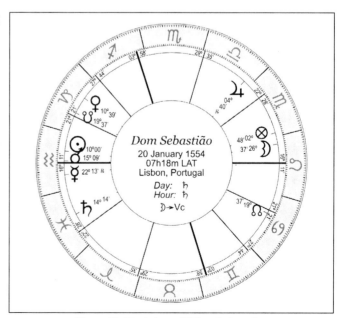

**Chart V. Nativity of King Sebastian**

The Sun, with its 15° orb, also reaches Mercury,

forming a conjunction. It is a weaker conjunction than that of Mars because the distance is even larger, but it is also a mutual application. As to other aspects, the Moon was considered, Venus and Saturn are in adjacent signs (and therefore without aspect), and Jupiter is out of orb for a trine.

Note the aspects this way:

☿ ☌ ☉ a

☿ ☌ ♂ a

Venus, which is next in speed, is at 10° Capricorn 39′ and its orb runs from 3°39′ to 17°39′. There are no planets next to Venus to form a conjunction, nor planets in opposition. The Sun, Mars, and Mercury are in an adjacent sign and do not form an aspect. The Moon is in the sign next to the opposition; therefore, it does not form an aspect. If we follow in the direction of the signs, we find Saturn in Pisces, to where Venus projects a sextile. Saturn is at 14°14′ of the sign and therefore within the rays of Venus. In turn, Saturn also touches Venus with its orb. We therefore have a Venus-Saturn sextile. It is an applying aspect because Venus, the faster planet, is approaching an exact aspect to Saturn. Because Venus projects a sextile in the order of the signs, it is also a sinister aspect.

If we look in the direction contrary to the order of the signs, we find Jupiter at 4° Libra 40′, and Venus in Capricorn projects a dexter square. Jupiter is within the rays of Venus (which runs to 3°39′) and also touches it with its own orb (which runs to 13°40′). There is, therefore, a square between both planets. The aspect is separating because Venus is 10° in front of Jupiter and is faster.

Note the aspects this way:

♀ □ ♃ s (dexter)
♀ ⚹ ♄ a (sinister)

The Sun is at 10° Aquarius 00′ and its orb runs from 25° Capricorn 00′ to 25° Aquarius 00′. In Aquarius we also find Mercury (whose conjunction to the Sun was already identified) and Mars at 15°09′. Mars and the Sun are within each other's orbs and form a conjunction because they are only 5°09′ apart. Since the Sun is faster and is approaching Mars, the conjunction is applying. In the opposite sign is the Moon, whose aspects we've already considered. Venus and Saturn are in inconjunct signs and form no aspect with the Sun. Jupiter is in Libra, a sign of the same element as Aquarius, allowing the possibility of a trine with the Sun. Since Jupiter is at 4°40′ and the Sun at 10°00′, we find that they are within each other's orb, which confirms a trine between them. The aspect is separating because the Sun, the faster of the two, is ahead of Jupiter. It is dexter because it is projected in the direction contrary to the order of the signs.

Note the aspects this way:

☉ ☌ ♂ a
☉ △ ♃ a (dexter)

Next, turn to Mars at 15° Aquarius 09′, whose orb runs from 7°09′ to 22°09′ of the sign. Since we noted all of the aspects of the planets faster than Mars, it is only necessary now to look for aspects from Mars to Jupiter and Saturn, which are slower. Saturn is in the adjacent sign, and therefore no aspects are formed. Jupiter is in Libra, where Mars projects a trine. However, Mars' orb does not reach Jupiter, and Jupiter's orb (extends to 12°40′) also does not reach Mars. Thus, no aspect is formed.

As to Jupiter, all that is left is to see if it forms an aspect with Saturn. Since they are in inconjunct signs in this chart, there are no aspects between them. The aspects between Saturn and the other planets have already been considered.

There are no feral planets because all the planets are involved in an aspect. Next, check to see if there are any planets that are void of course. For this we only need to see if there are any applying aspects:

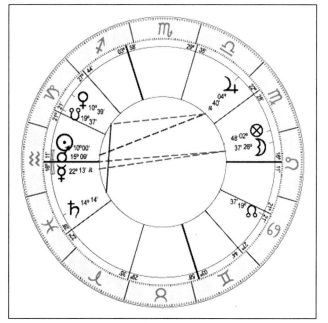

- The Moon has two separating aspects but no applying ones. It is, therefore, void.
- Mercury applies to Mars and the Sun.
- Venus applies to Saturn.
- The Sun forms a mutual application with Mercury.
- Mars also forms a mutual application with Mercury.
- Jupiter does not apply to any planet, and is therefore void.
- Saturn also has no applications and is void.

We can then make a list of all the aspects in King Sebastian's chart:

☽ ☍ ☿ s          ☿ ☌ ☉ a          ♀ □ ☉ s dexter
☉ ☌ ♂ a          ♃ voc            ♄ voc
☽ ☍ ♂ s          ☿ ☌ ♂ a          ♀ ✳ ♄ a sinister
☉ △ ♃ s dexter
☽ voc

**Figure 20. Aspects in King Sebastian's Chart**

We can then separately note the aspects formed to the Ascendant (ASC), the Midheaven (MC) and the Part of Fortune, which in this chart are:

☉ ☌ Asc          ☽ □ MC          ☽ ☌ P
☿ ☌ Asc          ☉ ✳ MC
♂ ☌ Asc          ♃ ✳ MC
☽ ☍ Asc

## Interpretation

### The Nature of the Aspects
Each aspect represents a specific type of interaction (or relationship) between the planets. This relationship is defined by the geometrical (the angle) and the zodiacal (signs) nature of the aspect. The first step in interpreting the aspects is to know their natures well.

### Conjunction
The conjunction is the most intense of all aspects since it directly unites the planets. It occurs when they are in an angle close to 0° and generally in the same sign. However, it is not a true aspect because it results from a "physical" connection between celestial bodies and not from an angular relationship (of rays).

Its nature is one of union because it mixes the qualities of the planets, and they can become so identified that their individual natures are confused. Despite its intensity, we may say that the conjunction is a neutral aspect. Its quality depends upon the nature of the planets involved and of the sign where it occurs. If the planets are compatible, the conjunction generates ease and flow; if the planets are of very different natures, it generates friction and obstruction. This aspect is also known as a "bodily conjunction" or synod.

## Opposition

The opposition relates planets in opposite signs, at an angle close to 180°. Its nature comes from the interaction between opposing sides and not from the actual signs involved, as in the remaining aspects. Since it puts two zodiacal polarities in contact, it indicates confrontation and manifests in a tense, difficult manner. If we compare the opposition to a dialogue, this would be an open discussion where the two parties are in direct conflict, producing discomfort and obstruction. This aspect is also known as a **diameter**.

## Trine

The trine corresponds to 120°. It relates planets in signs of the same element and which, therefore, share the same primary qualities (temperament) It thus, indicates an easy, smooth, and stable relationship between the planets involved. If this aspect were a dialogue, we could imagine two people who speak about the same things and agree with each other. This aspect is also known as a **triangle**.

## Square

The square relates two planets that are 90° apart. It relates signs of the same mode but of incompatible elements. It indicates tension between the planets involved, which generally manifests as pressure and internal conflict. It is externalized as struggle and resistance. Because of this, the square is often a source of stress and frustration. If it were a dialogue, the square would be a tense, uncomfortable conversation, full of provocations. Because the square cuts the zodiac into four parts, it is also known as a **quartile**.

## Sextile

The sextile corresponds to an angle of 60°. It represents a harmonious relationship because it relates signs of the same temperature (hot and cold). Nonetheless, the sextile is less intense than the trine because the signs involved have different elements and modes.

As a dialogue, the sextile would be a conversation where the two people agree on the main points, although with slight differences in their approaches. It is an aspect that represents cooperation and understanding, where the planets have a functional and pleasant expression. This aspect is also known as a **hexagon** because it divides the circle into six parts.

## Aspects and the Rulership Scheme

The aspects derive fundamentally from the natural relationships between signs. However, we can also relate the natures of the aspects with the natures of the planets. This relationship is established through the rulership scheme, in which the relationship between planets and luminaries (when placed in the signs they rule) reflects and compliments the nature of the aspects.

The luminaries—symbols of life, order, and abundance—rule over the signs of greatest daylight and heat: Cancer, ruled by the Moon, and Leo, ruled by the Sun. In the rulership scheme, the malefic planets Saturn and Mars form tense aspects with the lights. Saturn, the greater malefic, is in direct opposition with the Sun and the Moon because it occupies Capricorn (opposite Cancer) and Aquarius (opposite Leo). Mars, the lesser malefic, forms squares to the lights by way of its signs of rulership, Aries and Scorpio. From Aries, it is square the Moon's sign, Cancer, and from Scorpio, it is square the Sun's sign, Leo.

In turn, the benefic planets, Jupiter and Venus, form favorable aspects to the luminaries' signs from the signs they rule. Jupiter, the greater benefic, forms a trine to the Sun from Sagittarius and another to the Moon from

Pisces, while Venus, the lesser benefic, forms a sextile to the Sun from Libra and another to the Moon from Taurus.

Mercury is a special case because it is too close to the Sun to form an aspect. Its position in the rulership scheme mirrors this pattern: its signs of rulership, Gemini and Virgo, are adjacent to the signs of the lights. This image makes clear the symmetry that relates the planets with the aspects according to the type of relationship they create. Thus:

- The opposition has a nature similar to Saturn; it impedes, obstructs and creates tension.
- The square has the nature of Mars; it generates friction and misunderstanding.
- The trine has the nature of Jupiter; it unites with perfection and understanding.
- The sextile has the nature of Venus; it unites with friendship and moderation.
- The conjunction has the neutral nature of Mercury because its effect depends upon the planets involved.

Note that the symmetry of this scheme also reinforces the masculine/diurnal and feminine/nocturnal expression of the planets. The planets in their diurnal rulerships (Mercury in Gemini, Venus in Libra, Mars in Aries, and Jupiter in Sagittarius) form sextiles and trines with the Sun, the masculine light and lord of the day, while the planets in their nocturnal rulerships (Mercury in Virgo, Venus in Taurus, Mars in Scorpio, and Jupiter in Pisces) form sextiles and trines to the Moon, the feminine light and lady of the night. Only Saturn, the most malefic of all the planets, is opposed to the lights in any situation (in its diurnal rulership over Aquarius, it is opposite the Sun in Leo, and in its nocturnal rulership over Capricorn, it is opposite the Moon in Cancer).

It is also possible to observe a similar symmetry in the system of joys attributed to the astrological houses. In this system, the pairs Sun-Moon (the lights) and Jupiter-Venus (the benefics) have their joys in houses which symbolically make aspects to the Ascendant (first). The third house, joy of the Moon, and the eleventh house, joy of Jupiter, form sextiles to the Ascendant, while the ninth, joy of the Sun, and the fifth, joy of Venus, form trines.

On the other hand, the malefics are located in houses that do not aspect the Ascendant, the twelfth, and the sixth. This way, when they are in a position of power, they do not "damage" the Ascendant. Due to its neutral and ambivalent nature, Mercury is not matched up; it is positioned in the Ascendant so that it will be in good relationships with the lights and benefics.

**Interpreting the Aspects**

There are basically two types of aspects: harmonious and challenging. The aspects considered harmonious, the trine and sextile, represent comfortable relationships, wherein the natures of the planets combine easily. In the ancient texts they are called aspects of friendship and love, referring to the easy relationship that is established between the planets involved. The opposition and the square imply difficult planetary

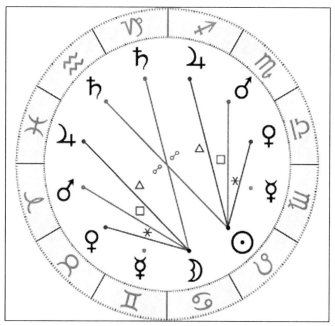

**Figure 21. Correlation Between Aspects and the Rulership Scheme**

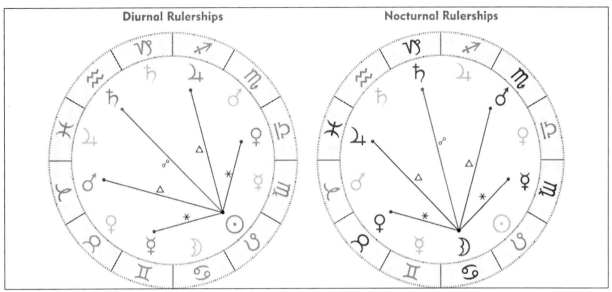

**Figure 22. Aspects in Diurnal and Nocturnal Rulerships**

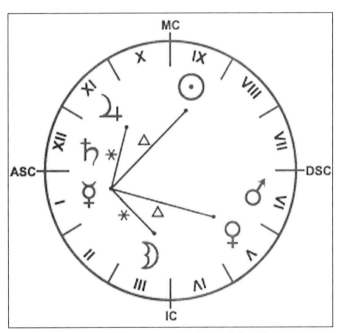

**Figure 23. Aspects and the Joys of the Planets**

relationships wherein tension and friction are predominant factors. In the ancient texts, they are called aspects of enmity and hatred, once more alluding to the type of relationship between the planets. The conjunction is considered neutral because the outcome of the combination depends upon the nature of the planets involved. The conjunction between two planets whose nature is compatible (such as Venus and the Moon) will be harmonious. On the other hand, the conjunction between two planets naturally antagonistic (such as Moon and Mars) will be disharmonious.

Without minimizing the information above, it should be noted that the quality and expression of each aspect depends in great part upon the planets involved. Besides the nature of the aspect and the compatibility between planets, dignities and debilities must also be considered. If we compare an aspect to a relationship, the quality of the relationship depends upon the participants themselves. The pleasant conversations (represented by trines and sextiles) can be frivolous and unproductive if the planets involved are in bad condition in the chart (debilitated). On the other hand, even the liveliest discussions (represented by squares and oppositions) can produce interesting results if the participants are intelligent individuals (dignified planets). The planets involved are thus always the most important factor in the interpretation of an aspect.

## Importance and Intensity of an Aspect

Not all aspects have the same "weight" in a horoscope. Some are very significant, while others are more secondary. To determine their significance, the following factors should be taken into consideration:

- The exactness of the aspect makes it more significant.
- The aspects where both planets are within each other's orbs are more intense.
- Out-of-sign aspects are weaker (except if very tight, less than 5°).
- Applying aspects tend to be more intense than separating aspects.
- Aspects at the end of the orb are very weak, especially if separating or out-of-sign.

In practice, these considerations help to establish a type of hierarchy for the aspects of a chart. In this way, undue importance will not be given to irrelevant aspects, or secondary status to important aspects, thus undermining the quality of the interpretation.

## Basic Significations

The basic signification of any aspect results from the delineation of two factors. The first concerns the type of aspect involved: the flowing aspects facilitate the combined expression of the planets, while the tense aspects challenge it. The other factor to keep in mind is the "mixing of the natures" of the two planets: compatible natures produce easy interactions, while incompatible natures produce instability. At the root if this compatibility issue are the primary qualities and temperaments of the planets.

For example, Mars and the Moon are essentially incompatible because they have adverse temperaments: one is hot and dry, the other cold and moist. Saturn and the Moon, although antagonistic in their significations, do have one thing in common: they share the cold quality, which contributes toward stabilizing their interactions. With Jupiter, the Moon has better compatibility because they share the moist quality; the differences in temperature are in this case of lesser importance because the heat of Jupiter, although moderated, does not interfere with the coldness of the Moon.

If two planets of compatible nature form an aspect, the resulting combination will always be positive. Nevertheless, the type of aspect that the planets form can alter this situation. The flowing aspects (trine and sextile) reinforce the compatibility of the planets, allowing each to share in what is good about the other. The tense aspects (square and opposition) disrupt this compatibility without, however, destroying it; the interaction

> Note: Since the aspects stand out quite a bit in the horoscope, students tend to place excessive emphasis on them, sometimes to the detriment of other factors. According to the rules of interpretation, the aspects should only be considered after one has interpreted the planet's overall condition (dignity/debility, position by sign, position by house). If the approach follows this order, the delineation of the aspects will be placed within its proper context and will furnish more meaningful and comprehensive information than if it were made first. *In summary, never start an interpretation from the aspects.*

continues to have an agreeable outcome, although its expression may be unstable and uncoordinated. In the case of compatible planets, the conjunction is considered a flowing aspect.

In combinations involving naturally incompatible planets, the tension is an ever-present factor, whatever the aspect being formed. Nonetheless, the flowing aspects (trine and sextile) minimize part of the tension, emphasizing what is best about the combination. The tense aspects (square and opposition) reinforce the characteristics that are already difficult about the shared interaction. In these cases, the conjunction functions like a tense aspect.

### The Friendship and Enmity of the Planets

The compatibilities and incompatibilities of the planets are presented in various ways in traditional astrology, and friendship and enmity are two that are most often referenced. They are used in planetary combinations in more advanced interpretative techniques (for example, the compatibility between two people). Although there are variations between different authors, the one presented here is the more common.

Figure 23 results from the compatibility in the natures of the planets, and from other considered factors (sect, general signification, etc.) For example, Venus is friendly with all planets except Saturn. This results not only from planetary temperament (sanguine and melancholic, respectively) but because everything that Venus signifies is totally averse to what Saturn signifies: while Venus is joyful, soft and colorful, Saturn is serious, somber and gray.

In some cases, friendship is not necessarily reciprocated. For example, many authors claim that the Sun is friends with Saturn because its heat ameliorates the coldness of the planet; but Saturn does not reciprocate its friendship in the same manner because its cold and dark nature is too contrary to the heat and luminosity of the Sun. Incidentally, these planets are naturally opposed in the zodiac, whether in the rulerships (Leo-Aquarius) or in the exaltations (Aries-Libra).

The friendly planets mutually reinforce one another. If there is a flowing aspect between them (sextile or trine), the reinforcement will be more evident; if there is a tense aspect (square or opposition) between them, this reinforcement will be less noticeable. In the case of enemy planets, the difference between their natures prevails, producing division between them. If the aspect is tense, the enmity reinforces it; if it is flowing, it retains its facilitating nature, although the enmity between the planets also remains. Obviously, the compatibility between planets is especially evident in the case of conjunctions. For example, aspects between Saturn and Venus always represent difficult qualities to reconcile, independently of their aspect. Even a trine between these planets will be colored by a melancholic intensity that is present even in situations of harmony.

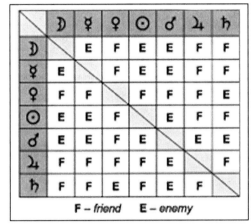

**Figure 24. Friendships and Enmities Between the Planets**

## A Guide for Planetary Combinations

Listed below are some general delineations of the various planetary combinations. These refer to natal charts, but the same combinations in other contexts can describe events or even alterations in climate, rather than personality traits.

*The Moon*

The Moon represents the emotional component of human beings, their moods, habits, and instincts. Because it is the fastest planet, it is also the most receptive. When it aspects a planet, it is strongly colored by the other planet's qualities. In contrast, because it is a luminary, it intensifies the potential of the planets it aspects.

Moon-Mercury combinations stimulate mental perception and agility, favoring communication, learning, and memory; these qualities may manifest in a more or less stable manner, depending upon the type of aspect being formed.

With Venus, the Moon indicates aesthetic and emotional sensibility, sometimes with artistic propensity. It is associated with a touch of levity and futility, and in some cases accompanied by laziness, self-indulgence, and some neglect.

With Mars, the Moon suggests temperamental behaviors, susceptibility, irritability, and aggression. When there is a flowing connection, the tension referred to is channeled to constructive actions, although the agitation remains.

With the Sun, the Moon has a special relationship. The contact between both lights always produces a powerful configuration that manifests via the phases of the Moon, in the **lunation cycle** (see Chapter X).

With Jupiter, the Moon bestows an optimistic and expansive side, with a good dose of self-confidence. There can be a tendency toward exaggeration and unrealistic expectations, particularly in the emotional realm.

With Saturn, the Moon generates emotional contention because the rigid nature of Saturn diminishes the adaptable nature of the Moon. The free expression of emotions and needs is challenged by defensiveness and a degree of pessimism. On a more positive note, it conveys pragmatism, self-sufficiency and a realistic perspective, protecting the individual from emotional disillusionment.

*Mercury*

Mercury is connected with communication and thought. As with the Moon, it is very fast and thus easily colored by the planets with which it comes into contact. Its neutral nature also contributes to this process.

With Venus, it can only form conjunctions and sextiles because these planets are never more than 76° apart. The combination of their natures produces pleasant, agreeable, and friendly, but also not very profound, communications.

Mercury has a special relationship with the Sun. Since these two bodies are never more than one sign apart, they never form any aspect other than the conjunction. The proximity to the Sun makes Mercury excessively subjective and centered on its own perception; greater distance corresponds to greater objectivity.

With Mars, it produces a wounding tendency, a sharp tongue, and argumentativeness. The harmonious aspects represent verbal persuasiveness and conviction, while in the tense aspects, there is a tendency toward argument and confrontation.

With Jupiter, Mercury produces optimism and magnanimous communications, but can also indicate a tendency toward exaggeration, boasting, and even lying.

With Saturn, Mercury brings intellectual insecurities and potential difficulties in learning, but it can also bestow depth of thought and the propensity for study. The mind is serious and analytical.

*Venus*

Venus represents the expression of affection, individual tastes, and pleasures. When aspected, Venus lends its yielding and conciliatory nature to the other planets.

With the Sun, Venus only forms conjunctions. In special cases, it can form a sextile, but this is always a weak aspect that never perfects and, therefore, has little impact on the horoscope. The proximity to the Sun gives the individual an agreeable expression, but also removes from Venus its natural receptivity, making it less empathetic.

With Mars, Venus produces a passionate and impetuous nature with the need to conquer affection. This contact has a seductive or even sexual quality to it. At its best, it produces enchantment and a mixture of charm and daring; at its worse, it produces competition, rudeness in interactions, and potential jealousies.

With Jupiter, Venus bestows dignity, optimism, and self-confidence that turn into good fortune. Generosity, honesty, and companionship are patent qualities of this combination, although the tense aspects add instability and self-indulgence.

With Saturn, the affective expression becomes more serious and melancholic. These characteristics may express as sobriety and emotional reserve, or as affective inhibitions and difficulty relating.

## *The Sun*

The Sun represents affirmation and authority. When in aspect with other planets, it bequeaths its energy, power and vitality unto them. However, the conjunction with the Sun obfuscates the planets and "burns up" their qualities. This condition is known as **combustion** (see Chapter X).

With Mars, the Sun bestows courage, daring, great personal affirmation, natural leadership, and boldness; at its worse, it may manifest as brutality, arrogance, and a lack of compassion.

With Jupiter, the Sun produces magnanimity, a regal stance, self-confidence, and generosity; but in the tense aspects, it is colored by loftiness and haughtiness.

With Saturn, the Sun indicates seriousness and responsibility, but with difficult aspects it suggests problems with authority figures, pessimism, and lack of confidence.

## *Mars*

Mars signifies fighting, aggression, and conquest. It bequeaths unto aspected planets a choleric and aggressive character, but can also add daring, courage, and activity. It all depends upon the type of aspect and on the condition of Mars itself in the horoscope.

With Jupiter, it produces a daring, adventurous, and optimistic nature, but which can be colored by tinges of irresponsibility and exaggeration. Thus, the defense of ideas and opinions typical of this combination can become heated, imposing, and doctrinaire.

With Saturn, Mars indicates rigorous, strategic, and calculating actions, but also difficulties and shame in self-assertion. In extreme cases, there can be cruelty, cowardice, and vengeful actions.

## *Jupiter*

Jupiter represents faith, honor, and temperance. Known as the great benefic, Jupiter bestows temperance and optimism to the planets it contacts. When debilitated, it can also transmit haughtiness and bravado.

Jupiter-Saturn aspects are especially studied in the context of mundane astrology because they are linked to 20-year cycles and have a generational impact. In a nativity, these aspects are related to one's capacity to relate to social structures and can be seen as a sign of honors. The flowing aspects are associated with good relationships with law and order. Tense aspects indicate difficulties of insertion in the social fabric of life due to countercultural choices.

## *Saturn*

Saturn receives connections with all the other planets, but because of its slow motion, it rarely applies to others.[21] It therefore emerges as a burdensome, halting, and obstructive element. It represents the obstacles and fears that impede action.

Contacts of Saturn to the other planets are always colored by seriousness, restriction, and rigor. Its more positive side bestows perseverance, responsibility, pragmatism, resiliency, and a sense of duty.

## Specific Signification in the Context of the Chart

Following is the most important factor and the key to an accurate interpretation of an aspect. Notwithstanding the general indications already mentioned, an understanding of the aspects can only be completed when one knows the role of the planets involved in the context of the chart. In this manner, an aspect should only be interpreted after discerning:

- The function of the planets in the horoscope (its significations and what houses it rules). Besides the natural signification of the planet, there are other factors to bear in mind: the house where the planet is posited indicates the area of life where the action manifests, and the houses ruled by the planet reveal topics underlying that manifestation.
- The strength of the planet to execute its purpose (dignity and debility). The essential state of the planet can significantly alter the final outcome of an aspect. Dignified planets act in a more orderly manner, contributing their strength and stability, whereas debilitated planets operate erratically, transmitting their instability to any aspect.

These considerations, when well understood and applied, allow us to go beyond vague, partial, and noncontextualized interpretations typical of astrological "cookbooks."

For example, the Moon-Mercury opposition in the chart of King Sebastian, it is not enough to say that his moods (Moon) interfere (opposition) with his communication and understanding (Mercury). Although correct, this interpretation is insufficient. We need to place it within a larger context of the chart to reveal deeper levels of meaning. Mercury is in Aquarius, indicating natural curiosity and a lively thought process. To these qualities we add the assertiveness of Mars and the radiance of the Sun, which, conjunct Mercury, contributes a lively, sharp, and extremely assertive mind that is expressed in a stubborn manner because Aquarius is a fixed sign. The Moon in Leo suggests an intense and assertive expression of emotions and moods that manifests above all in his relationships with others (seventh house).

Thus, the contact between the Moon and Mercury reflects an argumentative and brusque manner (opposition) marked by a sharp assertiveness (triple conjunction) but colored by insecurities in relation to his recognition by others (Moon in Leo). Since the opposition occurs in the first and seventh houses, it creates difficulties in the relationships of this king, often described as having a choleric and difficult temperament.

The Venus-Saturn sextile can be interpreted in the same manner. This combination is not naturally easy because they are unfriendly planets with incompatible natures: Saturn is a cold and dry planet, while Venus is hot and moist. Saturn, the slower of the two, imposes its cold, dry nature upon Venus, imparting sobriety to its affective expression and cooling its natural sensibility. Since they are linked by a sextile, the interaction is somewhat facilitated, although it remains naturally difficult.

Venus in Capricorn indicates an affective expression that is inhibited and pragmatic, and Saturn in Pisces adds a degree of sentimental withdrawal. His affection is contained and sober, with hints of melancholy colored by feelings of compassion, sacrifice, and suffering. For this king, affection is associated with severity and inhibition. We can see that the final outcome is always determined by the planets, although the nature of the aspect defines the manner in which they will combine.

Besides the general significations of the planets, which were just considered, now look at the general context of the chart. In this chart, Saturn is the Ascendant ruler and is posited in the first house, which defines to a great extent the motivations of the king. Venus is ruler of the ninth house, associated with religion and faith, and is posited in the eleventh house of friends and allies. King Sebastian had as strong allies people with strong religious convictions (rulers of the eleventh and ninth) who contributed greatly to his personal goals (sextile to Saturn, ruler of the Ascendant).

---

[21]The only exceptions are cases of mutual applications.

We just looked at a flowing aspect between planets of incompatible natures. Now we will look at a reverse example from the same chart: a tense aspect between friendly planets with compatible natures. In the Venus-Jupiter square, the planets are posited in signs indicating rigor and protocol (Capricorn, ruled by Saturn, and Libra, its exaltation), thereby suggesting a sober and restrained expression. It is nonetheless a square, which produces dissonance between pragmatic Venus in Capricorn and the idealistic expectations of Jupiter in Libra. Since Jupiter rules the Midheaven (the aspiration of life, career, and power) this configuration has a direct impact on the ambitions of the king. Venus rules the ninth house (ideals) and is positioned in the eleventh (allies), so the convictions of the king and his choice in allies interfered in his career. Because it is a square, it caused instability and greatly disturbed his kingdom. King Sebastian was poorly advised and launched the disastrous campaign of Alcácer-Quibir, where he lost his life.

### Interpretation of Non-planetary Aspects

To interpret an aspect between a planet and a non-planetary point, one must add the quality of the planet to the signification of the point in question. The planet contributes its qualities (natural and accidental) and the non-planetary point receives them. For instance, a dignified Saturn in aspect with the Ascendant adds to the personal expression a note of seriousness and pondering, whereas a debilitated Saturn gives it a more uncouth and suspicious manner.

On the other hand, the nature of the aspect shapes the contribution of the planet: if the aspect is flowing, the planet more easily integrates its nature to the signification of the point; if it is tense, the planet manifests in a less stable manner. For instance, a dignified Saturn in trine to the Ascendant indicates that the seriousness and pondering already mentioned are expressed in a constant and stable manner. However, if the same dignified Saturn is in square to the Ascendant, these qualities will be more inconstant to the point where it may harm the expression of the individual.

Now we will look at a practical example of the combination of both factors: the quality of the planet and the nature of the aspect. The charts of Friedrich Nietzche and Johannes Kepler have an aspect between a dignified Jupiter in Pisces and the Ascendant. However, in Nietzsche's chart, the aspect is a trine, while in Kepler's chart, it is a square. In both cases, the personal expression is colored by the qualities of justice and liberty, although in Kepler's case, these qualities have an erratic expression because of the square.

# Antiscia

There are other types of interactions between signs, of which the most well-known and used are the **antiscia**. Antiscia (antiscion in the singular) is a term of Greek origin meaning "shade" or "reflex." It is said that two zodiacal points are in antiscion when they occupy positions that are equidistant from the celestial equator. This happens when they are at the same distance from the solstice points, the Cancer-Capricorn axis.

The planets situated in Cancer have their "mirror points" in Gemini and vice-versa. In the same way, the antiscia connect the pairs Leo-Taurus, Virgo-Aries, Libra-Pisces, Scorpio-Aquarius, and Sagittarius-Capricorn. Antiscia are also called "days of equal light" because when the Sun transits degrees that are in antiscion, the duration of daylight is the same at those two times of the year. This means the degrees of antiscion are points in the zodiac where the amount of daylight given off by the Sun on those days is equal.

### Calculating Antiscia

The mirror image relationship establishes a correspondence not only between signs but also between the degrees and minutes of each sign. Thus, a planet situated in the first degree of a sign will have its antiscion in the *last degree* of the reflected sign. For example, 1° Virgo has its antiscion at 29° Aries. The same occurs with all the other signs: 2° Virgo corresponds to 28° Aries, 3° to 27°, and so on successively. The minutes are mirrored in an identical manner: 00° 01′ of one sign has its antiscion at 29° 59′ of the mirror sign, 00° 02′ has an antiscion at 29° 58′, 00° 03′ has its antiscion at 29° 57′, and so on successively.

To obtain the antiscion degree merely subtract from 30° the degrees and minutes of the planetary position. For instance, to calculate the antiscion of Venus at 8° Scorpio 20′:

- Find the mirror sign; in the case of Scorpio, it is Aquarius.
- Subtract that degree from 30°; subtract the minute from 60′ (to subtract 8° 20′ from 30°00′, "borrow"1 degree and turn it into minutes so that 30°00 becomes 29°60′). Then, 29°60' - 8° 20' = 21° 40'.

Thus, we see that Venus at 8° Scorpio 20′ projects its antiscion to 21° Aquarius 40′.

You can also convert the antiscia using the tables in Figure 26.

The point opposite to the antiscion is called contra-antiscion. For example, Venus at 8° Scorpio 20′ projects its antiscion to 21° Aquarius 40′. Its counter-antiscion is in the opposite degree: 21° Leo 40′.

Note: the counter-antiscion may also be thought of as a projection along the 0° Aries-0° Libra axis.

In practical terms, antiscia and counter-antiscia are only considered if there are planets or other chart factors activating those points. They are considered compliments to interpretation and are not interpreted by themselves.

Two planets in antiscion are thought of as a type of conjunction. This combination of planets in antiscion is less intense than a "bodily" conjunction and for it to be considered it must occur within 2° of being exact. For example, consider Mars at 19° Aries and the Moon at 10° Virgo. Mars projects its antiscion to 11° Virgo and the Moon projects its antiscion to 20° Aries. Therefore, Mars and the Moon are in antiscion. This means that the Moon is going to take on martial characteristics and that Mars is going to acquire a greater volatility, characteristic of the Moon. Just as in a conjunction, the antiscia fuse the qualities of both planets. The principal difference being that with the antiscion, it is possible to combine very different houses and signs, which does not occur with a normal conjunction.

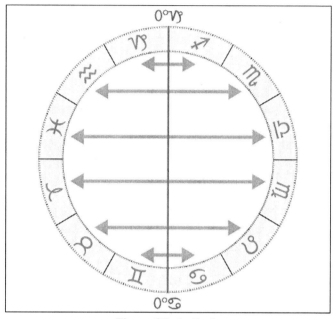

**Figure 25. Antiscia**

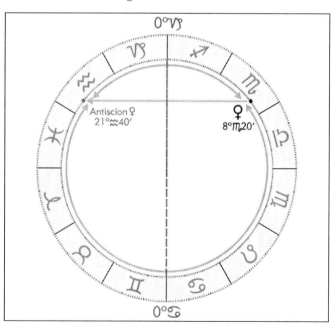

**Figure 26. Antiscion of Venus**

| Antiscia of degrees | Antiscia of minutes | |
|---|---|---|
| 00 ↔ 30 | 00 ↔ 60 | 16 ↔ 44 |
| 01 ↔ 29 | 01 ↔ 59 | 17 ↔ 43 |
| 02 ↔ 28 | 02 ↔ 58 | 18 ↔ 42 |
| 03 ↔ 27 | 03 ↔ 57 | 19 ↔ 41 |
| 04 ↔ 26 | 04 ↔ 56 | 20 ↔ 40 |
| 05 ↔ 25 | 05 ↔ 55 | 21 ↔ 39 |
| 06 ↔ 24 | 06 ↔ 54 | 22 ↔ 38 |
| 07 ↔ 23 | 07 ↔ 53 | 23 ↔ 37 |
| 08 ↔ 22 | 08 ↔ 52 | 24 ↔ 36 |
| 09 ↔ 21 | 09 ↔ 51 | 25 ↔ 35 |
| 10 ↔ 20 | 10 ↔ 50 | 26 ↔ 34 |
| 11 ↔ 19 | 11 ↔ 49 | 27 ↔ 33 |
| 12 ↔ 18 | 12 ↔ 48 | 28 ↔ 32 |
| 13 ↔ 17 | 13 ↔ 47 | 29 ↔ 31 |
| 14 ↔ 16 | 14 ↔ 46 | 30 ↔ 30 |
| 15 ↔ 15 | 15 ↔ 45 | |

**Figure 27. Antiscia (degrees and minutes)**

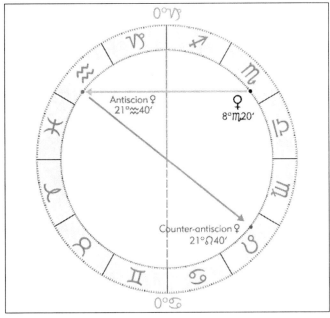

**Figure 28. Counter-antiscia**

Counter-antiscia is interpreted as a type of opposition. Using the previous example, Mars at 19° Aries would have its counter-antiscion at 11° Pisces; if Mercury is at 12° Pisces, it is in counter-antiscion to Mars, which translates to a certain irritability in communication.

There are two cases of antiscia in the horoscope of Friedrich Nietzche. The first is between Mercury at 4° Libra and Jupiter at 26° Pisces. These two planets form a very weak aspect (at the end of the orb). However, the presence of the antiscion, which is practically exact, reinforces the connection between them. The antiscion Mercury-Jupiter links the objective mind (Mercury in Libra) with an idealistic and devotional strain (Jupiter in Pisces), a contrasting combination that is well mirrored in its orb. Note that the involvement of Mars in this configuration (conjunct Mercury and opposite Jupiter) contributes to the bellicose and critical tone, so very characteristic of this author.

The second case of antiscia involves Saturn at 0° Aquarius and the Ascendant at 29° Scorpio. The personal expression (Ascendant) becomes colored by a strong Saturnine component, which manifested in the severe depressions that shaped his whole life.

**Other Relationships Between Signs**

Besides the antiscia, there are other non-aspectual relationships between signs that are presented in the tradition as targeted concepts applied in very specific contexts. The most well known is the relationship between signs that command and those that obey. According to Ptolemy, Aries, Taurus, Gemini, Cancer, Leo and Virgo are signs that command, because when the Sun is in them the day is longer than the night, since they correspond to the spring and summer

Note: since antiscia are mirror-image points without physical body, we **never** interpret the sextiles, squares or trines of these points. The only aspects that count are the conjunction and opposition for the reasons given above.

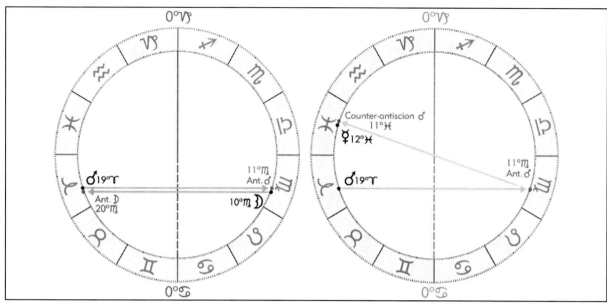

**Figure 29. Antiscia and Counter-antiscia**

months.[22] Complimenting these are the signs that obey, Libra, Scorpio, Sagittarius, Capricorn, Aquarius, and Pisces, which correspond to the autumn and winter months, since when the Sun is in them, the nights are longer than the days.[23]

This type of attribution is used to compare the power between signs. For instance, we can compare the relative strength of the Moon (emotions) and Mercury (reason) in a natal chart. If Mercury is in a sign that commands and the Moon in a sign of obedience, then reason tends to prevail over the emotions. In the inverse situation, the emotions easily overshadow reason.

The same type of reasoning was followed for other considerations, as is the case with signs that observe and those that listen, etc. Together with the antiscia, these techniques add new data to the study of planetary relationships and enrich the interpretation of a horoscope.

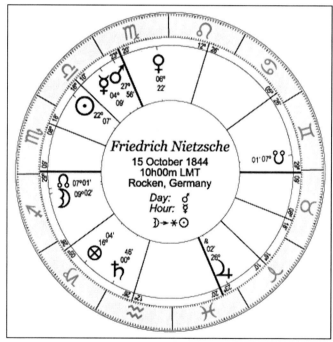

**Chart 1. Nativity of Friedrich Nietzsche**

Note: the antiscia presented here as examples are associated with aspects (the first corresponds to a weak opposition and the second to an out-of-sign sextile). However, an antiscion does not necessarily have to also involve an aspect. Their interpretation is valid in itself and is independent of the aspects.

---

[22]Recall that this consideration has the seasons in the northern hemisphere as its basis.

[23]There are some variations on the concept of commanding and obeying; in this manual we present the most utilized, and for which we have some examples. Some Arabic authors associate the signs that command to the signs of right ascension, and the signs obeying to the signs of oblique ascension. This is a slightly different opinion.

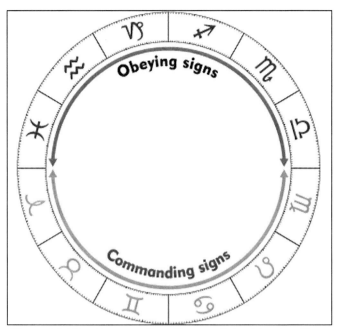

**Figure 30. The Commanding Signs and the Obeying Signs**

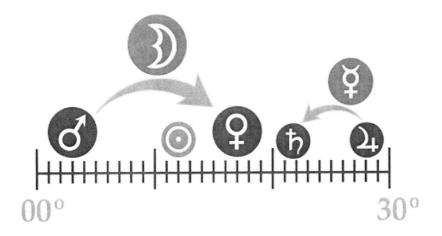

## Chapter IX
# Chart Dynamics

### Aspects in Motion

The aspects form a web of interaction between the planets in a chart. This chapter focuses on the more complex patterns of planetary dynamics: the interaction by aspect of several planets and the combination of these aspects with their essential dignities. In practice, this type of interaction is primarily analyzed with respect to horary astrology and occasionally in mundane or natal astrology.

### Combined Movements

When specific topics are studied in a chart, certain planets are designated as *significators*, which represent the action being studied. In a question about career, for example, the significators are the planets that rule the Ascendant (the person) and the Midheaven (the career). Any relationship (or lack of one) between significators describes the development of that action and conveys in more detail the "plot" of the story. This relationship is generally represented by an aspect. Nonetheless, the contact between the significators may be reinforced, impeded, or negated by other planets. In some cases, the planetary interactions are brought about through changes in the direction of the planet's movement, while in others they occur as a byproduct of the application and separation of aspects involving a third planet.

What is most important in this type of analysis, is to have some idea of the motion of the planets (i.e., relative speed and direction). Also important is to be aware that an aspect has three phases: the application, perfection (the moment when it is exact), and the separation. These concepts are essential to understanding the information in this chapter.

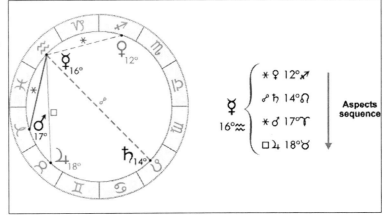

**Figure 7. Sequence of Aspects**

**The 30° Ruler**

A simple and practical way of visualizing the movement of the planets is to use a diagram consisting of a 30° ruler. This ruler is an alternate way of representing the planetary positions in the Zodiac, placing all of them within a space of 30 degrees, irrespective of their sign position (which is noted next to each planet, allowing for aspect distinctions). For example, in the horoscope of King Sebastian (see page 118) the planetary positions on the ruler are as follows:

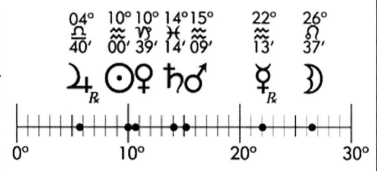

Figure 1. Example of the 30° Ruler

The ruler shows the distance between planets, which aids in the calculation of aspects and in seeing planetary movement. Visually, this allows the planets that are near each other by degree to be seen. The planets that are near each other on the ruler will form aspects as long as they are in signs that aspect each other. For example, Mercury and the Moon are about 4° from each other on the ruler in opposite signs (Aquarius and Leo respectively); thus, they form an opposition.

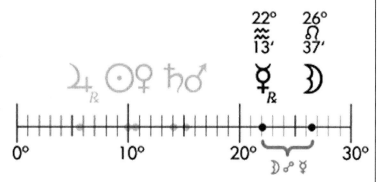

Figure 2.

Additionally, the ruler also shows planets that are located near each other by degree, but which are in signs that do not aspect one another. This is the case with the Sun-Venus pair, situated at 10° Aquarius and 10° Capricorn, respectively, and with the Mars-Saturn pair, located respectively at 15° Aquarius and 14° Pisces.

On the other hand, the Sun and Mars are only 5° apart and in the same sign, thereby forming a conjunction. While Venus and Saturn, being only 3° apart, form a sextile.

The ruler also makes it easier to observe whether the movement of the planets are applying or separating from an aspect. For example, if we look at

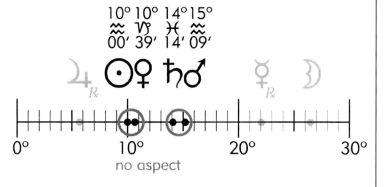

Figure 3.

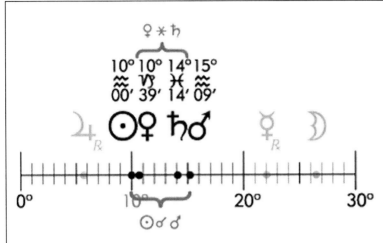

**Figure 4.**

the ruler, we see that the Venus-Saturn sextile is applying because Venus, the faster planet, is moving toward Saturn, the slower planet. Also, Mars and Mercury are 7° apart in the same sign, thereby forming a conjunction. Mercury, the faster body, is moving toward Mars by retrograde motion, therefore it is applying to the conjunction.

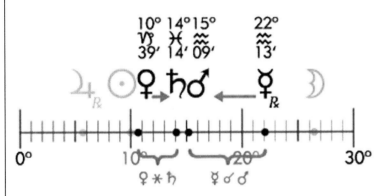

**Figure 5.**

Another useful function of the ruler is that it allows us to immediately detect any planets that are void of course. For example, the Moon is in the last degrees of a sign (in this case Leo) and does not apply to any aspects before leaving this sign. In this case, the Moon's orb extends past the 30 degrees of the ruler. Thus we must return to the ruler's beginning (0°) to complete the extension of the Moon's orb. Remember that when this happens, the sign always changes; in this case, the Moon's orb extends as far as 8° Virgo 37. As we can see by the ruler, the orb appears to touch Jupiter. However, Jupiter is in Libra, the sign next to Virgo, and therefore does not aspect it.

The 30° ruler was first proposed by English astrologer Derek Appleby. (1937-1995)

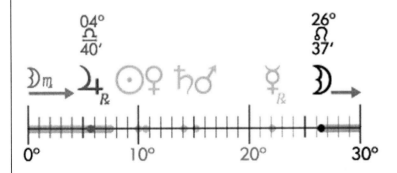

**Figure 6.**

The perfection of an aspect is the most important dynamic situation in the movement of a chart. The aspect is only considered *perfected* when it has become exact. For example, in Figure 7, Mercury at 16° Aquarius forms a sextile to Mars at 17° Aries and another to Venus at 12° Sagittarius. It also forms a square to Jupiter at 18° Taurus and an opposition to Saturn at 14° Leo. Every aspect is within orb. Nevertheless, from a dynamic perspective, only two aspects are considered: the last one formed (separating aspect) and the next one to complete (applying aspect)—in this case, the separation from Saturn and the applying sextile to Mars. Dynamically, neither the sextile to Venus (which occurred before the opposition to Saturn) nor the square to Jupiter (which only becomes exact after the sextile to Mars) need be considered.

### Translation of Light

Translation of light occurs when faster planet A separates from slower planet B and applies to planet C. In such a case, it is said that planet A transmits (or translates) the light from planet B to planet C. In other words, planet A connects the other two in the same way that a relay racer might transport the characteristics of planet B to planet C. In practical terms, translation of light has two effects:

1. It establishes a connection that would not otherwise exist when the faster planet unites two that do not aspect each other. For example, suppose that Mars at 12° Sagittarius and Jupiter at 20° Taurus are the significators. They do not form any apect because they are in inconjunct signs (150° apart). However, Venus at 15° Aquarius is separating from a sextile to Mars and is applying to a square with Jupiter. In this case, Venus unites two planets, transferring the light (and its nature) from Mars to Jupiter.

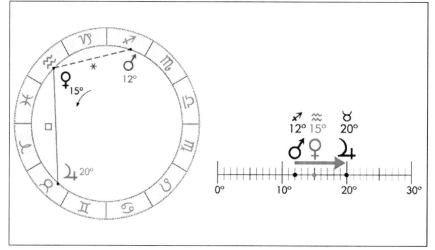

**Figure 8. Translation of Light, Example 1**

2. It reinforces a union when a faster planet unites two slower planets that are separating. For example, suppose Mars at 10° Cancer and Mercury at 15° are the significators. Mercury is separating from a sextile to Mars, which means the aspect has completed and is dissolving. However, the Moon at 12° Capricorn comes to reinforce the connection between them because it is separating from an opposition to Mars and applying by trine to Mercury, reactivating their connection.

Let's imagine a horary astrology example in which the following question is posed: "Will I get the job?" The chart for the question has 18° Sagittarius rising and 7° Libra on the Midheaven. In this case, the

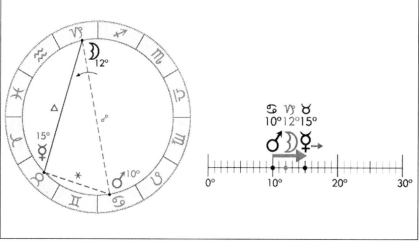

**Figure 9. Translation of Light, Example 2**

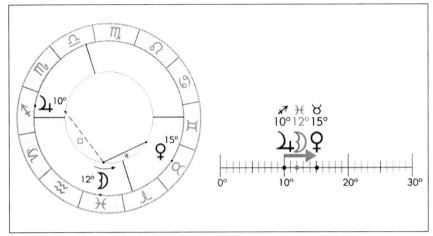

**Figure 10. Translation of Light, "Will I get the job?"**

significator for the querent (the person asking the question) is Jupiter (ruler of the Ascendant), which is at 10° Sagittarius. The significator for the job is Venus (ruler of the MC), which is at 15° Taurus.

Since the significators do not have any contact with each other by aspect, we might say at first glance that the querent will not get the job. Notwithstanding, the movements of the Moon imply the opposite. At 12° Pisces, the Moon unites both planets through translation of light: it separates from a square to Jupiter and applies to a sextile with Venus. We can therefore give a positive answer to this question: the querent will obtain the job, possibly through an intermediary (the Moon) who establishes a connection between the querent (Jupiter) and the job (Venus).

Had this configuration come up in a birth chart, it would indicate a tendency in the native (Jupiter) toward reaching his goals (Venus) with the assistance of intermediaries (Moon). In this case, it speaks to a tendency that would have to be judged within the larger context of the natal chart.

## Collection of Light

Collection occurs when two planets that do not aspect each other apply to a third slower planet. In such a case, it is said that the slower planet collects the light of the other two, bringing together their qualities and acting as a unifying agent. It can represent a situation or a person who functions as an intermediary who facilitates the action (the type of action is indicated by the two other planets). For example, suppose the Sun at 7° Libra and the Moon at 10° of Pisces are the significators. They are in inconjuct signs and do not therefore aspect each other. However, both are forming applying aspects to Mars, which is at 12° Gemini (the Sun forms a trine and the Moon a square). Since Mars is the slower planet, we say that Mars collects the light from the other two and thereby connects them.

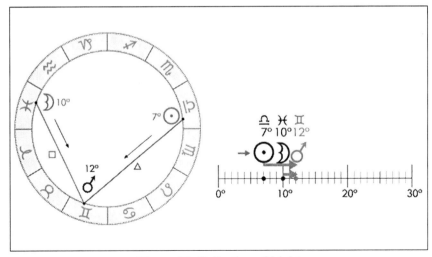

**Figure 11. Collection of Light**

Here is another horary question: "Will I find my lost necklace?" (see Figure 12). In this chart, the Ascendant is 11° Virgo. The significator of the querent is Mercury (ruler of the Ascendant), which is at 18° Scorpio. The lost object is represented by the ruler of the second house of possessions, which has 11° Libra on the cusp. Venus, its ruler, is at 21° Libra.

There are no aspects between Mercury (the querent) and Venus (the quesited, i.e., the necklace), which indicates a negative response. Nevertheless, both planets are applying to Mars, which is at 25° Capricorn (Mercury by sextile and Venus by square). We can then conclude that Mars gathers or collects the light from both planets, acting as an intermediary who reunites the two. In this case, Mars might represent a friend that finds the lost object (Venus) and safeguards it until the owner (Mercury) can recover it.

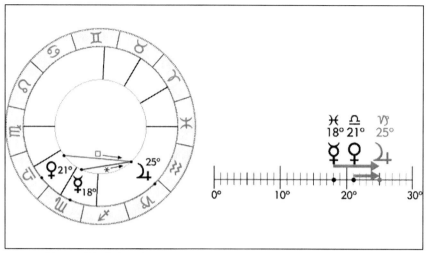

**Figure 12. Collection of Light, "Will I find my lost necklace?"**

## Prohibition of Light

A prohibition of light occurs when a third planet interferes in the perfection of an aspect between two others, impeding its realization. Prohibition exists when:

- Planet A applies to planet B, but before it can reach it, it first forms an aspect with planet C; thus, planet C impedes planet A from communicating with planet B. For Example, suppose Mercury at 5° Leo and Jupiter at 10° Libra are the significators. Mercury applies by sextile to Jupiter, but before it can complete the aspect, it forms a square with Mars at 7° Scorpio. In such a case, Mars prohibits the significators from finding each other and blocks their action.

- Planet A applies to planet B, but before it can reach it, it is aspected by planet C. For example, suppose Mars at 15° Leo and Saturn at 20° Taurus are significators. Mars is applying to Saturn by square, but before it can complete the aspect, Venus, which is at 12° Sagittarius, aspects it by trine. In such a case, Venus the faster of the three, prohibits the action promised through the square of Mars and Saturn.

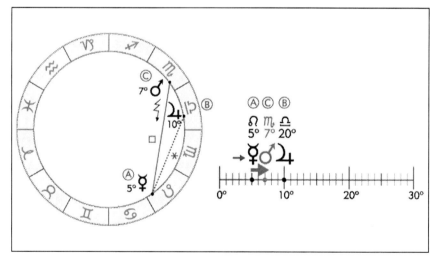

**Figure 13. Prohibition of Light, Example 1**

- Planet A applies to planet B, but before it can reach it, planet C aspects planet B. For example, Mars at 15° Aries and Jupiter at 25° Leo are the significators. Mars applies by trine to Jupiter, but before it can complete the aspect, Mercury at 14° Scorpio, completes a square to Jupiter. In this case, the faster Mercury, prohibits the connection between the significators.

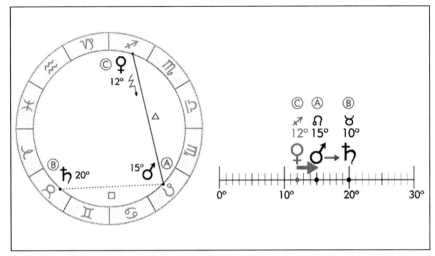

**Figure 14. Prohibition of Light, Example 2**

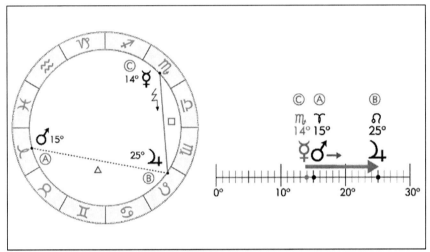

**Figure 15. Prohibition of Light, Example 3**

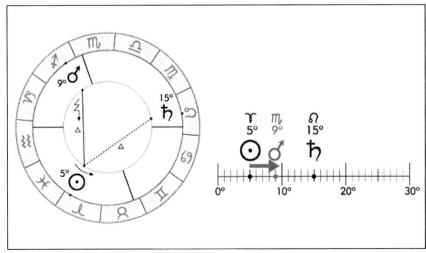

**Figure 16. Prohibition of Light, "Will she date me?"**

There are many variations of prohibition, some of which are given specific names by some authors. But the main idea to keep in mind is that in prohibition a third planet impedes in one way or another the realization of an aspect between two other planets. A simple example of prohibition of light from horary astrology can be seen in a question about relationships. Consider the chart for this question: "Will she date me?" The Ascendant of the chart is 5° Aquarius. In this case, the significator for the querent is Saturn (ruler of the Ascendant), located at 15° Leo. The significator of the quesited (the woman in question) is the Sun (ruler of the Descendant), located at 5° Aries.

The Sun (her) looks to be applying by trine to Saturn (him), suggesting that they will date. However, a closer look reveals that the Sun will not complete its aspect with Saturn because it will first form a trine with Mars at 9° Sagittarius. We can therefore say that she (the Sun) will initiate a relationship with a person represented by Mars and will not end up dating the person who posed the question (Saturn).

**Frustration of Light**

Frustration of light is a variation on prohibition. It occurs when planet A applies to planet B, but before the aspect is completed, B makes an aspect to C. One can say then that planet A is frustrated in its course of action. For example, suppose Mercury at 15° Gemini and Mars at 22° Aquarius are significators. In this case, Mercury is applying by trine to Mars, but before it can complete the aspect, Mars perfects to a conjunction with Saturn at 25° Aquarius. We say then, that the connection between Mercury and Mars was frustrated.

## Refranation of Light

Refranation occurs when two planets are applying to each other; but before they can complete the aspect, the faster planet changes direction, thus

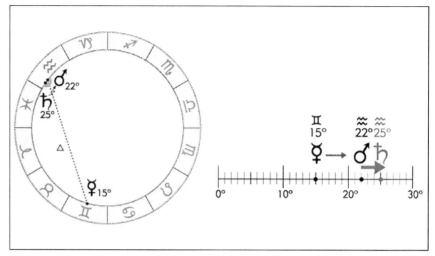

**Figure 17. Frustration of Light**

impeding the aspect from completion. For example, suppose Mercury is at 14° Virgo and Saturn at 18° Cancer. Mercury applies to Saturn by sextile, but before it can complete the aspect, Mercury stations and enters retrograde motion at 16° Virgo. In such a case, the aspect never completes, which means the action regresses and is not realized.

Refranation may be considered a sub-set of prohibition that involves only two planets and wherein the agent of impediment entails a change in one planet's direction.

As another example of refranation from horary astrology, consider this question: "Will we reconcile?" It was posed by someone who recently ended a relationship. In this chart, the Ascendant is at 18° Aries. The significator of the querent in this case is Mars (ruler of the Ascendant), lo-

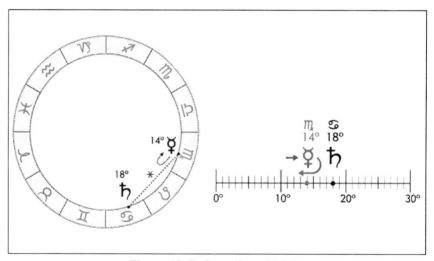

**Figure 18. Refranation of Light**

cated at 10° Scorpio. The partner is represented by a retrograde Venus (ruler of the Descendant) at 14° Scorpio. In its retrograde movement, Venus is applying to a conjunction with Mars, which suggests a reunion of the couple. However, Venus stations and returns to direct motion at 13° Scorpio before it can complete the conjunction to Mars. Because it is faster, Venus begins to distance itself from Mars as soon as it turns direct. Mars, moving more slowly, is unable to catch up to it. We can therefore conclude that a reconciliation between the couple does not take place. At first, the partner seems interested in returning (his ruler is retrograde) but then changes his mind and distances himself.

The planetary interactions presented here are the most important ones you will encounter. There are variations on these, and some have different technical names. However, what is most important is to come away with an understanding of planetary motion and that the chart is always a mirror of action.

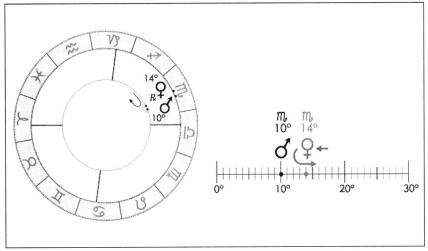

**Figure 19. Refranation of Light, "Will we reconcile?"**

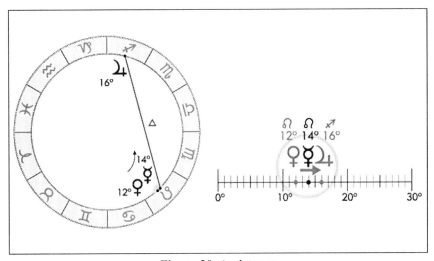

**Figure 20. Assistance**

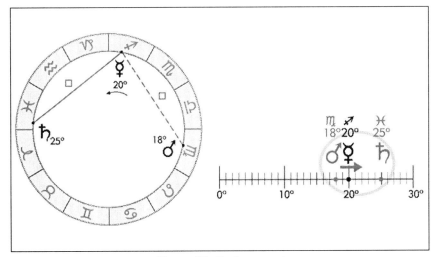

**Figure 21. Besiegement**

## Assisted and Besieged Planets

In certain circumstances the aspects have a direct impact on the capacity of the planet to express itself, at times amplifying that expression greatly, and at others, hindering it. This happens when soft aspects are combined with benefic planets or when hard aspects are combined with malefic planets. There are two extreme cases of this type of interaction: *assistance* and *besiegement*.

### Assistance

When a planet separates from one of the benefics and applies to another, it is said to be assisted. In assistance only the conjunction, trine, and sextile are considered (the conjunction is the most powerful). As the name itself indicates, assistance represents a situation in which the planet (and whatever it signifies in the chart) has external help. Assistance suggests positive circumstances with the possibility of success. For example, Mercury is at 14° Leo, Venus at 12° of the same sign, and Jupiter at 16° Sagittarius. Mercury is separating from a conjunction to Venus and applying by trine to Jupiter, thereby being assisted by the benefics. Anything that is signified by Mercury in that chart (an individual, event, or action) is therefore surrounded by good conditions.

### Besiegement

Besiegement is the opposite of assistance. A planet is besieged when it separates from one of the malefics and applies to the other. In besiegement only the conjunction, square and opposition are considered (the conjunction is the most powerful). Just as when a city is besieged, the planet experiences difficult circumstances from which it will have difficulty escaping. It is comparable to the proverbial expression of being "stuck between a rock (Saturn) and a hard place (Mars)." The planet and anything it signifies in the chart is surrounded by adverse circumstances. For example, consider Mercury at 20° Sagittarius, Mars at 18° Virgo and Saturn at 25° Pisces. In this case, Mercury is separating from a square to Saturn and applying, also by square, to Mars. Everything that Mercury signifies in this chart is encountering serious difficulties.

Some authors consider the Sun to be the only exception to the besiegement rule because they believe the Sun cannot be besieged, at least by conjunction, because of its inherent power. In such a case, it is the Sun that "consumes" the planets that are in conjunction with it, concealing their action.

### Examples of Assistance and Besiegment

There is an example of assistance in the chart of poet and writer Edgar Allen Poe. The Moon at 9° 49′ separates from a conjunction to Venus at 9° 07′ and applies to a conjunction of Jupiter at 16° 52′; all the planets are in Pisces, close to the cusp of the fifth house. Since the Moon is on the fifth house cusp and rules the ninth, it suggests that this assistance will benefit the matters relating to leisure and pleasures (fifth house), as well as learning, publishing, and travel (ninth house). Nevertheless, it should be noted that the Moon and Venus square Saturn, which also suggests some difficulties in these areas.

The benefits would therefore at times be marked by reversals, impasses, and losses. In effect, Poe's life was always met with difficulties and his literary success came about only after his death. Since Saturn is located in the first house (the individual), these setbacks may have originated from Poe's own actions (which is corroborated by Mars in a very debilitated state in the twelfth house). Many of Poe's problems were in fact tied to his propensity for alcohol, which would eventually lead to his death.

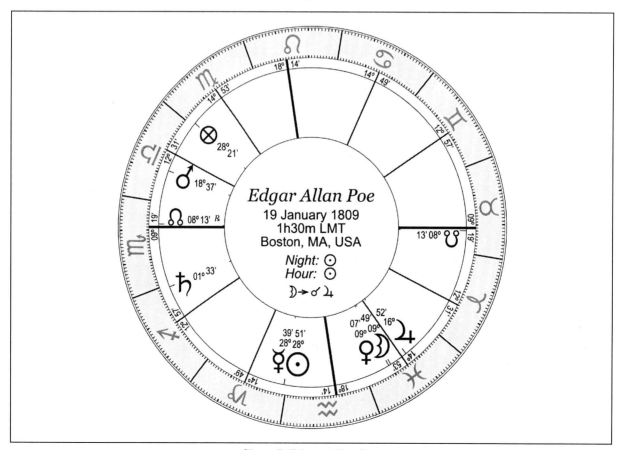

**Chart 7. Edgar Allen Poe**

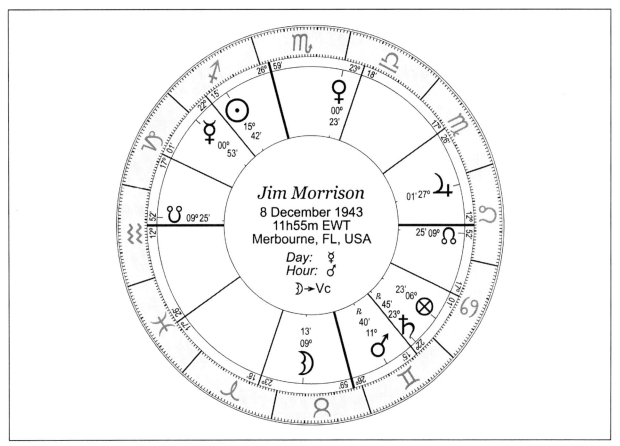

**Chart 8. Jim Morrison**

The chart of Jim Morrison, lead singer of *The Doors,* illustrates *besiegement.* The Sun at 15° Sagittarius 42 is separating from an opposition to Mars at 11° Gemini 40 and is applying to an opposition to Saturn at 23° Gemini 45. The Sun is located in the tenth house and rules the seventh, indicating the areas affected by the besiegement. In effect, the fame and success (tenth house) achieved by Morrison were marked by polemics: some of his musical performances were actually interrupted by the authorities and his conduct onstage condemned for its lack of decency. His personal relationships (seventh house) were equally marked by conflict and enmity.

As can be seen from these examples, cases of *assistance* and *besiegement* must always be examined within the larger context of the rest of the chart. Only in this way can their expression be fully seen in a specific chart, as well as their relative weight in the life of the native.

## Reception

At the same time that aspects allow for the connection between two planets, they also enable the sharing of dignity and power between them. It is from the combination of aspects and essential dignity that arises the concept of *reception*.

Recall that a planet that rules the dignity of a particular degree or zodiac sign is the dispositor of whichever planet (or other point in the chart) happens to be posited there. While the term "dispositor" is generally applied to the ruler or owner of the sign, it can also refer to a disposition by exaltation, triplicity, term, or face. Reception is an extension of the idea of disposition and occurs when planet A makes an aspect to planet B, when planet A is located in a sign over which planet B has some dignity. It is said that planet B receives planet A and gives it its disposition, nature and virtue, which means it transmits to it its dignity, making it stronger.

For example, consider Mars at 10° Pisces and Jupiter at 15° Taurus. Mars makes a sextile to Jupiter and is located in a sign ruled by Jupiter. Therefore, Mars is in reception (or is received) by Jupiter. In another example, let's suppose that the Moon is at 5° Aries and in a trine with the Sun at 15° Sagittarius. Here, the Moon is received by the Sun in its sign of exaltation, Aries. We can compare the planet that receives to a host who welcomes (receives) those who enter his home.

Reception is said to be perfect when planet A finds itself in the sign owned or exalted by planet B; in those cases the interaction between the two planets is fortified. When the reception involves the lesser dignities (triplicity, term, or face) it is considered weak or imperfect. For many authors, reception by the minor dignities is only considered when the planet received is located in a degree over which two simultaneous minor dignities are held by the dignifying planet. For example, consider Mars at 15° Virgo in aspect to Venus at 12° Gemini. Because Venus holds two minor dignities (triplicity and term) in 15° Virgo, it is considered to be in reception with Mars.

When the two planets in aspect are in each other's dignities (A in the dignity of B and B in the dignity of A), they are said to be in *mutual reception*. The relationship between the two planets is therefore considered to be more intense. An example of this is Mercury in Capricorn forming a trine to Saturn in Virgo; Mercury is in the sign ruled by Saturn, and Saturn is in the sign ruled by Mercury. Mutual receptions may also be mixed, when planet A is in the sign ruled by planet B, and planet B is in the sign of planet A's exaltation. An example of this would be Mercury in Pisces square Venus in Gemini; in this case it is a mutual but mixed reception because Mercury is received in exaltation by Venus, while Venus is received in rulership by Mercury.

In practice, we may look upon reception as a sign of good will by the dignifying planet to help out the visiting planet, which becomes stronger in its ability to act. In a sense, reception highlights the softer aspects (trine and sextile) and alleviates the more discordant circumstances (opposition and square).

Reception also indicates the predisposition and motivation behind particular actions. A planet that is received in rulership confers great importance onto its dispositor (in the same way that a visitor will honor the host). If the reception occurs through exaltation, it can represent excitement on the part of the planet received. The same occurs with the minor dignities, but on a smaller scale.

The debilities may also be included in an interpretation, although their impact is less noticeable and easily nullified by other configurations. They nevertheless represent a sort of "negative disposition" between the planets. For example, consider the Sun in Cancer forming a sextile with Saturn in Virgo. In this case, the Sun aspects Saturn from its sign of detriment (Cancer) such that Saturn does not hold him in regard.

As a more practical example, we return to the previous horary question: "Will she date me?" The Ascendant of the chart is 5° Aquarius. As we saw, the significator for the querent is Saturn (ruler of the Ascendant), located at 15° Leo. The significator of the quesited (the woman in question) is the Sun (ruler of the Descendant), located at 5° Aries.

The previous conclusion was that a relationship would not occur because she (the Sun) preferred to date another man (Mars), rather than the querent (Saturn). Now, from an examination of the receptions involved, we will look at the underlying motivations of each of these characters. The significator of the querent is Saturn, which, in Leo, is disposed by the Sun, significator of the woman. This indicates that he has a great interest in her and that in a manner of speaking he is under her dominion (Saturn is under the rulership of the Sun: he is

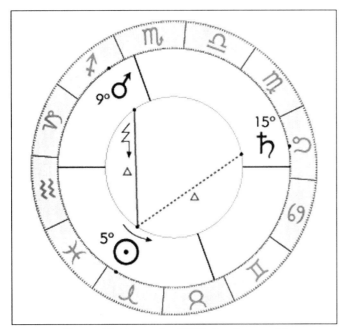

**Figure 22. Example, "Will she date me?"**

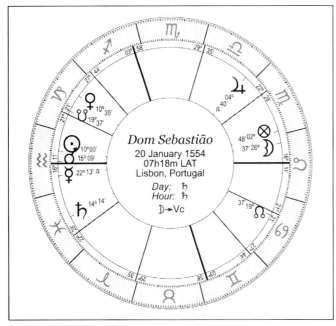

**Chart 5. King Sebastian**

in her "kingdom"). Unfortunately he is in a detrimented position (Saturn in Leo), so is not in a strong position to make his wishes come true.

She has a good social position, represented by the exaltation in Aries; which receives Saturn in the sign it rules. Saturn can only receive the Sun by triplicity, but in its weak condition of detriment this will not be greatly noticeable. Besides, she (the Sun) is in the sign of Saturn's detriment (Aries), which brings into play some sort of resentment or envy on his part toward her (she, the Sun, is in the sign of Saturn's exile; that is, in a position/status uncomfortable to him). The strongest feelings on her part are reserved for the other man, signified by Mars. Since the Sun (her) is in Aries, a sign ruled by Mars, we can say that she is under his dominion, and that he has a certain power over her (she is in his "kingdom").

Now we will look at an interpretation of these conditions in a natal chart. In the chart of King Sebastian, there are two examples of reception. In the square between Venus and Jupiter we have an example of simple reception: Jupiter in Libra is received by Venus, lady of the sign, posited in Capricorn. This reception reinforces the intensity of the aspect because it makes concrete the association of ideals with ambitions. Note that Jupiter, ruler of the Midheaven (ambition) is received by Venus, ruler of the ninth house (ideals).

The second example occurs with the sextile between Venus and Saturn. In this case, we have a mixed mutual reception: Venus is in the sign ruled by Saturn (Capricorn), and Saturn is in the exaltation of Venus (Pisces). The emotional rigor indicated by the planets (see Chapter VIII for an explanation of aspect delineation) is reinforced and intensified through the mutual reception. In the larger context of the life, this sextile represents King Sebastian's relationship with his allies (Venus in the eleventh). The mutual reception suggests that those allies attributed great force and power to him (Saturn disposes Venus), and that in return the King responded to these expectations with excitement (Venus disposes Saturn in exaltation).

The strength of reception thus functions at two levels: in *mutual reception*, the strongest, the interaction of both planets is greatly intensified; and in *simple reception*, the interaction helps to make the aspect more concrete (if the aspect is applying it makes the reception even more effective). In the above example, the reception between Venus and Saturn is not only strong because it is mutual, but also because it is an applying aspect. In comparison, the reception between Venus and Jupiter is less noticeable because the aspect is separating.

Some authors speak of the existence of reception without the presence of an aspect between the planets. In these cases, the reception is very weak. There may exist an "expectation" between the planets involved (represented by the reception), but this expectation is not acted upon (represented by the aspect). We might say that there is a latent motivation between the planets, but there lacks an aspect to realize it. For example, the Moon at 2° Sagittarius disposed by Jupiter at 16° Libra is colored by the expectations and optimism of Jupiter. Nonetheless, because there is no aspect between both bodies, that expectation does not express itself in a specific action. Instead, it remains an underlying disposition in the nature of the Moon. In this case, the correct term to be used should be *disposition* and not reception. Throughout this book we use the term reception to refer only to those cases where an aspect is present; in the absence of an aspect, we use the term *disposition*. (Some authors suggest that mutual reception has enough strength to function even without an aspect to connect the pertinent planets).

In the horoscope of King Sebastian, the conjunction of Mercury, Sun, and Mars in Aquarius is disposed by Saturn, which is in Pisces. In this case, there is no reception because there is no aspect between the conjoined planets and Saturn. Notwithstanding, even without reception, the disposition is not without its influence; it indicates a motivation underlying the actions of the disposed planets. In this way, the impetuosity and expansiveness represented by the Mercury-Sun-Mars conjunction in an air sign (Aquarius) are somewhat emotionally constricted due to the disposition of Saturn in a water sign (Pisces). Note that, while important, this characteristic is not always noticeable in the actions of the native.

---

### Additional Concepts

There are some concepts of minor importance related to reception that are limited to very specific uses of the chart and should be looked at as secondary indicators that strengthen or diminish the strength of the aspect and the planets involved.

#### Emission of Virtue

Emission of power occurs when a planet in one of its major dignities (rulership or exaltation) makes an aspect to another planet. It is said to then send emit its power to the other planet. For example, the Moon exalted at 13° Taurus in trine to Mercury at 10° Capricorn emits or discharges its power to Mercury which is peregrine, and thus, aided. In practice, this concept tells us that a planet in its own major dignities is not only powerful, but can transmit that strength to others it contacts. In otherwords, a dignified planet can strengthen and assist other planets it aspects.

#### Return of Virtue

When a planet is received by another, but it is combust, retrograde or cadent, it cannot receive the strength and virtue of its dispositor and returns it. For example, Venus retrograde at 8° Aries in the sixth house, trines Mars at 10° Leo in the tenth house. Mars receives Venus and sends her his virtue or nature. But because Venus is retrograde and cadent, she returns what he sends. The idea that this concept is conveying is that a planet that is very debilitated in a chart does not benefit greatly from reception. This means reception can strengthen what already exists, but does not have the power in itself to remove a planet's debilitated condition.

*Chapter X*

# The Condition of the Planets

In addition to the essential dignity and debility of the planets, there are other conditions that can increase, decrease, or modify the expression of a planet. These conditions are based upon the repetition, to a greater or lesser extent, of the idealized astrological scheme. With regard to this topic, the Moon will be considered separately because it is a luminary and not a planet.

## Sun and Planet Relationships

The Sun is the engine of the astrological scheme. Its movement produces the zodiac and the seasons of the year, and its central position in the celestial sphere determines the essential nature of the planets. The Sun also defines day and night. Its light is so bright that no planet, with the exception of the Moon, can be seen during the day. Because of its overarching power, the Sun plays a pivotal role in the dynamic relationship among the planets.

### Increase and Decrease of Light

In astrology, there is a direct relationship between luminosity and strength: the more light a planet has, the stronger it is in the horoscope because its light and visibility are the root of astrological interpretation. The amount of light that a planet appears to display to a terrestrial observer (the solar light it reflects to earth) is determined by its position in relation to the Sun. When a planet is very close to the Sun, its light is overwhelmed by the Sun's glare. As it distances itself from the Sun (or the Sun from it) the planet gradually becomes more luminous, and consequently more visible. It is said then to be **increasing in light**. The planet reaches its greatest luminosity when it is farthest from the Sun. From that point on, the process reverses itself and the planet is next said to be **decreasing in light**. The phase of least luminosity corresponds to the conjunction with the Sun.

In the case of the slower, superior planets (Saturn, Jupiter, and Mars), this condition is established from its proximity or distance from the Sun. The cycle begins with the conjunction, during which the planet is not visible to a terrestrial observer due to solar glare. As the Sun distances itself from the planet, it gradually becomes brighter and therefore stronger. This increase in light culminates with the opposition, the point at which the planet reflects the greatest amount of solar light. After this, the Sun begins once more to approach the planet, which starts to decrease in light and is therefore weakened. The decrease culminates with a new conjunction to the Sun.

For the inferior planets (Venus and Mercury) the cycle is different due to their proximity with the Sun. Their cycles exhibit two different phases of increase in light: one when they detach from the Sun during direct motion, and one when they move away from the Sun during retrograde motion. Similarly, they also exhibit two phases corresponding to a decrease in light: one when direct, and one when retrograde. To determine the phase of the cycle in which the planets find themselves in a particular horoscope, it is necessary to observe the direction of its movement in relation to the Sun.

*Practice Example:*
*Increase and Decrease in Light*
The chart of Florbela Espanca illustrates the increase and decrease of light of the inferior planets.

In the chart of Florbela Espanca, first look at the inferior planets, Mercury and Venus. Venus is conjunct the Sun and therefore not visible. Because it is faster than the Sun, Venus is beginning to move away from it and thus beginning to increase in light. Mercury, on the other hand, is nearing the Sun and thus in a phase of decreasing in light. The conclusion then is that Venus is becoming stronger and Mercury is moving toward a weaker state.

Regarding the superior planets (Saturn, Jupiter, and Mars), Saturn and Jupiter are both in a phase of increased light because the Sun, the

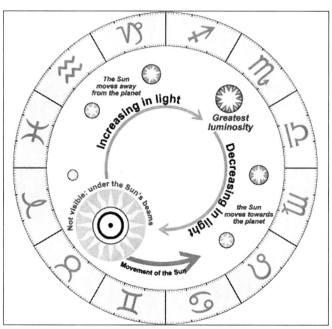

**Figure 1. Increase and Decrease of Light of the Superior Planets**

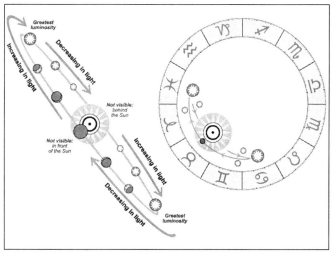

**Figure 2. Increase and Decrease of Light of the Inferior Planets**

faster body, is separating from them. Saturn is in its initial phase, with the Sun relatively close by, while Jupiter is close to culminating its cycle because the Sun is nearing its maximum distance (the opposition). The conclusion is thus that both are strengthening. Mars, in turn, is in a phase of decreased light because the Sun is gradually approaching it. The Moon is increasing in light because it is also moving away from the Sun. Note: Although this contributes to the general study of the chart, this condition is not interpreted in isolation.

## Under the Beams, Combustion, and Cazimi

When a planet nears the Sun, its light is concealed by the heavenly king. As it advances into the area of solar glare, its light becomes ever more difficult to see until it is ultimately completely hidden. The glare of the Sun projects to about 17° to either side of the Sun. It is this glare that can be seen at dusk, just after the Sun has set (when the star-king crosses the Descendant). It only disappears after the Sun has descended to about 17° below the horizon. This glare is also visible at dawn. It is the dawn light that announces the start of a new

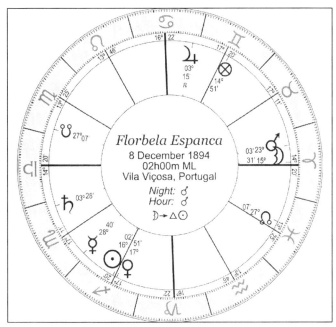

**Chart 3. Nativity of Florbela Espanca**

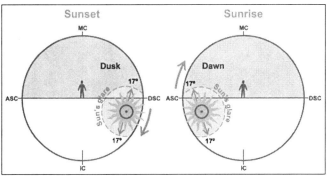

**Figure 3. Dusk and Dawn**

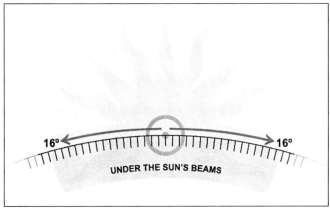

**Figure 4. Under the Sun's Beams**

day, before the Sun's rise, when it is 17° below the Ascendant (the day only really begins when the Sun crosses the Ascendant.

When a planet enters into this glare, it is said to be **under the beams of the Sun**. Its visibility is compromised as soon as it is fewer than 17° from the star-king. A planet in these conditions is slightly weakened because it cannot shine at its maximum strength.

When the proximity to the Sun is within 8° it is said to be **combust**. In this case, its light is no longer visible under the Sun's rays. The qualities of the planet are also very weakened. Combustion, by the way, is considered a greater debility. It removes from the planet a great part of its capacity to act, weakening its expression, whether for good or bad.

In a natal chart, a combust planet indicates a degree of inhibition with regard to the matters signified by the planet in that horoscope. The repercussions of this situation depend upon the relative importance of the planet and its functions in the chart. For example, if the combust planet is the ruler of one of the angles of the chart, the condition tends to be more noticeable; in other cases, it may be relatively inconsequential.

In specific situations, such as horary astrology, combustion may indicate weakness, disease, anxiety, fear, imprisonment, or even death (depending obviously on the question and the context). This occurs because the state of combustion is similar to a "burn": the planet (and what it signifies) is burned up by the Sun. For example, if the combust planet is the ruler of the Ascendant in a horary chart, it suggests a worried person under pressure or in some way weakened; if it is the significator of an object that one wishes to purchase, it raises questions regarding the satisfactory condition of the article. In another context, combustion can also be associated with hidden things, which correlates to the invisibility of the planet.

Combustion affects each planet in a different way in accordance with the different natures of the planets. Mercury, a naturally dry planet, is little affected by combustion. Its effects manifest as a slight loss of objectivity. Besides that, the frequent proximity of Mercury to the Sun makes combustion relatively common. Mars, an exceedingly hot and dry planet, possesses a nature that is exacerbated under combustion. Nonetheless, that excess in itself becomes a limiting factor on the actions of the planet. On the other hand, for the feminine planets (Venus and the Moon) whose principal characteristic is moistness, combustion is particularly damaging because it contradicts the essence of these planets. Combust Jupiter loses the wetness that is characteristic of it, thus diminishing its temperance. As for Saturn, the excessive heat of combustion disturbs its cold nature and produces rigidity.

**Figure 5. Combustion**

Returning to Florbela's horoscope, Venus is combust (at 1°49′ from the Sun). Because Venus is the Ascendant ruler, combustion will affect something intrinsic to her personal expression, which in this case is a strong interest in love and romance. Nonetheless, combustion diminishes the sensibility that is characteristic of Venus. We thus get a strong expression of "emotional greed," where there is a powerful focus on feelings and personal and subjective experiences, combined with difficulty in understanding the feelings of others. Note that this dynamic expression occurs in the third house of communication and writing.

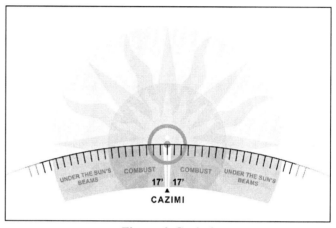

**Figure 6. Cazimi**

There exists a special case of combustion wherein the planet is strengthened rather than weakened. This occurs when the planet is in exact conjunction with the Sun, or more precisely, when it is at 17′ or less of the center of the solar disc. This condition is known as **cazimi**, which means "in the heart of the Sun." It corresponds to a state of great power, where the planet is supported and facilitated by the power of the star-king.

The outcome of this special situation depends on the condition of the planet: if it is dignified, cazimi adds to it a strong ability to project itself; if it is debilitated, the strength conferred by the condition of cazimi may accentuate the difficulties. A good example of the first case would be in a chart with Saturn, ruler of the Midheaven, dignified in Aquarius and cazimi. In this case, the native has a good chance of receiving recognition and fame. The seriousness and work ethic of dignified Saturn are enhanced by the Sun. For the second case, consider a chart where Saturn, ruler of the Midheaven, is simultaneously in fall and cazimi. Here, the Sun also grants fame, but not for the best of reasons (Saturn is debilitated).

In whatever case, what needs to be highlighted is that cazimi only enhances whatever is already present in the horoscope.

In the chart of Edgar Allen Poe, Mercury, planet of communication and writing, is cazimi and only 0°12′ from the Sun. Mercury is therefore greatly strengthened by the Sun. Because in this chart the Sun rules the Midheaven, its action manifests as fame. The conjunction occurs in the third house of communication and

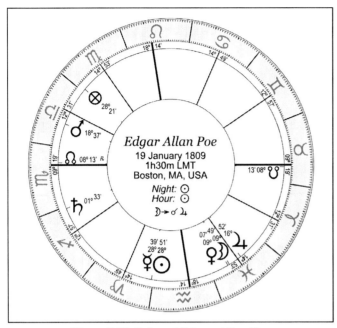

**Chart 7. Nativity of Edgar Allan Poe**

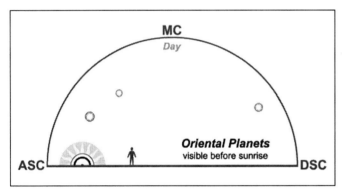

**Figure 7. Oriental Planets**

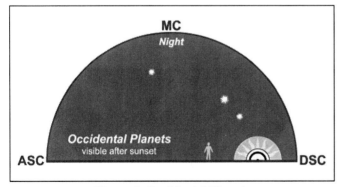

**Figure 8. Occidental Planets**

writing, indicating that fame will come from these activities. The strong connection between Mercury and Saturn (by aspect and disposition) describes the somber quality of his writings. In addition, Mercury rules the eighth house, which also contributes to his style of literary writing, which is marked by morbid themes and psychological undertones.

**Orientality and Occidentality**

These conditions are also defined by the position of the planets in relation to the Sun. A planet is **oriental** when it rises in the sky before the Sun because at that time it is visible and to the east (orient). When it rises after the Sun, it is **occidental** because it will only be visible in the west (occident) after the Sun has set. This concept is probably as old as astrology itself and derives from the direct observation of the movement of the planets. The first interpretive prehistoric techniques were based in large part on this type of relationship between the planets and the Sun.

*Determining Oriental and Occidental Planets*

Because horoscopes may have the Sun in any position (and not just on the Ascendant), new students may encounter difficulties determining orientality and occidentality. Most important is to remember that one's point of reference is always **the relationship of the planets to the Sun** and not the position of the Sun in the houses. Thus, to determine the position of the planets, imagine that the Sun is rising over the horizon (conjunct the Ascendant). This establishes an imaginary horizon that divides the chart into two parts: the planets that are above this imaginary horizon are oriental, and those that are below are occidental. To help visualize this, you can turn the chart.

The oriental planets, those that precede the Sun, were envisioned as "spear-bearers" of the star-king, signaling the vitality of a new day. Thus, an oriental planet was considered to have masculine characteristics, giving it a more direct, outward, and assertive manner. On the other hand, occidental planets, which follow the Sun, were envisioned as the entourage that follows the solar court. Occidental planets exhibit feminine qualities, expressing themselves in a more discreet, contemplative, and withdrawing manner. Note that these qualities must be added to the characteristics that the planets acquire via their positions by sign, house, etc. There is little point in interpreting them independently.

The superior masculine planets (Saturn, Jupiter, and Mars) are strengthened when oriental in position because they have their masculinity reinforced. On the other hand, the inferior feminine planets (Venus, Mercury, and the Moon) are strengthened when occidental by position because this position reinforces their feminine natures.

The orientality of masculine planets and the occidentality of feminine planets repeats the order of the celestial spheres: the superiors are above the Sun when oriental because they rise before him, while the inferior planets are below the Sun when occidental because they rise after him.

When the natural order of the celestial spheres is repeated in a horoscope, the planets are in their idealized positions in relationship to the Sun and therefore strengthened. Mercury, a neutral planet, is a special case. Contrary to the others, all of which have a defined gender (masculine or feminine), Mercury's gender is determined by its position in relationship to the Sun. It is considered masculine when oriental and feminine when occidental.

Orientality and occidentality also has an effect on the primary qualities that characterize each planet. Depending upon the planet's position in relation to the Sun, one of its primary qualities is emphasized. Thus, Saturn, naturally cold and dry, tends to be colder when oriental, and drier when occidental. When oriental, it tends to acquire some humidity, thereby moderating its qualities. Jupiter, hot and moist, gets hotter when oriental, and wetter when occidental. Mars reinforces its heat when oriental and its dryness when occidental. Just like Jupiter, Venus is hotter when oriental and wetter when occidental. Mercury also increases its heat when oriental, but occidentality reinforces its dryness. The Moon, because it is a luminary, follows special rules explained later in this chapter.

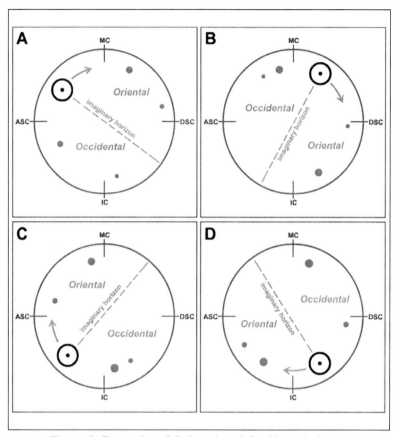

**Figure 9. Examples of Oriental and Occidental planets**

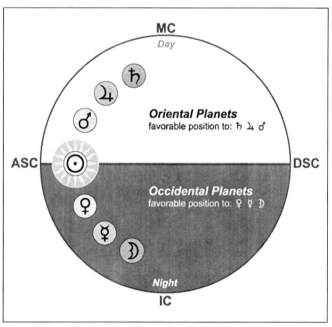

**Figure 10. Correlation Between the Ptolemaic Scheme and Orientality**

*Practice Example for Orientality and Occidentality*

In the chart of Florbela Espanca there are three oriental and three occidental planets. Mercury, Saturn, and Jupiter rise before the Sun, so they are oriental. In terms of strength, orientality favors Jupiter and Saturn, and occidentality favors the Moon. The same might be said of Venus if this state were not nullified by its excessive proximity to the Sun (combustion). In the case of Mars, which is dignified in this chart (in rulership and angular), occidentality merely removes the capacity for assertiveness from it. The leadership of Mars is still felt, but it is colored by hesitation and doubt. Because Mars is in the seventh house, this situation tends to be experienced in the area of relationships (especially in her tumultuous marriages). By being oriental, Mercury acquires speed and vitality in this horoscope (although it is considered to be favored in occidentality because it is an inferior planet).

*Other Orientality Concepts*

There are other planetary classifications with regard to orientality. These are based upon the placement of the planets in the hemispheres and quadrants of the chart and not on their relationship with the Sun, as in the previous cases. This type of classification is known as *orientality in mundo.* According to this concept, a planet is oriental when it is in the east in oriental quadrants (twelfth, eleventh, tenth, and sixth, fifth, fourth houses) and occidental when in western quadrants (ninth, eighth, seventh, and third, second, first houses). This classification is used in different contexts and has no relationship to the concept of orientality with regard to the Sun, described here.

## The Conditions of the Moon

Due to its status as a luminary, the Moon's dynamic relationships are different from the other planets. It shares with them the same conditions (orientality, combustion, etc.) but also has its own characteristics (velocity, amount of light, and others) that make it unique.

### The Lunation Cycle

At the root of the Moon's dynamic interaction is its unique relationship with the Sun. Because it is the fastest planet, it is the Moon that sets the pace of that relationship. The Sun-Moon cycle has four distinct phases. The first, known as the First Quarter, begins with the conjunction of the lights (New Moon) and lasts until the square (First Quarter). During this phase, the Moon gradually distances itself from the Sun's rays. Because its visibility increases, it is said to be **waxing in light**. The Second Quarter phase follows, which begins with the square of the lights and ends at the opposition (Full Moon). In this phase, the Moon, which is increasing in light, reaches the point of its greatest distance from the Sun. The Third Quarter phase lasts from the opposition to the next square (Last Quarter). After it has attained its greatest distance and brightness, the Moon begins once more to approach the Sun. Its visibility, which is still great, now begins to diminish. It is said then to be **waning in light**. The Fourth Quarter phase begins with the square and ends at a new conjunction. In this phase, the Moon loses a large part of its brightness and

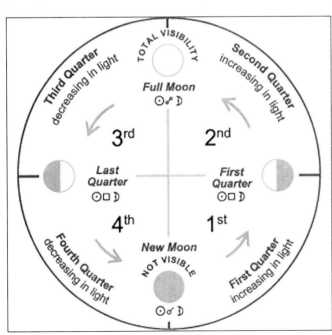

**Figure 11. The Lunation Cycle**

continues to wane in light until it is conjunct the Sun and is no longer visible. Each quarter extends for approximately one week, totaling a complete cycle of 29½ days (that is, a lunar month).

The primary qualities of the Moon are altered as it travels along the course of its cycle. Although its natural essence remains cold and moist, the various phases add slight shades of heat and dryness to it. In the first quarter, the Moon appears hot and moist, which gives it a sanguine temperament. The heat remains in the second quarter, but the waxing light adds dryness to it, thus producing a choleric temperament. With the decrease in light of the Third Quarter phase, the Moon cools but retains its dryness, producing a melancholic temperament. In the last phase of the cycle, the Moon recovers its moistness, which will combine with the cold, producing a phlegmatic temperament.

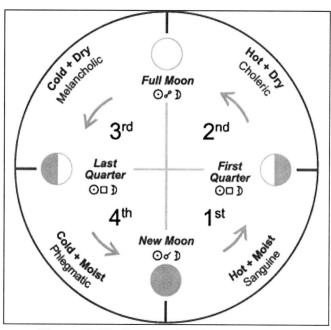

**Figure 12. The Primary Qualities of the Moon**

For a deeper interpretation, the Moon's temperament is combined with the characteristics given to it by its sign position. While the position by sign indicates the general attitude, its position by phase (temperament), defines the manner in which it is externalized. For example: a Taurus Moon, which is oriented toward security, stability, and comfort (earth + fixed), will have a different expression according to its lunar phase. If it is choleric (hot + dry), this need becomes more dynamic and urgent, actively seeking security. If it is phlegmatic (cold + moist), the search has a more passive and expectant tenor ("be still," "don't make waves") and the conditions for security will eventually come to the native. In the general interpretation of a nativity, the Moon's sign and its phase are considered together with other factors to determine the individual's character. This determination is crucial in the overall characterization of an individual.

*Orientality and Occidentality of the Moon*
In the waxing phases (the first two quarters), the Moon is occidental to the Sun, so this phase is considered hotter and therefore more dynamic. In the waning phase (the last two quarters), the Moon is oriental to the Sun and therefore colder and more withdrawn.

*Determining the Moon's Phase*
First look at the position of the Sun. From this, note the points to which the Sun emits rays for the opposition and the two squares. If the Moon is positioned between the point of the conjunction and the first quarter (in the direction of the order of the signs), it is in the **First Quarter**. If it is between that square and the opposition, it is in the **Second Quarter**. If it is after the opposi-

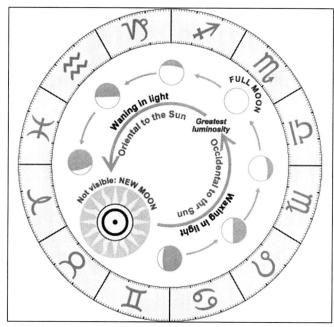

**Figure 13. Orientality and Occidentality**

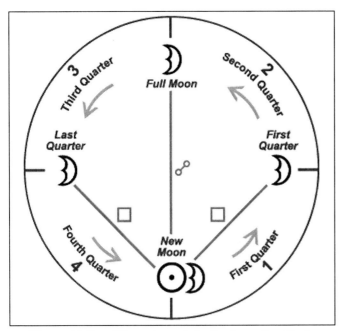

**Figure 14. Sun-Moon Aspects in the Lunation Cycle**

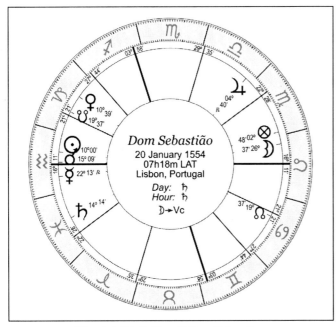

**Chart 5. Nativity of King Sebastian**

tion but before the second square (toward which the Sun's rays are emitted in the direction contrary to the order of the signs), the Moon is in the **Third Quarter** phase. If it is between that square and the conjunction, it is in the **Fourth Quarter**. The transition places of the Moon's phases are the points of exact aspects. For the divisions into quarters, no orbs are used.

For example, in the horoscope of Florbela Espanca, the Sun is at 16° Sagittarius. It emits an exact opposition to 16° Gemini and exact squares to 16° Pisces (first square) and 16° Virgo (second square). The Moon is at 15° Aries, therefore located between the first square (of Pisces) and the opposition (in Gemini). It is therefore in the second quarter, which corresponds to a choleric temperament (hot and dry). In this case, the naturally dynamic and impatient attitude of the Moon in Aries (fire + cardinal) is exacerbated by the Moon's choleric condition.

In another example from the chart of King Sebastian, the Moon is positioned right after the opposition and before the second square and is thus in the third quarter. This phase corresponds with a melancholic temperament. The need for assertiveness and self-recognition characteristic of the Moon in Leo (fire + fixed) acquires a more rigid and controlled expression due to the melancholic temperament (cold + dry).

**The Syzygies or Lunations**

The two principal phases of the Moon's cycle are the New Moon and Full Moon. It is at the New Moon, during the Sun-Moon conjunction, that the Moon becomes subject to the Sun's power. Due to its luminosity, the Moon only falls under the beams when it is fewer than 12° from the Sun (the other planets fall under the beams when they are within 16°). After that, there follows the phase of conjunction, when the Moon loses a good deal of its power, as happens with the planets. This phase only ends when the Moon is 12° apart from the Sun and visible once more. The New Moon marks the beginning of the cycle and symbolizes birth and beginnings.

The Full Moon signals the culmination of the lunation cycle. It corresponds to the exact opposition between the Sun and Moon. The Moon is then at its greatest brightness and strength. After this point, it begins to decrease in light, initiating the waning phase, which will culminate in a new conjunction.

The New Moon and Full Moon are called **lunations** or **syzygies** (a term from the Greek * σίαίᾱββά*, which means conjunction, but which in this context can also be applied to the opposition). In mundane astrology, the monthly syzygies signal important transition points, whether as climaxes or as initiators of events. In natal charts, it is especially important to determine the **prenatal syzygy**. If an individual was born after the New Moon and before the Full Moon, the prenatal syzygy will be the degree of the New Moon. It is then said that the individual's horoscope is **conjunctional**. If the birth occurs after the Full Moon and before the next New Moon, the pre-natal syzygy will be the degree where the Moon was opposite the Sun.[24] In this case, the horoscope is said to be **preventional**.

The prenatal syzygies act as sensitive points in the horoscope and are used in advanced predictive techniques. Florbela Espanca's chart is an example of a conjunctional chart. The Moon is in a waxing phase, inching its way toward a Full Moon. The prenatal syzygy was a New Moon at 5° Sagittarius 09. The chart of King Sebastian is as example of a preventional case as he was born shortly after the Full Moon. In this instance, the previous syzygy was the actual Full Moon, which occurred at 6° Leo 27′, the position of the Moon at the moment of the opposition.

### Occidentality and Orientality of the Planets to the Moon

In astrological texts, references are often made to the orientality and occidentality of the planets in relation to the Moon. As with the Sun, a planet is oriental of the Moon when it rises before the Moon and occidental when it sets after it.

This is a concept rarely utilized; it is only referred to in very specific interpretative methods. Obviously, this condition does not apply to the Sun. A planet is considered strengthened when it is occidental to the Moon. In this condition, the planet acts as maidservant to the Queen, carrying the train of her gown.

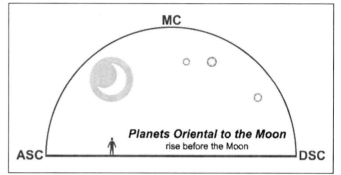

Figure 15. Planets Oriental to the Moon

### Conditions Specific to the Moon

There are some conditions that are specific to the Moon and that speak to its condition as luminary and fastest planet.

*The Via Combusta*

When the Moon is located between the last half of Libra and the first half of Scorpio, it is said to be in the **via combusta**.[25] This position, consid-

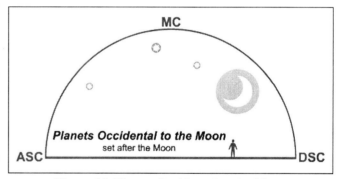

Figure 16. Planets Occidental to the Moon

ered a slight debility, imparts a degree of discomfort and instability to the Moon. It is particularly used in horary astrology. In certain questions, the Moon in via combusta can indicate a negative answer or a situation of distress.

---

[24]In the case of the Full Moon, some authors affirm that the degree of the luminary that is above the horizon at the moment of the lunation should be considered. This idea seems to originate with Ptolemy but was not unanimously accepted.

[25]Some authors apply the concept of the via combusta to all the planets.

| | Lunar Mansion | | Star (approximate) | Position (beginning) | | | |
|---|---|---|---|---|---|---|---|
| N. | Name | Meaning | | 1900 | 1950 | 2000 | 2050 |
| 1 | Al Thuraiya | the many little ones | Pleiades | 28°♉36' | 29°♉18' | 29°♉59' | 00°♊41' |
| 2 | Al Dabaran | the follower | Aldebaran | 08°♊24' | 09°♊05' | 09°♊47' | 10°♊29' |
| 3 | Al Hak'ah | a white spot | Al Hecka | 23°♊23' | 24°♊05' | 24°♊47' | 25°♊29' |
| 4 | Al Han'ah | a brand or mark | Alhena | 07°♋43' | 08°♋25' | 09°♋06' | 09°♋48' |
| 5 | Al Dhira | the forearm | Castor | 18°♋51' | 19°♋33' | 20°♋15' | 20°♋56' |
| 6 | Al Nathra | the gap or crib | Praesaepe | 05°♌57' | 06°♌39' | 07°♌20' | 08°♌02' |
| 7 | Al Tharf | the glance (of the lion's eye) | Alterf | 16°♌29' | 17°♌10' | 17°♌52' | 18°♌34' |
| 8 | Al Jabhah | the forehead | Regulus | 28°♌26' | 29°♌08' | 29°♌50' | 00°♍31' |
| 9 | Al Zubrah | the mane | Zosma | 09°♍55' | 10°♍37' | 11°♍19' | 12°♍10' |
| 10 | Al Sarfah | the changer (of the weather) | Denebola | 20°♍13' | 20°♍55' | 21°♍37' | 22°♍19' |
| 11 | Al Awwa | the barker | Zavijava | 25°♍45' | 26°♍27' | 27°♍10' | 27°♍52' |
| 12 | As Simak | the unarmed | Spica | 22°♎27' | 23°♎09' | 23°♎51' | 24°♎32' |
| 13 | Al Ghafr | the covering | Syrma | 02°♏23' | 03°♏05' | 03°♏47' | 04°♏29' |
| 14 | Al Zubana | the claws | Zubenelgenubi | 13°♏41' | 14°♏23' | 15°♏05' | 15°♏46' |
| 15 | Al Iklil al Jabhah | the crown of the forehead | Abrab | 01°♐48' | 02°♐29' | 03°♐11' | 03°♐53' |
| 16 | Al Kolb | the heart | Antares | 08°♐22' | 09°♐04' | 09°♐46' | 10°♐27' |
| 17 | Al Shaula | the sting | Shaula | 23°♐11' | 23°♐52' | 24°♐34' | 25°♐16' |
| 18 | Al Na'am | the ostrich | Ascella | 12°♑14' | 12°♑56' | 13°♑38' | 14°♑20' |
| 19 | Al Baldah | the city | Albaldah | 14°♑51' | 15°♑32' | 16°♑14' | 16°♑56' |
| 20 | As Sa'd al Dhabi | the lucky one of the slaughterers | Giedi | 02°♒22' | 03°♒04' | 03°♒46' | 04°♒27' |
| 21 | As Sa'd al Bula | the good fortune of the swallower | Albali | 10°♒19' | 11°♒01' | 11°♒42' | 12°♒24' |
| 22 | As Sa'd al Su'ud | the luckiest of the lucky | Sadalsud | 22°♒00' | 22°♒42' | 23°♒23' | 24°♒05' |
| 23 | As Sa'a al Ahbiyah | the lucky star of hidden things | Sadalmelek | 02°♓01' | 03°♓03' | 03°♓45' | 04°♓27' |
| 24 | Al Fargh al Mukdim | the fore-spout or the water bucket | Markab | 22°♓06' | 22°♓47' | 23°♓29' | 24°♓11' |
| 25 | Al Fargh al Thani | the second or lower spout | Algenib | 07°♈46' | 08°♈28' | 09°♈09' | 09°♈51' |
| 26 | Al Batn al Hut | the belly of the fish | Mirach | 29°♈01' | 29°♈42' | 00°♉24' | 01°♉06' |
| 27 | Al Sharatain | the two signs | Sheratan | 02°♉34' | 03°♉16' | 03°♉58' | 04°♉40' |
| 28 | Al Butain | the belly | Botein | 19°♉27' | 20°♉09' | 20°♉51' | 21°♉33' |

**Figure 17. Lunar Mansions (according to Al-Biruni)**

| | Lunar Mansion (tropical) | | Position (beginning) | Ruler |
|---|---|---|---|---|
| N. | Name | Meaning | | |
| 1 | Alnath | the horns of the ram | 00°♈00' | ☉ |
| 2 | Allothaim ou Albochan | the belly of the ram | 12°♈51' | ☽ |
| 3 | Achaomazon ou Athoray | the Pleiades | 25°♈43' | ♂ |
| 4 | Aldebaram | the eye of the bull | 08°♉34' | ☿ |
| 5 | Alchatay ou Albachay | the white spot | 21°♉26' | ♃ |
| 6 | Alhanna ou Alchaya | the small star of great light | 04°♊17' | ♀ |
| 7 | Aldimiach ou Alarzach | the arm of the twins | 17°♊09' | ♄ |
| 8 | Alnaza ou Anatchtraya | the nebula | 00°♋00' | ☉ |
| 9 | Archaam ou Arcaph | the eye of the lion | 12°♋51' | ☽ |
| 10 | Algelioche ou Albgebh | the forehead of the lion | 25°♋43' | ♂ |
| 11 | Azobra ou Ardurf | the mane of the lion | 08°♌34' | ☿ |
| 12 | Alzarpha ou Azarpha | the tail of the lion | 21°♌26' | ♃ |
| 13 | Alhaire | the dog star or the wings of Virgo | 04°♍17' | ♀ |
| 14 | Achurethor | the ear of corn of Virgo | 17°♍09' | ♄ |
| 15 | Agrapha ou Algarpha | the covering | 00°♎00' | ☉ |
| 16 | Azubene ou Ahubene | the claws of Scorpio | 12°♎51' | ☽ |
| 17 | Alchil | the crown of Scorpio | 25°♎43' | ♂ |
| 18 | Alchas ou Altob | the heart of Scorpio | 08°♏34' | ☿ |
| 19 | Allatha ou Achala | the sting of Scorpio | 21°♏26' | ♃ |
| 20 | Abnahaya | the beam | 04°♐17' | ♀ |
| 21 | Abeda ou Albeldach | the desert | 17°♐09' | ♄ |
| 22 | Sadahacha ou Zodeboluch | the sheppard | 00°♑00' | ☉ |
| 23 | Zabadola ou Zobrach | the swallower | 12°♑51' | ☽ |
| 24 | Sadabath ou Chadezoad | the star of fortune | 25°♑43' | ♂ |
| 25 | Sadalbracha ou Sadalachia | the butterfly | 08°♒34' | ☿ |
| 26 | Alpharg ou Phragol Mocaden | the first spout | 21°♒26' | ♃ |
| 27 | Alcharya ou Alhalgalmoad | the second spout | 04°♓17' | ♀ |
| 28 | Albotham ou Alchalcy | the fishes | 17°♓09' | ♄ |

**Figure 18. Tropical Lunar Mansions**

The term *via combusta* should not be confused with the concept of combustion. In this use, the term "combusta" refers to a region of the zodiac considered difficult for the Moon and not to its proximity to the Sun. Some authors state that this condition derives from the fact that Libra and Scorpio are the signs of the fall of the luminaries.

## Gemini Moon

Another situation that specifically weakens the Moon is its position in Gemini, since this is the twelfth sign from its rulership. Therefore, a Gemini Moon is considered to be in a sort of twelfth house position and, because of this, more limited in its expression.

## Late Degrees of a Sign

When the Moon is located in the last degrees of a sign, it is also considered to be partially weakened. Because it is close to changing signs, it represents unexpected behavior. In addition, at the end of the signs the Moon is always in the terms of a malefic planet (Mars and Saturn). The combination of these two conditions generates discomfort and instability, which are prejudicial to the nature of the Moon. Once more, this concept is used largely in horary and electional astrology. In a horary chart, it suggests that something is soon about to change (a situation, a price, an opinion, etc., depending upon the context of the question).

## Lunar Mansions

Just as the zodiac is divided into 12 signs, corresponding to the annual motion of the Sun, the path of the Moon in the sky can be divided into 28 houses or lunar mansions. The positions of the stars are used to divide them, in contrast with the signs, which rely on the seasons to mark their boundaries.

Another version of the Lunar Mansions uses the tropical zodiac as its point of reference instead of the stars. In this system, beginning with the first section at 0° Aries, each mansion is equivalent to approximately the path traveled by the Moon in one day. All 28 divisions have equal lengths of 12° 51'. This is in effect an exact transposition of a sidereal system onto a tropical one since the significations of each mansion remain the same.

*Practical Meaning of the Lunar Mansions*

Each mansion has a particular signification that is activated by the transit of the Moon. The particular significations are especially useful in electional charts. Their use in natal and mundane astrology is relatively uncommon. Following is the significance of the Lunar Mansions in elections:

| Sidereal Mansion | Tropical Mansion | Name | When the moon is posited here... |
|---|---|---|---|
| 1 | 3 | the many little ones | **Good for:** planting and sawing<br>**Avoid:** weddings and journeys by water |
| 2 | 4 | the follower | **Good for:** business, traveling and marriage |
| 3 | 5 | a white spot | **Good for:** begin wars<br>**Avoid:** sawing or undertake any good |
| 4 | 6 | a brand or mark | **Good for:** plowing and sawing<br>**Avoid:** travels |
| 5 | 7 | the forearm | **Good for:** travels and to take medicine |
| 6 | 8 | the gap or crib | **Good for:** navigation |
| 7 | 9 | the glance<br>*(of the lion's eye)* | **Good for:** planting, building and marriage<br><br>**Avoid:** travels |
| 8 | 10 | the forehead | **Good for:** sawing, planting, and releasing prisoners<br>**Avoid:** purgative remedies |
| 9 | 11 | the mane | **Good for:** planting and marriage<br>**Avoid:** navigation |
| 10 | 12 | the changer<br>*(of the weather)* | **Good for:** travels, navigation, sawing, plowing, marriage and sending messengers |
| 11 | 13 | the barker | **Good for:** sawing, planting and to take medicine<br>Avoid: travel and marriage |
| 12 | 14 | the unarmed | **Good for:** digging<br>**Avoid:** marriage and travels |
| 13 | 15 | the covering | **Avoid:** all activities |
| 14 | 16 | the claws | **Good for:** buying cattle<br>**Avoid:** navigation |
| 15 | 17 | the crown of the forehead | **Good for:** building, sawing, planting and navigation<br>**Avoid:** marriage |
| 16 | 18 | the heart | **Good for:** plant, saw, travel, go to war |
| 17 | 19 | the sting | **Good for:** buying cattle, hunting<br>**Avoid:** marriage |
| 18 | 20 | the ostrich | **Good for:** building, asking favors<br>**Avoid:** marriage |
| 19 | 21 | the city | **Good for:** taking medicine, navigation, putting on new clothes |

| Sidereal Mansion | Tropical Mansion | Name | When the moon is posited here... |
|---|---|---|---|
| 20 | 22 | the lucky one of the slaughterers | **Good for:** taking medicine, travels<br><br>**Avoid:** lending money and marriage |
| 21 | 23 | the good fortune of the swallower | Good for: marriage, sawing, taking medicine, leading an army |
| 22 | 24 | the luckiest of the lucky | **Good for:** building, marriage, making friends, and travels |
| 23 | 25 | the lucky star of hidden things | **Good for:** taking medicine<br><br>**Avoid:** everything else |
| 24 | 26 | the fore-spout or the water bucket | Good for: planting, sawing, bargaining, and marriage<br>**Avoid:** navigation |
| 25 | 27 | the second or lower spout | Good for: marriage, taking medicine, pursuing business<br>**Avoid:** traveling and lending money |
| 26 | 28 | the belly of the fish | **Good for:** travels and taking purgatives |
| 27 | 1 | the two signs | **Good for:** buying cattle, planting and travels |
| 28 | 2 | the belly | **Good for:** buying and selling<br>**Avoid:** sea activities |

In astrological elections these significations are activated when a favorable moment is selected for the start of a particular action. Since the Moon is the fastest moving celestial body, its position describes the action of the moment. Thus, one selects a moment when the Moon is located in a mansion whose meaning is appropriate to the endeavor being initiated. For example, if the objective is to elect a marriage, one should avoid the position of the Moon in the twentieth mansion (As S' ad al Dhabi), which is unfavorable for unions. The wedding ceremony should be delayed until the Moon transits into the twenty-first lunar mansion (As S'ad al Bula), which is more favorable for marriage.

## Other Planetary Conditions

In addition to the conditions derived from the planet's position in relation to the Sun, there are other specific conditions. These act as a sort of addendum"to the general condition of the planet (essential dignity, position by house, etc.), either reinforcing or disturbing it.

### Hayz

*Hayz* means "natural position" or "preferential position." While the planetary states studied earlier are illustrations of the repetition of the astrological scheme, *hayz* derives from a synthesis of various forms of compatibility between the nature of the planet and the position it occupies.

Compatibility exists whenever a planet is located in a place that reinforces its nature. One of the forms of compatibility has to do with its sect: diurnal planets located in a diurnal hemisphere or nocturnal planets located in a nocturnal hemisphere. Recall that the diurnal hemisphere is always the one in which the Sun is positioned. In a diurnal chart, it is in the upper hemisphere (the one that contains the twelfth, eleventh, tenth, ninth, eighth, and seventh houses); in a nocturnal chart, it is in the bottom hemisphere (containing the seventh, sixth, fifth, fourth, third, second, and first houses).

The other form of compatibility is related to gender: masculine planets are comfortable in masculine signs, and feminine planets in feminine signs.

When these two forms of compatibility combine, the planet is said to be in *hayz*. It thus gains greater than usual strength and stability.

The dignity of *hayz* exists when two conditions are met: the planet located in the hemisphere corresponding with its sect, and in a sign corresponding with its gender. Thus, Jupiter and Saturn are in *hayz* when they are in masculine signs, above the horizon in a diurnal chart, or below the horizon in a nocturnal chart. Mars, which is nocturnal, must be below the horizon by day and below the horizon by night; but because it is a masculine planet, it must be in a masculine sign. The *hayz* condition of Mercury depends upon its position in relation to the Sun: when oriental, it has masculine, diurnal qualities, and when occidental, it has feminine, nocturnal qualities. The Sun is also a special case because it defines both day and night; it is in *hayz* only when it is located above the horizon in a masculine sign. When it is below the horizon, it is in a nocturnal chart and therefore out of sect.

A planet in *hayz* is within its sphere of influence and thus very comfortable. This condition reinforces a dignified planet and bestows some stability upon a debilitated one.

The state of *hayz* can also be reinforced by other factors. If, in addition to the conditions already mentioned, the planet is also located in a quadrant of the same gender—that is, a masculine planet in a masculine quadrant (first and third) and a feminine planet in a feminine quadrant (second and fourth)—it is said to be **conforming by quadrant**.

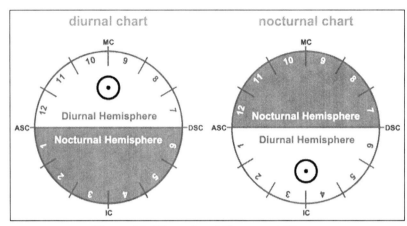

Figure 19. Diurnal and Nocturnal Charts

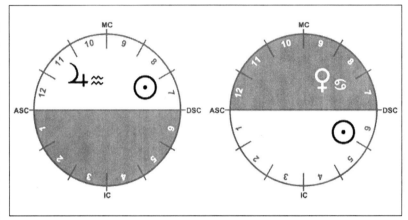

Figure 20. Example of a Diurnal Planet (Jupiter) and a Nocturnal Planet (Venus) in *Hayz*

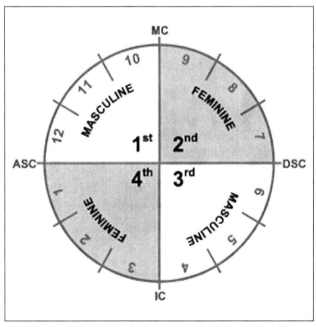

Figure 21. Masculine and Feminine Quadrants

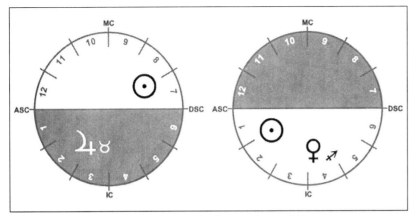

**Figure 22. Planets in Contrariety of *Hayz***

When a planet is in conditions that are the complete opposite of *hayz*, it is said to be **contrary to *hayz***. This condition lightly weakens the planet, even if it is dignified.

In Figure 22, Jupiter, a masculine and diurnal planet, is positioned in a feminine sign and in a nocturnal hemisphere. Venus, a feminine, nocturnal planet, is in a masculine sign and in a diurnal hemisphere. Both are therefore, contrary to *hayz*.

*Example of Planets in Hayz*

The horoscope of Florbela Espanca is nocturnal. Because the Sun is below the horizon, the lower hemisphere is diurnal, and as a result, the upper is nocturnal. In order to be in *hayz* in this chart, the diurnal planets must be below the horizon (in the same hemisphere as the Sun) and in masculine signs; the nocturnal planets must be above the horizon and in feminine signs in the case of Venus and the Moon; and Mars (nocturnal, masculine planet) must also be above the horizon, but in a masculine sign.

Saturn, Mercury, Venus, and the Sun are in the diurnal hemisphere. Saturn, a diurnal, masculine planet, is in a diurnal hemisphere but a feminine sign. Because it only fulfills one of the conditions, it is not in *hayz*. Mercury is oriental and therefore considered diurnal and masculine; it is in a diurnal hemisphere but in a feminine sign, so does not meet the necessary conditions. Venus is nocturnal and feminine but positioned in the diurnal hemisphere in a masculine sign. It is therefore in a condition opposite to that of *hayz*, and is said to be contrary to *hayz* (which reinforces the weakened state caused by combustion).

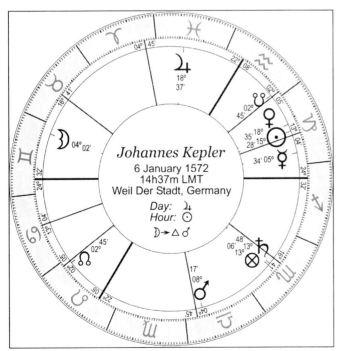

**Chart 6. Nativity of Johannes Kepler**

Because this is a nocturnal chart, the Sun can never be in *hayz* even if, as is the case, it is in a masculine sign. The Moon, Jupiter, and Mars are in the nocturnal hemisphere. Despite being nocturnally placed, the Moon is in a masculine sign, which removes the possibility of its being in *hayz*. Jupiter, a masculine and diurnal planet, is in a nocturnal hemisphere and feminine sign, also contrary to *hayz*. Mars is in *hayz* because it is a nocturnal and masculine planet, located in a nocturnal hemisphere and in a masculine sign.

We will now compare the condition of *hayz* in a diurnal chart using the chart of mathematician Johannes Kepler.

Because Johannes Kepler's chart has the Sun above the horizon, the upper hemisphere is diurnal and the one below is nocturnal. In order to be in *hayz*, the diurnal planets must be above the horizon and in masculine signs; the nocturnal planets must be below the horizon and in feminine signs (except Mars, which must be in a masculine sign).

In the diurnal hemisphere are both lights as well as Mercury, Venus, and Jupiter. The Moon and Venus are automatically excluded because they are nocturnal planets. The Moon is contrary to condition because, in addition to being diurnal, is in a masculine sign. The Sun and Jupiter are masculine and diurnal, but are both located in feminine signs and are therefore also excluded from the possibility of *hayz*. This is true also for Mercury, which in this case is masculine (since it is oriental), but in a feminine sign.

In the nocturnal hemisphere are Saturn and Mars. Saturn is contrary to *hayz* because it is diurnal and masculine, but in a nocturnal, feminine sign. Mars is nocturnal and in a masculine sign, which agrees with its nocturnal, masculine nature, and therefore it is in *hayz*. Because it is also positioned in a masculine quadrant (conforming by quadrant), it reinforces the condition of *hayz*.

The condition of *hayz* gives stability to the expression of the planet. In the case of dignified planets, it reinforces their power; with debilitated planets, it slightly softens the debility, bringing greater coherence to its expression. *Hayz* imparts some instability to the planets, even to those that are dignified. In general terms, *hayz* can be compared to comfort or discomfort.

### *Dustoria* or Security

This is a very specific condition that encompasses within it many other conditions. In practical terms, it is rare that a planet has this configuration. When it occurs, it is considered a sign of fame and success. A planet is considered *dustoria* when it applies to all of the following conditions:

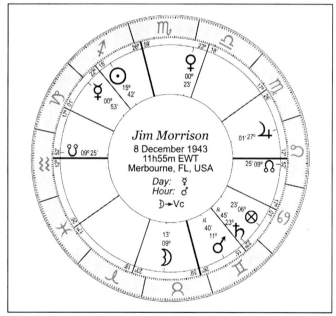

- *Hayz* (which is itself a composite condition).
- Posited in an angular house.
- Oriental to the Sun (in a diurnal chart) or occidental to the Moon (in a diurnal chart), with the luminary posited in an angular house, which forms a 90° angle to the house of the planet (in practice, this implies that the planet must be 10 houses away from the Sun and four houses away from the Moon).

This is a very complex condition, which explains its rarity.

In Jim Morrison's chart, Jupiter is in *dustoria*. In effect, Jupiter meets all of the requirements

**Chart 8. Nativity of Jim Morrison**

necessary for this condition. First, it is in *hayz* because it is a diurnal planet in a diurnal hemisphere and masculine sign; it is also **angular**, in the seventh house, and oriental to the Sun, which is the luminary of the hour. In turn, the Sun is also angular in the tenth house, located 90° from Jupiter's house (the seventh). Jupiter is a benefic planet, which makes this configuration a clear indicator of success and fame. The remaining interactions of the chart reinforce this configuration: the lights are strong, and there are important fixed stars conjunct Jupiter and the Midheaven.

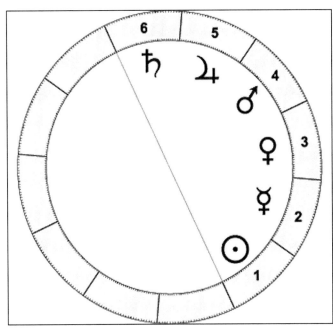

**Figure 23. Almugea to the Sun**

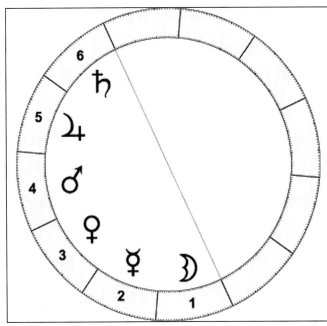

**Figure 24. Almugea to the Moon**

### Almugea (or Proper Face)

This accidental dignity derives from the position of the planets in relation to the Sun or Moon as dictated by the rulership scheme. Thus, whenever a planet is the same number of signs away from the Sun or the Moon as it is in the rulership scheme, it is said to be in a state of **almugea** or **proper face** (independently of the signs where they are posited). In order to be in almugea to the Sun, the planet must be in the signs following the Sun (in the order of the signs). The *almugea* to the Moon requires that the planet be in the signs before the Moon, that is, the almugea to the Sun occurs in one half of the zodiac and that of the Moon in the other half. The *almugea* of the Sun is more pertinent in a diurnal chart, and that of the Moon in a nocturnal chart.

- Mercury is in this state if it is in the sign preceding the Moon or in the sign following the Sun.
- Venus, if it is two signs before the Moon and two after the Sun.
- Mars, three signs before the Moon, and three after the Sun.
- Jupiter, four signs before the Moon, and four signs after the Sun.
- Saturn, five signs before the Moon and five after the Sun.

A planet in *almugea* is slightly strengthened in its expression because it is in its natural position relative to the light. For obvious reasons, the condition of *almugea* does not apply to the luminaries.

Note: The term "proper face," a synonym for *almugea*, should not be confused with "face" (or decanate), which refers to the divisions of the signs by 10 degrees.

### Example of Planets in Almugea

In the chart of Florbela Espanca, there is only one instance of *almugea*. Saturn is in *almugea* to the Moon because it is five signs before this luminary. This *almugea* will be particularly significant because this is a nocturnal birth. There are various examples of *almugea* to the Sun in the chart of Agatha Christie.

Mercury, Venus, and Mars are all in *almugea* because they are ahead of the Sun by the same number of signs as they are in the rulership scheme. Mercury is in the next sign, Venus is two signs ahead, and Mars is three signs ahead of the Sun. Nonetheless, since this is a night birth, the almugeas to the Sun are less relevant.

## Reconciling Apparently Contradictory Conditions

It is common to see horoscopes where there is an apparent contradiction between the dignities of a planet and its other conditions. In reality the contradiction does not exist because the various states of the planet are combined without negating each other. The dignities and debilities always indicate the quality of manifestation of a planet, while the other conditions serve to reinforce or diminish that basic tendency.

Let's look at two practice examples. In the horoscope of Florbela Espanca there are two dignified planets that are also in some debilitating conditions. Jupiter in Cancer is exalted and is the most elevated planet, which indicates a strong position. Nevertheless, it is also contrary to *hayz*, which weakens it a bit. How are these

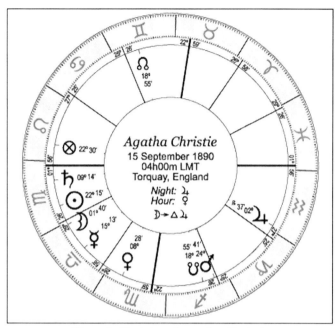

**Chart 2. Nativity of Agatha Christie**

conditions synthesized? In practice, the planet's exaltation and elevation would be enough to consider the planet strong because these are important conditions. The exaltation indicates ease of action, while the elevated state highlights the planet in the chart. The contrary condition of *hayz* indicates that despite all this strength the planet exhibits a degree of instability and discomfort in its expression. The horoscope suggests a good capacity for study (Jupiter is in the ninth house of study), which is hampered by instability and hesitation.

In the same horoscope, Mars is in a similar situation. It is in rulership, angular, and in *hayz*, but occidental. Occidentality does not remove its strength; it merely alters it, making it more introverted and discreet, less assertive and direct.

An inverse situation is found in Johannes Kepler's horoscope, in which a planet is debilitated but in conditions that fortify it. Mars is debilitated in Libra, but also oriental and in *hayz*. The debility of Mars indicates difficulties in the expression of assertiveness, but orientality imparts a more active and sharp tenor, while *hayz* stabilizes its overall expression, giving it more confidence. The debility does not disappear, but its expression is softened.

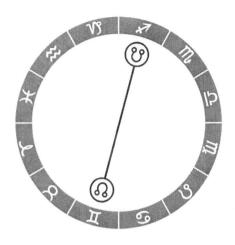

*Chapter XI*

# Lunar Nodes

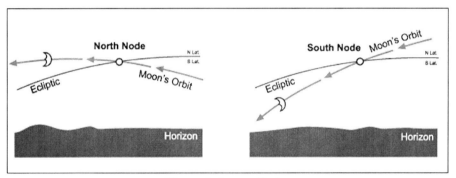

**Figure 1. Lunar Nodes**

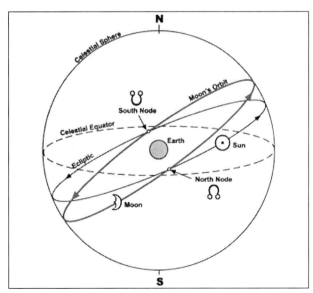

**Figure 2. Lunar Nodes in the Celestial Sphere**

The lunar Nodes are mathematical points, not celestial bodies. They derive from the intersection of the Moon's orbit with the ecliptic (the apparent course of the Sun around the Earth, which demarcates the zodiac), which occurs because the Moon's orbit has a five-degree offset from the ecliptic. This means that during half of its trajectory the Moon is north of the ecliptic (thus having north latitude) and during the other half, it is south of the ecliptic (having south latitude), thus coinciding with the ecliptic at two points (during which it is at 0° latitude). The point at which the Moon crosses the ecliptic moving from south to north is called the **North Node**; the opposite point, where it moves from north to south is called the **South Node**. The symbols of the Nodes are ☊ (North Node) and ☋ (South Node).

The movement of the Nodes in the zodiac is always retrograde. For each lunar cycle (a complete revolution of the Moon around the zodiac) the Nodes retrograde 1° 30′ of arc of the ecliptic. Their daily motion is about 3′ of arc, completing a cycle in a total of 18.6 years.

The significance of the lunar Nodes comes from their relationship to the eclipses. The Nodes mark the intersection points of the path of the Sun and the path of the Moon. At these points, the lights have 0° latitude and are in perfect alignment with Earth. Whenever the lights simultaneously also pass the Nodes, there is an eclipse. Because they imply the darkening of one of the lights (the Sun or Moon, depending on the kind of eclipse), the eclipses are considered disturbing phenomena of a celestial order. For this reason, the Nodes, which are the points where this occurs, become somewhat significant. The ancients designated the North Node to be the **Head of the Dragon** and the South Node, the **Tail of the Dragon**; in Latin, this is *Caput Draconis* and *Cauda Draconis*, respectively.

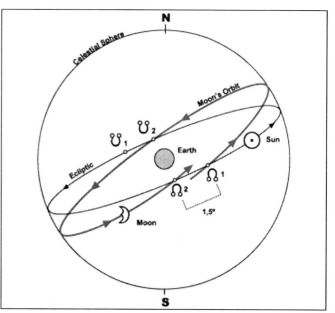

**Figure 3. Movement of the Nodes on the Ecliptic**

Because the Nodes are connected to the occurrence of eclipses, the Nodes represent areas of disturbance in the horoscope because they are believed to disturb the expression of any planet that is located near them. In chart interpretation, the North Node is looked upon more favorably than the South Node. The North Node is given a nature similar to the benefic planets (Jupiter and Venus) and is related to abundance and fertility. Therefore, when a planet is conjunct the North Node, its expression is amplified and its outcome depends upon the condition of that planet. On the other hand, the South Node is looked upon unfavorably. It partakes of the nature of the malefic planets (Saturn and Mars) and is thus connected to barrenness.

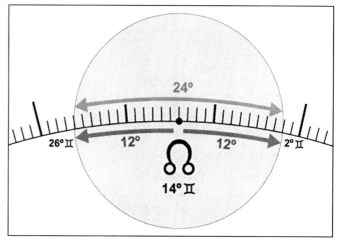

**Figure 4. Node's Orb of Influence**

Because they are not visible, the Nodes cannot form aspects nor be aspected (the word "aspect" means "to see"). For this reason, their delineation refers only to the conjunction of the planets to the Nodes, not to any of the other aspects. The orb of influence begins 12° before and extends to 12° after the Node.

**Interpretation of the Nodes**

In interpretation, it should be noted that the Nodes affect the signs and houses where they are placed. They represent increases and decreases of the matters of the houses where they are placed and they disturb the expression of the sign where they are located. The North Node brings with it a more positive alteration because it amplifies and bestows a degree of prosperity. Nevertheless, its benefits are rarely long-lasting and can imply some inconstancy. The South Node always represents a diminution or some type of alteration that damages the significations of the houses, signs, and planets. From this perspective, the North Node is considered a benefic and the South Node a malefic.

For example, in Nietzsche's horoscope the adventurous and enthusiastic behavior of the Sagittarius Moon is amplified by its conjunction to the North Node, which also adds a trace of instability to the moods of the phi-

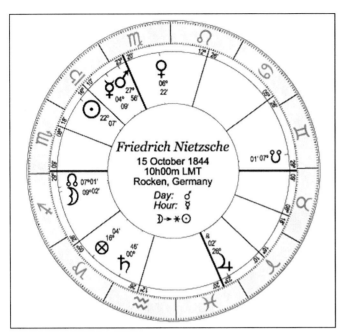

**Chart 1. Nativity of Friedrich Nietzsche**

**True Node and Mean Node**

In the tables of planetary motion, two types of Nodes are listed: the mean Node and the true Node, which are calculated using different formulas. The true Node is an astronomically exact point. Its calculation takes the Sun's gravitational interaction with the Moon into account. It exhibits some fluctuations in its motion and can be stationary or retrograde.

The Mean Node, as its name indicates, is a calculation of the average position of the Nodes. Since it does not take other gravitational interferences into account, it exhibits a regular retrograde motion. The difference between the true and mean Nodes is never greater than 2°.

losopher. In Agatha Christie's horoscope, there is a conjunction of the South Node with Mars. This configuration bestows a trace of abruptness and recklessness to the naturally passionate and adventurous actions of Mars in Sagittarius. The square between Mars and the lights also contributes to this attitude.

## The Exaltations of the Nodes

Because they are not planets, the Nodes do not rule signs of the zodiac. Nevertheless, the tradition does attribute to them places of exaltation and fall. The North Node is exalted in Gemini and has its fall in Sagittarius, the opposite sign. The South Node, in turn, is exalted in Sagittarius and in fall in Gemini. These attributions are of little practical use because the Nodes never function as rulers of houses or dispositors. They indicate, if anything, a difference in the intensity of the nodal effects.

Traditional authors explain this attribution by stating that the North Node, by virtue of its dual nature (Jupiter and Venus combined), has its exaltation in the first dual sign of the zodiac, Gemini. The South Node, its opposite, and also of a dual nature (Saturn and Mars), is exalted in the opposite dual sign Sagittarius.

# Eclipses

An eclipse occurs whenever a lunation occurs in the proximity of the Nodes. It is only at these points that the paths of the Sun and Moon cross, giving rise to a perfect alignment between the Sun, Moon, and Earth. It is this alignment that causes an eclipse. There are two types of eclipses: solar and lunar.

## Solar Eclipse

The solar eclipse occurs during a new Moon when the Moon passes between the Sun and Earth, obscuring the solar disc.

A solar eclipse always results when the New Moon occurs at fewer than 18° from one of the Nodes; the closer the lights are to the Nodes, the more complete will be the occultation. Thus, a solar eclipse may have several degrees of intensity:

- A total eclipse, when it occurs very close to the Node and the Moon completely covers the Sun.
- A partial eclipse, when the lunation occurs a bit farther from the Node and the Moon covers only a portion of the Sun.
- An annular eclipse, a special case, when the

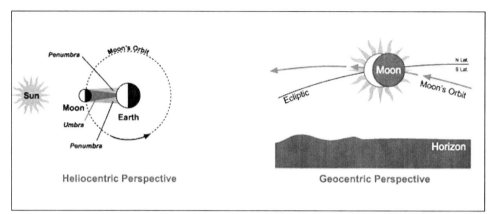

**Figure 5. Solar Eclipse**

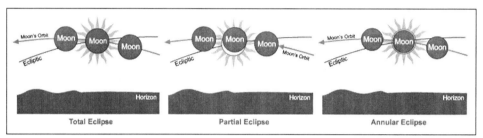

**Figure 6. The Three Types of Solar Elipse**

Moon is farther from the Earth; here, its apparent diameter covers only the central portion of the Sun, leaving visible the outer perimeter of the solar disc, which forms a "ring of light."

Because the Moon is smaller than Earth, its shadow reaches only some parts of the globe. For this reason, eclipses are only visible in certain regions or countries. On the other hand, because Earth rotates on its axis, and the Moon is also in motion, the shadow projected from the Moon traces a path along the terrestrial globe. The path of the eclipse traces the areas where the occultation is visible in its greatest intensity.

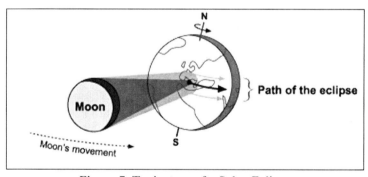

**Figure 7. Trajectory of a Solar Eclipse**

## Lunar Eclipses

A lunar eclipse occurs during a Full Moon, when Earth projects its shadow on the Moon and occults it.

A lunar eclipse always results when a Full Moon occurs less than 12° 30′ from one of the Nodes. There are three kinds of lunar eclipses:

- Total eclipse, when the Moon completely crosses the shadow of the Earth.

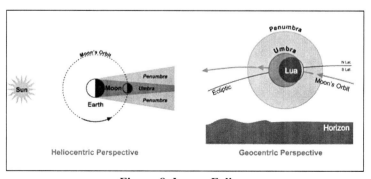

**Figure 8. Lunar Eclipse**

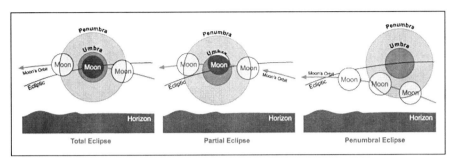

**Figure 9. The Three Kinds of Lunar Eclipse**

- Partial eclipse, when the Moon partially crosses the shadow of the Earth.
- Penumbral eclipse, when the Moon merely crosses the penumbra (these are not considered in astrology because they are not visible to a terrestrial observer.

Lunar eclipses can be observed in any part of the globe as long as the Full Moon is above the horizon (regions where it is nighttime).

**Periodicity of Eclipses**

Every year there are at least four eclipses, two solar and two lunar. The solar eclipses correspond to the two New Moons that occur close to the Nodes, one conjunct the North Node and the other conjunct the South Node. Lunar eclipses correspond to the two Full Moons that occur together with each of the Nodes. The four annual eclipses thus occur at opposite points of the zodiac.

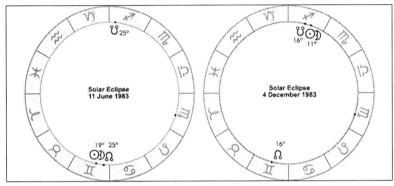

**Figure 10. The Four Eclipses Occurring Every Year**

For example, in 1983, there were four eclipses. The first was a solar eclipse at 19° Gemini on June 11; the eclipse took place close to the North Node, which on that date was at 25° Gemini. Six months later, on December 4, there was another solar eclipse, this time at 11° Sagittarius (conjunct the South Node, which was at 16° Gemini).

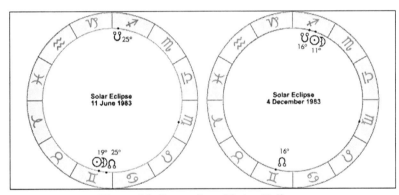

**Figure 11. Examples of Solar Eclipses**

The first lunar eclipse occurred June 25 (on the Full Moon following the first solar eclipse). The Moon was at 3° Capricorn (with the Sun at 3° Cancer) and the Nodes were at 24° Gemini-Sagittarius. Because the distance

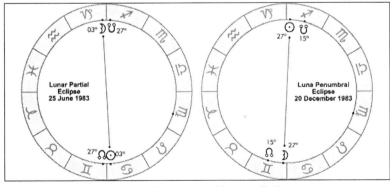

**Figure 12. Examples of Lunar Eclipses**

between the lights and the Nodes was less than 12°, a partial lunar eclipse still took place. Six months later, on December 20 (on the Full Moon that followed the second solar eclipse) there was a second eclipse of the Moon. Because it was at 27° Gemini and the Nodes were at 15° Gemini-Sagittarius (exactly on the 12° limit), the eclipse was merely penumbral; the Moon never touched the shadow of the Earth.

We thus see that eclipses occur in pairs: each occultation of the Sun is associated with an occultation of the Moon. In the previous example, a solar eclipse was followed by a lunar one 14 days later. Six months later, the sequence repeated on the other side of the zodiac. The 14 or 15 day gap is obviously tied to the lunar cycle: it is the time between the New Moon and Full Moon. In this example, the solar eclipses preceded the lunar ones, but in other cases, the reverse occured. The order depends upon the relative positions of the lunations and Nodes. More than four eclipses per year can take place. This happens when the distance between the lights and the Nodes allows for a fifth eclipse.

Figure 13. Symbols of the Eclipses

In the tables of planetary motion the eclipses are often indicated by a shaded conjunction symbol (solar eclipse) and an opposition symbol (lunar eclipse). The solar eclipse symbol is also used to symbolize the occultation of another planet by conjunction.

**Interpreting Eclipses**

Because they involve the temporary disappearance of one of the luminaries (sources of life and light), eclipses are sometimes looked upon with apprehension, and by some, as omens of disaster. Nevertheless, their astrological interpretation is not necessarily catastrophic. Eclipses have a particular relevance in the context of mundane astrology. They signal points of reversals and sudden change, particularly at the social and political levels. The impact of the eclipse is principally borne out in the regions of the world where it is visible.

In mundane astrology, only visible eclipses are considered. In the case of solar eclipses, only those visible at the location under study are considered. The same applies to lunar eclipses. In horary, the penumbral eclipses are not considered because they are not visible to a human observer. The kind of eclipse (solar or lunar) suggests different things. Lunar eclipses are associated with events of short duration (in the order of months) and rapid change, while solar elipses are related to more noticeable changes of longer duration (in the order of years). A deeper astrological interpretation of an eclipse follows very specific rules whose explanation is beyond the scope of this book.

**Planetary Nodes**

Just like the Moon, the planets also have planetary nodes. They correspond to the points where the apparent path of the planet crosses the ecliptic and there is a change in latitude. Due to the geocentric perspective, the nodes of the five planets do not correspond to two opposing points. For example, the Nodes of Mercury, just like the planet, never drift more than 28° from the Sun. The planetary nodes are not a part of the classical interpretative system; they are merely used as astronomical references in the evaluation of the planet's latitude; they serve to determine if a planet is moving toward a north or south latitude. Its interpretive value, if any, is still to be determined.

Currently many astrologers use the heliocentric planetary nodes because they are more consistent over time, and similar to the lunar Nodes, correspond to exactly opposite points. However, this practice mixes two different systems: the geocentric system, which is the basis for astrology, and the heliocentric coordinate system, whose nature is astronomical. Its validity is therefore debatable.

*Chapter XII*
# Fixed Stars

The designation "fixed star" is attributed to all of the visible stars. As groups, the stars form the constellations and constitute the background upon which the planets move. They are called "fixed" because their relative position to each other is constant. The fixed stars are part of the firmament, the highest of the celestial spheres. They are located beyond the planetary spheres, which, in a horoscope, makes them function at a different level from the planets. Because they are fixed and immutable, they transmit their qualities to any planet (or chart factor) that is conjunct one of them.

Whenever a planet is conjunct a fixed star, its action is strengthened and it acquires characteristics that are not defined by any other configuration in the chart. Each star imparts very specific characteristics. Those of a beneficial nature impart honors, fame and success, while others of more negative symbolism, disturb the vitality of a planet. The stars of greater magnitude are more potent in their effect; those of a lesser intensity merely add secondary shadings to the interpretation.

While powerful, the effects of the fixed stars are actually shaped by other chart factors. Since their power is carried by the planets, they can only effectively transmit their characteristics if these same characteristics are corroborated by the chart itself; without this reinforcement their efficacy is weak. For example, if a star promises fame and honors, but there is no configuration in the chart to support this tendency, the most likely scenario is that this fame will not manifest, or if it does, that it will not endure. Without the support of the planets, which move within the intermediary spheres, the action of the fixed stars cannot "descend to Earth."

### Nature of the Fixed Stars
Each star is unique; its particular nature derives from visible characteristics (brightness, intensity, and color) and from the symbolism of the constellation to which it belongs. Nonetheless, it is possible to associate with each star one or two planets whose natures are similar to the characteristics of the star. This association serves as an interpretive guideline for the fixed stars, allowing us to group them under a common planetary theme so that we may understand their general meaning. The stars associated with the same planet thus share the same general effects. When more than one planet defines the nature of the star, one should pay particular attention to the one mentioned first because this planet will define the principal characteristics, while the other adds a secondary theme.

**Stars associated with Saturn signify**: jealousies, greed, work, struggles, falls, imprisonment, poverty, and meanness; nevertheless, if they are conjunct beneficial planets, this effect is negated, making the meaning about serious thoughts, inheritances and sobriety.

**Saturn-Jupiter**: mental ability; the capacity to judge, magnanimity, and some form of riches.

**Saturn-Mars**: betrayal, talkativeness, aggression, confrontations, precipitations, cruelty and torture.

**Saturn-Venus**: envy, slander, jealousy, loneliness, greed, shameful actions, mediocrity.

**Saturn-Mercury**: studiousness, profound intellect, if poorly configured, they indicate slander, betrayals, and theft.

**Stars associated with Jupiter signify**: good manners, justice, modesty, faith, magnanimity, piety, honors and riches.

**Jupiter-Mars**: the capacity for command and conquest, a taste for grand actions, daring, competitiveness, great accomplishments, does not like mediocrity. Although fortunate, this combination can also indicate aggression and obstinacy.

**Jupiter-Venus**: physical beauty, honesty, piety, justice, fidelity, liberty, honors and riches from friends, or relationships with women.

**Jupiter-Mercury**: favorable for teaching and administration, ingenuity, knowledge of languages, good spoken and verbal expression.

**Stars associated with Mars signify**: aggression, fights, violence and dangers, can indicate losses, assassinations, injuries; if favorably configured, they bestow honors from activities of a martial nature.

**Mars-Sun**: daring, bellicosity, leadership, difficulty with authority, when poorly configured, they can signify cruelty and danger by fire.

**Mars-Venus**: unexpected luck, inheritances and riches if configured to benefics, otherwise, it is associated with desires, passions, and luxury.

**Mars-Mercury**: lively and daring spirit, but colored by rage, irritability, and a lack of patience, associated with spying, treason, and swindling.

**Mars-Moon**: violence, poverty, hard work, misery; propensity for drink, associated with travel and exile.

**Stars associated with Venus signify**: beauty, grace, harmony, artistic sensibility, sociability.

**Venus-Mercury**: ingenuity, talent, charm, softness, subtlety, artistic talent and goodness.

**Stars associated with Mercury signify**: intellect and capacity for learning, fortune and success through trade, books, and intellectual activities.

In traditional astrology there are no cases of stars associated with the Sun and Moon, nor with the combinations Saturn-Sun, Saturn-Moon, Jupiter-Sun, Jupiter-Moon, Venus-Moon and Mercury-Moon. These combinations only appear in the works of more recent authors (19th and 20th centuries).

## Principal Fixed Stars

The positions and characteristics of the fixed stars most commonly used in the tradition are presented here, with the positions indicated for 2000. At the end of this chapter is a more complete list of fixed stars, their positions, and characteristics.

**Algenib**: Pegasus' wing (09° Aries 09'). Of the nature of Mars and Mercury; favors notoriety, although it can also bring dishonor and violence.

**Alpheratz**: The head of Andromeda (14° Aries18'). Of the nature of Jupiter and Venus; bestows honor and abundance. It is associated with independence and liberty.

**Algol**: The head of Medusa (26° Taurus 10'). It is the most malefic star in the sky. Imparts instability, stubbornness, and violence. Commonly used in elective astrology to obtain victory in battle. It is of the nature of Saturn and Jupiter combined.

**The Pleiades**: The shoulder of the Bull/the seven sisters (01° Gemini 00'). Of the nature of the Moon and Mars; associated with ambition, greed, and turbulence.

**Aldebaran**: The southern eye of the Bull (09° Gemini 47'). Intelligence, eloquence, integrity, popularity and courage, but also ferocity and revolt; can lead to the loss of honor and benefits. Of the nature of Mars.

**Rigel**: Orion's left foot (16° Gemini 50'). Bestows renown, honor, and glory. Also associated with ingenuity and inventiveness. Of the nature of Jupiter and Saturn.

**Capella**: The little goat (21° Gemini 51'). Of the nature of Mars and Mercury combined. Courage, inquiring spirit (sometimes sarcastic), love of novelty. Riches and renown, sometimes accompanied by envy.

**Betelgeuse**: Orion's right shoulder (28° Gemini 45'). It is one of the most beneficial stars in the sky. Of the nature of Mars and Mercury; promises honor and prosperity, but can also indicate some instability.

**Sirius**: The mouth of the great dog (dog-star) (14° Cancer 05'). Considered very beneficial, bestows great honor, renown and riches. It is above all associated with fidelity and devotion. Because it is of the nature of Jupiter and Mars, it can indicate petulance, boldness, and pride.

**Canopus**: The ship's captain (the Argo) (14° Cancer 58'). Bestows dignity, religiosity and knowledge. Star of the nature of Saturn and Jupiter; frequently associated with travels.

**Castor**: The northern Twin (the mortal twin) (20° Cancer 15'). Of the nature of Mercury; bestows acute intellect; the law and publications can bring success, although it is not always durable.

**Pollux**: the southern Twin (the immortal twin) (23° Cancer 13'). Of the nature of Mars; indicates an inventive and daring spirit, but with a tendency toward impatience and even cruelty.

**Procyon**: The little dog (25° Cancer 48'). Provocative behavior, petulant and prideful, but expressed in a tentative and timid manner. Of the nature of Mercury and Mars.

**Asellus Borealis** and **Asellus Australis**: The northern and southern donkeys (07° Leo 32' and 08° Leo 43'). Stars of the nature of Mars and the Sun. They indicate generosity and courage, but also danger of violence and accidents. Traditionally tied to eyesight problems.

**Alphard**: The heart of the Hydra (27° Leo 17'). Of the nature of Saturn and Venus; bestows wisdom and artistic gifts, which are hindered by strong passions and excesses.

**Regulus**: The heart of the Lion (29° Leo 50'). Honor, magnanimity, and desire for power; if misused, can lead to violence and destruction. Of the nature of Mars and Jupiter.

**Denebola**: The tail of the Lion (21° Virgo 37'). Bestows nobility and good judgment. Nonetheless, it is frequently associated with despair, regret, and anxiety. Of the nature of Saturn and Venus.

**Algorab**: The crow's right wing (13° Libra 27'). Of the nature of Mars and Saturn; bestows malevolence, destructiveness, lies and slander.

**Spica**: The sheaf of wheat (23° Libra 51'). Beneficial star, bestows renown, riches, love of art and science. Of the nature of Venus and Mars.

**Arcturus**: The knee of the herdsman (24° Libra 15'). Of a nature similar to Mars and Venus. Indicates great determination, honor and renown, but also anxiety and extravagance.

**Alphecca**: the most brilliant jewel in the crown (12° Scorpio 18'). Star of the nature of Venus and Mercury; bestows brilliance and honor. It is associated with poetic and artistic talents.

**Zuben Elgenubi**: The southern claw/the southern scale (15° Scorpio 05'). Malefic tied to betrayals and poisonings. Of the nature of Saturn and Mars, indicating difficulty forgiving.

**Zuben Elschemali**: The northern claw/the northern scale (19° Scorpio 22'). Benefic, tied to fortune, honor and happiness. Of the nature of Jupiter and Mercury.

**Unukalhai**: The head (or the heart) of the Serpent (22° Scorpio 04′). Malefic star, of the nature of Saturn and Mars. It is tied to intrigue, jealousy, and accidents.

**Agena**: The right leg of the Centaur (23° Scorpio 48′). Of the nature of Venus and Jupiter; this star bestows good health, honor, friends, and refinement.

**Rigel Centaurus**: The foot of the Centaur (29° Scorpio 32′). Beneficence, friends and positions of honor. Of the nature of Venus and Jupiter; it bestows refinement.

**Antares**: The heart of the Scorpion (09° Sagittarius 46′). Of the nature of Mars and Jupiter; it bestows liberty and impatience, which easily turn to stubbornness and destructiveness.

**Lesath**: The sting of the Scorpion (24° Sagittarius 01′). Malefic star of the nature of Mercury and Mars. It indicates malevolence, envy, and a sharp tongue.

**Facies**: The face of the Archer (08° Capricorn 18′). Of the nature of the Sun and Mars. It is related to eye problems and accidents.

**Vega**: Handle of the lyre (15° Capricorn 19′). Benefits, idealism, and hope; colored by a certain sobriety. Of the nature of Venus and Mercury.

**Altair**: The eagle (01° Aquarius 46′). Of the nature of Mars and Jupiter; it is associated with daring, confidence and bravery. Abrupt fortune but of short duration. Excessive daring may lead to excess and violence.

**Deneb Algedi**: The tail of the goat (23° Aquarius 32′). Star of the nature of Saturn and Jupiter; bestows ambiguous gifts. It can either be a carrier of success or of misfortune. Imparts honors and dignity, but always with great effort and struggle.

**Formalhaut**: The mouth of the southern fish (03° Pisces 51′). Benefic star; of the nature of Venus and Mercury. Bestows great honors, but there is always the danger of corruption.

**Deneb Adige**: The tail of the swan (05° Pisces 20′). Of the nature of Venus and Mercury; it bestows an ingenious nature, lively intellect, and ease of learning.

**Achernar**: The end of the river (15° Pisces 19′). Benefic star of the nature of Jupiter. Bestows honors and good fortune, inclines toward religion and charity.

The above list contains general indications about the signification of the stars. For more detail, see *The Fixed Stars and Constellations* by Vivian Robson (see recommended bibliography).

### Movement of the Fixed Stars

Due to the precession of the equinoxes, the fixed stars travel about one degree of longitude in the zodiac every 72 years. This can be seen in the table presented here by comparing the star positions for 1900, 1950, and 2000. Due to this movement, the stars of a given constellation may actually be located in the following sign, depending upon the date used. For example, Spica, of the Virgo constellation, is currently situated in Libra. Antares, the heart of the Scorpion, is currently in Sagittarius. This means that the current positions are very different from those of the past. When dealing with ancient charts, one must calculate the necessary adjustments to determine the position of the fixed stars for the date under study. If we know that a star moves one degree every 72 years, we can conclude that in one year it has moved 50 seconds. This ratio permits a very approximated position.

For example, in 2000, Antares was at 09° Sagittarius 46′. From this information, the approximate position of Antares in the chart of Nietzsche, who was born in 1844, can be calculated. Since his birth, 156 years have passed. To determine the distance the star traveled during this time, simply divide 156 by 72 (the number of years that the star takes to travel 1°), giving 2.17. Then convert the decimal into minutes of arc (0.17 x 60 = 10.2 – approximately, 10 minutes of arc). This star, at its recalculated position, was 2°10′ from the 2000 position, or at 7°36′ of Sagittarius.

## Fixed Stars in the Horoscope

Before interpreting the fixed stars of a horoscope, one must make a selection of the most relevant stars from all of those in the sky. (An attempt to use all of the hundreds of stars in existence is impractical.) There are two criteria for this selection or filtering process: its **magnitude** (brightness) and its **proximity to the ecliptic.** The magnitude of each star depends upon its visibility and brightness. In accordance with these criteria, the stars are classified by a **magnitude scale**. The brightest and most visible stars are considered to be of the 1st magnitude. These are the stars that stand out in the night sky and are visible even when seen through the light pollution of a city. The remaining stars gradually diminish in brightness until the 6th magnitude of the scale; the stars that are the most faint to human eyes are included in this last group.[26]

Note: Technically, the fixed stars are not really fixed. The passage of time alters not only their position in the zodiac but their distances relative to one another. Besides the shift caused by precession of the equinoxes, each star also has its own motion, which leads to a gradual alteration of the shape of the constellations. This alteration takes thousands of years to become apparent since the motion is extremely slow. In astrological practice, the individual motion of each star is not very relevant.

In interpretation, the stars of 1st magnitude are those that produce the most intense effects. Those of the 2nd and 3rd magnitude also produce noticeable effects, but the remaining fainter stars are not much considered. The smallest and least visible stars are generally used in very specific interpretations (for example, in medical questions). As to distance, priority is given to the stars that belong to the 12 zodiacal constellations, or that, although they belong to other constellations, are close to the ecliptic.[27] The reason for this selection has to do with the movement of the planets and lights because priority is given to the stars that are situated within the zodiacal band where the planets circulate. The others are of minor importance.

With a few exceptions, the list presented earlier contains only stars of 1st and 2nd magnitude that are situated close to the ecliptic.

## Interpreting the Fixed Stars

The stars function only by conjunction. The other aspects are not relevant to the astrological interpretation of stars. Because they are luminous objects, the stars possess an orb, just like the planets. In a conjunction between a star and a planet, the only orb to keep in mind is that of the star, never the orb of the planet. This is because the star is found in a celestial sphere superior to that of the planets and is thus hierarchically superior.

The orbs used in these conjunctions vary according to the magnitude of the star; the orb of the planet or of the luminary has no bearing. Following are the orbs for fixed stars:

| Star's magnitude | Orb (radius) |
|---|---|
| 1st Magnitude | 7°30′ |
| 2nd Magnitude | 5°30′ |
| 3rd Magnitude | 3°30′ |
| 4th Magnitude | 1°30′ |

---

[26]This is the traditional scale, which is based upon visibility. A more recent scientific scale is used in astronomy to catalogue the brightness of celestial bodies. Although it does not have much use in astrological interpretation, it is this scale that is normally presented in a great majority of astrological software and books.

[27]Some contemporary astrologers argue that the latitude of a star has no significance and include in their interpretations stars which are very distant from the ecliptic, such as Ursa Major and Minor and Draco. Recently, stars visible in the southern hemisphere (which are not a part of the original tradition) have also been included. Their astrological validity remains to be defined.

A conjunction takes place the moment the body of the planet comes into contact with the orb of the star. When stars of a lesser magnitude are used, the conjunction should be very exact (about 30'). Although the stars of 1st and 2nd magnitude possess large orbs, their influence will be that much more emphasized the greater the proximity of the planet is to the star. A conjunction of a planet or angle at the edge of the star's orb, is considered to be weak and not very relevant. The student should evaluate these factors before interpreting. A star of a 1st magnitude can override the influences of 2nd and 3rd magnitude stars, but not negate them, particularly if the stars of a lesser magnitude are closer to the planet.

In practice, only the stars that are conjunct important points, namely the planets, the lights, and the angles (particularly the Ascendant and Midheaven) are considered in a chart. In interpretation, one must add the theme of the star to the characteristics of the planet. If the nature of the star coincides with that of the planet, the effects reinforce each other, making them more obvious. For example, Regulus has a nature similar to Mars and Jupiter combined; if in a chart, it is conjunct Mars, it combines its martial nature with that of the actual planet, intensifying its bellicose and domineering nature; the Jupiter undertone adds grandiosity to it. On the other hand, if Regulus is conjunct a planet that does not share its nature, this reinforcement does not take place. If the conjunction is with Venus, for example, the martial and jovial nature of the star is simply added to the planet, which therefore adds to the sociable and easy-going nature of Venus a touch of assertiveness (Mars) and magnanimity (Jupiter).

*Fixed Stars Example*
There are several relevant fixed stars in Frederick Nietzsche's chart.

In the Ascendant is Dschuba, a star of 2nd magnitude of the nature of Mars and Saturn. This star contributes an aggressive and talkative behavior, adding a tendency toward confrontation with others. Also in the first house is a conjunction of the Moon and Antares, a star of the 1st magnitude of the nature of Mars and Jupiter. This combination adds a domineering and confident attitude to the expansiveness and versatility of the Moon in Sagittarius. Antares also bestows great mental breadth, love of philosophy, popularity, and power. Because the possibility of loss is also present in every star of great power, in this case it would manifest through overinflated, extravagant actions.

Note that the Sun, the other light, is closely conjunct the fixed star Arcturus, also of 1st magnitude, and of the nature of Jupiter and Mars. This star bestows success and fame, but since the Sun is in fall in Libra, the fame promised by the star is affected by arrogance and egocentrism (negative expressions of a debilitated Sun).

When this information is combined with that of Moon-Antares, a clear influence of Jupiter and Mars is detected. This combination indicates fame and recognition (luminaries strengthened by stars of the 1st magnitude), but also contains the possibility of excess. Continuing a bit further with this interpretation, we note that Mars and Jupiter (which define the nature of these stars) are the most angular planets of this chart. This angularity reinforces a promise of popularity and notoriety suggested by the stars, but because there is a tense aspect (opposition) be-

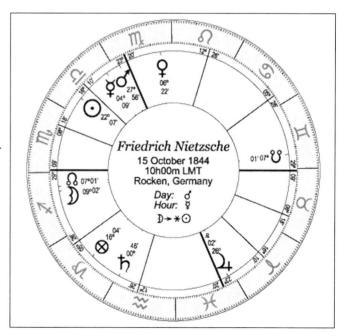

**Chart 1. Nativity of Friedrich Nietzsche**

tween the planets, the possibility of loss is also reinforced. We thus have an indication of fame shadowed by restless, unreflective behavior.

Note also that not only the Midheaven and Mars but also the IC and Jupiter are conjunct stars of the nature of Mercury and Mars, which are in the tenth house (Zavijava on the Midheaven; Markab and Scheat on the IC). This combination imparts argumentation, critical thinking and audacity, which will be projected onto both the career and the public image of this philosopher. All of this is reinforced by the position of Mercury and Mars in the tenth house.

| Name | Location | Nature |
|---|---|---|
| Andromeda, *the chained woman* | 13°♈ – 29°♉ | ♀ |
| Aries, *the ram* | 19°♈ – 21°♉ | *Zodiacal* |
| Cassiopeia, *the enthroned queen* | 26°♈ – 01°♊ | ♄ ♀ |
| Triangulum, *o triangle* | 05°♉ – 14°♉ | ☿ |
| Taurus, *the bull* | 16°♉ – 24°♊ | *Zodiacal* |
| Perseus, *the warrior* | 13°♉ – 09°♊ | ♃ ♄ |
| Lepus, *the hare* | 06°♊ – 04°♋ | ♄ ☿ |
| Orion, *the hunter* | 07°♊ – 03°♋ | ♃ ♄ |
| Auriga, *the charioteer* | 11°♊ – 04°♋ | ♂ ☿ |
| Ursa Minor, *the greater bear* | 00°♋ – 08°♍ | ♄ ♀ |
| Canis Major, *the greater dog* | 01°♋ – 01°♌ | ♀ |
| Gemini, *the twin* | 02°♋ – 24°♋ | *Zodiacal* |
| Argo Navis, *the ship* | 11°♋ – 21°♎ | ♄ ♃ |
| Canis Minor, *the lesser dog* | 19°♋ – 29°♋ | ☿ ♂ |
| Cancer, *the crab* | 23°♋ – 17°♌ | *Zodiacal* |
| Hydra, *the water serpent* | 06°♌ – 24°♏ | ♄ ♀ |
| Leo, *the lion* | 13°♌ – 23°♍ | *Zodiacal* |
| Crater, *the cup* | 14°♍ – 04°♎ | ♀ ☿ |
| Coma Berenices, *Berenice's Hair* | 18°♍ – 13°♎ | ☽ ♀ |
| Virgo, *the virgen* | 23°♍ – 06°♏ | *Zodiacal* |
| Bootes, *the herdsman* | 28°♍ – 08°♏ | ☿ ♄ |
| Centaurus, *the centaur* | 03°♎ – 29°♏ | ♀ ☿ ♃ |
| Corvus, *the raven* | 06°♎ – 16°♎ | ♂ ♄ |
| Hercules, *the kneeled man* | 29°♎ – 03°♑ | ☿ |
| Corona Borealis, *the northern crown* | 03°♏ – 18°♏ | ♀ ☿ |
| Libra, *the scales* | 08°♏ – 29°♏ | *Zodiacal* |
| Serpens, *the serpent* | 14°♏ – 16°♑ | ♄ ♂ |
| Lupus, *the wolf* | 16°♏ – 08°♐ | ♄ ♂ |
| Scorpius, *the scorpion* | 24°♏ – 27°♐ | *Zodiacal* |
| Ophiuchus, *the serpent-holder* | 28°♏ – 28°♐ | ♄ ♀ |
| Ara, *the altar* | 11°♐ – 01°♑ | ♀ ☿ |
| Sagittarius, *the archer* | 28°♐ – 02°♒ | *Zodiacal* |
| Corona Australis, *the southern crown* | 03°♑ – 13°♑ | ♄ ☿ |
| Lyra, *the harp* | 11°♑ – 00°♒ | ♀ ☿ |
| Ursa Major, *the greater bear* | 11°♑ – 28°♍ | ♂ |
| Aquila, *the eagle* | 13°♑ – 16°♒ | ♂ ♃ |
| Sagitta, *the arrow* | 18°♑ – 10°♒ | ♂ ♀ |
| Capricornus, *the water goat* | 26°♑ – 23°♒ | *Zodiacal* |
| Delphinus, *the dolphin* | 09°♒ – 20°♒ | ♄ ♂ |
| Aquarius, *the water-bearer* | 10°♒ – 27°♓ | *Zodiacal* |
| Pisces Australis, *the southern fish* | 16°♒ – 06°♓ | ♀ ☿ |
| Cygnus, *the swan* | 23°♒ – 27°♓ | ♀ ☿ |
| Pegasus, *the winged horse* | 28°♒ – 11°♈ | ♂ ☿ |
| Pisces, *the fishes* | 16°♓ – 27°♈ | *Zodiacal* |
| Eridanus, *the river* | 16°♓ – 01°♊ | ♄ |
| Cetus, *the sea monster* | 18°♓ – 14°♉ | ♄ |
| Cepheus, *the king* | 18°♓ – 01°♋ | ♄ ♃ |
| Draco, *the dragon* | *Circumpolar* | ♄ ♂ ♃ |

**Figure 1. Constellations and Their Nature**

A study of the tormented life of Nietzsche mirrors the behaviors indicated by the configurations seen in his chart. This interpretation is a good example of the interaction between the fixed stars and the horoscope because since it clearly demonstrates how the influence of the fixed stars is corroborated by the configurations of the chart, reinforcing the effects of the planets.

## Constellations

The actual constellations can also be an integral part of interpretation. Their use emerges primarily in the context of mundane astrology, particularly in the interpretation of comets, but also in meteorological forecasts. The table presented here indicates the approximated positions of the traditional constellations in the tropical zodiac for 2000. Just as with the fixed stars, the constellations are also associated with planets that reflect their nature. In the case of the 12 zodiacal constellations, we've omitted the planetary correlate because no single planet uniformly correlates with all the stars of each constellation. For a more detailed discussion of the influence of each constellation, see *The Fixed Stars and Constellations* by Vivian Robson.

Note that in many cases the brightest star of the constellation possesses a nature different from the others and from the group as a whole. This is due to the particular character given to the stars of greater magnitude and visibility. Thus, for example, the constellation of Orion is primarily composed of stars of a Jupiter and Saturn nature. This is also the nature attributed to the constellation as a whole. Nevertheless, its two brightest stars, Betelgeuse and Bellatrix, are of a Mars and Mercury nature.

## Parans

The term paran is an abbreviation of the Greek term *paranatellonta* and means "to rise simultaneously." In an astrological context, two stars are considered to be paranatellonta when they coincide at the angles, such as when a star rises in the east (on the Ascendant) while another culminates (on the Midheaven) or sets in the west (on the Descendant).

The concept of paran is, above all, used in astrological/astronomical observation to compensate for a possible lack of visibility. If an observer knows that the rising of star A corresponds to the position of star B, then whenever star B is seen, the observer knows immediately that star A is rising, even when the meteorological or geographical conditions do not allow for a direct observation of the heavens. Another practical application of the parans is in meteorological forecasting. The stars that rise and set at the same time as the Sun (or the planets) are interpreted in terms of climatological changes. For example, when the eye of the Bull (Aldebaran) rises with the Sun, "it brings rain and wind and sometimes thunder." Note that Aldebaran is a star of the nature of Mars, which is why it is associated with bad weather.

Some contemporary authors defend that the concept of parans contributes to the construction of the celestial mythology. They affirm that the simultaneous rising of a particular celestial figure and the culmination of another gives rise to a series of associations of a symbolic nature.

## Fixed Stars and their Nature

| Name and planetary nature | | Mag. | Zodiacal Longitude | | | | Constellation |
|---|---|---|---|---|---|---|---|
| | | | 1900 | 1950 | 2000 | 2050 | |
| Deneb Kaitos – the tail of the whale | ♄ | 2 | 01°♈11' | 01°♈53' | 02°♈35' | 03°♈17' | Cetus |
| Algenib – the tip of Pegasus wing | ♂ ☿ | 3 | 07°♈46' | 08°♈28' | 09°♈09' | 09°♈51' | Pegasus |
| Alpheratz – the head of Andromeda | ♀ | 2 | 12°♈55' | 13°♈37' | 14°♈18' | 15°♈00' | Andromeda |
| Baten Kaitos – the belly of the wale | ♄ | 4 | 20°♈33' | 21°♈15' | 21°♈57' | 22°♈39' | Cetus |
| Al Pherg – of the tale of the fish | ♄ ♃ | 4 | 25°♈26' | 26°♈07' | 26°♈49' | 27°♈30' | Pisces |
| Vertex – of Andromeda's head (Galaxy) | ♀ | 5 | 26°♈28' | 27°♈09' | 27°♈51' | 28°♈33' | Andromeda |
| Mirach – of Andromeda's chain | ♀ | 2 | 29°♈01' | 29°♈42' | 00°♉24' | 01°♉06' | Andromeda |
| Mira – of the wale | ♄ | 3 | 00°♉07' | 00°♉49' | 01°♉31' | 02°♉13' | Cetus |
| Sheratan – the northern horn of Aries | ♂ ♄ | 3 | 02°♉34' | 03°♉16' | 03°♉58' | 04°♉40' | Aries |
| Hamal – the head of Aries | ♂ ♄ | 2 | 06°♉16' | 06°♉58' | 07°♉40' | 08°♉22' | Aries |
| Schedar – of Cassiopeia | ♄ ♀ | 2 | 06°♉24' | 07°♉05' | 07°♉47' | 08°♉29' | Cassiopeia |
| Almak – the left foot of Andromeda | ♀ | 2 | 12°♉50' | 13°♉32' | 14°♉13' | 14°♉55' | Andromeda |
| Menkar – the jaw of the wale | ♄ | 3 | 12°♉55' | 13°♉37' | 14°♉19' | 15°♉01' | Whale |
| Zaurak – of the river Eridanus | ♄ | 3 | 22°♉28' | 23°♉10' | 23°♉52' | 24°♉34' | Eridanus |
| Capulus – of Perseus' sword (Cluster) | ♂ ☿ | 4 | 22°♉49' | 23°♉30' | 24°♉12' | 24°♉54' | Perseus |
| Algol – the head of Medusa | ♄ ♃ | 2 | 24°♉46' | 25°♉28' | 26°♉10' | 26°♉52' | Perseus |
| Pleiades (Alcyone) – the seven sisters (Cluster) | ☽ ♂ | 3 | 28°♉36' | 29°♉18' | 29°♉59' | 00°♊41' | Taurus |
| Hyades – the seven mourners (Cluster) | ♄ ☿ | 4 | 05°♊28' | 06°♊10' | 06°♊52' | 07°♊34' | Taurus |
| Ain – the northern eye of Taurus | ♄ ☿ | 3 | 07°♊04' | 07°♊46' | 08°♊28' | 09°♊10' | Taurus |
| Aldebaran – the southern eye of Taurus | ♂ | 1 | 08°♊24' | 09°♊05' | 09°♊47' | 10°♊29' | Taurus |
| Rigel – the left foot of Orion | ♃ ♄ | 1 | 15°♊26' | 16°♊08' | 16°♊50' | 17°♊32' | Orion |
| Bellatrix – the left shoulder of Orion | ♂ ☿ | 2 | 19°♊33' | 20°♊15' | 20°♊57' | 21°♊39' | Orion |
| Capella – the little goat | ♂ ☿ | 1 | 20°♊28' | 21°♊10' | 21°♊51' | 22°♊34' | Auriga |
| Mintaka – from the belt of Orion | ♃ ♄ | 2 | 21°♊01' | 21°♊43' | 22°♊24' | 23°♊06' | Orion |
| El Nath – the northern horn of Taurus | ♂ | 2 | 21°♊11' | 21°♊53' | 22°♊34' | 23°♊17' | Taurus |
| Ensis – from Orion's sword (Nebula) | ♂ ☽ | 4 | 21°♊36' | 22°♊17' | 22°♊59' | 23°♊41' | Orion |
| Alnilam – from the belt of Orion | ♃ ♄ | 2 | 22°♊04' | 22°♊46' | 23°♊28' | 24°♊10' | Orion |
| Al Hecka – the southern horn of Taurus | ♂ | 3 | 23°♊23' | 24°♊05' | 24°♊47' | 25°♊29' | Gemini |
| Betelgeuse – the right shoulder of Orion | ♂ ☿ | 1 | 27°♊21' | 28°♊03' | 28°♊45' | 29°♊27' | Orion |
| Menkalinan – the shoulder of the Charioteer | ♂ ☿ | 2 | 28°♊31' | 29°♊13' | 29°♊55' | 00°♋37' | Auriga |
| Propus – between the shoulders of the twins | ☿ ♀ | 3 | 02°♋03' | 02°♋45' | 03°♋26' | 04°♋08' | Gemini |
| Tejat Posterior – the left foot of Castor | ☿ ♀ | 3 | 03°♋55' | 04°♋36' | 05°♋18' | 06°♋00' | Gemini |
| Alhena – the left foot of Pollux | ☿ ♀ | 2 | 07°♋43' | 08°♋25' | 09°♋06' | 09°♋48' | Gemini |
| Sirius – the mouth of the greater dog | ♃ ♂ | 1 | 12°♋42' | 13°♋24' | 14°♋05' | 14°♋46' | Canis Major |
| Canopus – the pilot of the ship Argus | ♄ ♃ | 1 | 13°♋35' | 14°♋16' | 14°♋58' | 15°♋40' | Argus |
| Wasat – the right arm of Castor | ♄ | 3 | 17°♋08' | 17°♋50' | 18°♋31' | 19°♋13' | Gemini |

| Name and planetary nature | | Mag. | Zodiacal Longitude | | | | Constellation |
|---|---|---|---|---|---|---|---|
| | | | 1900 | 1950 | 2000 | 2050 | |
| Castor – *the northern twin* | ☿ | 2 | 18°♋51' | 19°♋33' | 20°♋15' | 20°♋56' | Gemini |
| Pollux – *the southern twin* | ♂ | 1 | 21°♋50' | 22°♋32' | 23°♋13' | 23°♋54' | Gemini |
| Procyon – *the lesser dog* | ☿♂ | 1 | 24°♋24' | 25°♋06' | 25°♋48' | 26°♋29' | Canis Minor |
| Praesaepe – *the manger* (Cluster) | ♂☽ | 4 | 05°♌57' | 06°♌39' | 07°♌20' | 08°♌02' | Cancer |
| Asellus Borealis – *the northern ass* | ♂☉ | 5 | 06°♌09' | 06°♌50' | 07°♌32' | 08°♌14' | Cancer |
| Asellus Australis – *the southern ass* | ♂☉ | 4 | 07°♌19' | 08°♌01' | 08°♌43' | 09°♌25' | Cancer |
| Acubens – *the south claw of Cancer* | ♄☿ | 4 | 12°♌15' | 12°♌57' | 13°♌38' | 14°♌20' | Cancer |
| Algenubi – *the mouth of the Lion* | ♄♂ | 3 | 19°♌18' | 20°♌00' | 20°♌42' | 21°♌24' | Leo |
| Alphard – *the heart of the Hydra* | ♄♀ | 2 | 25°♌53' | 26°♌35' | 27°♌17' | 27°♌59' | Hydra |
| Adhafera – *the mane of the Lion* | ♄☿ | 3 | 26°♌11' | 26°♌52' | 27°♌34' | 28°♌16' | Leo |
| Al Jabhah – *the forehead of the Lion* | ♄☿ | 3 | 26°♌31' | 27°♌13' | 27°♌54' | 28°♌36' | Leo |
| Regulus – *the heart of the Lion* | ♂♃ | 1 | 28°♌26' | 29°♌08' | 29°♌50' | 00°♍31' | Leo |
| Zosma – *the back of the Lion* | ♄♀ | 2 | 09°♍55' | 10°♍37' | 11°♍19' | 12°♍10' | Leo |
| Denebola – *the tail of the Lion* | ♄♀ | 2 | 20°♍13' | 20°♍55' | 21°♍37' | 22°♍19' | Leo |
| Labrum – *the cup* | ♀☿ | 4 | 25°♍18' | 26°♍00' | 26°♍41' | 27°♍23' | Crater |
| Zavijava – *the head of Virgo* | ☿♂ | 4 | 25°♍45' | 26°♍27' | 27°♍10' | 27°♍52' | Virgo |
| Markeb – *the hull of the ship Argo* | ♄♃ | 3 | 27°♍32' | 28°♍13' | 28°♍53' | 29°♍35' | Argus |
| Zaniah – *of Virgo's wing* | ☿♀ | 4 | 03°♎08' | 03°♎50' | 04°♎31' | 05°♎13' | Virgo |
| Vindemiatrix – *of Virgo's wing* | ♄☿ | 3 | 08°♎33' | 09°♎15' | 09°♎57' | 10°♎38' | Virgo |
| Algorab – *the right wing of the crow* | ♂♄ | 3 | 12°♎04' | 12°♎45' | 13°♎27' | 14°♎09' | Corvus |
| Seginus – *the left should of the hunter* | ☿♄ | 3 | 16°♎16' | 16°♎58' | 17°♎40' | 18°♎29' | Boötes |
| Foramen – *the mast of the ship Argos* | ♄♃ | 3 | 20°♎47' | 21°♎28' | 22°♎09' | 22°♎50' | Argus |
| Spica – *the ear of grain of Virgo* | ♀♂ | 1 | 22°♎27' | 23°♎09' | 23°♎51' | 24°♎32' | Virgo |
| Arcturus – *the knee of the hunter* | ♃♂ | 1 | 22°♎49' | 23°♎32' | 24°♎15' | 24°♎56' | Boötes |
| Princeps – *of the hunter* | ☿♄ | 3 | 01°♏45' | 02°♏27' | 03°♏09' | 03°♏09' | Boötes |
| Khambalia – *the left foot of Virgo* | ♀♂ | 4 | 05°♏34' | 06°♏15' | 06°♏57' | 06°♏57' | Virgo |
| Alphecca – *the brightest of the crown* | ♀☿ | 2 | 10°♏53' | 11°♏35' | 12°♏18' | 13°♏00' | Corona Boreal |
| Zuben Elgenubi – *the southern claw* | ♄♂ | 3 | 13°♏41' | 14°♏23' | 15°♏05' | 15°♏46' | Libra |
| Zuben Eschemali – *the northern claw* | ♃☿ | 3 | 17°♏59' | 18°♏40' | 19°♏22' | 20°♏04' | Libra |
| Unukalhai – *the head (or heart) of the snake* | ♄♂ | 3 | 20°♏40' | 21°♏22' | 22°♏04' | 22°♏46' | Serpens |
| Agena – *the left foot of the centaur* | ♀♃ | 1 | 22°♏24' | 23°♏06' | 23°♏48' | 24°♏29' | Centaurus |
| Rigel Centaurus – *the foot of centaur* | ♀♃ | 1 | 28°♏10' | 28°♏51' | 29°♏32' | 00°♐06' | Centaurus |
| Yed Prior – *the left hand of the serpent holder* | ♄♀ | 3 | 00°♐54' | 01°♐36' | 02°♐18' | 03°♐00' | Ophiuchus |
| Dschubba – *of the head of Scorpio* | ♂♄ | 2 | 01°♐10' | 01°♐52' | 02°♐34' | 03°♐16' | Scorpius |
| Acrab – *of the head of Scorpio* | ♂♄ | 3 | 01°♐48' | 02°♐29' | 03°♐11' | 03°♐53' | Scorpius |
| Han – *the left knee of the serpent holder* | ♄♀ | 3 | 07°♐50' | 08°♐31' | 09°♐13' | 09°♐13' | Ophiuchus |
| Antares – *the heart of Scorpio* | ♂♃ | 1 | 08°♐22' | 09°♐04' | 09°♐46' | 10°♐27' | Scorpius |

| Name and planetary nature | | Mag. | Zodiacal Longitude | | | | Constellation |
|---|---|---|---|---|---|---|---|
| | | | 1900 | 1950 | 2000 | 2050 | |
| Ras Algethi – the head | ♂ ♀ | 3 | 14°♐45' | 15°♐27' | 16°♐09' | 16°♐50' | Hercules |
| Graffias – the head of Scorpio | ♂ ♄ | 4 | 15°♐51' | 16°♐32' | 17°♐14' | 17°♐55' | Scorpius |
| Sabik – the left knee of the serpent holder | ♄ ♀ | 2 | 16°♐34' | 17°♐16' | 17°♐58' | 18°♐40' | Ophiuchus |
| Ras Alhague – the head of the serpent holder | ♄ ♀ | 2 | 21°♐03' | 21°♐45' | 22°♐27' | 23°♐08' | Ophiuchus |
| Lesath – the sting of Scorpio | ☿ ♂ | 3 | 22°♐37' | 23°♐19' | 24°♐01' | 24°♐42' | Scorpius |
| Aculeus – of the sting of Scorpio (Nebula) | ♂ ☽ | 5 | 24°♐20' | 25°♐02' | 25°♐43' | 26°♐25' | Scorpius |
| Acumen – of the sting of Scorpio (Nebula) | ♂ ☽ | 3 | 27°♐21' | 28°♐03' | 28°♐45' | 29°♐26' | Scorpius |
| Sinistra – the left hand of the serpent holder | ♄ ♀ | 3 | 28°♐21' | 29°♐03' | 29°♐45' | 00°♑26' | Ophiuchus |
| Spiculum – the tip of the arrow (Nebula) | ♂ ☽ | 6 | 29°♐40' | 00°♑21' | 01°♑03' | 01°♑45' | Sagittarius |
| Polis – the bow of the archer | ♃ ♂ | 4 | 01°♑49' | 02°♑30' | 03°♑12' | 03°♑54' | Sagittarius |
| Facies – the face of the archer (Cluster) | ☉ ♂ | 6 | 06°♑54' | 07°♑36' | 08°♑18' | 08°♑59' | Sagittarius |
| Nunki – the arrow of the archer | ♃ ☿ | 2 | 10°♑59' | 11°♑41' | 12°♑23' | 13°♑04' | Sagittarius |
| Ascella – the shoulder of the archer | ♃ ☿ | 3 | 12°♑14' | 12°♑56' | 13°♑38' | 14°♑20' | Sagittarius |
| Manubrium – of the archer | ☉ ♂ | 4 | 13°♑35' | 14°♑17' | 14°♑59' | 15°♑41' | Sagittarius |
| Wega – of Lira | ♀ ☿ | 1 | 13°♑55' | 14°♑37' | 15°♑19' | 16°♑00' | Lyra |
| Deneb Okab – the tail of the eagle | ♂ ♃ | 3 | 22°♑14' | 22°♑56' | 23°♑38' | 24°♑20' | Aquila |
| Terebellum – the tail of the archer | ♀ ♄ | 5 | 24°♑27' | 25°♑09' | 25°♑50' | 26°♑33' | Sagittarius |
| Albireo – the head of the swan | ♀ ☿ | 3 | 29°♑52' | 00°♒33' | 01°♒14' | 01°♒56' | Cygnus |
| Altair – the eagle | ♂ ♃ | 1 | 00°♒22' | 01°♒04' | 01°♒46' | 02°♒28' | Aquila |
| Giedi a1 – of the southern horn of the goat | ♀ ♂ | 5 | 02°♒22' | 03°♒04' | 03°♒46' | 04°♒27' | Capricornus |
| Giedi a2 – of the southern horn of the goat | ♀ ♂ | 4 | 02°♒28' | 03°♒10' | 03°♒51' | 04°♒33' | Capricornus |
| Dabir – the left eye of the goat | ♄ ♀ | 3 | 02°♒39' | 03°♒21' | 04°♒03' | 04°♒44' | Capricornus |
| Oculus – the right eye of the goat | ♄ ♀ | 5 | 03°♒19' | 04°♒01' | 04°♒42' | 05°♒24' | Capricornus |
| Bos – the face of the goat | ♄ ♀ | 5 | 03°♒46' | 04°♒28' | 05°♒09' | 05°♒51' | Capricornus |
| Armus – the heart of the goat | ♂ ☿ | 5 | 11°♒21' | 12°♒02' | 12°♒44' | 13°♒26' | Capricornus |
| Dorsum – the back of the goat | ♄ ♃ | 4 | 12°♒27' | 13°♒08' | 13°♒50' | 14°♒32' | Capricornus |
| Castra – the belly of the goat | ♄ ♃ | 5 | 18°♒48' | 19°♒30' | 20°♒11' | 20°♒53' | Capricornus |
| Nashira – the tail of the goat | ♄ ♃ | 4 | 20°♒23' | 21°♒05' | 21°♒47' | 22°♒29' | Capricornus |
| Sadalsuud – the left shoulder of Aquarius | ♄ ☿ | 3 | 22°♒00' | 22°♒42' | 23°♒23' | 24°♒05' | Aquarius |
| Deneb Algedi – the tail of the goat | ♄ ♃ | 3 | 22°♒09' | 22°♒50' | 23°♒32' | 24°♒14' | Capricornus |
| Sadalmelek – the right shoulder of Aquarius | ♄ ☿ | 3 | 02°♓22' | 03°♓03' | 03°♓45' | 04°♓27' | Aquarius |
| Fomalhaut – the mouth of the fish | ♀ ☿ | 1 | 02°♓27' | 03°♓09' | 03°♓51' | 04°♓33' | Piscis Austrinus |
| Deneb Adige – the tail of the swan | ♀ ☿ | 1 | 03°♓57' | 04°♓38' | 05°♓20' | 06°♓00' | Cygnus |
| Skat – the left leg of Aquarius | ☿ ♄ | 3 | 08°♓02' | 08°♓10' | 08°♓52' | 09°♓34' | Aquarius |
| Achernar – the end of the river | ♃ | 1 | 13°♓54' | 14°♓36' | 15°♓19' | 16°♓01' | Eridanus |
| Markab – the wing of Pegasus | ♂ ☿ | 2 | 22°♓06' | 22°♓47' | 23°♓29' | 24°♓11' | Pegasus |
| Scheat – the left leg of Pegasus | ♂ ☿ | 2 | 27°♓59' | 28°♓41' | 29°♓22' | 00°♈04' | Pegasus |

About the table: Some star names may vary according to different epochs and cultures. In the following list are some of the main variants.

## Alternative Names for Some Stars

Acubens: Seratan

Agena: Beta Centauri

Algol: Rasalgul

Alphecca: Gemma

Alpheratz: Sirrah ou Schedar

Altair: Vultur Volans

Capella: Alannaz, Hircus, Alayodi

Castor: Apollo

Deneb Kaitos: Difda

Pollux: Hercules

Algenubi: Ras Elased Australis

Spica: Arista, Azimech

Rigel Centaurus: Toliman, Bungula, Alpha Centauri

Wega: Vultur Cadens

**Nature of the stars**: The planetary associations presented in the table originated from our research into the Ptolemaic tradition and also from authors whose practice reveals the recurrent usage of the stars. There are other more recent tables that present several variations to the tradition, including the addition of the modern planets. These associations where disregarded in this manual even though they are mentioned in *Fixed Stars and Constellations in Astrology* by Vivan Robson.

**Magnitude**: The magnitude value corresponds to the traditional classification, and not to the astronomical scale of magnitudes.

**Other celestial bodies**: Some stars in the list are not real stars, but celestial bodies of another kind, namely galaxies (the M31 in Andromeda), nebulas, and star clusters, which are identified in the table.

**Positioning**: The stars' placements in the zodiac are calculated by projecting their position onto the ecliptic (taking in account their latitude, right ascension, and declination).

*Chapter XIII*
# *The Parts*

The parts are mathematical points derived from the combination of three factors in the astrological chart. This interaction produces a fourth point, the part, which combines the significations of the other factors involved. In an astrological chart, the parts are significators of specific matters. Their function is to complement the interpretation of the major significators.

To calculate a part, the zodiacal distance from point A to point B is projected from point C. The zodiacal degree obtained is where the part is located. This distance between points A and B is always measured in the direction of the order of the zodiac, meaning in the order of the signs. Points A and B are, generally speaking, planets (although they can also be other factors in the chart) chosen in function of their natural significations. The meaning of the part that is formed derives from the interaction of these two planetary significations. Point C, from where the part is projected, is almost always the Ascendant, which signifies the individual or the event being analyzed in the chart.

For example, the Part of Children, used to complement interpretations relating to children and fertility, is calculated by taking the zodiacal distance between Jupiter and Saturn. These planets were chosen as significators since Jupiter represents fertility and Saturn as that which limits it. The part is obtained by projecting the distance between these two planets from the Ascendant, which represents the native. Thus, we are measuring fertility (Jupiter) and its limitations (Saturn) in the context of the native's life (Ascendant).

The calculation of the parts is often determined by the sect of the horo-

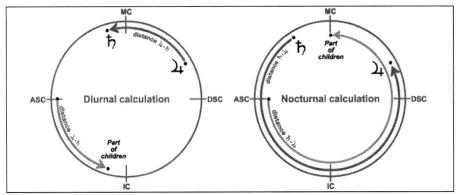

**Figure 1. Calculating a Part**
**(Diurnal and Nocturnal Charts)**

scope. As a general rule, the calculations differ in diurnal and nocturnal charts, although the planets involved remain the same. Returning to the example of the Part of Children, take the distance from Jupiter to Saturn in diurnal charts, and from Saturn to Jupiter in nocturnal charts. In either case, the projection is always made from the Ascendant.

The parts are often called "Arabic" because for a long time their development was attributed to the Arabs. This occurred because Ptolemy did not mention them in *Tetrabiblos*. During the Renaissance, *Tetrabiblos* became a sort of canon of "good" astrology. As a consequence, any technique that was not found in it was thought to lie outside of the classical nucleus of astrology. Thus, the parts began to be looked upon as a superfluous addendum and fell into disuse. However, all of the other Hellenistic authors who were contemporaries of Ptolemy do include abundant references to the various parts (they are known in the Hellenistic texts as Lots). For reasons unknown to us, Ptolemy appears to be the only one who excludes the parts from his treatise. Additionally, recent studies have revealed that these mathematical points were already an integral part of interpretation during the Hellenistic period and that the Arabs merely refined and greatly expanded upon their use.

The only part mentioned by Ptolemy in *Tetrabiblos* is the **Part of Fortune**. This is the only part to have survived and to have continued to be used in charts from antiquity until the current age. Nonetheless, after the 19th century, Fortune lost its practical significance in interpretation and began to be treated as a relic from ancient times. Various attempts by authors of the 20th century to recover the parts were not successful because instead of studying the original techniques and their practical application, they merely adapted the parts to their own preconceived notions. The emergence of various ineffectual interpretive techniques led to the complete loss of their original signification. As a result, the Part of Fortune began to be considered useless by a large number of astrologers. Another consequence of the loss of this doctrine is the recent development of new parts without any technical basis or practical signification. Only recently, with the translation and study of ancient works, has the original understanding of the parts and their practical application been recovered. An important interpretive complement, which is as old as astrology itself, has thus been returned to the discipline.

## The Various Parts and their Use

In addition to Fortune, there are many other traditional parts, each with its own specific meaning. Some are used in all horoscopes, while others are restricted to a particular branch of astrology (natal, horary, mundane, etc.).

Among the most important parts in natal astrology are the planetary parts associated with the planets. This is a group of seven parts, each one corresponding to the qualities of the planet that produces it. The most important are the Part of the Moon, or Part of Fortune, and the Part of the Sun, or Part of Spirit. They are calculated from the angular distance between the two luminaries. The remaining planetary parts are extracted from these two principal parts. They are produced by projecting from the Ascendant the distance between the planet and one of these two principal parts (Fortune or Spirit, depending on each part's formula).

The **Part of Saturn** or **The Heavy Part** is calculated from the distance between Saturn and Fortune in diurnal charts, or between Fortune and Saturn in nocturnal charts.

The **Part of Jupiter** or **Part of Victory and Triumph** is given by the distance between Spirit and Jupiter in diurnal charts, and between Jupiter and Spirit in nocturnal charts.

The **Part of Mars** or **Part of Daring and Courage** is obtained from the distance between Mars and Fortune in diurnal charts, and between Fortune and Mars in nocurnal charts.

The **Part of Venus** or **Part of Love and Concord** is given from the distance between Spirit and Venus in diurnal charts, and between Venus and Spirit in nocturnal charts.

The **Part of Mercury** or **Part of Necessity** is calculated from the distance between Mercury and Fortune in diurnal charts, and between Fortune and Mercury in nocturnal charts.[28]

These parts complement the delineation of the planet to which they are associated, and help to describe the manner in which the individual expresses the natural significations of that planet. For example, the Part of Daring and Courage, tied to Mars, complements the delineation of Mars in a chart by giving indications as to the manner in which the native expresses courage (or the lack of it).

Another group of parts is associated with the astrological houses. For example, the seventh house has several parts associated with it, the most well known being the **Part of Marriage**, which complements the most obvious signification of this house: relationships and marriages. In addition to this one, there are other parts associated with this house, such as the **Part of Contests**, for situations involving face to face conflict, or the **Part of Lawsuits**, for questions involving lawsuits. Note that the designation "Parts from the Houses" simply establishes a semantic relationship between the meaning of the part and the topic of the house; in contrast with the parts extracted from the planets, this designation does not imply that the house cusp is necessarily involved in the extraction of these parts. The list of parts associated with each house and their respective formulas is too long to include in this book (see *The Book of Instruction in the Elements of the Art of Astrology* by Al-Biruni and *On the Arabic Parts* by Guido Bonatti).

We may yet consider another group of parts that do not belong to the categories just described. These parts have a variety of uses and are as a general rule applied to horary and mundane astrology. Among them are the Part of Victory and Battles, obviously used for military matters; the Parts of Rain, of Wind, and of Clouds, for meteorological purposes; and the Parts of Secrets, of Truth and Lies, and of Lost Animals, used in horary questions. Other parts have curious names, such as the Part of Onions, of Honey, of Apricots, and of Wheat, which were used in matters relating to trade or to forecast the annual harvest.

The parts are complements for specific interpretations and must be interpreted in their appropriate context. It is a waste of time to interpret all the parts in every horoscope, but rather to determine which part or parts are appropriate for the particular topic under study. For example, in an inquiry about resources and assets, one would evaluate the general indicators (the second house, planets in the second, its ruler, etc) that reveal the native's capacity to generate material resources. In this scenario, an examination of the Part of Substance may add information about the source of income of the individual.

In addition to their meaning in the horoscope, the parts can be examined in the directions, transits, etc. and therefore become good indicators of events related to their symbolism. Just as with the planets, a part is affected by aspects and by antiscia, but in contrast to the planets, it does not cast aspects because parts lack an orb. Their dynamics are similar to those of the chart angles, which do not form applications or separations. On the other hand, the parts may be affected by combustion and by conjunctions with fixed stars. In interpretation, the most important factor is the planet dispositing the part. The position of the dispositor by sign and house, as well as the aspects that it receives and its condition, determines the effect of the part. The position of the part by house and sign must also be considered.

---

[28]The formulas indicated for the Part of Venus and Mercury are found in the Greek tradition. Later, in the Middle Ages, other variations were developed. The Part of Venus starts being calculated by taking the distance from the part of Fortune to the Part of Spirit and projecting it from the Ascendant (the reverse at night); the Part of Mercury was then calculated by taking the distance from the Part of Spirit to the Part of Fortune and projecting that from the Ascendant (the reverse at night). In this handbook, we use the Greek formula, which includes in the calculation the planets that give them their name.

## The Part of Fortune

This is the most important Arabic part. It has been present in astrological interpretation since the beginnings of horoscopy. Its symbol is a circle with an enclosed cross—⊕.

Its calculation is extracted from the position of the luminaries. In a day chart, take the distance from the Sun (the "luminary of the hour" in a day chart) to the Moon and project this distance from the Ascendant. In a night chart, take the distance from the Moon (the "luminary of the hour" for a night chart) to the Sun and project it from the Ascendant.

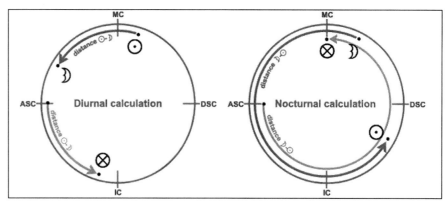

**Figure 2. Diurnal and Nocturnal Calculation for the Part of Fortune**

A way to tell whether the calculation of the Part of Fortune is correct is to compare the lunar phase and the distance of the part to the Ascendant. The distance between the Sun and the Moon (lunar phase) should be the same as the distance between Fortune and the Ascendant. Thus, in a horoscope with a New Moon (that is, with a conjunction between the Sun and Moon), Fortune should be very close to the Ascendant. In a horoscope with a Full Moon (a Sun-Moon opposition), the part should be very close to the Descendant.

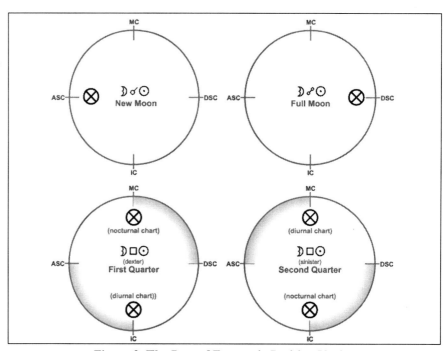

**Figure 3. The Part of Fortune's Position Varies According to the Phase of the Moon**

For the other phases of the Moon, one must take into account whether the horoscope is diurnal or nocturnal. In charts with a waxing moon, Fortune is always located below the horizon in diurnal charts, and above in nocturnal charts. In charts with a waning moon, Fortune is always above the horizon in diurnal charts and below in nocturnal charts. Conjunctions of Fortune with the Midheaven or IC always occur in charts where the luminaries are in square aspect (waxing or waning square, as the case may be).

*Example: Calculation of the Part of Fortune*

Friedrich Nietzsche's chart is diurnal, so the Sun is the luminary of the hour. The part is calculated by measuring the distance from the Sun to the Moon and projecting it from the Ascendant. The Sun is at 22° Libra

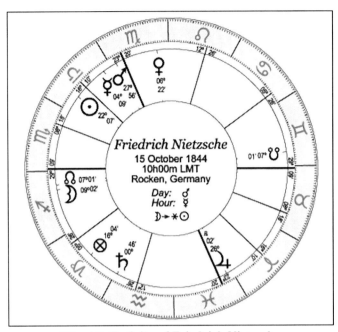

**Chart 1. Nativity of Friedrich Nietzsche**

07′ and the Moon at 09° Sagittarius 02. The distance between the lights is 46° 55′: 7° 53′ (from the Sun to the end of Libra) + 30° (all of Scorpio) + 9° 02′ (from the beginning of Sagittarius to the Moon). This distance is added to the Ascendant to find the part. The 46° 55′ consists of 30° (or a whole sign) plus 16° and 55′. Therefore, add 30° (a whole sign) to the Ascendant: 29° 09′ Scorpio + 30° = 29° 09′ Sagittarius. Now add the remaining 16° 55′. There are 51′ from 29° 09′ to the end of Sagittarius. This leaves 16° 04′ that now belongs to the following sign. Therefore, the Part of Fortune is at 16° Capricorn 04.

Note: Calculating the Part of Fortune may seem complicated, but is less so if it is visualized directly onto the chart.

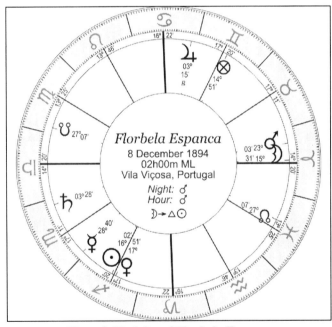

**Chart 3. Nativity of Florbela Espanca**

In the horoscope of Florbela Espanca, the Moon is the luminary of the hour because this is a nocturnal chart. In this case, the Part of Fortune is calculated by taking the distance from the Moon to the Sun and projecting it from the Ascendant. The Moon is at 15° Aries 31′ and the Sun at 16° Sagittarius 02′. Note that in this case the larger arc is used because the direction is always of the order of the signs. The distance between the lights is 240° 31′, which corresponds to 8 whole signs plus 31′, or 240° 31′ is equal to 14° 29′ (from the Moon until the final sign of Aries) + 210° (seven whole signs) + 16° 02′ (from the beginning of Sagittarius to the Sun). All that is left is to add 240° 31′ to the Ascendant, which is at 14° Libra 20′. By advancing 8 signs from this point, the result is 14° Gemini 20. Then add the remaining 31′ to obtain 14° Gemini 51′, which is the position of the Part of Fortune.

The Part of Fortune is considered one of the vital points of the horoscope because its significators are the Sun, source of life, and the Moon, symbol of the body and of substance. Thus, it is almost as important as the actual luminaries, making it a key point of the horoscope. It is one of the few parts that can be interpreted in isolation because it synthesizes the critical points of any chart: the Ascendant, Moon, and Sun.

The term "fortune" does not necessarily signify money, but rather comfort, well-being and benefits in general. It represents an area of life or a situation in which the individual is fortunate or has luck. The use of this part is varied and depends upon the interpretive context. It is primarily used in matters having to do with wealth and health. Essentially, the Part of Fortune represents the substantiation of things. In a nativity it signifies that which gives comfort and well-being to the native. It represents the material aspects of life, namely the wealth and prosperity of an individual, as well as that which supports and sustains individual actions (conditions, people, areas of life).

*Interpretation Examples for the Part of Fortune*

In Nietzsche's chart, Fortune is located at 16° Capricorn 04' in the second house, which highlights matters connected to material security and economic prosperity. Saturn, the dispositor of the part, is also the ruler of the second house and is posited there, which reinforces the importance of the topic. Because Saturn is involved, there is without a doubt an indication of struggle and hard work connected with well-being and material security. However, the planet is dignified and therefore can assist with these objectives. The position of Saturn in Aquarius (an air sign)

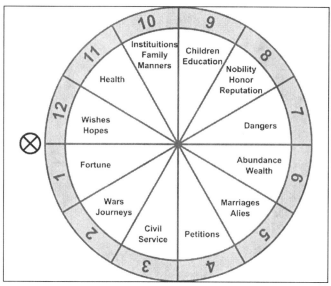

**Figure 4. The Houses from the Part of Fortune**

suggests that the well-being indicated by the Part of Fortune is tied to depth of thought, to concepts and ideas. Note also that Saturn rules the third house of writing, teaching, and communication activities through which Nietzsche attained not only material resources but great satisfaction.

The Part of Fortune in Florbela Espanca's chart is at 14° Gemini 51' in the ninth house, which signifies that this poet got great satisfaction from intellectual stimulation (Gemini) and from cultural discussions (the ninth house). Florbela belonged to the intellectual circles of her time and was one of the first women to attend the university. These activities were nevertheless marked by strong emotion because Mercury, the dispositor of the part and ruler of the ninth, is in Scorpio. It is also posited in the second house, which is important to someone who, through her writing, obtained not only material resources but also great personal satisfaction.

*Houses From the Part of Fortune*

In older systems of astrology, namely those of the Hellenistic period, the part of Fortune was so important that it was turned into a sort of Ascendant. From this new Ascendant, a new system of houses could be derived with significations completely different from those of the normal houses. The interpretive technique for these houses did not survive intact from ancient times, but the examples that do survive reveal the crucial importance of this part to astrological interpretation. The only list of meanings that survive is presented by Manilius (ca. 14 AC) in his work *Astronomica*.

Another variation is presented by Vettius Valens (ca. 120-175 AC) in his work *Anthology*, which calls the eleventh house from Fortune the "place of Acquisition" and associates it with riches and prosperity. This author also gives great weight to the angularity of the planets in relation to the Part of Fortune (namely planets placed in the tenth house from Fortune). The Part of Spirit was interpreted in a similar manner.

**The Part of Spirit**

This part, also known as the Part of the Sun, is a complement to the Part of Fortune. In its calculation we use the same elements as those in Fortune, but reverse the order. It is therefore a sort of counterpart to the Part of Fortune. To obtain the Part of Spirit in diurnal charts, take the distance from the Moon to the Sun; in nocturnal charts, take the distance from the Sun to the Moon. Once more, these distances are projected from the Ascendant. Note that because they have an inverted calculation, the Parts of Fortune and Spirit will always be at

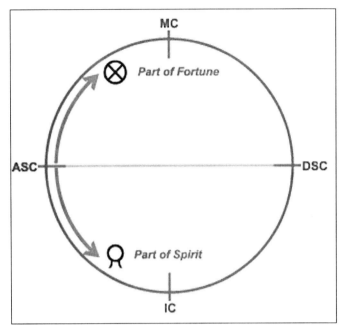

**Figure 5. The Parts of Fortune and Spirit as Mirror Images of One Another**

identical distances from the Ascendant, but in opposite hemispheres. They form a mirror image with the horizon as their axis.

As the name indicates, the Part of Spirit signifies the attitude of the individual with regard to matters of spirituality. Just as with Fortune, it is related to well-being, but in this case it pertains to a more philosophical or intellectual outlook. It is also associated with the personal concept of divinity, the interpretation that each person makes of what is divine. The Part of Spirit is the only part, except for Fortune, that has its own symbol. It is represented by a globe from which descend two rays of light.

In Friedrich Nietzsche's horoscope, the Moon is at 09° Sagittarius 02′ and the Sun at 22° Libra 07′. Because it is a day chart, take the distance from the Moon to the Sun, in the order of the signs. The sum is 313° 05′, or 10 signs (from Sagittarius to Libra = 300°) + 13° 05′. This distance is projected from the Ascendant at 29° Scorpio 09′, which gives the Part of Spirit at 12° Libra 14′.

In this chart, the Part of Spirit is in Libra, an air sign, which suggests that Nietzsche's attitude toward beliefs is primarily intellectual. Because it is also in a cardinal sign, the part points toward someone actively spreading his beliefs (religious, philosophical, or others). However, Venus, the dispositor of the part, is debilitated in Virgo, which adds a strong pragmatic quality that is somewhat disillusioned. The critical attitude of this philosopher toward religious and social institutions is well known. On the other hand, Venus is in the ninth house and the Part of Spirit is conjunct the Sun, ruler of the ninth, which greatly emphasizes Nietzsche's studious and philosophical tendencies.

**Figure 6. Symbol for the Part of Spirit**

### Part of Faith

This part is used in the delineation of the ninth house and gives additional information about the manner in which the individual approaches his or her faith (from within a religious or secular existence). Important: this part does not indicate the *degree* of religiosity of the individual, but rather *the approach* with regard to matters of faith. It can therefore manifest in the chart of the very devout or of the atheist, indicating only different attitudes to the topic.

It is calculated by taking the distance from the Moon to Mercury and projecting that from the Ascendant in diurnal charts; and in nocturnal charts, the distance from Mercury to the Moon and projecting that from the Ascendant. For example, in Friedrich Nietzsche's chart the Moon is at 09° Sagittarius 02′ and Mercury at 04° Libra 09′. Since it is a day chart, take the distance from the Moon to Mercury. From the Moon at 09° Sagittarius 02′, advance in the order of the signs (Sagittarius, Capricorn, etc.) until Mercury, which is at 04° Libra 09′. This is a total of 259° 07′. Or, there are 10 signs (from Sagittarius to Libra = 300°) minus 4° 53′ (the difference in degrees between both planets). This distance is then projected from the Ascendant at 29° Scorpio 09′, which places the Part of Faith at 24° Virgo 16′.

In this case, it is very tightly conjunct the Midheaven (23° Virgo 20′), a position that is highly significant to a philosopher who spent most of his life questioning matters of a religious nature. Note that there is no incompatibility between Nietzsche's anticlerical views and this extremely highlighted Part of Faith in his horoscope. In this case, since it is in Virgo, a mutable earth sign, and governed by Mercury, his vision of faith is exceedingly pragmatic. In addition to this, it is conjunct Mars, which gives him a contesting and critical attitude toward religions. Much of his philosophical work is based upon the critical analysis and dispute of religion and its effect on societies. Matters of faith are therefore indeed highlighted in his life, albeit by way of his rational opposition to them.

## Part of Substance

This part contributes to the delineation of material resources and values in a horoscope and indicates possible sources of income. It is thus designated as a second house part. It is calculated by taking the distance from the ruler of the second house to the cusp of the second house and projecting that from the Ascendant. In contrast to the cases already presented, this calculation does not vary with sect; it is the same whether in a diurnal or nocturnal chart.

In the chart of Florbela Espanca, the Part of Substance is found in the seventh house, suggesting that a part of her material resources would come from marriage. The part is located at 08° Taurus 28′, and Venus, the dispositor, is found in the third house, which points to another of her sources of income: writing, and the publication of literary works. Since Venus is combust, it is to be expected that her income could fall short of expectations. Note that the delineation of this part serves as a complement to Fortune with regard to matters of material resources. In this chart, there in fact does exist a notable correspondence between both parts.

## Part of Marriage

This part gives additional information about relationships in natal charts. It integrates the delineation of the seventh house and complements the interpretation of the principal factors involved. To calculate the Part of Marriage, use Venus (love and relationships) and Saturn (contracts and obligations) as significators, and project their distance from the Ascendant (the individual). In this case, the calculation varies according to the gender of the individual: in a man's horoscope, take the distance from Saturn to Venus, and in a woman's chart, take the distance from Venus to Saturn. In both cases, project the obtained arc from the Ascendant.

Before proceeding to a chart example, recall that the Part of Marriage only makes sense when integrated within the interpretation of the seventh house and of the other relationship significators. An interesting case to study is that of Princess Maria, the youngest daughter of King Manuel of Portugal. This princess was promised in marriage to the most important kings of her time, but for political and economic reasons, she never married. She remained known throughout history with the epithet "forever betrothed."

In the chart of Princess Maria, the Part of Marriage is located at 24° Gemini 33′ in the seventh house. It is impeded because it is combust and its dispositor is cadent and retrograde, conditions which make it difficult to form a lasting and official union. Nevertheless, the possibility of relationships should not be ruled out because

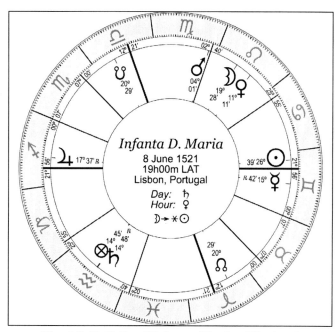

**Chart 9. Nativity of Princess Maria of Portugal**

the part is in a mutable sign and aspected by various planets. Because it is combust in the seventh house, there is a strong indication of hidden relationships—that is, those not officially sanctioned. It should be noted that Princess Maria was one of few royal women of her time to have her own home and to live from her own income, which gave her a degree of liberty and privacy uncommon in her time. This information is corroborated by Mercury, dispositor of the part and ruler of the seventh house. Mercury is in a mutable (or double-bodied) sign, and the same is true for the cusp of the seventh, which reinforces the possibility of there being various relationships.

There are other parts related to marriage, which sometimes generates confusion. The most well known is the Part of Marriage according to Hermes: in a man's horoscope it is obtained by projecting the distance between the Sun and Venus from the Ascendant; and in a woman's chart, one projects the distance between the Moon and Mars.

## Part of Children

This part is used to complement the assessment of fertility, both in nativities and horary astrology. It is calculated by taking the distance from Jupiter to Saturn in diurnal charts and from Saturn to Jupiter in nocturnal charts and projecting it from the Ascendant. Its interpretation should always be made in conjunction with other significators of the fifth house.

The Part of Children in Agatha Christie's horoscope is at 25° Capricorn 19′. This is a moderately barren sign, which indicates few children. This judgment is reinforced by the position of Saturn, its dispositor, in Virgo, a barren sign. In fact, Agatha had only one daughter, born from her first marriage. The proximity of this part to the cusp of the sixth house (illnesses) suggests the existence of some debility or medical condition that interferes with fertility.

## Parts of the Father and the Mother

These parts are used in the evaluation of the fourth and tenth houses respectively, and provide additional information regarding the parents of the native. The Part of the Father is calculated by taking the distance from the Sun to Saturn and projecting it from the Ascendant; while the Part of the Mother is obtained by taking the distance from Venus to the Moon and projecting from the Ascendant. If the nativity is nocturnal, the Part of the Father is obtained from distance from Saturn to the Sun, and the Part of the Mother from the Moon to Venus.

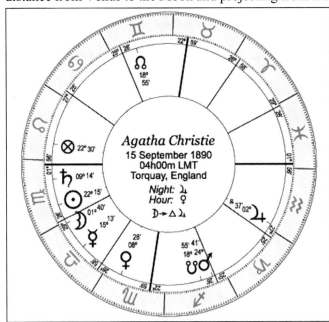

In Nietzsche's case, which is diurnal, the Part of the Father is calculated from the arc of the Sun to Saturn. The part is located in the third house at 7° Pisces 48′. Its dispositor is Jupiter, which is dignified and also in Pisces in the fourth house, which imparts unto the father the qualities of devotion, religiosity and honor. The Part of the Mother, curiously, is also located in the third house and in Pisces, at 1° 49′, which bestows unto the mother very similar qualities. It is a well-known fact that all of Nietzsche's family was devoutly religious and that his father was a Lutheran minister.

**Chart 2. Nativity of Agatha Christie**

The indications given by the parts should always be combined with other relevant significators in order to obtain a complete and precise image. In this case, the Parts of the Father and the Mother are in the same sign and house, which suggests a certain agreement. However, the other significators of the parents should also be taken into consideration. For instance, there is an opposition between Jupiter, ruler of the fourth house (father) and Mercury, ruler of the tenth house (mother), which suggests a difference in attitude between the parents. These and other indications should be considered together with those given by the parts in order to attain a more complete picture.

Other interesting parts for the astrological practice are:
- Part of Brothers (from Saturn to Jupiter, projected from the Ascendant), associated with the third house.
- Part of Illnesses (from Saturn to Mars, projected from the Ascendant; reversed in night charts), interpreted in the context of sixth house matters.
- Part of Death (distance from the Moon to the eight house, projected from Saturn), related to the eighth house.
- Part of Travels (distance from the ruler of the ninth to the cusp of the ninth, projected from the Ascendant), another part related to the ninth house.
- Part of Friends (from the Moon to Mercury, projected from the Ascendant), related to the eleventh house.
- Part of Enemies (from the twelfth house ruler to the twelfth house cusp, projected from the Ascendant), associated with the twelfth house.

## Computers and Arabic Parts: Some Practical Considerations

When using a computer to calculate the Arabic parts it is necessary to keep in mind the following points:

- The majority of software applications mix the names and formulas of the traditional parts with modern names and formulas. Determine the formula used by the program; otherwise, the part may be different from the one intended.
- Not all applications differentiate between day and night calculations for the parts.

Generally, programs list the parts that are conjunct the planets in a horoscope, instead of simply listing their position. These lists of conjunctions are completely useless for interpretation and derive from a lack of understanding on the part of programmers of the philosophy and interpretive technique pertaining to the parts.

*Chapter XIV*
# Power of the Planets

## Strength of the Planets: Accidental Dignities

A planet's capacity to act is dependent upon two factors: the quantity and quality of its expression. The **quality of a planet's expression** is measured by a planet's **essential dignity**. A planet with dignity can fulfill its potential because its expression is stable and enduring. In other words: a dignified planet keeps its promise. In contrast, a debilitated planet has difficulty being true to its nature and can be maladjusted. The **quantity of a planet's expression** is measured through the **accidental dignities**. These originate from the particular conditions in which a planet finds itself in a given horoscope.[29]

While the essential dignities refer to the conditions pertaining to the planet's (essential) nature, the accidental dignities are states or conditions that reinforce or impede the expression of that nature. The most obvious example of this type of dignity is the planet's position by house: in the angular houses, the planets are accidentally dignified. Other examples of accidental dignity and debility are combustion, orientality, and retrogradation. In practice, the essential dignities are more powerful, since they refer to the planet's state, but the accidental dignities are the more noticeable because they affect the planet's power to express.

The combination of these two factors—essential and accidental dignities and debilities—is an important key to understanding the role of each planet in the chart. For example, a planet that has essential dignity and that is also accidentally dignified is like an individual with a good resume, and which, in addition to this, also has an important job where his or her worth can be demosntrated. However, if the planet with essential dignity is accidentally debilitated, the individual also has a good resume, but a less important job. In the context of business, the first case is that of a competent individual with a leadership position, and the second is that of an individual with the same personal skills, but who is the doorman. No matter how skilled the second individual is, he or she will never attain the same level of importance in the firm as the first person.

---

[29]The term "accidental" is not used here with the negative connotations that it has in everyday language. In an astrological context, this term means "by accident" or "particularity". In this context it is used to designate a condition that changes from chart to chart, such as the placement of a planet in a particular house.

On the other hand, there are also cases where an essentially debilitated planet is accidentally dignified. In this case, the planet also achieves great prominence, although its intrinsical qualitiy is poor.

Returning to the business analogy, a similar situation is one where a person without the proper skills, for one reason or another (possibly nepotism), is placed in a position of leadership. The visibility afforded by the position allows for sufficient action, but may also expose his or her inadequacies and its consequences (the mistakes of the boss are generally more prejudicial to a firm than those of the doorman). Finally, in an extreme case, a very weak planet that has essential and accidental debility is comparable to a person with very few skills who has an equally mediocre position.

## Accidental Dignities and Debilities and Their Scoring

In previous chapters the topic of the essential dignities, their importance, and respective systems of scoring were discussed. This concept will now be expanded to include the accidental dignities, and in this manner obtain a complete picture of the planet's capacity for expression in the horoscope. The system is therefore an extension of the essential dignities and follows a similar framework. Thus, positive points are attributed to the accidental dignities, and negative ones to the accidental debilities. The number of points given or removed naturally depends upon the relative importance of the dignity or debility in question. While the essential dignities originate simply from the position of the planets in the signs, the accidental dignities arise from a diverse series of factors and conditions. Many of these conditions have already been explained. Now, they will be systematized into groups and attributed their respective scores.

### Position by House

The most significant condition is the position of the planet by house, which determines a large part of the planet's quantity of expression. With respect to the houses, there are two forms of dignity: angularity and joy.

*Angularity:* A planet expresses its capacity in its totality when in an angular house, about half, when in a succedent house, and about a quarter when in a cadent house. In general, a planet that is angular is considered to be accidentally dignified, while a cadent planet is accidentally debilitated. Its position in the succedent houses is also a dignified state, although it does not have the same strength as when in an angular position. At first though, one might simply associate a dignified condition with the angular and succedent houses and a debilitated one with the cadent positions. However, this interplay is much more complex because there are differences among the houses. In practice, each house has its own specific strength that leads to a more complex system of scoring.

The positioning of planets in the first and tenth houses, which are the most important angles, corresponds in practice to the highest score: 5 points. The remaining angles, the seventh and fourth houses, and the eleventh house (which, although succedent, is very strong) each receive 4 points. Next are the fifth and second (succedent) houses with 3 points, and the ninth (cadent) with 2 points, and the third with 1 point. The planets located in any of these houses are accidentally dignified, albeit with different degrees of intensity, as is obvious from their scores.

As seen earlier, the sixth, eighth, and twelfth houses are considered malefic because they do not aspect the Ascendant. A planet located in these houses is thought to be accidentally debilitated and receives a negative score. The most debilitated of all is the twelfth, with -5 points awarded, followed by the eighth with 4 points, and the sixth with 3 negative points.

*Joy:* The joys are also an accidental dignity and function in a manner similar to angularity. They give the planet some prominence, although their effects are not as strong as those of angularity. Therefore, a planet in its house of joy receives 2 points.

*Relationship to the Sun*

This accidental dignity pertains to the manner in which the Sun can enable or debilitate the expression of a planet. In this topic there are several criteria to quantify.

*Under the Beams and Combustion*: These conditions are considered debilities because the excessive proximity to the Sun weakens the planet's capacity to express. The under-the-beams condition is given a -4 score. In turn, combustion attains the greatest of the negative scores: -6 points. Although a combust planet is technically under the beams of the Sun, these conditions are not cumulative: one either scores under-the-beams or the combustion. In practice, a combust planet receives -6 points, but these are not added to the -4 points given to the planet when under the Sun's beams. Combustion is simply an aggravated version of being under the beams and the score already reflects this.

These conditions are so significant that the opposite condition is also significantly scored: when a planet is free from the influence of the Sun (outside of the areas of combustion or under-the-beams) it receives 5 points.

*Cazimi*: The particular condition of cazimi (within 17′ of the Sun) is also considered a dignity and corresponds to 5 points. For the reasons already mentioned above, this score is also not cumulative with combustion or under-the-beams.

*Increasing and Decreasing in Light*: Similarly, a planet increasing in light receives 1 point; in the decreasing phase it loses 1 point.

*Orientality and Occidentality*: This position of the planet relative to the Sun can be quantified because it significantly augments or deters from its nature and, consequently, the intensity of its expression. As already stated, the superior and masculine planets are slightly favored when oriental of the Sun and receive 2 points; when they are occidental, they lose the same number of points. Similarly, the feminine planets from the lower celestial spheres are favored by occidentality and receive 2 points; they lose 2 points when oriental.

*Motion*

The motion of the planet is also an important accidental state because its fluidity strongly conditions the planet. With respect to this topic, two distinct factors need be considered: velocity and direction.

*Velocity*: A planet may be fast or slow in relation to its average speed. Those that are in a state of rapid motion are considered to be slightly dignified and receive 2 points; similarly, those which are slow are penalized with -2 points.

*Direction*: When in direct motion, a planet follows its normal course and hence is considered dignified and receives 4 points. Retrograde motion is considered more debilitated and gives the planet -5 points.

Obviously, this condition does not apply to the Sun and Moon, which are always in direct motion. In the case of stationary planets moving toward retrograde, they receive the same score as for retrograde motion; if the station is from retrograde to direct, they receive the direct motion score.

*Aspects*

The contacts a planet makes by aspect are very important in the evaluation of its expression. Aspects with other planets, or even the absence of aspects, are significant in the scoring of dignity and debility.

*Aspects with Malefic and Benefic Planets*: In terms of accidental dignity, aspects of a planet with the benefics (Venus and Jupiter) are particularly noteworthy. Thus, a planet is considered accidentally dignified if it forms a facilitating aspect (sextile or trine) or if it is conjunct the benefic planets. The conjunction receives 5 points, the trine, 4 points, and the sextile 3 points. Similarly, a planet is considered accidentally debilitated if it forms a tense aspect (square and opposition) or is conjunct the a malefic (Mars and Saturn). The conjunction receives -5 points, the opposition -4 points, and the square, -3 points. The sextile, trine, square or opposition aspects should be applying or very close.

The conditions of assistance and besiegement are also included in this category as extreme cases. Thus, an assisted planet receives 5 points, while a besieged planet receives -5 points.

*Void of Course and Feral*: These two conditions are considered debilitated states. A feral planet is thought to be very debilitated and receives -3 points. A void planet is considered slightly less debilitated and is penalized with -2 points. Both scores are not cumulative; that is, the planet is either feral or void and is scored by one or the other, but never both simultaneously.

## Conformity

Conformity speaks to a combination of conditions wherein the natural predisposition of the planet is reinforced. The most significant of these conditions are *hayz* and *joy by sign*.

### Hayz

Because it gives the planet some stability in its expression, the condition of hayz equals a score of 3 points. The contrariety of hayz, considered a little less debilitated, equals only -2 points.

### Joy by Sign

This is also a dignity because a planet in the sign of its joy has the ideal conditions to express its nature. This dignity gives 3 points; it has no equivalent debility.

The conditions of *conformity by quadrant* and of *dustoria* are also included in this group of accidental dignities. In practice, though, they are simply secondary reinforcements of the *hayz* condition and are not always included in the tables. Conforming to quadrant is given 2 points; dustoria, due to its rarity, receives 5 points.

## Conjunction to the Lunar Nodes

The tradition considers both Nodes as points of instability and the contact of a planet to the lunar Nodes is considered a debility. The conjunction with the South Node is considered more debilitated and receives -5 points. The conjunction with the North Node is not as damaging, equaling -3 points.[30]

## Lunar Condition

To the Moon are attributed various specific conditions, of which the most important in terms of scoring is *via combusta*, to which -2 points are awarded. Other lunar conditions that may be scored are the following:

- The position in Gemini, or at the end of signs, which awards it -2 points.
- An eclipsed Moon, which awards it -5points (this condition may also be applied to the Sun).

These conditions have greater significance in horary and mundane horoscopes.

---

[30]Some authors consider the North Node to be positive due to its benefic nature. In this case, the conjunction to the node receives 3 points.

## Conjunction to Fixed Stars

The conjunction of a planet with a fixed star of the 1st or 2nd magnitude and of a benefic nature awards it 5 points; in parallel, the conjunction to a star of a malefic nature, also of the 1st and 2nd magnitude, equals -5 points.

The following stars are suggestions for interpretation:
- Benefics: Regulus, Spica, Agena, Rigel Centaurus, Vega, Formaulhaut, Achernar, Sirius, and Rigel.
- Malefics: Algol, Antares, Markab, Alphard, Hamal, Zosma, Denebola, Sabik and Ras Alhague.

The majority of traditional authors that include this scoring in their tables limit themselves to Regulus and Spica as benefics and Algol as a malefic.

## Other Accidental Dignities and Debilities

There is yet another series of conditions of more minor importance, which may also be considered. Although there are points assigned to them, their practical use is limited to a mere mention, which is secondary or even completely omitted from the general scoring of the horoscope. Among them are:

*Ascension to the Midheaven*

This condition relates to a planet that is moving toward culmination, meaning located between the IC and the Midheaven on the side of the Ascendant; it is given 2 points. The corresponding debility—Descendant to Midheaven—equals -2 points and refers to a planet that moves away from culmination (between the Midheaven and the IC on the side of the Descendant).

*Latitude of the Planet*

A planet that moves from southern latitude to northern latitude receives 2 points because this movement increases its visibility (and consequently, its power). The movement in the inverse direction is considered a debility and corresponds to a penalization of -2 points.

*Ascension to its Auge*

As already mentioned, the *auge* corresponds to a planet's proximity to its apogee (the point farthest from the Earth). The debility corresponds to the approximation of the planet to perigee (the point closest to the Earth). They receive 2 and -2 points, respectively.

*Favorable and Unfavorable Degrees*

When a planet is posited in one of the favored degrees it is considered slightly dignified and given 1 point. When in unfavorable degrees it is considered debilitated and given -1 point. The tables for these degrees and their respective explanations can be found in Appendix 3.

### Final Scoring: the Table of Strengths and Debilities of the Planets

The scoring system discussed here can be organized into a scoring table, which is one of the essential instruments of the astrological tradition. This table evaluates the relative strength of each planet in the horoscope and assists in interpretation. According to this system, the strength of each planet is indicated by the sum of all of its dignities and debilities, both the essential and accidental ones. Each planet thus obtains a numerical value that facilitates a comparison of strengths. The table below summarizes the most significant scores[31]:

The scores for each planet are given in columns. Not all of the boxes will be filled because all of the indicated conditions do not apply to every planet. Furthermore, some conditions do not occur for particular planets (for example, the Sun cannot be combust nor retrograde); in these cases, the relevant box is shaded. At the end, the points for each column are added and a sum total is obtained for each planet. The essential dignities are scored in the first part of the table. In this first scoring a subtotal is obtained that indicates the essential quality of each planet. To this result are added two new elements: the condition of **peregrine** and **mutual reception**.

A peregrine condition is normally not scored because it corresponds to 0 dignity points. Nevertheless, in this

**Table of Strengths and Debilities of the Planets**

| Strengths: | | ♄ | ♃ | ♂ | ☉ | ♀ | ☿ | ☽ | | Debilities: |
|---|---|---|---|---|---|---|---|---|---|---|
| Rulership | +5 | | | | | | | | -5 | Detriment |
| Exaltation | +4 | | | | | | | | -4 | Fall |
| Triplicity | +3 | | | | | | | | - | |
| Term | +2 | | | | – | | | – | - | |
| Face | +1 | | | | | | | | - | |
| Essential Dignities - Total: | | | | | | | | | | |
| | - | | | | | | | | -5 | Peregrine |
| Mutual Reception by House | +5 | | | | | | | | - | |
| Mutual Reception by Exalt. | +4 | | | | | | | | - | |
| In the 1st or 10th House | +5 | | | | | | | | -5 | In the 12th House |
| In the 7th, 4th or 11th House | +4 | | | | | | | | -4 | In the 8th House |
| In the 5th or 2nd House | +3 | | | | | | | | -3 | In the 6th House |
| In the 9th House | +2 | | | | | | | | - | |
| In the 3rd House | +5 | | | | | | | | - | |
| In the Sign of its Joy | +5 | | | | | | | | - | |
| In the House of its Joy | +5 | | | | | | | | - | |
| Cazimi | +5 | | | | – | | | | -6 | Combust |
| Free from the Sun's beams | +5 | | | | – | | | | -4 | Under Sun's beams (☽<12°) |
| Increasing in Light | +1 | | | | – | | | | -1 | Decreasing in Light |
| ♄, ♃, ♂ Oriental | +2 | | | | – | – | – | – | -2 | ♄, ♃, ♂ Occidental |
| ♀, ☿, ☽ Occidental | +2 | – | – | – | – | | | | -2 | ♀, ☿, ☽ Oriental |
| | - | | | | | | | | -3 | ☌ ☊ |
| | - | | | | | | | | -5 | ☌ ☋ |
| Direct | +4 | | | | – | | | – | -5 | Retrograde |
| Fast in motion | +2 | | | | | | | | -2 | Slow in motion |
| ☌ ♃ or ♀ | +5 | | | | | | | | -5 | ☌ ♄ or ♂ |
| Applying △ to ♃ or ♀ | +4 | | | | | | | | -4 | Applying ☍ to ♄ or ♂ |
| Applying ✶ to ♃ or ♀ | +3 | | | | | | | | -3 | Applying □ to ♄ or ♂ |
| Assisted (between ♃ and ♀) | +5 | | | | | | | | -5 | Besieged (between ♄ and ♂) |
| | - | | | | | | | | -2 | Void of course |
| | - | | | | | | | | -3 | Feral |
| Haiz | +3 | | | | | | | | -2 | Contrariety of Haiz |
| | - | – | – | – | – | – | – | | -5 | ☽ in *Via Combusta* |
| Final Score: | | | | | | | | | | |

**Figure 1. Planetary Strengths**

[31]There are many versions of this table in the traditional literature, but its underpinning is always the same. The variations are due to minor differences in the scoring or in the factors that other authors considers to be more significant.

global scoring system, it is penalized with -5 points. The reason for this is to give more weight to planets that have essential dignities by elevating them in the final scores. A planet with some dignity is always more functional than a peregrine one, and thus should be emphasized in the final score.

Mutual reception is considered here because it involves a combination of essential and accidental dignities: rulership (or exaltation) and aspect. In the case of a mutual reception,[32] each planet is given the score that it would have had if it had been in the sign where it has dignity. Thus, 5 points are given to planets in mutual reception by rulership, and 4 points to those in mutual reception by exaltation. The mixed reception (rulership-exaltation) is rarely scored because it is considered less noticeable. However, a planet that is in the exaltation of the other receives 4 points, and the one that is in the rulership of the other receives 5 points.

The remaining lines refer to the accidental dignities described above. Note that in each line the dignity is indicated to the left and the corresponding debility to the right. For example, rulership corresponds to the debility of detriment, and direct motion corresponds to the debility of retrogradation. In some cases this correspondence does not exist. For example, the triplicity, term, and face dignities do not have equivalent debilities.

In addition to the counting of points, this table also serves as a memorandum where all of the conditions of the planets are indicated.

**Scoring Example**

Using Florbela Espanca's chart as an example, the table will be completed step by step.

Begin with the essential dignities and give each planet the score relative to its state of dignity or debility. The following dignities are present in Florbela Espanca's chart:

- Mars in rulership in Aries, receives 5 points
- Jupiter exalted in Cancer, receives 4 points
- The Sun in triplicity in Sagittarius, receives 3 points
- Mars also in term at 23° Aries, receives 2 more points

There are no planets in detriment or fall.

The first subtotal for the essential dignities is thus:

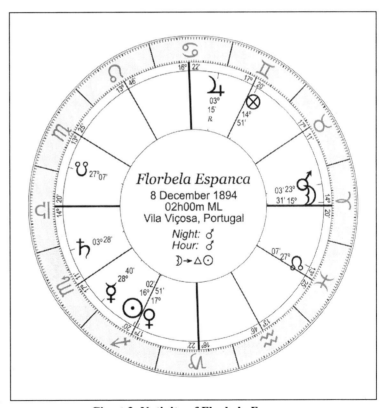

**Chart 3. Nativity of Florbela Espanca**

---

[32]We recall that mutual reception requires the existence of an aspect between planets, as was referred in the chapter on aspectual dynamics. However, not all authors agree with this rule; some attribute points to mutual reception even when no aspect exists.

| | ♄ | ♃ | ♂ | ☉ | ♀ | ☿ | ☽ | |
|---|---|---|---|---|---|---|---|---|---|
| Rulership | +5 | | | +5 | | | | -5 | Detriment |
| Exaltation | +4 | | +4 | | | | | -4 | Fall |
| Triplicity | +3 | | | +3 | | | | . | |
| Term | +2 | | +2 | – | | | – | . | |
| Face | +1 | | | | | | | . | |
| Essential Dignities - Total: | | 0 | 4 | 7 | 3 | 0 | 0 | 0 | |

**Figure 2. Scoring the Essential Dignities**

Next, the totals for peregrine planets and mutual reception are added to the essential dignities subtotal. From the previous table, observe that there are four peregrine planets, meaning without essential dignity—Saturn, Venus, Mercury, and the Moon. Each is therefore penalized with -5 points. There are no mutual receptions. The result is:

| | | ♄ | ♃ | ♂ | ☉ | ♀ | ☿ | ☽ | |
|---|---|---|---|---|---|---|---|---|---|
| | . | -5 | | | | -5 | -5 | -5 | -5 | Peregrine |
| Mutual Reception by House | +5 | | | | | | | . | |
| Mutual Reception by Exalt. | +4 | | | | | | | . | |

**Figure 3. Scoring the Conditions of Peregrine and Mutual Reception**

Next, the **accidental dignities**, are evaluated. This involves several sections. Begin by attributing the scores relevant to their **position by house**. The result is:

- Saturn in the first receives 5 points
- Mars and the Moon in the seventh each receive 4 points
- Mercury in the second house receives 3 points
- Jupiter in the ninth house receives 2 points
- The Sun and Venus in the third house each receive 1 point

Because there are no planets in the twelfth, eighth and sixth houses, no negative points are attributed. The result is:

| | | ♄ | ♃ | ♂ | ☉ | ♀ | ☿ | ☽ | |
|---|---|---|---|---|---|---|---|---|---|
| In the 1st or 10th House | +5 | +5 | | | | | | | -5 | In the 12th House |
| In the 7th, 4th or 11th House | +4 | | | +4 | | | | +4 | -4 | In the 8th House |
| In the 5th or 2nd House | +3 | | | | | | +3 | | -3 | In the 6th House |
| In the 9th House | +2 | | +2 | | | | | | . | |
| In the 3rd House | +5 | | | | | +1 | +1 | | . | |

**Figure 4. Scoring House Positions**

The concept of joy by sign and house is derived from the position of the planets by sign and house. In this example, there are no planets in either position.

Next score the planets with regard to their positions relative to the Sun. In this section, the Sun is not scored because for obvious reasons none of the conditions apply to it. The first factor to be evaluated is the planet's proximity to the Sun, which produces the conditions of combustion, under-the-beams, and cazimi. In this

| | | ♄ | ♃ | ♂ | ☉ | ♀ | ☿ | ☽ | | |
|---|---|---|---|---|---|---|---|---|---|---|
| Cazimi | +5 | | | | – | -6 | | | -6 | Combust |
| Free from the Sun's beams | +5 | +5 | +5 | +5 | – | | +5 | +5 | -4 | Under Sun's beams (☽<12°) |
| Increasing in Light | +1 | +1 | +1 | -1 | – | +1 | -1 | +1 | -1 | Decreasing in Light |
| ♄, ♃, ♂ Oriental | +2 | +2 | +2 | -2 | – | – | – | – | -2 | ♄, ♃, ♂ Occidental |
| ♀, ☿, ☽ Occidental | +2 | – | – | – | – | +2 | -2 | +2 | -2 | ♀, ☿, ☽ Oriental |

**Figure 5. Scoring the Planet's Relationships to the Sun**

chart, Venus is combust, so it receives -6 points. All of the others are free of combustion and outside of the Sun's beams and therefore receive 5 points. There are no cazimi planets.

Next, look for increase in light, another condition derived from the planet's relationship to the Sun. In this chart, the slow planets Saturn and Jupiter are increasing in light because the Sun is moving away from them. The same occurs with Venus and the Moon, which are moving away from the Sun. For this condition they each receive 1 point. Diminishing in light is Mercury, which is approaching the Sun, and the slower Mars, to which the Sun is approaching. These planets each receive -1 point.

As to orientality, Saturn and Jupiter are oriental, each receiving 2 points. Venus and the Moon also receive 2 points each because they are occidental. As to the debilities, Mars is occidental and Mercury is oriental; therefore, each is penalized with -2 points.

| Planet | Daily average speed | Speed on Florbela's chart |
|---|---|---|
| ♄ Saturn | 00°02' | 00°06' |
| ♃ Jupiter | 00°05' | 00°07' ℞ |
| ♂ Mars | 00°31' | 00°12' |
| ☉ Sun | 00°59' | 01°01' |
| ♀ Venus | 00°59' | 01°15' |
| ☿ Mercury | 00°59' | 01°26' |
| ☽ Moon | 13°11' | 12°49' |

**Figure 6. Velocity of the Planets in Florbela Espanca's Chart**

In Florbela Espanca's chart there are no planets conjunct the lunar Nodes.

Next, evaluate the motion of the planets, which includes direction and velocity. With respect to direction, all of the planets are scored except the Sun and the Moon, which are never retrograde. In this chart, all of the planets are direct and receive 4 points, with the exception of Jupiter, which is retrograde and receives -5 points.

The evaluation of velocity is possibly the least obvious in this table. It requires prior knowledge of the average speed of the planets and also the velocity of each planet of the chart under study (which is not always indicated by the astrological software programs). By comparing the velocities of the planets in this chart with the correspondent average velocities we verify that:

- Saturn, Mars, the Sun, Venus and Mercury are fast, and therefore they receive 2 points each
- Mars and the Moon are slow, so they receive 2 negative points each

If a planet's velocity corresponds to the average, it receives 0 points (neither fast nor slow). The result is shown in Figure 6.

| | | ♄ | ♃ | ♂ | ☉ | ♀ | ☿ | ☽ | | |
|---|---|---|---|---|---|---|---|---|---|---|
| Direct | +4 | +4 | -5 | +4 | – | +4 | +4 | – | -5 | Retrograde |
| Fast in motion | +2 | +2 | +2 | -2 | +2 | +2 | +2 | -2 | -2 | Slow in motion |

**Figure 7. Scoring the Planet's Movement**

Next is the evaluation of the accidental dignities by aspect: conjunctions (both applying and separating) with the benefic planets, Venus and Jupiter; applying aspects of sextile and trine to the same planets, or the condition of assistance.

The corresponding debilities are: conjunctions to the malefic planets, Mars and Saturn; applying squares and oppositions to the same planets, and the condition of besiegement.

In the chart of Florbela Espanca the Sun receives 5 points for its conjunction to Venus, and the Moon loses 5 points for its conjunction to Mars; Mars and the Moon receive 4 points each, due to the applying trine of Venus.

In this case 4 points are also attributed to Saturn because of the trine from Jupiter; although separating, this aspect is extremely exact, with both planets within the same degree and only 13′ apart.

There are no conditions of assistance or besiegement in this horoscope.

As to the other conditions related to the aspects, there is only one void of course planet, Mars, which receives 2 negative points, and a feral planet, Mercury, which receives 3 negative points. Although strictly speaking Saturn and Jupiter are not applying to any planet, they form a very close aspect and so are not considered void of course.

Note that the conditions of feral and void are not cumulative (remember that the feral condition includes, by definition, the void of course condition). The results are:

| | | ♄ | ♃ | ♂ | ☉ | ♀ | ☿ | ☽ | | |
|---|---|---|---|---|---|---|---|---|---|---|
| ☌ ♃ or ♀ | +5 | | | | +5 | | | -5 | -5 | ☌ ♄ or ♂ |
| Applying △ to ♃ or ♀ | +4 | +4 | | +4 | | | | +4 | -4 | Applying ☍ to ♄ or ♂ |
| Applying ✱ to ♃ or ♀ | +3 | | | | | | | | -3 | Applying □ to ♄ or ♂ |
| Assisted (between ♃ and ♀) | +5 | | | | | | | | -5 | Besieged (between ♄ and ♂) |
| | - | | | -2 | | | | | -2 | Void of course |
| | - | | | | | | -3 | | -3 | Feral |

**Figure 8. Scoring the Aspects**

There is only the condition of *hayz* and its contrariety left to evaluate. In Florbela's horoscope one planet is in *hayz*, Mars, which receives 3 points, and two in contrariety, Jupiter and Venus, which each receive -2 points.

Lastly, the condition of being in the *via combusta* is examined. This applies solely to the Moon. In the example under study, the Moon is not in the *via combusta* and therefore does not receive a score.

The final tally is shown in Figure 10.

In this case, Mars is clearly the most distinguished planet with 20 points, followed by Saturn with 18. The predominance of Mars becomes evident at the very start of the scoring because it is the planet with the most essential dignity. Its final score is therefore of no surprise.

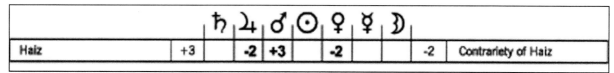

| | | ♄ | ♃ | ♂ | ☉ | ♀ | ☿ | ☽ | | |
|---|---|---|---|---|---|---|---|---|---|---|
| Haiz | +3 | | -2 | +3 | | -2 | | | -2 | Contrariety of Haiz |

**Figure 9. Scoring the Conditions of *Hayz* and Contrariety of *Hayz***

| Strengths: | | ♄ | ♃ | ♂ | ☉ | ♀ | ☿ | ☽ | | Debilities: |
|---|---|---|---|---|---|---|---|---|---|---|
| Rulership | +5 | | | +5 | | | | | -5 | Detriment |
| Exaltation | +4 | | +4 | | | | | | -4 | Fall |
| Triplicity | +3 | | | | +3 | | | | · | |
| Term | +2 | | | +2 | – | | | – | · | |
| Face | +1 | | | | | | | | · | |
| Essential Dignities - Total: | | 0 | 4 | 7 | 3 | 0 | 0 | 0 | | |
| | · | -5 | | | | -5 | -5 | -5 | -5 | Peregrine |
| Mutual Reception by House | +5 | | | | | | | | · | |
| Mutual Reception by Exalt. | +4 | | | | | | | | · | |
| In the 1st or 10th House | +5 | +5 | | | | | | | -5 | In the 12th House |
| In the 7th, 4th or 11th House | +4 | | | +4 | | | | +4 | -4 | In the 8th House |
| In the 5th or 2nd House | +3 | | | | | | +3 | | -3 | In the 6th House |
| In the 9th House | +2 | | +2 | | | | | | · | |
| In the 3rd House | +5 | | | | +1 | +1 | | | · | |
| In the Sign of its Joy | +5 | | | | | | | | · | |
| In the House of its Joy | +5 | | | | | | | | · | |
| Cazimi | +5 | | | | – | -6 | | | -6 | Combust |
| Free from the Sun's beams | +5 | +5 | +5 | +5 | – | | +5 | +5 | -4 | Under Sun's beams (☽<12°) |
| Increasing in Light | +1 | +1 | +1 | -1 | – | +1 | -1 | +1 | -1 | Decreasing in Light |
| ♄, ♃, ♂ Oriental | +2 | +2 | +2 | -2 | – | – | – | – | -2 | ♄, ♃, ♂ Occidental |
| ♀, ☿, ☽ Occidental | +2 | – | – | – | – | +2 | -2 | +2 | -2 | ♀, ☿, ☽ Oriental |
| | · | | | | | | | | -3 | ☌ ☊ |
| | · | | | | | | | | -5 | ☌ ☋ |
| Direct | +4 | +4 | -5 | +4 | – | +4 | +4 | – | -5 | Retrograde |
| Fast in motion | +2 | +2 | +2 | -2 | +2 | +2 | +2 | -2 | -2 | Slow in motion |
| ☌ ♃ or ♀ | +5 | | | | +5 | | | -5 | -5 | ☌ ♄ or ♂ |
| Applying △ to ♃ or ♀ | +4 | +4 | | +4 | | | | +4 | -4 | Applying ☍ to ♄ or ♂ |
| Applying ⚹ to ♃ or ♀ | +3 | | | | | | | | -3 | Applying □ to ♄ or ♂ |
| Assisted (between ♃ and ♀) | +5 | | | | | | | | -5 | Besieged (between ♄ and ♂) |
| | · | | | -2 | | | | | -2 | Void of course |
| | · | | | | | | -3 | | -3 | Feral |
| Haiz | +3 | | -2 | +3 | | -2 | | | -2 | Contrariety of Haiz |
| | · | – | – | – | – | – | – | | -5 | ☽ in *Via Combusta* |
| Final Score: | | 18 | 9 | 20 | 11 | -3 | 3 | 4 | | |

**Figure 10. Final Score in Florbela Espanca's Nativity**

Saturn is in second place exclusively because of the accidental dignities, of which angularity, orientality, direct motion, swiftness, and an applied trine from Jupiter are highlighted. This case exemplifies how a planet without essential dignity ends up being important in the overall scoring.

### Important Considerations Regarding the Practical Use of the Table

It is of the utmost importance to remember that each of these accidental dignities has a specific value and that not all weigh the same in the interpretation. The most important is, without a doubt, the planet's placement by house because it is the strongest and most evident of all of the accidental dignities. Its consideration should be made first and serve as a basis for the others, which add small variations to the expression of the planet. It is of paramount importance to keep in mind that this table gives us only a *quantification* of each planet's conditions. These data must be approached within the context of the interpretation where they are treated not in terms of quantity but rather in terms of quality.

In practice, these dignities are cumulative and never nullify each other. Each one gives the planet its own specific ease or difficulty. The additions and subtractions of this table serve only to facilitate the scoring; the totals obtained should be viewed as an instrument that allows for a comparison of the relative strengths of the planets in the horoscope. They should not be viewed as absolute values because this approach does not take into account the gradations that the majority of situations present. For example, two planets situated in the same house will have different intensities if one is very close to the cusp and the other is at the end of the house. Nonetheless, both receive the same score. In another example, a planet that is moving away from combustion and is already at the limit of the eighth degree from the Sun receives the same -6 point score as another planet that is only 2 degrees away from the Sun. In the first case, although still combust, the planet is in a slightly better condition than the second. These and other gradations, which are fundamental to proper interpretation, can only be detected by closely examining the chart. In reality, the chart is always the starting and ending point: it should be studied before erecting a table and examined again after the scoring in order to properly contextualize the obtained results.

It is important to resist the tendency to immediately interpret any value that is obtained from a calculation, since, in the majority of the cases, this value only makes sense in the context of the delineation. This is, incidentally, a problematic aspect of the current astrological trend: the necessity, often inappropriate, to interpret everything independently of a context. Note that many times this problem is generated by automatic scoring and by other shortcuts resulting from the use of computers. As for interpreting the results, it is always important to note that the planetary scores are only valid when placed within the general context of the table. Therefore, it is of no use to interpret a planet in isolation; this interpretation only makes sense when its score is compared with that of the others.[33]

In summary, although the importance of this scoring table is recognized, its value is relative since it quantifies that which should be qualified. It is a tool for interpretation but cannot in any circumstance substitute for a study of the horoscope itself. Its objective is simply to augment the student's own capacity to interpret. It is important that it be fully understood and applied since its inappropriate use leads to instant and noticeably incongruent interpretations.

Having said that, planetary scoring should be made with care. One should dedicate the necessary time and effort, since it is of fundamental assistance to delineation. We encourage students to do these calculations manually because they prepare the way for delineation.

Because we live today in a society that values "fast and easy," there may be a desire to skip the effort needed to make these calculations. Computer programs encourage this laziness, offering all manner of precalculated tabulations. However, the student should always keep in mind that this attitude impairs one's interpretation results.

### Examples of the Scoring Table

*Florbela Espanca*
Returning again to the chart for Florbela Espanca, the essential dignity of the planets will be compared with their overall power in the horoscope.

Mars, the planet with the greatest essential dignity, retains its prominence in the final tally. This emphasis of Mars characterizes the pioneering and bold attitude that marked the life of this poet.

On the other hand, Saturn's highlighted position points to an entirely different aspect to her nature. This planet is strong but without essential dignity and located in a water sign, which suggests a melancholic and disagreeable personality with a tendency toward depressive episodes. Notice that Saturn is in the first house, which contributes directly to the characterization of Florbela's personality and even overrides the indications given by Mars, in spite of its higher score. This combination of traits results in a comportment that os-

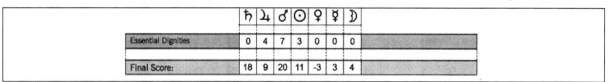

| | ♄ | ♃ | ♂ | ☉ | ♀ | ☿ | ☽ |
|---|---|---|---|---|---|---|---|
| Essential Dignities | 0 | 4 | 7 | 3 | 0 | 0 | 0 |
| Final Score: | 18 | 9 | 20 | 11 | -3 | 3 | 4 |

**Figure 11. Essential Dignities and Scoring in the Chart of Florbela Espanca**

[33]In the same way, it is of little use to compare the scores of two charts since each is valid only within its own context.

cillates between "poetic melancholy" (Saturn) and the bold impulsivity (Moon-Mars) that characterize her life and her work.

*Friedrich Nietzsche*

The planetary scores for this philosopher's horoscope are as follows:

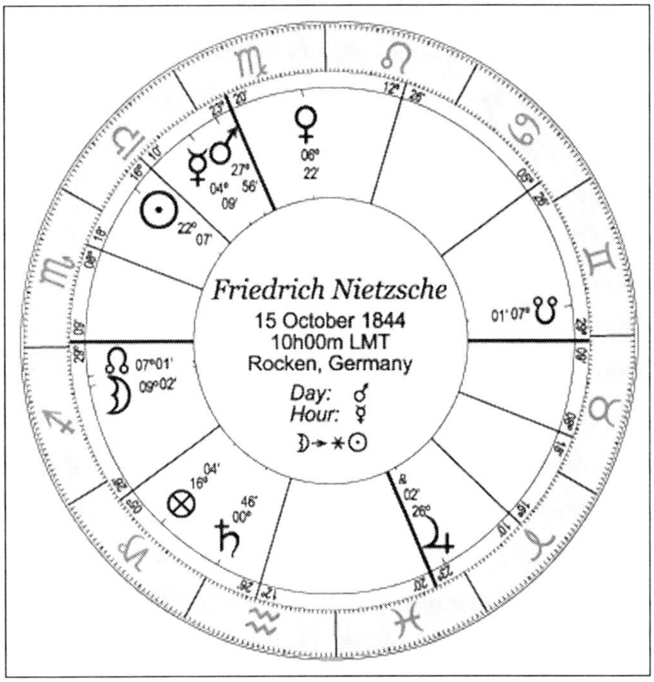


**Chart 1. Nativity of Friedrich Nietzsche**

In this case we observe a clear predominance of Mars followed by Saturn and Mercury, planets which will characterize the general coloring of the individual. We note in the chart that Mars and Mercury are conjunct, which suggests a personality given to arguments, discussions and to critique. Saturn, the other highlighted planet, contributes with the depth of thought typical of a philosopher, but also accents the tendency to diverge from current trends.

Jupiter is also interesting. The planet is essentially dignified but, contrary to what is expected, it has a low final score because it includes several accidental debilities. In practice, the essential dignity of Jupiter imparts conviction and the courage of one's beliefs (in this case, strong anti-clerical convictions), but the total of accidental debilities keeps these from manifesting with much power. From the work of this philosopher we find that the expression of his more profound beliefs (dignified Jupiter but not very prominent) is concealed by his natural tendency toward questioning and dispute (very prominent Mars, Mercury and Saturn).

| Strengths: | | ♄ | ♃ | ♂ | ☉ | ♀ | ☿ | ☽ | | Debilities: |
|---|---|---|---|---|---|---|---|---|---|---|
| Rulership | +5 | +5 | +5 | | | | | | -5 | Detriment |
| Exaltation | +4 | | | | -4 | -4 | | | -4 | Fall |
| Triplicity | +3 | +3 | | +3 | | +3 | +3 | | · | |
| Term | +2 | | | +2 | – | | | – | · | |
| Face | +1 | | | | | | | | · | |
| Essential Dignities - Total: | | 8 | 5 | 5 | -4 | -1 | 3 | 0 | | |
| | · | | | | -5 | | | -5 | -5 | Peregrine |
| Mutual Reception by House | +5 | | | | | | | | · | |
| Mutual Reception by Exalt. | +4 | | | | | | | | · | |
| In the 1st or 10th House | +5 | | | +5 | | | +5 | +5 | -5 | In the 12th House |
| In the 7th, 4th or 11th House | +4 | | +4 | | +4 | | | | -4 | In the 8th House |
| In the 5th or 2nd House | +3 | +3 | | | | | | | -3 | In the 6th House |
| In the 9th House | +2 | | | | | +2 | | | · | |
| In the 3rd House | +5 | | | | | | | | · | |
| In the Sign of its Joy | +5 | +3 | | | | | | | · | |
| In the House of its Joy | +5 | | | | | | | | · | |
| Cazimi | +5 | | | | – | | | | -6 | Combust |
| Free from the Sun's beams | +5 | +5 | +5 | +5 | – | +5 | +5 | +5 | -4 | Under Sun's beams (☽<12°) |
| Increasing in Light | +1 | -1 | -1 | +1 | – | -1 | -1 | +1 | -1 | Decreasing in Light |
| ♄, ♃, ♂ Oriental | +2 | -2 | -2 | +2 | – | – | – | – | -2 | ♄, ♃, ♂ Occidental |
| ♀, ☿, ☽ Occidental | +2 | – | – | – | – | -2 | -2 | +2 | -2 | ♀, ☿, ☽ Oriental |
| | · | | | | | | | -3 | -3 | ☌ ☊ |
| | · | | | | | | | | -5 | ☌ ☋ |
| Direct | +4 | +4 | -5 | +4 | – | +4 | +4 | – | -5 | Retrograde |
| Fast in motion | +2 | -2 | +2 | +2 | +2 | +2 | +2 | +2 | -2 | Slow in motion |
| ☌ ♃ or ♀ | +5 | | | | | | -5 | | -5 | ☌ ♄ or ♂ |
| Applying △ to ♃ or ♀ | +4 | | | | | | | | -4 | Applying ☍ to ♄ or ♂ |
| Applying ✶ to ♃ or ♀ | +3 | | | | -3 | | | | -3 | Applying □ to ♄ or ♂ |
| Assisted (between ♃ and ♀) | +5 | | | | | | | | -5 | Besieged (between ♄ and ♂) |
| | · | -2 | -2 | | | -2 | -2 | | -2 | Void of course |
| | · | | | | | | | | -3 | Feral |
| Haiz | +3 | | -2 | -2 | +3 | | +3 | | -2 | Contrariety of Haiz |
| | · | – | – | – | – | – | – | | -5 | ☽ in *Via Combusta* |
| Final Score: | | 16 | 4 | 22 | -3 | 7 | 12 | 7 | | |

**Figure 12. Planetary Strengths for Nietzsche's Nativity**

*Agatha Christie*

The chart of Agatha Christie has the following planetary scores:

The scoring of essential dignities indicates that Mercury and Jupiter are the more powerful planets, which is not surprising brcause this is the chart of a writer. However, surprisingly, the final score clearly underscores Venus, a planet that is in detriment and cadent! The distinction of Venus in the life of this writer becomes easy to understand if we examine the chart. Venus rules the Midheaven (career and fame) and is posited in the third house (writing, communication). In fact, this author is known for extensive literary work whose theme is crime, mystery and passion—situations described by a debilitated Venus in Scorpion. In any event, Mercury is the second most highlighted planet, which makes complete sense in the chart of a person who dedicated her life to writing.

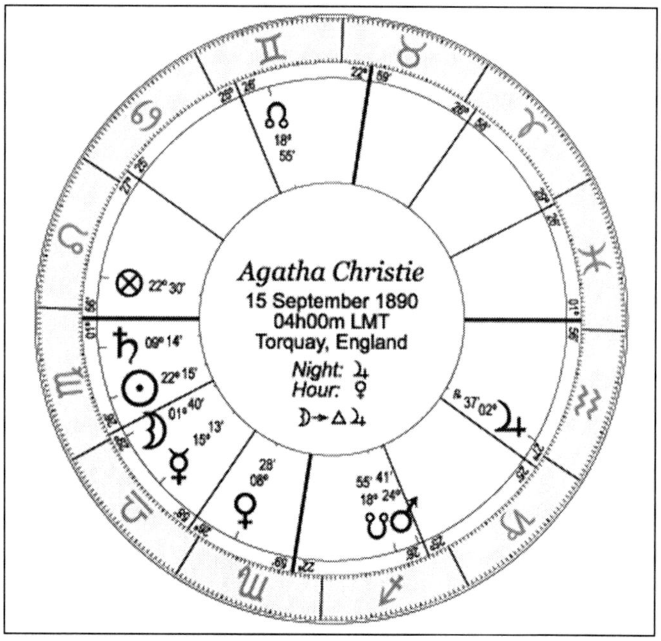


**Chart 2. Nativity of Agatha Christie**

These are some examples of the application of this table to natal charts. Let's now look at how it might be applied to horary charts.

*Broken Computer*

There was a potentially serious problem with a broken computer, possibly the need to replace the motherboard, which would be very costly. This question was asked: "Is the motherboard of the computer broken?"

The computer is signified by the second house (since it is a possession), by the ruler and by the planets that are posited there. The second house has Leo on the cusp, which makes the Sun its ruler. The Sun has no dignity whatsoever (peregrine) and is in the sixth house, a weak cadent house, which depicts its poor or weakened condition. Also in the second house is the Moon, it too in a weakened condition: it is peregrine, slow in motion and applying to a square with Mars.

After completing the full scoring, the Sun and Moon have negative scores, meaning their accidental condition reinforces their weakened state. Conclusion: the motherboard did indeed have to be replaced. Although it retained some of its functions, it nonetheless had an irreparable problem.

| Strengths: | | ♄ | ♃ | ♂ | ☉ | ♀ | ☿ | ☽ | | Debilities: |
|---|---|---|---|---|---|---|---|---|---|---|
| Rulership | +5 | | | | | -5 | | | -5 | Detriment |
| Exaltation | +4 | | | | | | | | -4 | Fall |
| Triplicity | +3 | | +3 | | | +3 | +3 | | • | |
| Term | +2 | | | | – | +2 | | – | • | |
| Face | +1 | | | | | | | +1 | • | |
| Essential Dignities - Total: | | 0 | +3 | 0 | 0 | 0 | +3 | +1 | | |
| | • | -5 | | -5 | -5 | | | | -5 | Peregrine |
| Mutual Reception by House | +5 | | | | | | | | • | |
| Mutual Reception by Exalt. | +4 | | | | | | | | • | |
| In the 1st or 10th House | +5 | +5 | | | +5 | | | | -5 | In the 12th House |
| In the 7th, 4th or 11th House | +4 | | | | | | | | -4 | In the 8th House |
| In the 5th or 2nd House | +3 | | -3 | +3 | | | +3 | +3 | -3 | In the 6th House |
| In the 9th House | +2 | | | | | | | | • | |
| In the 3rd House | +5 | | | | | +1 | | | • | |
| In the Sign of its Joy | +5 | | | | | | | | • | |
| In the House of its Joy | +5 | | | | | | | | • | |
| Cazimi | +5 | | | | – | | | | -6 | Combust |
| Free from the Sun's beams | +5 | -4 | +5 | +5 | – | +5 | +5 | -4 | -4 | Under Sun's beams (☽<12°) |
| Increasing in Light | +1 | +1 | -1 | -1 | – | +1 | -1 | +1 | -1 | Decreasing in Light |
| ♄, ♃, ♂ Oriental | +2 | +2 | -2 | -2 | – | – | – | – | -2 | ♄, ♃, ♂ Occidental |
| ♀, ☿, ☽ Occidental | +2 | – | – | – | – | +2 | +2 | +2 | -2 | ♀, ☿, ☽ Oriental |
| | • | | | | | | | | -3 | ☌ ☊ |
| | • | | | -5 | | | | | -5 | ☌ ☋ |
| Direct | +4 | +4 | -5 | +4 | – | +4 | +4 | – | -5 | Retrograde |
| Fast in motion | +2 | +2 | -2 | +2 | 0 | +2 | -2 | -2 | -2 | Slow in motion |
| ☌ ♃ or ♀ | +5 | | | | | | | | -5 | ☌ ♄ or ♂ |
| Applying △ to ♃ or ♀ | +4 | | | | +4 | | | +4 | -4 | Applying ☍ to ♄ or ♂ |
| Applying ✶ to ♃ or ♀ | +3 | +3 | | | -3 | | | | -3 | Applying □ to ♄ or ♂ |
| Assisted (between ♃ and ♀) | +5 | | | | | | | | -5 | Besieged (between ♄ and ♂) |
| | • | -2 | | -2 | | | | | -2 | Void of course |
| | • | | | | | | -3 | | -3 | Feral |
| Haiz | +3 | | +3 | | -2 | | -2 | -2 | -2 | Contrariety of Haiz |
| | • | – | – | – | – | – | – | | -5 | ☽ in *Via Combusta* |
| Final Score: | | 6 | -2 | -1 | -1 | 15 | 9 | 3 | | |

**Figure 13. Planetary Strengths for Agatha Christie's Nativity**

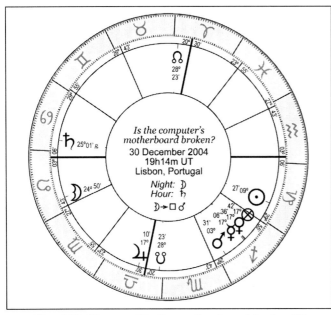

**Chart 10. Horary: "Is the motherboard broken?"**

| | ♄ | ♃ | ♂ | ☉ | ♀ | ☿ | ☽ |
|---|---|---|---|---|---|---|---|
| Essential Dignities | -5 | 5 | 0 | 0 | 0 | -3 | 0 |
| Final Score: | -6 | 30 | 10 | -8 | 14 | 19 | -7 |

**Figure 14. Planetary Strengths for chart 10**

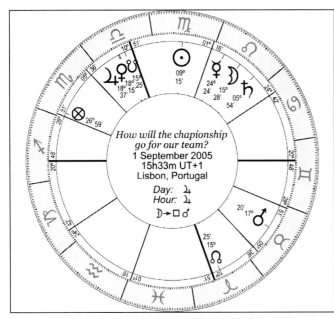

**Chart 11. Horary: "How will the championship go for our team?"**

| | ♄ | ♃ | ♂ | ☉ | ♀ | ☿ | ☽ |
|---|---|---|---|---|---|---|---|
| Essential Dignities | -1 | 5 | -2 | 1 | 5 | 0 | 0 |
| Final Score: | 10 | 19 | 9 | 3 | 22 | -9 | -18 |

**Figure 15. Planetary strengths for chart 11**

## Sports Championship

On the eve of an international sports championship, the captain of a team wanted to know how the competition would result. Figure 11 is the chart of the question: "How will the championship go for our team?"

The significators are Jupiter, ruler of the Ascendant and significator of the team, and Venus, ruler of the Midheaven and significator of the honors obtained and the yearned-for position. We observe in the horoscope that these planets are in exact (partile) conjunction, well-positioned in the tenth house, and essentially dignified, which indicates quite clearly that the competition will go well and that the team will obtain a good placement. Examining the table we verify that the complete scoring of planetary strength confirms the good condition of Jupiter and Venus, as would be expected.

Nonetheless, Jupiter and Venus are close to the South Node, a significator of disturbance and loss, which means the positive meaning of the planets will in some way be diminished. In fact, the team did lose the championship by a few points and had to become content with an honorable second place.

This is a good example of the absolute necessity to look at the chart, despite the information given by the scoring table. The numerical information merely *quantifies* the strength of the planets to attain the desired result. It does not *interpret* those results. If we consider the table without looking at the chart, we would judge victory as a certain outcome (because the planets are certainly very strong). However, we only get a complete picture from the interpretation, which reveals a factor that is vital for the outcome: the South Node. This factor indicates that the level of success is reduced and stops short of what is desired. This is the difference between *quantifying* (using the table) and *qualifying* (interpreting the chart).

## Home Purchase

Excited about a house he had seen, the prospective buyer wanted to confirm whether the property was of quality. The horoscope for the question is shown in Figure 12.

The house is signified by Venus, ruler of the fourth house (immovable property). In the horoscope Venus is essentially debilitated, representing therefore a house in poor condition. The conjunction to the South Node reinforces the idea of the poor condition.

However, a look at the table reveals that Venus is the most highly scored planet of the chart, which would lead to a rash judgment that the house is of good quality. We are faced with an apparent contradiction: on the one hand, Venus is highly scored, on the other, it is essentially debilitated. Which is the correct answer?

First, realize that the elevated score of Venus merely indicates its *prominence*, not its *quality*. In reality, the buyer was enchanted by the house and was tempted to precipitously purchase the property. This enchantment corresponds with the high distinction of Venus. Nevertheless, the horoscope reveals that this house, charming upon first glance, does not live up to expectations because it is represented by an essentially

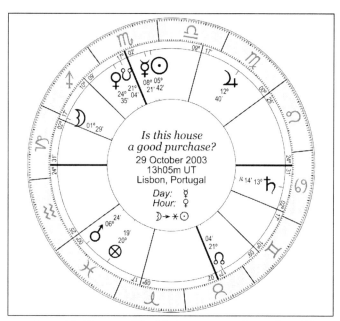

**Chart 12. Horary: "Is this house a good purchase?"**

| | ♄ | ♃ | ♂ | ☉ | ♀ | ☿ | ☽ |
|---|---|---|---|---|---|---|---|
| Essential Dignities | -5 | -5 | 3 | 0 | -1 | 0 | -2 |
| Final Score | -6 | -4 | 10 | 4 | 10 | 3 | 8 |

**Figure 15. Planetary strengths for chart 12**

debilitated planet. Therefore, no contradiction in reality exists. What exists is a powerful projection (elevated score) without the reciprocated worth (essential debility). On the basis of this and other information that the chart offers, we conclude that the house was not worth the asking price and that given the circumstances, it would be best not to make the purchase. This example once again highlights the importance of interpreting the correct context for the values given by the table.

# The Astrological Symbols

Because astrological symbols have evolved over time, this appendix presents the main variants of each symbol from the Greek, Medieval, and Renaissance periods.

## Planetary Symbols

Initially, the planets did not have their own symbols; they were represented in charts by their written names. As time went by, the writing became abbreviated and some names were gradually reduced to their initials, which eventually evolved into symbols. According to some authors, this is the origin of the symbols for Jupiter, Saturn, and Venus. The acronym for Jupiter derived from the letter zeta (Z), because the planet's Greek name is Zeus; the one for Venus comes from the letter Phi (Φ), *the initial of one of its Greek names, Phosphoros (meaning bright); the one for Saturn comes from Kappa* (K), from the name Kronos, one of Saturn's epithets.

Other symbols would have probably evolved from the attributes of the Greek gods they are associated with. This is the case of Mercury, whose symbol is the caduceus of Hermes, and the case of Mars, represented by the spear of Ares, god of war. There are symbols, which are direct representations of the planet, as is the case of the Moon.

## Symbols of the Signs

The symbols of the signs are, generally speaking, direct representations of the animal for which they are named. However, these symbols vary according to period and culture.

| Name | Greek Symbol | Medieval Symbol | Renaissance Symbol | Present time Symbol |
|---|---|---|---|---|
| Sun | ♂ | ☉ | ☉ | ☉ |
| Moon | ☾ | ☾ | ☽ | ☽ |
| Mercury | ☿ | ☿ | ☿ | ☿ |
| Venus | ♀ | ♀ | ♀ | ♀ |
| Mars | ♂ | ↑ | ♂ | ♂ |
| Jupiter | Z | ♃ | ♃ | ♃ |
| Saturn | ♄ | ♄ | ♄ | ♄ |

**Figure 1. Symbols of the Planets Throughout Time**

## Symbols of the Nodes

The lunar Nodes are represented by two circles united by an arc or semicircle, one arc is facing upward (the North Node), while the other is facing downward (the South Node). The glyph's circles represent the two Nodes and the arc connecting them is the path of the Moon, either the northern (upper) or the southern (lower) path.

The symbols of the Nodes have remained almost the same over time, with one important exception: by the end of the Middle Ages there was an exchange of glyphs between the North Node and the South Node. Therefore, until the end of the Medieval period, the North Node was represented by the symbol which is now used for the South Node, and vice-versa. This inversion may be due to the standardization of North at the top of maps. In earlier maps (for example in the Arabic culture) South was placed on the upper part of a chart. So, in earlier representations the South Node had the down-curving arc, and the North Node the up-curving arc.

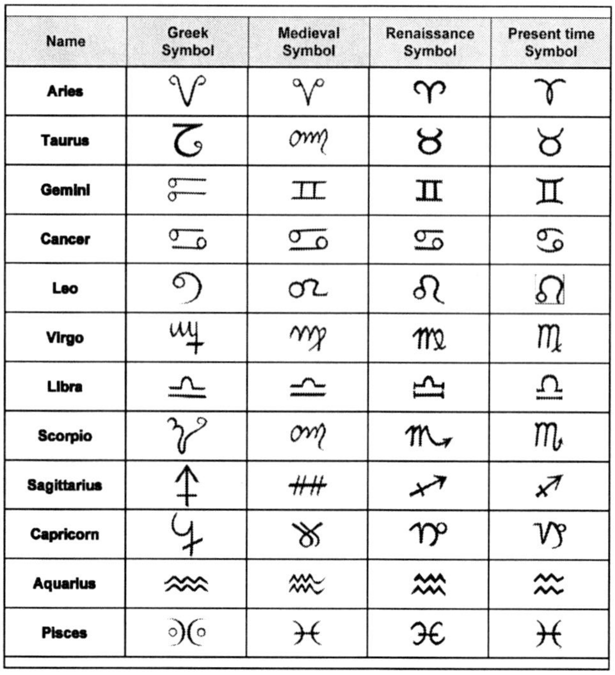

| Name | Greek Symbol | Medieval Symbol | Renaissance Symbol | Present time Symbol |
|---|---|---|---|---|
| Aries | | | | |
| Taurus | | | | |
| Gemini | | | | |
| Cancer | | | | |
| Leo | | | | |
| Virgo | | | | |
| Libra | | | | |
| Scorpio | | | | |
| Sagittarius | | | | |
| Capricorn | | | | |
| Aquarius | | | | |
| Pisces | | | | |

**Figure 2. Symbols of the Signs Throughout Time**

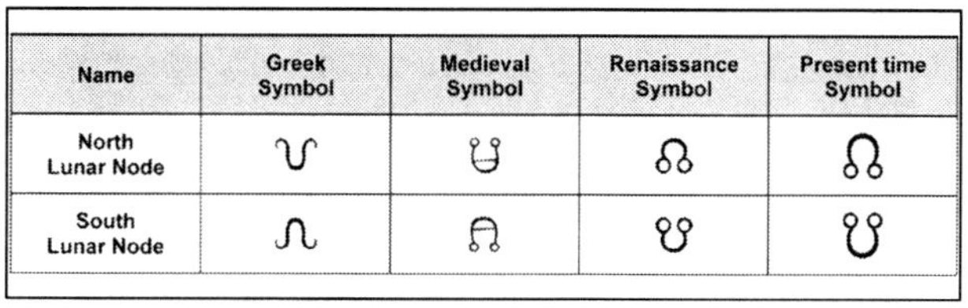

| Name | Greek Symbol | Medieval Symbol | Renaissance Symbol | Present time Symbol |
|---|---|---|---|---|
| North Lunar Node | | | | |
| South Lunar Node | | | | |

**Figure 3. Variants in the Node's Symbols**

*Appendix 2*
# *The Modern Planets*

The development of optical instruments in the 18th century allowed for the discovery of new celestial bodies that are not visible to the naked eye due to their small size and distance from Earth. In 1781, English astronomer John Herschel (1792-1871) discovered Uranus. In 1801, Italian astronomer Giuseppe Piazzi discovered the first asteroid, Ceres. In the following years Pallas, Juno, and Vesta were discovered, along with thousands of other asteroids. Neptune was detected in 1846, with the official discovery being attributed to German astronomer Johann Gottfried Galle (1812-1910), whose work was based on the calculations of the French mathematician Urbain Le Verrier (1811-1877).[34]

On the heels of these discoveries, new perceptions about the motion and relative position of the planets developed in just a few decades, eventually leading to the current concept of the solar system. The new celestial bodies were not immediately included in the astrological system and in the beginning they were ignored by astrologers. Uranus and Neptune only became a regular part of chart interpretation at the end of the 19th century. In 1930, they were joined by Pluto, which initially was classified with the planets, but is now considered a dwarf-planet.

The asteroids begin to appear in astrological charts in the 1970s. Their application in astrology peaked after the discovery of the planetoid Chiron in 1977. The last decades have witnessed the continual discovery of many new celestial bodies beyond the orbits of Neptune and Pluto, which has generated a state of confusion, whether from an astronomical or astrological perspective.

This appendix offers some thoughts regarding the inclusion and interpretation of these celestial bodies in the astrological system.

---

[34]Galileo had already discovered this planet, but thought it to be a star. Other renowned astronomers had suspected the existence of a planet beyond Uranus, without however being able to incontrovertibly prove it.

## Modern or Trans-saturnian Planets

### Uranus, Neptune and Pluto

From an astrological perspective, Uranus and Neptune are undoubtedly the more significant of all the new celestial bodies, followed closely by Pluto. The systematic interpretation of Uranus and Neptune in astrological charts began only at the end of the 19th century, during the astrological revival. The new planets are, in reality, an integral part of the "new" astrological system used at this time and which is the cornerstone of so-called modern astrology. During the process of astrological revival, the traditional system (by then severely misunderstood and lacking competent practitioners) was altered to make room for Uranus and Neptune. In order to accomplish this, an attempt was made to attribute to them some astrological signification and to define their nature. These attributions became widely accepted and are the ones used by the majority of present-day astrologers. However, the natures and characteristics attributed to the new planets are based upon a weak premise. This weakness derives from the method employed to derive these attributes. Because no empirical significations were available for these planets, astrologers resorted to mythology (generally what was associated with the name of the planet) and to the social and political events occurring at the time of the planet's discovery.

Therefore, because **Uranus** was discovered around the time of the French and American revolutions, it became associated with revolutions, unexpected events, ruptures, shocks, and unusual situations. These concepts are vaguely corroborated by the mythology of the Greek god Ouranos, who was dispossessed of his power by the rebellion of his son, Chronos (Saturn). The planet also became associated with genius, inventions and the new technologies, supposedly because there was an increase in scientific breakthroughs and technology after its discovery.

The qualities of spirituality, mystery, and mysticism were attributed to **Neptune** because its discovery coincided with the spiritual revival of the 19th century. On the other hand, it also becomes the planet of dreams, illusions, and escapism because its discovery coincides with certain medical innovations, such as anaesthesiology and hypnotism. In Neptune's case, the connection to mythology is tenuous at best since the attributes of Poseidon (the turbulent god of the oceans, the Greek equivalent of Neptune) bear little resemblance to the significations given to the planet. The only detectable association is a vague poetic correlation between the sea and its mysteries.

**Pluto** appeared some decades later, in the period between the two great wars, and thus became associated with destruction, death, catastrophes, and the abuse of power. For this reason, it also assumes rulership over atomic energy and its destructive power. Most of Pluto's astrological significations derive from the mythology of Hades (Pluto), the Greek god of the Underworld and thus attributes of death and rebirth as well as hidden and profound matters.

> Note: Pluto is now considered a dwarf-planet. As this change of status is very recent it is too soon to know its impact in the astrological community. The new classification will certainly affect the future interpretation of this dwarf-planet.

In the case of Pluto these significations were attributed almost immediately after the planet's discovery, without any experimental period to empirically test their validity. Note also that most of the attributes given to this planet had already been assigned in the beginning of the century to a hypothetical planet bearing the same name.[35] The coincidence of names led to the direct superimposition of the hypothetical planet's qualities onto newly discovered Pluto without much thought on the matter.

---

[35]This is a reference to the hypothetical planet currently known as Wemyss-Pluto, proposed by the Scottish astrologer Maurice Wemyss (1892-1960?), as a possible ruler of Cancer.

Much of the present symbolism of these celestial bodies is also said to be supported by octave theory. According to this theory, the three modern planets would stand as "superior" equivalents, or octaves, of Mercury, Venus, and Mars. In this perspective Uranus would signify the "collective mind" and the power of "individualized" thought, thus functioning as a higher vibration of Mercury, the "common" mind. Neptune would be "universal love," the higher octave of "personal love," signified by Venus. Pluto would stand for "transformation," a superior manifestation of the "destruction," signified by Mars. However, there are several attributes of the modern planets that are not explained by the theory of the octaves. For instance, the qualities of rebelliousness and rupture commonly attributed to Uranus are in the traditional system related to Mars and not to Mercury; illusion and dream, associated with Neptune, are attributes of the Moon, not Venus; the issues of power presently related to Pluto are traditionally the Sun's domain. Furthermore, in traditional astrology the higher quality or "superior" expression of a planet's action is related to its essential condition, as given by the essential dignity system, not by another planet. The "sharing" of a class of attributes by two planets creates a sort of "short-circuit" in the astrological interpretation system. There are other versions of the octave theory, but none is completely satisfactory.

Notwithstanding these misgivings, the advocates of this theory consider the modern planets to be agents of transformation, acting upon the traditional planets (referred to in this context as personal or social planets) and inducing the personality to transcend their limitations. For this reason, the modern planets are commonly referred to as the transpersonal planets.

## The Question of Modern Rulerships
As part of the attempt to integrate the modern planets into the astrological system, the rulership of a sign was assigned to each one. This assignment was not made quietly. For a long time, several propositions were argued for, each one gathering its passionate defenders. In the end, the English/American version eventually predominated over the French and German suggestions. It gives the sign Aquarius to the rulership of Uranus, Pisces to Neptune, and Scorpio to Pluto and currently enjoys almost unanimous acceptance. In contrast, the assignment of the exaltations was never clarified, and the assignment of the remaining essential dignities (triplicity, term, and face) was never even attempted since contemporary astrologers, who were unfamiliar with their practical application, considered them obsolete.

It is important to note that the inclusion of the new planets in the scheme of rulerships runs contrary to the principles upon which the system rests. Instead of basing the scheme upon the order of the celestial spheres and the seasons of the year—which establish the traditional rulerships—the rulership of the new planets is based upon a supposed similarity between the planets' and signs' attributes. From this point, the situation gets even more complicated because the connection based on similarity between sign and planet leads to the transference of the sign and house attributes onto the planets themselves. For instance, Pluto justifies its signification of death through its association with Scorpio, the eighth sign and also (incorrectly) to the eighth house of death.

## Astrological Associations of the Trans-saturnian Planets
The amalgamation of mythological and historical associations combined with attributes "borrowed" from the signs and houses has resulted in the following associations:

**Uranus**: liberty, inventiveness, originality, independence, revolution, innovation, inspiration, eccentricity, unpredictability, unrest, everything that breaks boundaries, sudden changes, long distance travels, telecommunications, computers electricity; some also argue that it rules astrology and astrologers.

**Neptune**: idealism, spirituality, devotion, intuition, fantasy, yearning, mysticism, universal love, dissolution and sacrifice; escapism, illusion, victimization, unpredictability, drugs, anesthesia, hypnosis, cinema and publicity.

**Pluto**: transformation, transmutation illumination, but also obsession, dependency, control, manipulation; nuclear energy, terrorism and organized crime.

| Planet | Most common symbol | Alternative Symbols | | | |
|--------|--------------------|---------------------|--|--|--|
| Uranus | ♅ | ⊙ | | | |
| Neptune | ♆ | ♆ | | | |
| Pluto | ♇ | ♇ | ♇ | ♇ | ☽ |

**Figure 1. Symbols of the Modern Planets**

It should be noted that all of the attributions of the modern planets were "borrowed" from the traditional planets, as has been stated. The association of astrology with Uranus is in truth borrowed from Mercury, which has always ruled astrological knowledge.

Despite this smorgasbord of significations, attributions, and rulerships, the nature of the modern planets was never clearly defined. No primary qualities were ever attributed to them, nor were any temperaments, sect, or gender.[36] Because of this, the modern planets lack an essential foundation that defines their effects. Instead, an enormous collection of significations have been grouped over the last decades. In practice, their interpretations appear to be applied subjectively, which leaves open the question of their astrological effects. There are arguments that attempt to justify this lack of consistency by considering that they operate on a superior level and that, therefore, their effects are unknowable. This very statement can undermine the astrological application of these planets. Because astrology is essentially a predictive instrument (whether of individual behavior or of unfolding events), it is crucial that interpretations be clear and objective. If it is impossible to know the effects of Uranus, Neptune, or Pluto, their astrological (and therefore predictive) value becomes greatly diminished.

### The Matter of Speed

Another question related to these planets concerns their slow speed. Because they are very distant from the Sun, they have very slow cycles. Uranus takes 84 years to complete its orbit around the Sun. Neptune, which is even more distant, takes 164 years and Pluto takes 248. This means that Uranus takes on average seven years to pass through each sign. Neptune takes roughly 13 years. Pluto is a special case, since its orbit, which is inclined in relation to the ecliptic, causes variations in its apparent motion. Thus, its passage through a sign varies between 13 and 35 years, depending upon what area of the zodiac it is traversing.

As a comparison, recall that Saturn, the slowest of the visible planets, takes two and a half years to cross a sign and completes a revolution of the zodiac in 29 years. Jupiter completes a cycle in 12 years and therefore, spends only a year in each sign. The speed of the remaining planets is even faster: Mars takes two years to complete a revolution, while Venus and Mercury, always close to the

---

[36]Some modern astrologers have proposed the nature of hot and dry for Uranus and of cold and moist for Neptune. However, this attribution is dubious because it is based upon the supposed characteristics of the planet and not on its position in the celestial spheres, from where the visible planets derive their qualities. In the celestial spheres model, the new planets would be located beyond Saturn and before the sphere of the fixed stars. Therefore, Uranus could never be hot, since it is beyond Saturn, which is cold and dry and very far from the Sun, which imparts heat. Similarly, Neptune, the most distant of the planets, could never be moist, since humidity derives from its proximity to the Moon and the Earth (or from the interposition between two hot and cold extremes, as is the case with Jupiter).

Sun, take about one year each. The Moon, which is extremely fast, completes a cycle in less than 28 days.

The slow speed of the trans-saturnian planets implies that all people born around the same period have these planets in similar configurations. For this reason, some authors suggest that their influence should be considered to apply on the collective rather than individual levels. Astrological generations determined by the zodiacal positions of these planets are often referred to. For instance, all of the people born between November 1974 and November 1981 have Uranus in Scorpio, Neptune in Sagittarius, and Pluto in Libra (although obviously in different degrees of each sign depending on the birth date) and therefore, share the symbolism attributed to these zodiacal positions.

### The Matter of Visibility

The astrological system is based upon direct observation of the heavens. It is thought that light is the medium by which the planets transmit their properties, since light is what allows us to see (that is, in the sense of understanding or interpreting). It is for this reason that the planets that cannot transmit their light to Earth (for example, a planet obscured by the Sun's rays or an eclipsed luminary) are interpreted as being devoid of power and capacity to act. From this perspective, the modern planets would be considered non-functioning in the astrological system, since they are not visible to the naked eye.

This non-visibility also has repercussions in the matter of the aspects. As we've explained, the aspects relate to the planet's capacity to "see" (from the Latin term *aspectare*, "to see"). Thus, it is not possible to aspect (see) something which is not visible. Therefore, a planet invisible to the naked eye also cannot form aspects.

### Conclusion

Taking all this into consideration, some authors have proposed that the modern planets be included in a special category of invisible bodies that would operate on a different level from the visible ones.

It is the authors' opinion that the interpretation of Uranus, Neptune, and other similar bodies should be refrained from until their natures have been defined in an objective and consistent manner.

Furthermore, the discovery of new astrological objects should not be used as a pretext for neglecting the study of astrology's fundamental principles. Even if these new objects prove to be valid in astrological interpretation, they should always be considered as adjuncts to the traditional system and never as their substitutes.

*Notwithstanding the chosen approach to astrology (modern, psychological, purely traditional, or other), a committed student must master the traditional interpretation techniques in which the new planets are not included, for they are the core of the astrological system.*

## The Asteroids and Other Minor Bodies

There are, in our solar system, thousands of celestial bodies that fall into this classification. The most well-known are the asteroids that orbit between Mars and Jupiter. The first, Ceres, was discovered in 1801; in 1802, Pallas was discovered, followed by Juno (1804) and Vesta (1807). In the subsequent decades, hundreds of others were discovered. Today, there are several thousand asteroids catalogued.

The inclusion of the asteroids in the astrological interpretation dates from the 1960s. Of the thousands of known celestial bodies, the most frequently used are Ceres, Pallas, Juno, and Vesta—the first to have been discovered and also the largest of the group (Ceres, the largest of all, was classified as a dwarf-planet in 2006). The astrological interpretation of the asteroids is based upon the mythology associated with the asteroid's name: Ceres, which receives its name from the Roman goddess of the harvest, is interpreted as an indicator of "nutritional capabilities." Pallas, baptized in honor of the Greek goddess Pallas Athene, is frequently associated with "combat and strategy" characteristics of this goddess. Juno, which gets its name from Jupiter's goddess consort, is held as a symbol of the "capacity to manage relationships." Vesta, whose name evokes the goddess who protects the hearth and its fire, is generally connected with "integrity and personal discipline."

As is apparent, all of these attributes can be related to the classical planets: Ceres' attributes are borrowed from the Moon; those of Pallas, from Mercury and Mars; those of Juno from Venus; and Vesta's from the Sun.

Another celestial body "adopted" in some astrological circles is the asteroid Chiron, which was discovered in 1977. It is a small celestial body whose orbit lies between that of Saturn and Uranus. The name Chiron also comes from Greco-Roman mythology: it is the name of a centaur and son of Zeus who was the instructor of many heroes.

This discovery made a big splash among some astrologers, who considered it to be a tenth planet and immediately began to theorize about its possible astrological effects. Among the more popular meanings is the association of this celestial body with healing and teaching because the mythology of Chiron depicts him as a healer and teacher. Despite its huge popularity, the interpretation of Chiron has remained largely theoretical and in practice the results have been largely ineffectual and rather vague.

For some time, this planetoid was thought to be the sole one of its kind. This notion proved to be incorrect when after 1990, many bodies similar to Chiron began to be detected in that region of the solar system. They were generically classified as centaurs and the convention was adopted to baptize them all with names of centaurs from Greek mythology or mythological figures related to them. Today, dozens of centaurs are known. They make up a heterogeneous group with different shapes and sizes. Their orbits are very eccentric and in many cases they cross the planetary orbits. Among those most cited in astrology, aside from Chiron, we also find Pholus, Nessus, and Chariklo.

Other minor celestial bodies have been discovered in the past few years, particularly in the region situated beyond

| Symbol | Asteroid |
|--------|----------|
| ⚳ | *Ceres* |
| ⚴ | *Pallas* |
| ⚵ | *Juno* |
| ⚶ | *Vesta* |

**Figure 2. Asteroid Symbols**

| Symbol | Centaur |
|--------|---------|
| ⚷ | *Chiron* |
| ⚷ | *Pholus* |
| ⚷ | *Nessos* |

**Figure 3. Centaur Symbols**

The large number of discoveries has exhausted the names from Greco-Roman mythology and made it necessary to adopt names from the mythologies of other cultures or from mundane life itself (the latter used mainly to name the smaller asteroids). Currently, it is even possible to purchase the right to name an asteroid.

the orbits of Neptune and Pluto. The detection of numerous bodies in that region of space (one of them larger than Pluto itself) has led the International Astronomical Union to redefine a dwarf planet. Among the newly discovered bodies are Quaoar, Sedna, Ixion, Varuna, and Orco, to mention just a few of those already named. Many others exist but which have yet to be named and are currently referenced through their catalog number.

## The Matter of Interpretation

The speed with which these discoveries occurred makes any coherent attempt at integrating the new celestial bodies into astrological interpretation impossible. Each time a new astronomical body is discovered new significations, rulerships, and cycles are immediately attributed to them. However, these proposals, lacking maturity and practical testing, turn out to be simply precipitous, theoretical speculations. The case of Sedna, one of the recently (November 2003) discovered planets, is emblematic of this situation. A few days after its name was announced (inspired by the name of an Inuit goddess of the sea), the first astrological articles appeared. The mythology of this goddess was immediately scoured for key-words which were themselves immediately applied in astrological interpretations. Many more inflated theories were proposed, none of which was testable in practice. Furthermore, no one remembered that Sedna takes 10,500 years to complete a revolution of the zodiac, which makes its inclusion in natal charts absurd.

This rush to interpret also applies to the asteroids, even those that are very small. Here too the interpretation follows the questionable method of extracting ideas from the mythology connected with the name and applying them directly to the planet. For example, the asteroid Eros is undoubtedly connected with erotic love, while Urania, another asteroid, is inevitably associated with astrology. With little imagination, one can produce a more or less coherent interpretation (but not necessarily a true one). The question is made more complicated when we try to interpret the asteroids with more mundane names, such as Dudu or Le Car. Obviously, these associations, when applied indiscriminately or without good sense, produce ridiculous interpretations without any relevance to the astrological perspective. Some astrologers go so far as to invent astrological interpretations for astronomical bodies whose discovery is so recent that they have yet to be named and are known merely by their catalog name.

The reality is that we are still in the process of determining the astrological significance of these astronomical bodies. Their discovery is too recent to have objectively researched their precise effects (if they exist at all) in an astrological chart. In addition, one must also consider that **the astrological system has been for thousands of years, perfectly functional and complete as is: it does not support the new elements, nor does it need to.** It is incorrect to think that all of the new astronomical discoveries must necessarily be included in the astrological system. **Astronomy and astrology are distinct areas with distinct approaches, criteria, and purposes**.

A competent professional astrologer makes interpretations without the need for new elements. The new discoveries are seen as interesting advances in astronomy whose application to astrology must be carefully considered.

## Hypothetical Planets

Some astrologers developed the concept of a hypothetical planet, a celestial body that is merely theoretical but which does not physically exist.

The hypothetical planets were very much in vogue at the turn of the 19th century, particularly in occult circles. While some of these "planets" arise from more or less scientific conjectures, others are the product of visions and psychic impressions. The fact that they do not objectively exist is justi-fied by their supposed esoteric existence, accessible only to the more spiritually advanced.

With the continued appearance of new "planets" of this type, the situation became even more ab-surd. We've reached a point where there now exist various hypothetical planets with different at-tributes sharing the same names or ruling the same signs. Many of these "planets" even have pub-lished ephemeredes (which establishes their orbits, speeds, positions, etc.), without ever having their existence—ethereal or otherwise—proven. After the discovery of Pluto in 1930, the theoreti-cal surge diminished and the hypothetical planets gradually disappeared from astrological interpre-tations.

Among the most well-known hypothetical planets are Vulcan, Transpluto, Proserpina, Adonis, Isis, and Osiris. Currently there are still some who use these bodies. This is the case of the Uranian school of astrology, which, besides the known planets, includes eight hypothetical planets in their interpretations: Admetos, Apollon, Cupido, Hades, Kronos, Poseidon, Vulcanus, and Zeus.

## Modern Non-planetary Points

In addition to the planets and asteroids already mentioned, there are still other secondary elements that some astrologers include in their interpretations. The most well-known is the **Black Moon** or **Lilith**, a point that results from the projection of the apogee of the Moon onto the ecliptic.[37] The at-tributions given to this point, such as rejection, non-conformity, and instability, are characteristics inspired by the mythology of Lilith, the first wife of Biblical Adam. There is some confusion around the name of this point, since it is given to three different elements: the Black Moon, asteroid #1181 (also named Lilith), and a hypothetical satellite named Dark Moon that supposedly orbits Earth.[38] For this reason, some less informed astrologers use the same interpretive attributes indiscriminately (as well as the same symbol) for all three elements.

Another point frequently mentioned by some astrologers is the **Galactic Center,** which as the name indicates, marks the position of the galaxy in relation to the zodiac. It is currently located at about 27° Sagittarius (26° 51′ in the year 2000) and moves at a velocity of 1° every 72 years, the rate of precession. The interpretive interest in this point seems to be more symbolic than practical and typi-cally refers to mundane astrology.

The **Vertex,** which gained popularity in the 1990s, arises from the intersection of the Prime Vertical with the ecliptic in the west. Its interpretation is ex-tremely speculative and is sometimes referred to as a sort of "second descendant" and associated with re-lationships. The opposite point is known as the anti-Vertex and no interpretative meaning is given to it.

| Symbol | Name |
|---|---|
| ⚸ | *Black Moon or Lilith* |
| ⊚ | *Galactic Center* |
| Vx or ⋔ | *Vertex* |

Figure 4. Symbols of the
Modern Non-planetary Points

---

[37]The apogee is the point in the orbit of the Moon, where it is at its greatest distance from the Earth.

[38]The Dark Moon, a hypothetical satellite of the Earth, was proposed by the authors Goldstein and Jacobson.

# Minor Dignities, Zodiacal Degrees, and Additional Tables

## Minor Dignities

In addition to the dignities mentioned in Chapter V, there are others of lesser importance whose practical application is more uncommon. Among these, the better known are the novenaria and the doudecima, both resulting from the division of the signs by nine and 12 equal parts, respectively.

Similar to the terms and the faces, these small segments of the signs are ruled by a planet.

## Novenaria

Novenaria are 03°20′ segments of a sign resulting from its division into nine equal parts. The first novenaria of the zodiac (0°00′-03°20′ Aries) is ruled by Mars; the following novenaria are attributed to the planets according to the order of the domiciles. In this way, Mars initiates the sequence because it rules the first sign, Aries, followed by Venus, ruler of the second sign (Taurus), Mercury (Gemini), the Moon (Cancer), the Sun (Leo), Mercury again (Virgo), Venus (Libra), Mars (Scorpio), Jupiter (Sagittarius), Saturn (Capricorn), Saturn once again (Aquarius) and finally Jupiter (ruler of the last sign, Pisces). The sequence then begins again

|  | 00°00′ | 03°20′ | 06°40′ | 10°00 | 13°20′ | 16°40′ | 20°00 | 23°20′ | 26°40′ |
|---|---|---|---|---|---|---|---|---|---|
| ♈ | ♂ | ♀ | ☿ | ☽ | ☉ | ☿ | ♀ | ♂ | ♃ |
| ♉ | ♄ | ♄ | ♃ | ♂ | ♀ | ☿ | ☽ | ☉ | ☿ |
| ♊ | ♀ | ♂ | ♃ | ♄ | ♄ | ♃ | ♂ | ♀ | ☿ |
| ♋ | ☽ | ☉ | ☿ | ♀ | ♂ | ♃ | ♄ | ♄ | ♃ |
| ♌ | ♂ | ♀ | ☿ | ☽ | ☉ | ☿ | ♀ | ♂ | ♃ |
| ♍ | ♄ | ♄ | ♃ | ♂ | ♀ | ☿ | ☽ | ☉ | ☿ |
| ♎ | ♀ | ♂ | ♃ | ♄ | ♄ | ♃ | ♂ | ♀ | ☿ |
| ♏ | ☽ | ☉ | ☿ | ♀ | ♂ | ♃ | ♄ | ♄ | ♃ |
| ♐ | ♂ | ♀ | ☿ | ☽ | ☉ | ☿ | ♀ | ♂ | ♃ |
| ♑ | ♄ | ♄ | ♃ | ♂ | ♀ | ☿ | ☽ | ☉ | ☿ |
| ♒ | ♀ | ♂ | ♃ | ♄ | ♄ | ♃ | ♂ | ♀ | ☿ |
| ♓ | ☽ | ☉ | ☿ | ♀ | ♂ | ♃ | ♄ | ♄ | ♃ |

**Figure 1. Novenaria**

with Mars, followed by Venus, Mercury, and so on until all the novenaria of the 12 signs are completed.

This way, we obtain the "unfolding" of the rulerships throughout the zodiac, which repeats the complete sequence nine times.

| | 00°00 | 02°30' | 05°00' | 07°30' | 10°00' | 12°30' | 15°00' | 17°30' | 20°00 | 22°30' | 25°00' | 27°30' |
|---|---|---|---|---|---|---|---|---|---|---|---|---|
| ♈ | ♈ | ♉ | ♊ | ♋ | ♌ | ♍ | ♎ | ♏ | ♐ | ♑ | ♒ | ♓ |
| ♉ | ♉ | ♊ | ♋ | ♌ | ♍ | ♎ | ♏ | ♐ | ♑ | ♒ | ♓ | ♈ |
| ♊ | ♊ | ♋ | ♌ | ♍ | ♎ | ♏ | ♐ | ♑ | ♒ | ♓ | ♈ | ♉ |
| ♋ | ♋ | ♌ | ♍ | ♎ | ♏ | ♐ | ♑ | ♒ | ♓ | ♈ | ♉ | ♊ |
| ♌ | ♌ | ♍ | ♎ | ♏ | ♐ | ♑ | ♒ | ♓ | ♈ | ♉ | ♊ | ♋ |
| ♍ | ♍ | ♎ | ♏ | ♐ | ♑ | ♒ | ♓ | ♈ | ♉ | ♊ | ♋ | ♌ |
| ♎ | ♎ | ♏ | ♐ | ♑ | ♒ | ♓ | ♈ | ♉ | ♊ | ♋ | ♌ | ♍ |
| ♏ | ♏ | ♐ | ♑ | ♒ | ♓ | ♈ | ♉ | ♊ | ♋ | ♌ | ♍ | ♎ |
| ♐ | ♐ | ♑ | ♒ | ♓ | ♈ | ♉ | ♊ | ♋ | ♌ | ♍ | ♎ | ♏ |
| ♑ | ♑ | ♒ | ♓ | ♈ | ♉ | ♊ | ♋ | ♌ | ♍ | ♎ | ♏ | ♐ |
| ♒ | ♒ | ♓ | ♈ | ♉ | ♊ | ♋ | ♌ | ♍ | ♎ | ♏ | ♐ | ♑ |
| ♓ | ♓ | ♈ | ♉ | ♊ | ♋ | ♌ | ♍ | ♎ | ♏ | ♐ | ♑ | ♒ |

**Figure 2. Duodenaria (by Sign)**

| | 00°00 | 02°30' | 05°00' | 07°30' | 10°00' | 12°30' | 15°00' | 17°30' | 20°00 | 22°30' | 25°00' | 27°30' |
|---|---|---|---|---|---|---|---|---|---|---|---|---|
| ♈ | ♂ | ♀ | ☿ | ☽ | ☉ | ☿ | ♀ | ♂ | ♃ | ♄ | ♄ | ♃ |
| ♉ | ♀ | ☿ | ☽ | ☉ | ☿ | ♀ | ♂ | ♃ | ♄ | ♄ | ♃ | ♂ |
| ♊ | ☿ | ☽ | ☉ | ☿ | ♀ | ♂ | ♃ | ♄ | ♄ | ♃ | ♂ | ♀ |
| ♋ | ☽ | ☉ | ☿ | ♀ | ♂ | ♃ | ♄ | ♄ | ♃ | ♂ | ♀ | ☿ |
| ♌ | ☉ | ☿ | ♀ | ♂ | ♃ | ♄ | ♄ | ♃ | ♂ | ♀ | ☿ | ☽ |
| ♍ | ☿ | ♀ | ♂ | ♃ | ♄ | ♄ | ♃ | ♂ | ♀ | ☿ | ☽ | ☉ |
| ♎ | ♀ | ♂ | ♃ | ♄ | ♄ | ♃ | ♂ | ♀ | ☿ | ☽ | ☉ | ☿ |
| ♏ | ♂ | ♃ | ♄ | ♄ | ♃ | ♂ | ♀ | ☿ | ☽ | ☉ | ☿ | ♀ |
| ♐ | ♃ | ♄ | ♄ | ♃ | ♂ | ♀ | ☿ | ☽ | ☉ | ☿ | ♀ | ♂ |
| ♑ | ♄ | ♄ | ♃ | ♂ | ♀ | ☿ | ☽ | ☉ | ☿ | ♀ | ♂ | ♃ |
| ♒ | ♄ | ♃ | ♂ | ♀ | ☿ | ☽ | ☉ | ☿ | ♀ | ♂ | ♃ | ♄ |
| ♓ | ♃ | ♂ | ♀ | ☿ | ☽ | ☉ | ☿ | ♀ | ♂ | ♃ | ♄ | ♄ |

**Figure 3. Duodenaria (by Planetary Ruler)**

## Duodenaria or Duodecimae (Twelfth-Parts )

Duodenaria are segments of 02°30' of a sign, resulting from its division into 12 equal parts. To each duodenaria is attributed one sign and the correspondent planetary ruler. In this way, each sign includes within itself a complete zdiac, with all of its rulers. The first duodenaria of each sign is always given to the sign itself. Thus, the first 02°30' degrees of Aries correspond to Aries, the first 02°30' degrees of Taurus correspond to Taurus, and so on. The other segments of each sign follow the natural order of the zodiac. For instance, the first duodenaria of Cancer is attributed to Cancer, the second to Leo, which is the following sign in the zodiac, and then by Virgo, Libra, Scorpio, Sagittarius, Capricorn, Aquarius, Pisces, Aries, Taurus, and Gemini. The duodenaria can also be represented by their planetary rulers.

## Practical Application

Although frequently mentioned by the ancient authors, the practical application of the novenaria and the duodenaria are seldom exemplified. They can be applied to any factor in the chart, providing additional information to its delineation. For example, the ruler of the novenaria and the sign of the duodenaria where the Moon in placed contribute to the delineation of the behavior of an individual (in a nativity) or the unfolding of the events in a horary figure (in a horary question).

For example, the Ascendant of Friedrich Nietzsche's chart is 29° Scorpio. It is in a duodenaria of Libra, and therefore, this sign and its ruler, Venus, contribute to determining his motivations. The duodenaria of Libra suggests sociability and communication (moveable air sign), which he expressed through his ideals and beliefs, as Venus is posited in the ninth house. It is, however, colored by rigor, severity (Virgo), and also some sadness (Venus is in fall). The Ascendant is also posited in a novenaria of Jupiter. This planet is dignified, which bestows upon him an idealistic nature with a strong sense of honor and dignity. Note, however, that all these considerations are always subordinate to the ruler of the Ascendant and its conditions. With Mars, the ruler of the Ascendant posited in Virgo in the Midheaven, Nietzsche wished to succeed in this projects (tenth house), although he projected a controversial image marked by criticism (Mars).

Another example: In the chart of King Sebastian, the Ascendant falls into a duodenaria of Leo, which gives him an assertive, imposing, and conquering manner. However, the duodenaria's planetary ruler, the Sun, is debilitated in Aquarius, somewhat limiting this assertiveness and tainting it with arrogance. The Ascendant is posited in a novenaria of Saturn, which is also the ruler of the Ascendant, and therefore corroborates and reinforces its traits.

### The Degrees of the Zodiac and their Properties

According to the tradition, the individual degrees of each sign also contain specific qualities that allow for greater detail in delineation. Degrees can be classified as feminine or masculine, fortunate, obscure, void, luminous, etc. This level of detail is used only in specific delineations and rarely tabulated in the study of an astrological chart.

The tables presented here are the more commonly used, but students should keep in mind that there are several other versions, as in the case of the terms.

It is important to note that the tables provided in this appendix present the real value of the degree. For instance, the third degree of the table starts at 03°00′00″ and ends at 03°59′59″. This differs from the tables presented in ancient books, where the number 3 usually means the third degree of a sign, that is from 02°00′00″ to 02°59′59″.

#### Masculine and Feminine Degrees
These degrees are useful in aiding the description in horary astrology. They can help determine gender, according to the position of the significator in a masculine or feminine degree.

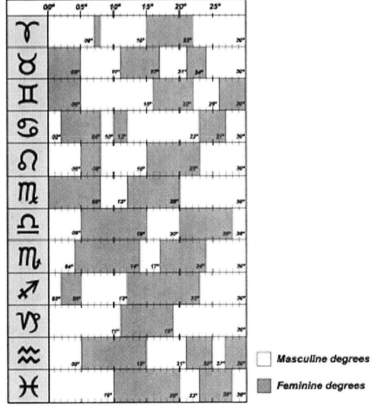

Masculine degrees
Feminine degrees

**Figure 4. Masculine and Feminine Degrees**

#### Light, Dark, Smoky and Void Degrees
These degrees are also used to describe individuals (generally in the context of a horary chart) and their interpretation is very straightforward. The light degrees indicate lighter or pale skin, dark degrees signify darker complexion, and smoky degrees suggest intermediate tones. In some delineations they are also used for aesthetic evaluation: a light degree suggests beauty and harmony of the face, a smoky degree is associated with average looks, and a dark degree with inharmonious features. Obviously, these descriptions reflect an aesthetic of beauty that was probably culturally specific to Hellenistic and Medieval Europe, and would have to be altered to reflect the cultural standards and mores of today.

The void degrees have to do with intellectual capabilities. If the Ascendant and the Moon are posited in void degrees, they suggest limited understanding (to be considered valid, this information must be corroborated by other factors in the chart).

Note: the light degrees are sometimes designated "lucid" or "luminous"; the dark degrees are also called "tenebrous" or "obscure."

## Pitted Degrees

According to the tradition, a planet posited in one of these degrees is like a person at the bottom of a pit, that is, blocked and immobilized. A significator posited in a pitted degree describes a person, an animal, or a situation that is impeded, restrained, and unable to overcome the problem without help.

## Azemene or Unlucky Degrees

Sometimes called "deficient" or "handicapped" degrees, they are also used in the description of individuals. They indicate congenital problems, such as distorted limbs, blindness, deafness, incurable diseases, and similar problems. The Ascendant and the Moon, as well as their respective rulers, posited in these degrees suggest some kind of physical deformity.

## Fortunate Degrees

As the name suggests, these degrees indicate good fortune and wealth, and represent fortunate individuals or abundance.

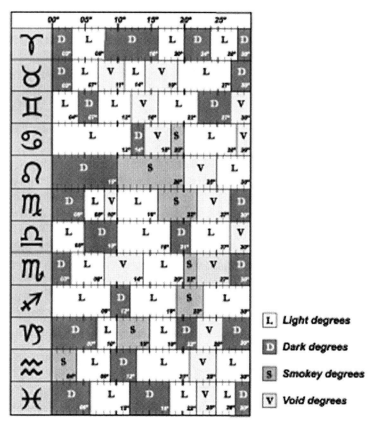

Figure 5. Light, Dark, Smokey, and Void Degrees

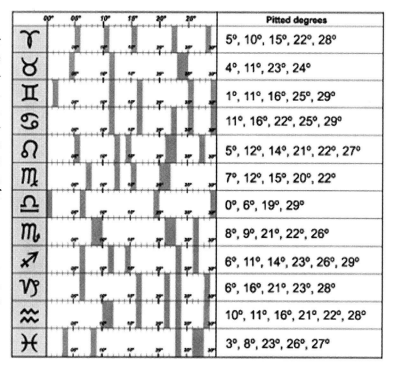

Figure 6. Pitted Degrees

| | Pitted degrees |
|---|---|
| ♈ | 5°, 10°, 15°, 22°, 28° |
| ♉ | 4°, 11°, 23°, 24° |
| ♊ | 1°, 11°, 16°, 25°, 29° |
| ♋ | 11°, 16°, 22°, 25°, 29° |
| ♌ | 5°, 12°, 14°, 21°, 22°, 27° |
| ♍ | 7°, 12°, 15°, 20°, 22° |
| ♎ | 0°, 6°, 19°, 29° |
| ♏ | 8°, 9°, 21°, 22°, 26° |
| ♐ | 6°, 11°, 14°, 23°, 26°, 29° |
| ♑ | 6°, 16°, 21°, 23°, 28° |
| ♒ | 10°, 11°, 16°, 21°, 22°, 28° |
| ♓ | 3°, 8°, 23°, 26°, 27° |

**Figure 7. Azemene (or Lame) degrees**

| | Fortunate degrees |
|---|---|
| ♈ | 18° |
| ♉ | 2°, 14°, 26° |
| ♊ | 10° |
| ♋ | 0°, 1°, 2°, 3°, 14° |
| ♌ | 1°, 4°, 6°, 18° |
| ♍ | 2°, 13°, 19° |
| ♎ | 2°, 14°, 20° |
| ♏ | 6°, 17°, 19° |
| ♐ | 12°, 19° |
| ♑ | 11°, 12°, 13°, 19° |
| ♒ | 6°, 15°, 16°, 19° |
| ♓ | 12°, 19° |

**Figure 8. Fortunate Degrees (or Degrees of Increasing Fortune)**

## Additional Tables

### Variants of the Terms

The exact arrangement of the Ptolemaic terms presents some problems and it is still a matter of debate, as several versions exist. The various extant tables vary with respect to the number of degrees of each term and to the sequence of the planetary rulers. As no original version of Ptolemy's *Tetrabiblos* has survived, there is no way to determine with certainty which of the several fragments available presents the correct version of the table of terms.

The more disseminated versions were the one presented in the F. E. Robbins translation (see bibliography), and the one included in *Christian Astrology* by William Lilly.

| | | | | | |
|---|---|---|---|---|---|
| ♈ | ♃ 06° | ♀ 14° | ☿ 21° | ♂ 26° | ♄ 30° |
| ♉ | ♀ 08° | ☿ 15° | ♃ 22° | ♄ 24° | ♂ 30° |
| ♊ | ☿ 07° | ♃ 13° | ♀ 20° | ♂ 26° | ♄ 30° |
| ♋ | ♂ 06° | ♃ 13° | ☿ 20° | ♀ 27° | ♄ 30° |
| ♌ | ♃ 06° | ☿ 13° | ♄ 19° | ♀ 25° | ♂ 30° |
| ♍ | ☿ 07° | ♀ 13° | ♃ 18° | ♄ 24° | ♂ 30° |
| ♎ | ♄ 06° | ♀ 11° | ☿ 16° | ♃ 24° | ♂ 30° |
| ♏ | ♂ 06° | ♀ 13° | ♃ 21° | ☿ 27° | ♄ 30° |
| ♐ | ♃ 08° | ♀ 14° | ☿ 19° | ♄ 25° | ♂ 30° |
| ♑ | ♀ 06° | ☿ 12° | ♃ 19° | ♄ 25° | ♂ 30° |
| ♒ | ♄ 06° | ☿ 12° | ♀ 20° | ♃ 25° | ♂ 30° |
| ♓ | ♀ 08° | ♃ 14° | ☿ 20° | ♂ 25° | ♄ 30° |

**Figure 9. Ptolemaic terms from *Tetrabiblos* (translation of F. E. Robbins)**

As a curiosity, we also include in this book a third version which appears in several Iberian works, among them *Os Almanaques de Madrid*(from the paper *Os Almanaques de Madrid*, Luís Albuquerque, Junta de Investigações do Ultramar, Coimbra 1961).

| | | | | | |
|---|---|---|---|---|---|
| ♈ | ♃ 06° | ♀ 14° | ☿ 21° | ♂ 26° | ♄ 30° |
| ♉ | ♀ 08° | ☿ 15° | ♃ 22° | ♄ 24° | ♂ 30° |
| ♊ | ☿ 07° | ♃ 13° | ♀ 20° | ♂ 26° | ♄ 30° |
| ♋ | ♂ 06° | ♃ 13° | ☿ 20° | ♀ 27° | ♄ 30° |
| ♌ | ♃ 06° | ☿ 13° | ♄ 19° | ♀ 25° | ♂ 30° |
| ♍ | ☿ 07° | ♀ 13° | ♃ 18° | ♄ 24° | ♂ 30° |
| ♎ | ♄ 06° | ♀ 11° | ☿ 16° | ♃ 24° | ♂ 30° |
| ♏ | ♂ 06° | ♀ 13° | ♃ 21° | ☿ 27° | ♄ 30° |
| ♐ | ♃ 08° | ♀ 14° | ☿ 19° | ♄ 25° | ♂ 30° |
| ♑ | ♀ 06° | ☿ 12° | ♃ 19° | ♄ 25° | ♂ 30° |
| ♒ | ♄ 06° | ☿ 12° | ♀ 20° | ♃ 25° | ♂ 30° |
| ♓ | ♀ 08° | ♃ 14° | ☿ 20° | ♂ 25° | ♄ 30° |

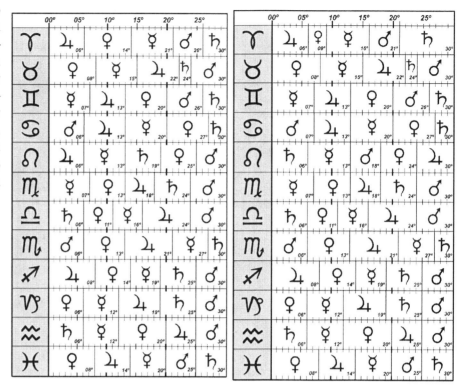

**Figure 10. Ptolemaic terms from William Lilly**

| | | | | | |
|---|---|---|---|---|---|
| ♈ | ♃ 06° | ♀ 09° | ☿ 15° | ♂ 21° | ♄ 30° |
| ♉ | ♀ 08° | ☿ 15° | ♃ 22° | ♄ 24° | ♂ 30° |
| ♊ | ☿ 07° | ♃ 13° | ♀ 20° | ♂ 26° | ♄ 30° |
| ♋ | ♂ 07° | ♃ 13° | ☿ 20° | ♀ 27° | ♄ 30° |
| ♌ | ♄ 06° | ☿ 13° | ♂ 18° | ♀ 24° | ♃ 30° |
| ♍ | ☿ 07° | ♀ 13° | ♃ 18° | ♄ 24° | ♂ 30° |
| ♎ | ♄ 06° | ♀ 11° | ☿ 16° | ♃ 24° | ♂ 30° |
| ♏ | ♂ 06° | ♀ 13° | ♃ 21° | ☿ 27° | ♄ 30° |
| ♐ | ♃ 08° | ♀ 14° | ☿ 19° | ♄ 25° | ♂ 30° |
| ♑ | ♀ 06° | ☿ 12° | ♃ 19° | ♄ 25° | ♂ 30° |
| ♒ | ♄ 06° | ☿ 12° | ♀ 20° | ♃ 25° | ♂ 30° |
| ♓ | ♀ 08° | ♃ 14° | ☿ 20° | ♂ 25° | ♄ 30° |

**Figure 11. Table of Ptolemaic terms (third variant)**

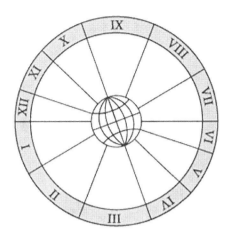

*Appendix 4*
# Additional Considerations Concerning the Houses

This appendix focuses on some technical aspects pertaining to the houses. The objective here is to cover various questions and the related ramifications that arise in astrological practice without addressing technical details that are beyond the scope of this book. Also included in this section is a supplement for house interpretation that includes the triplicity rulers.

### Brief Notes on the Origin and Development of the Houses

Despite their importance in delineation, the astrological houses had a relatively late development. This is explained by the difficulty that exists in precisely determining the degree of the Ascendant, which is a pivotal element in the calculation of the houses. Before accurate calculations existed, astrologers had recognized the importance of the angles and based their interpretations on the rising, culmination, and setting of the stars. However, at this stage, the astrological houses had not come into use.

The first house systems only appear around the 2nd century B.C. with the development of the mathematical calculation of the Ascendant. The oldest was the whole house system, in which a whole zodiacal sign is made to equal one house. In this system, the degree of the Midheaven is not considered. With the development of the requisite mathematics, the quadrant systems (explained in detail below) began to appear. Quadrant systems in general, make the Ascendant and Midheaven the cusps of the first and tenth houses, respectively. This method of calculation determines the angles with precision but leaves open the question of how to determine the remaining house cusps. Several house systems thus developed to address this question, which to this day continues under scrutiny.

The change from the whole-sign house system to a quadrant system coincides with a series of developments in astrology resulting from ever-more precise measurements. One of these is the attribution of orbs to the planets. The improvement of mathematical calculations, whose historical details are not completely known, signals the birth of astrology as we know it today.

## The Problem of House Systems

### Different Methods of Division

As mathematics and astronomy developed, several methods for calculating the house cusps emerged. Throughout history, astrologers have developed different methods for dividing the sky. Currently, they are still in disagreement as to the most effective method.

### Various House Systems

There are two categories of house division: the **natural division** and a **quadrant division**. The systems of natural division take a reference point—usually the Ascendant—and divide the sky into 12 equal parts from that point. The most well known and utilized systems under this class are the **whole-sign** and **equal** house systems.

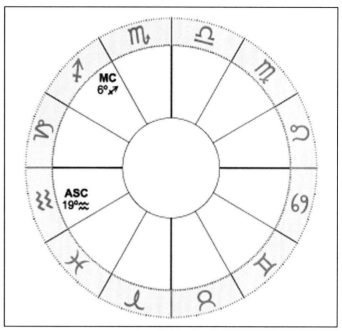

**Figure 1. Whole-sign System**

The whole-sign system, also known as the sign-house system, is the oldest. It takes the whole sign that is rising as the first house, the next whole sign as the second house, etc. This division does not use the exact Ascendant degree, nor the Midheaven for its cusps.

The equal house system takes the degree of the Ascendant as the first house cusp, the same degree of the next sign as the second house cusp, and so on successively. All of the houses therefore have exactly 30 degrees and all begin with the same degree of consecutive signs. The degree of the Midheaven is not used as the tenth house cusp.

The quadrant systems take the degree of the Ascendant as the first house cusp and

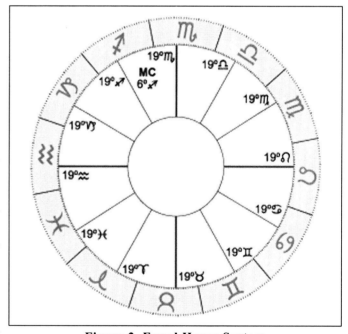

**Figure 2. Equal House System**

the degree of the Midheaven as the tenth house cusp. The differences between these systems lie in the manner in which they divide up the quadrants (semi-arcs) to obtain the cusps of the succedent and cadent houses. These are known as intermediary houses because they are situated between two angles.

There are two methods used to define the intermediary houses: divide the space, or divide up the time. Thus, while some divide the space into slices between the Ascendant and the Meridian, others divide the ascensional time from the zodiacal degree rising. There are various ways to do these calculations, all of which produce different house systems. The more well-known methods of spatial

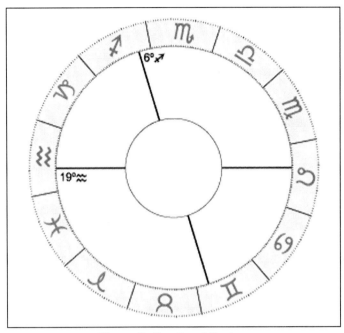

**Figure 3. Quadrant System**

division are the **Regiomontanus** and **Campanus**, and the most well-known methods of temporal division are **Placidus**, **Alchabitius**, and **Koch**.

There are two other systems of house division: **Porphyry** and **Topocentric**. The Porphyry system is one of the oldest quadrant systems; it directly divides the ecliptic into three parts using the distances between the Ascendant-Midheaven arc and IC-Ascendant arc. The Topocentric system was created in the 20th century and makes a very complex division from reference points located on the surface of the Earth.

**Most Popular Systems**

Although there are more than 20 known house systems, the truth is that throughout history only a handful have actually been

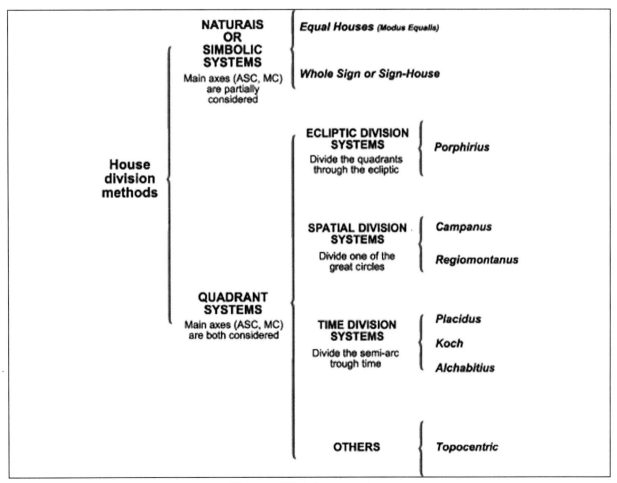

**Figure 4. Main house systems**

used. The oldest is the whole-sign or sign-house system, which is very simple and easy to calculate. It was so popular that its rationale is the basis for all the technical foundations of astrology. Even when the quadrant systems became the norm, it was always kept in use as an auxiliary system. Its use is clearly documented until the end of the Middle Ages.

The Porphyry system appears to be the one most used by Greek authors of the 1st millennium of the Christian Era. Later, during the Middle Ages and until the 16th century, the Alcabitius house system began to be more commonly used. Nevertheless, from the second half of the 15th century, the Regiomontanus system became the most popular.

The preference of one system over another is due to several factors. The Alcabitius system (also known as "the ancient system") seems to owe its use to the simplicity of its mathematics and to its very clear principles. In the 15th century, when Arabic techniques fell out of favor and were discriminated against (more for political and nationalistic reasons than for astrological ones), the Regiomontanus system, whose logical principles are also clear and simple, supplanted it. The fact that the tables needed to calculate this system were widely published became one more reason for its popularity. The existence of readily available tables saved the practitioner a great deal of time otherwise wasted in the manual calculations of the Alcabitius system. The Regiomontanus house division was widely used until the decline of astrology at the end of the 17th century.

Currently, the house division system most in use is Placidus, which was created in the 17th century by the mathematician Placidus of Titis. However, this system only became widespread at the end of the 19th century when it was included in Raphael's Tables, which at the time were the only ones in circulation. The ease of reference (coupled perhaps by the lack of knowledge by many practitioners of other house systems) contributed toward making Placidus the primary house system.

Because the current astrological software programs allow for the calculation of many house system divisions, other systems have begun to compete with Placidus for primacy. Of these, the most popular are Koch (created in the 20th century) and Regiomontanus (recovered by some practitioners of traditional astrology). The Alcabitius system, used throughout this work, is equally appropriate to traditional astrology, although for the time being it is not as well represented as Regiomontanus.

### Which is the Best System?

This is an open question. Different astrologers point to different house systems and all have reasonable reasons for their choices. Some state that one should use different systems for different purposes or techniques; others disagree, maintaining that the astrological system should be consistent and that therefore the same house system should be used in all branches of astrology. The answer will most certainly be found in practice, as astrological knowledge recovers its integrity and experimentation provides new data pertaining to this question.

### Higher Latitudes

Another problem that astrology faces with regard to house systems is the matter of higher latitudes. As one gets closer to the poles, most house systems become progressively more distorted. This happens because at very high latitudes there are degrees of the ecliptic that never rise on the horizon. For this reason, when one reaches latitudes greater than 66°, most house systems break down because it becomes impossible to calculate house cusps. Charts calculated for extreme latitudes often have a Midheaven that is very "close" to the Ascendant. In some cases, the degree of the Ascendant and the degree of the Midheaven may even coincide, which makes a quadrant house calculation impossible.

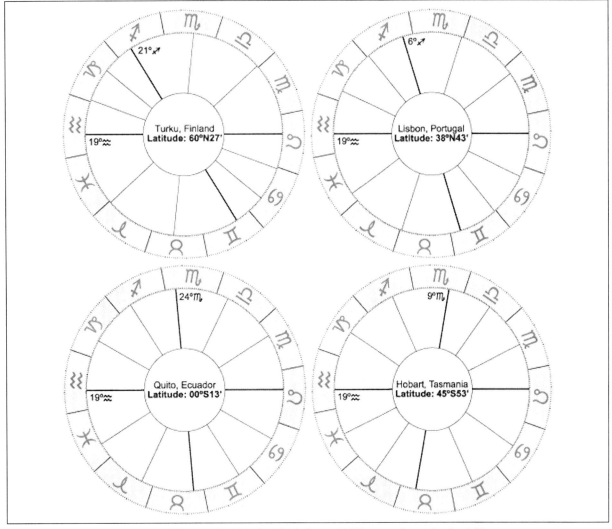

**Figure 5. Different Latitudes Originate Different Astrological Houses**

This extreme distortion of the houses (which ends up suppressing some of them) results from the discrepancy between the duration of night and day at those latitudes. In truth, the weakness of the system is a direct reflection of the life conditions in those regions of the globe, where at certain times of the year the Sun does not rise, while at others, it never sets.

## Technical Notes on Traditional House Systems

### Alcabitius

The Alcabitius house system gets its name from the Arabic mathematician Abu al-Saqr al-Qabîsî 'Abd al-'Azîz ibn 'Uthman (c. 967), known in the west as Alcabitius. Although this author was not in fact the creator of this method of house division, it is described quite clearly in his work. To the traditional authors this was known as the ancient method and the earliest evidence of its use appears in the Byzantine period (6th century C.E.).

Very simply, the method consists of dividing the arc or right ascension of the Ascendant into three equal parts. To obtain the cusps of the twelfth and eleventh houses, divide the arc of ascension from the Ascendant to the Midheaven; that is, divide the semi-arc that the zodiacal degree, rising at that moment, will traverse until it culminates at the meridian (Midheaven).

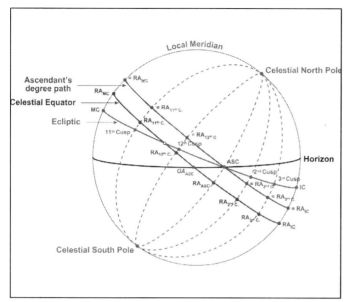

**Figure 6. Alcabitius System**

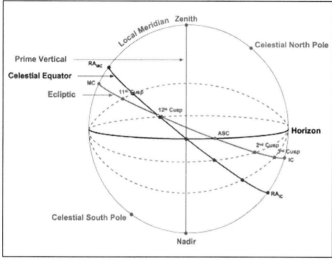

**Figure 7. Regiomontanus System**

The fifth and sixth houses are obtained directly from the eleventh and twelfth houses because they are at diametrically opposite points. To obtain the cusps of the second and third houses (and their opposites, the eighth and ninth) identically divide the semi-arc between the Ascendant and the IC.

### Regiomontanus

This system of house division became very popular after 1490, when its first house tables were published. It gets its name from its propagator, the mathematician Johann Müller (1436-1476), known by his Latin name Regiomontanus. As with the Alcabitius method, Regiomontanus was not its creator, but rather the one who popularized the system, since centuries earlier some Arabic authors mention a similar method.

The explanation for this method is a bit more complex than the previous one and requires some knowledge of celestial reference points. It consists of the division of the celestial equator[39] into 12 equal parts, using the horizon (Ascendant) and the meridian (Midheaven) as reference points. Then the space is divided into "slices," using the poles of the prime vertical.[40] The cusps of the intermediary houses are found at the points where each "slice" intercepts the ecliptic.

## The Triplicities of the Houses

Traditional interpretation is very detailed when it comes to the houses of the horoscope. In addition to the sign on the cusp of each house, the planets located in them, and the ruling planet, traditional authors also include the triplicity rulers in interpretation; that is, the three planets that rule over the element of the sign on the cusp. These planets deepen and provide specifics about the interpretation of each house. Each of the three triplicity lords has "rulership" over one of the topics of the house, which allows us to interpret in greater detail all of the topics associated with that area. In practice, the triplicity rulers complement the delineation of the houses and give details about specific matters

---

[39]The celestial equator is an extension into the celestial sphere of the terrestrial equator; it divides the celestial sphere into two equal parts.

[40]The prime vertical is a circle that divides the celestial sphere at the center, cutting it from East to West and passing through the Zenith and Nadir.

or times when the themes of the houses are activated. For example, the first ruler of the triplicity of the seventh house relates to marriage and romantic partners; the second triplicity ruler gives indications about conflicts and all manner of confrontations; the third refers to business partners and legal matters (contracts, etc.). These meanings are obviously subordinated to the more general meaning of the house, indicated by the planets located in the house and by the ruler of the house.

The meanings of each triplicity are shown below. Although some authors have minor deviations from these attributions, the table we present includes the most frequently cited meanings. Note: the meanings for the tenth, eleventh, and twelfth houses vary considerably from author to author.

| *House* | *First Triplicity* | *Second Triplicity* | *Third Triplicity* |
|---|---|---|---|
| First | Life and nature of the individual, his or her wishes and tastes; the first third of life | The body and its strength; the second third of life | Similar to the previous two; the third third of life |
| Second | Wealth in the beginning of life | Wealth in the middle part of life | Wealth in the later part of life |
| Third | Older brothers; brothers in general | Middle brothers; knowledge, learning | Younger brothers; short travels |
| Fourth | father | Property and estate | The end of things |
| Fifth | Older sons; sons in general | Middle sons; pleasure and love | Younger sons; messages, ambassadors, presents |
| Sixth | Infirmities | Servants, workers | Small animals |
| Seventh | Marriage, partners, sex | Conflict and confront | Business associates and legal matters |
| Eighth | Death | Old things | Inheritances, enterprises, anguish |
| Ninth | Travel and peregrination | Religion, honesty, faith, dreams | Dreams, vision, wisdom, knowledge |
| Tenth | The mother, the profession | Fame, dignities, honours, boldness and style of action | Brings stability to the other significators of this house, recognition |
| Eleventh | Hopes | Friends, allies | Grace, benefits |
| Twelfth | Enemies | Sadness and sorrow | Big animals |

## How to Determine Triplicity Rulers

The first step in identifying the rulers of the triplicities is to determine the element of the sign on the cusp of the house being studied. For each element there are three ruling planets, as was mentioned in Chapter VI (see Figures 8, 9, and 10 in that chapter). The second step is to determine whether the chart is diurnal or nocturnal. As was stated, this distinction is of crucial importance for interpreting, since it alters the order of the rulerships. For example, if the cusp of a house is occupied by a fire sign in a diurnal chart, the first ruler of the triplicity will be the Sun (the diurnal triplicity), the second will be Jupiter (the nocturnal triplicity) and the third will be Saturn (the participating triplicity). In a nocturnal chart, the sequence is Jupiter (nocturnal), the Sun (diurnal), and Saturn (participating).

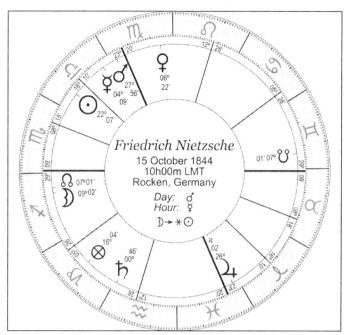

**Chart 1. Nativity of Friedrich Nietzsche**

## Interpretation Examples

In Nietzsche's chart, the ninth house starts at 12° Leo 25′. Since it is a fire sign in a diurnal chart, the triplicity rulers are (in this order) the Sun, Jupiter, and Saturn. Thus, the Sun has rulership over matters pertaining to trips, Jupiter has rulership over faith, religion and beliefs, and Saturn rules wisdom and dreams. Following is the condition of these planets:

- The Sun (ruler of trips) is posited in the eleventh house, which, to begin with, suggests a connection between trips and allies. In fact, Nietzsche traveled extensively throughout Europe and even adopted Swiss nationality when he was invited to lecture at a university in that country. However, the Sun is very debilitated (in fall in Libra and square Saturn), which means that his travels also involved a good deal of dissatisfaction. There is a permanent inconstancy (Libra is a cardinal sign) and many difficulties (square with Saturn). The majority of his travels were a search for a favorable climate for his health and thoughts—a climate which he never found.
- Jupiter (ruler of faith) is in the fourth house, dignified in Pisces, which indicates faith, honor, and dignity. Nevertheless, Jupiter is opposite Mars and Mercury, which indicates a critical and bellicose attitude in the expression of these themes. The harshness of his writing is very well known. In addition, Jupiter is retrograde, which suggests retractions in his attitude toward faith and religion.
- Saturn (ruler of wisdom) is also dignified in Aquarius, which implies a profound and highly qualified understanding, although colored by a large degree of individualism. The ideas that he advocated had little acceptance while he was alive.

Another example:

In the horary "Is this house a good purchase?" (see Chapter XIV) the second ruler of the fourth house provides further details about immovable property.

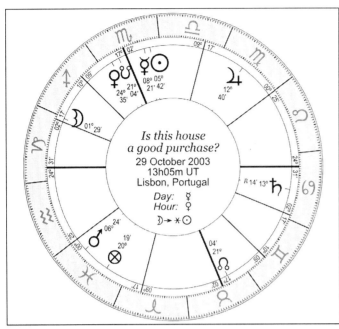

**Chart 12. Horary chart: "Is this house
a good purchase?"**

*Is this house
a good purchase?*
29 October 2003
13h05m UT
Lisbon, Portugal

Since this is a diurnal chart with earth on the cusp, the sequence of triplicities is Venus, Moon, and Mars. The Moon, ruler of the second triplicity is therefore significator of immovable property, and is debilitated because it is in Capricorn (its detriment), cadent in the weak twelfth house, and opposition Saturn. This configuration indicates that the property is not of good quality. This indication corroborates the actual ruler of the fourth house, Venus, which is debilitated in Scorpio, conjunct the South Node, and feral.

Note: For the beginner in horary astrology, there may be some confusion about the relative importance of all the rulers of a house: the ruler, exaltation, almuten, triplicity, etc. Our suggestion is that the initial interpretation be made solely with the ruler of the house. The triplicity significations of the houses are always secondary in relation to the ruler of the sign. If this ruler is weak, the triplicity rulers, even if strong, can only ameliorate this weakness. By contrast, the power of a well-positioned ruler can never be nullified by weak triplicity rulers. Furthermore, the interpretation of the rulers should always be framed within the appropriate chart context (since the information given by the triplicity lords it is not always pertinent). The correct integration of all the rulers of a house follows specific rules of delineation that are beyond the scope of this book.

## Co-significators of the Houses

This is a system that associates planets to the houses symbolically, according to the Chaldean order: Saturn is given to the first house, thus representing the enclosure of the soul in the physical body; Jupiter to the second of wealth; Mars to the third of brothers; the Sun to the fourth house of the father; Venus to the fifth of pleasures; Mercury to the sixth, the house of slaves; the Moon to the seventh of marriage; Saturn to the eighth of death; Jupiter to the ninth of religion; Mars to the tenth of achievements; the Sun to the eleventh house of friends and hopes; and Venus to the twelfth, signifying vices, according to some authors.

In theory, each co-significator acts as a natural significator of the matters ruled by that house, but in practice only a few are used in delineation of the houses:

| House | Co-significator | Usage as natural significator of the matters of the house |
|---|---|---|
| First | ♄ | not used |
| Second | ♃ | used as the natural significator of wealth and prosperity |
| Third | ♂ | used as the natural significator of brothers and travels (in this regard the Moon is also used to signify sisters as well as travel) |
| Fourth | ☽ | used as the natural significator of fathers (together with Saturn) |

| | | |
|---|---|---|
| Fifth | ♀ | (used only as a natural significator of pleasure; in matters of fertility it is used with Jupiter and Moon as a benefic planet and not as co-significator of the fifth) |
| Sixth | ☿ | (used only as a natural significator of employees) |
| Seventh | ☽ | used in the delineation of relationships and marriage as a natural significator of women (in female charts it is replaced by the Sun) |
| Eighth | ♄ | (used only as a natural significator of death) |
| Ninth | ♃ | used as the natural significator of religion and law |
| Tenth | ♂ | not used |
| Eleventh | ☉ | not used |
| Twelfth | ♀ | not used |

The signs can also be considered as co-significators of the houses. Thus Aries is co-significator of the first, Taurus of the second, etc. In practice, this association is used **only** in the delineation of illness, and each house corresponds to that part of the body ruled by the sign which is its co-significator. For example, the third house corresponds to the arms and shoulders, the parts of the body assigned to the sign of Gemini.

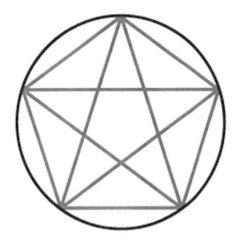

*Appendix 5*
# Minor Aspects and Aspect Configurations

## Minor Aspects

In addition to the five aspects already studied (conjunction, opposition, trine, square and sextile), there are the so-called minor aspects. These aspects were initially proposed by astrologer/astronomer Johannes Kepler (1571-1630), who considered other divisions of the sphere besides those acknowledged in the tradition. These aspects are derived from the division of the circle (the zodiac) by 5, 8, 10, and 12. The division by 5 produces the quintile (72°), from which we also get the biquintile (144°). The division by 8 produces the semi-square (45°) and the sesquiquadrate (135°). The division by 10 generates the semiquintile (36°), also known as the decile, from which derives the sesquiquintile (108°), also known as thetridecile. As to the division by 12, it produces the semi-sextile (30°) and the quincunx (150°). More recently (20th century) two new minor aspects have arisen in astrological circles, the septile and the novile, produced from the division of the zodiacal circle by 7 (51° 27') and by 9 (40°).

The assimilation of these aspects into astrological circles was gradual. Some were quickly received, such as the quincunx and the semi-sextile, while others were never popularly incorporated. The quincunx and semi-sextile are special cases. In contrast with the other minor aspects, these two aspects are directly related to the symmetry of the zodiac (see the chapter on aspects). They are the so-called inconjuncts which the tradition does not consider legitimate aspects. Despite this, some authors give them meaning: the semisextile is similar, although weaker, to the sextile, and the quincunx has a moderately malefic nature. Others give them both the meaning of instability and disconnect, which is in agreement with the natural state of inconjunction that relates to the signs that they connect. The remaining minor aspects are based upon mathematical and geometrical concepts, thereby completely losing the traditional relationship between signs. For this reason, they were never considered to be of great importance. The classical authors sometimes use them in directions,[41] but interpret the combination of planets involved, instead of the actual aspect; from the aspect one simply derives the ease or difficulty of the aspectual relationship.

---

[41]For example, William Lilly, in *Christian Astrology* (see Bibliography).

It was only in the 20th century that specific meanings were given to the minor aspects. These attributions were never based upon the relationships between the signs, as is the case in the tradition, but rather upon factors external to the geometry of the zodiac. Some aspects derive their meanings from numerical symbolism. For example, since the number five is associated with creativity in number symbolism, it is assumed that the aspects resulting from the division by 5 (quintile and biquintile) mean creativity (although the definition of what it means to have a "creative" relationship between two planets is never clearly defined). The septile aspects are given the meaning of fate, destiny, or fatality from the symbolism of the number seven. Other aspects get their meanings from the geometric divisions of the major aspects. For example, the semiquadrate and the sesquiquadrate, both derived from the square, mean tension and friction; the novile, which is a third of the trine, receives from the latter the meaning of harmony and success.

No orbs are used with the minor aspects because the range of the orbs would intersect with various aspects. Only very close aspects are considered (no larger than 2° or 3°). In any event, any interpretation that is attributed to them is always less important in the larger context of the chart.

### Minor Aspect Symbols

As with the major aspects, there are conventional symbols for the minor aspects, although not all astrologers are in agreement about them. Figure 1 shows the more commonly used glyphs.

### Parallels and Contraparallels

Parallels are planetary relationships that derive from the declination of the planets, meaning their position north or south of the celestial equator. Conceptually, they are completely different from the aspects, which are based upon the position of the planets on the ecliptic, that is, on the zodiac. Two planets are in parallel if both are equally distant from the celestial equator (they have the same declination). Planets in parallel are both north or south of the celestial equator, while in cases where one is north and the other south, but equally distant from the celestial equator, they are contraparallel. Generally, an orb of 1° is used. Below are the glyphs for the parallel and contraparallel.

| Glyph | Name | Angle |
|-------|------|-------|
| ⊻ | Semi-sextile | 30° |
| ⊼ | Quincunce | 150° |
| ∠ | Semi-square | 45° |
| ⊡ | Sesquiquadrate | 135° |
| Q | Quintile | 72° |
| ± | Biquintile | 144° |
| ⊥ | Semi-quintile | 36° |
| ⊥ | Sesquiquintile | 108° |
| S | Septile | 51° 26' |
| N | Novile | 40° |

**Figure 1. Minor Aspect Glyphs**

| Name | Glyph |
|------|-------|
| Parallel | ∥ |
| Contraparallel | ⫫ |

In terms of interpretation, a parallel is treated similarly to the conjunction and a contraparallel as an opposition. This concept is a modern derivation of antiscia. Although it's received some attention, those that use it in their practice are few in number.

### Harmonics

The harmonics concept developed as a part of a statistical study regarding aspects. Harmonics is a system used to detect patterns in the minor aspects and to interpret them according to numerological symbolism. This work, developed by British astrologer John Addey (1920-1982), among others, received some acceptance in the 1970s, although it was never widely used by practitioners. Although interesting, harmonics mixes elements of statistics with geometry and numerology and has little in common with the traditional astrological system.

# Aspect Configurations

It is very common to find the aspects of a horoscope grouped into geometric patterns (triangles, rectangles, diamonds, etc.) The interpretation of these patterns, known as "aspect configurations" is not a part of traditional astrology. Until the beginning of the 20th century, astrologers did not routinely trace aspects in a chart. It was only when the graphical representation of aspects became popular that astrologers began to highlight these patterns and attribute meanings to them. This new approach led to the patterning of aspect configurations and to their interpretations as geometric figures without actually considering the planets involved. This shift in focus resulted in a change in interpretative priorities: the focus was removed from the planets (which produce the dynamic relationships of the horoscope) and instead was placed on the aspects and their configurations. From such an approach, one can only obtain generalized interpretations, which are continually more abstract and removed from the unique meaning of each chart. The fascination that these geometric designs have engendered in new students ends up distracting them from the more important elements of a chart. Although they do not belong to the tradition, we mention the aspect configurations here because their use (and abuse) is common practice in astrology.

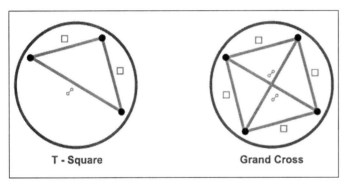

**Figure 2. T-square and Grand Cross**

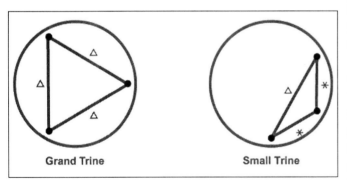

**Figure 3. Grand Trine and Small Trine**

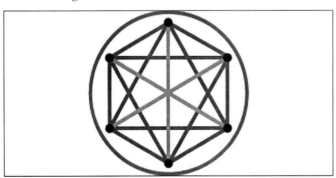

**Figure 4. The Star of David**

## T-square and Grand Cross

Both configurations are comprised of squares and oppositions and therefore represent tension. The T-square is comprised of three planets: two are in opposition to each other and the third that squares them both. The figure forms a right isosceles triangle.

The grand cross is a derivation of the above configuration: to the triangle is added a fourth planet, which opposes the third. The combination forms a square with a planet on each corner, diagonally criss-crossed by two oppositions.

## Grand and Small Trines

These two configurations are comrpised of different trines and therefore indicate harmony and ease. The grand trine is a triangle formed by planets that are 120° from each other. The small trine is a minor version of the grand trine in which two planets in trine form sextiles to a third.

The combination of two grand trines results in a configuration known as the "Star of David." It integrates six planets, all at 60° angles from one another, forming a six-pointed star. This is a configuration that is rarely formed in the sky, to which was given the meaning of good fortune and luck. In practice, its power is more imaginary than real.

Other common configuration figures are the kite and the popular mystic rectangle. The latter was all the rage in astrological circles when some students began to relate this configuration with "a noteworthy spirituality" (independently of the planets involved!). Obviously, this is an exaggeration. Even Dane Rudhyar, the astrologer who named it, said regarding its use: "At first I called it a 'mystical rectangle. . . . Later, I realized the inadequacy of the term, that it was confusing, especially considering the way it has been used and abused of late."[42]

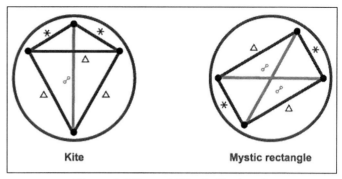

**Figure 5. Kite and Mystic Rectangle**

If we add the minor aspects to the major ones, the number of configurations increases, as does the imagination of some authors who attribute names and symbolism to them.

Because the planets involved in the aspect configurations are considered to be less important than the geometric patterns that they create, it has become common practice to include the trans-saturnian planets, planetoids, lunar Nodes, and other minor elements in order to "complete" these figures. This obviously increases the chances of finding "rare" and "exotic" patterns, while simultaneously diminishing even further their significance and meaning.

It is fair to suppose that these configurations may indicate a degree of tension or fluidity involved in the dynamic interactions of the chart and that they may even represent legitimate relationships between the planets. However, they always need to be interpreted from the perspective of the planets and not as independent patterns in themselves. It is the planets that form the aspects; therefore, it is *with them* that we anchor the delineation, not with the aspect. Nevertheless, the great majority of practitioners delineate the pattern by itself without paying proper attention to the planets involved—and therein lies a mistake. For example, a chart that has a T-square is interpreted as tense and problematic, while one with a grand trine is seen as harmonious and fluid. Although there is truth to these interpretations, they are meaningless if the nature of the planets involved and their function in the chart are not considered. A T-square between the Moon, Venus, and Jupiter, for example, will not present great tension, while a grand trine between Mars, Saturn and the Moon will never be completely carefree and easy.

> **The Huber Method**
>
> Also known as astrological psychology[43], this method was created by Bruno and Louise Huber around the mid 20th century. Its interpretation is based largely upon aspect configurations, thereby creating a specific methodological approach to the horoscope. It consists of studying the types of configurations formed by various aspects and giving them elaborate meanings. For this purpose, more than 30 geometrical configurations were catalogued. This method is also a derivation of the traditional system and includes very specific parameters, namely as it relates to orbs and house systems.

---

[42]Rudhyar, Dane. *Astrological Aspects*. Aurora Press. Santa Fe, NM. 1980.

[43]Not to be confused with psychological astrology, as this term encompasses several variations of astrological practice based on, or related to, psychology.

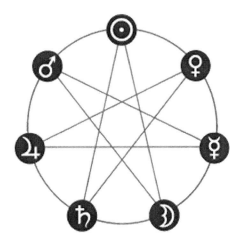

## *Appendix 6*
# *Planetary Hours*

According to the astrological tradition the planets and their attributes are present in every aspect of life. Consequently, every day of the week is under the dominion of one planet. The first day, Sunday, is consecrated to the Sun, the most important of the celestial bodies. Monday is dedicated to the Moon, Tuesday to Mars, Wednesday to Mercury, Thursday to Jupiter, Friday to Venus and Saturday to Saturn.

This astrological rulership can be found in the names given to the days of the week. In French and in Spanish this association is quite evident. Lundi and Lunes (Monday), originate from the Latin term *luna*, meaning Moon; Mardi and Martes (Tuesday) come from *mars*; the remaining days of the week follow the same pattern, as can be seen in their names; the only exception is Sunday (Dimanche, Domingo, respectively) which derives its name directly from the Latin term *dominus*, which means Lord, as in day of the Lord. As to the word Saturday, it derives from the Hebrew term *shabbath*, which refers to the day of Saturn (which in Hebrew is called *Shabbathai*).

The Anglo-Saxon names derive mostly from northern deities: Tuesday is Tiw's day (a god of war, like Mars), Wednesday is Wotan's (or Odin's) day (god of wisdom which is taken in this regard as equivalent to Mercury), Tuesday is Thor's day (god of thunders, like Jupiter) and Friday is Freya's or Frigg's day (goddess of love, similar to Venus). Sunday and Monday are very obviously Sun's

| | | **Figure 1. The Days of the Week in Several Languages** | | |
|---|---|---|---|---|
| *Week Day* | *Planet* | *Latin* | *French* | *Spanish* |
| Sunday | Sun | Sole | Dimanche | Domingo |
| Monday | Moon | Luna | Lundi | Lunes |
| Tuesday | Mars | Martis | Mardi | Martes |
| Wednesday | Mercury | Mercurii | Mercredi | Miércoles |
| Thursday | Jupiter | Iovis | Jeudi | Jueves |
| Friday | Venus | Veneris | Vendredi | Viernes |
| Saturday | Saturn | Saturni/Sabatum | Samedi | Sábado |

day and Moon's day.

Just as the days have planetary rulers, the hours are also ruled by the planets. The planetary rulers of the hours are assigned according to the order of the celestial spheres, or Chaldean order: Saturn, Jupiter, Mars, Sun, Venus, Mercury and the Moon. The first hour of each day determines the planetary ruler that rules the entire day. For instance; the first hour of Sunday, the day of the Sun, is attributed by the Sun, and the entire day is therefore, under its dominion. To determine the hour rulers of the remaining hours one just has to follow the order of the spheres. Therefore, after the hour of the Sun comes the hour of Venus (second hour of the day), then the hour of Mercury (third hour), then of the Moon (fourth hour), of Saturn (fifth hour), of Jupiter (sixth hour) and of Mars (seventh hour). After the seventh hour the sequence repeats itself: the eighth hour is again ruled by the Sun, the ninth by Venus, the tenth by Mercury, the eleventh by the Moon and finally the twelfth by Saturn.

At the end of the twelfth planetary hour the Sun sets, and Sunday night begins. However, the sequence of planetary hours continues without interruption: after the twelfth hour of Saturn follows the thirteenth hour of Jupiter, which is also the first planetary hour of the night; so, the night of Sunday is ruled by Jupiter. We have in this manner, a day of the Sun (Sun-day), to which corresponds the night of Jupiter. The night of Jupiter begins in the thirteenth hour, ruled by Jupiter, followed by the fourteenth hour, of Mars (second of the night), the fifteenth hour, of the Sun (third of the night), the sixteenth hour, of Venus (fourth of the night), the seventeenth hour, of Mercury (fifth of the night), the eighteenth hour, of the Moon (sixth of the night), the nineteenth hour, of Saturn (seventh of the night), the twentieth hour, again of Jupiter (eighth of the night), the twenty-first hour, of Mars (ninth of the night), the twenty-second hour, of the Sun (tenth of the night), the twenty-third hour, of Venus (eleventh of the night), and finally the twenty-fourth hour, of Mercury (twelfth of the night).

After the twenty-fourth planetary hour, the Sun rises again and a new day begins, in this case Monday. As Sunday ends with an hour of Mercury, Monday begins with one hour ruled by the Moon, the next planet in the Chaldean order. Therefore, Monday is the Moon's day.

The sequence of planetary hours continues uninterruptedly. It can be represented by a spiral which repeats itself every week.

Every day (a period of 24 hours) has a diurnal ruler and a nocturnal ruler. These pairs of rulers are always the same for each day of the week because the sequence of planetary hours never changes.

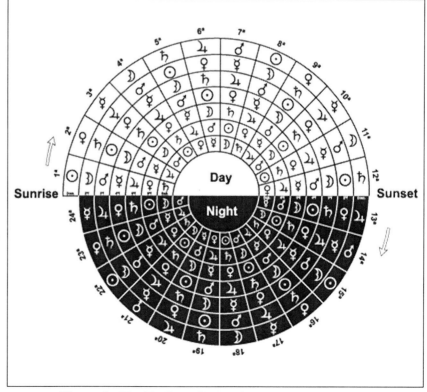

**Figure 2. The Endless Cycle of the Planetary Hours**

## Figure 3. Day and Night Planetary Rulers

| Week Day | Diurnal Ruler | Nocturnal Ruler |
|----------|---------------|-----------------|
| Sunday | ☉ | ♃ |
| Monday | ☽ | ♀ |
| Tuesday | ♂ | ♄ |
| Wednesday | ☿ | ☉ |
| Thursday | ♃ | ☽ |
| Friday | ♀ | ♂ |
| Saturday | ♄ | ☿ |

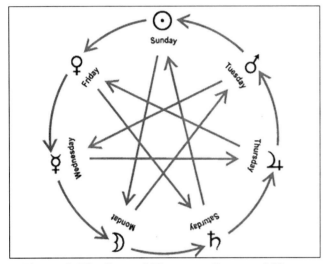

**Figure 4. The Star of Planetary Days and Hours**

The correlation between the days of the week and the planetary hours may be represented by a seven pointed star formed by the seven planets (see figure 4). The central arrows show the sequence of the days (and nights) of the week. The outer arrows show the sequence of planetary hours.

### Planetary Hours and Official Hours

It is important to note that the planetary days and hours do not correspond to the official days and hours. The astrological calendar is defined by the natural movements of the planets, and the official calendar is based upon standard time. Accordingly, the astrological days begin at sunrise and end at sunset (and of course the astrological nights begin at sunset and end at sunrise), while the official days run from the 00h00 (midnight) of one day to the 00h00 hours of the next. Therefore, although Monday officially begins at 00h00, astrological Monday only begins at sunrise (until then, it is still Sunday night).

The planetary hours, like the hours of a sundial, are sun-based and consequently they too are dependant upon the length of the day as timed from sunrise to sunset. The length of each hour depends upon the length of the day (from sunrise to sunset), which changes throughout the year. At the time of the spring equinox, day and night have the same duration; thus, both diurnal and nocturnal hours contain 60 minutes each. From then on, the diurnal hours increase gradually every day as days become longer. Conversely, the nocturnal hours decrease as nights become shorter. The culminating point occurs at the summer solstice, when we get the longest day and the shortest night. During this time of the year, the diurnal hours reach their longest duration and the nocturnal hours their shortest.

After the solstice, the days gradually shorten and the nights lengthen, and consequently so do their hours. By the autumn equinox, days and nights once again have the exact same duration (60 minutes for each hour). But the days continue to decrease until the shortest day of the year is reached at the winter solstice (the longest night of the year). At this time, diurnal hours are short and nocturnal hours long. After that, there is a gradual increase of the day (and a correspondent shortening of the night), until balance is achieved once more at the spring equinox—starting the cycle all over again.

In summary, in summer the diurnal planetary hours are longer and the nocturnal hours are shorter, and in winter the situation is reversed, with short diurnal planetary hours and long nocturnal hours.

This method of marking time is completely different from that of official hours, which always last 60 minutes, regardless of the season of the year. It is only at the equinoxes that the planetary hours and the official hours coincide, that is, when days and nights in both systems have the same exact duration.

## Calculating the Planetary Hours

To calculate the planetary hours of a given day it is necessary to know the exact time for sunrise and sunset of that day and also for the next day's sunrise. This information is easily found in astronomical almanacs, in some newspapers, and in official reports published by the astronomical observatories. To calculate the diurnal planetary hours of a given day it is necessary to subtract the sunrise hour from the sunset hour in order to obtain the length of that day. This value is then divided by 12, to obtain the length of each hour. Then add this number to the sunrise hour and each successive hour thereafter in order to determine the beginning of each planetary hour.

For example, using Jauary 1, 2006 in Lisbon:

Sunrise at: 7 hours 55 minutes

Sunset at: 17 hours 26 minutes (always use military time by adding 12 to the PM hours)

Therefore, the day had a duration of 9 hours and 31 minutes (17h26m – 7h 55m = 9h 26m)

Since we have 12 diurnal hours, it is necessary to divide 9h 31m by 12.

To make it easier the minutes can be converted to a decimal by cross-multiplying:

So, the 31 minutes correspond to 0.52 hours.

*If one hour corresponds to 60 minutes, then:*

> 1 h — 60m
>
> **a** — 31m          **a** = (31 x 1)/60 = 0.52h

This number is added to the 9 hours, to obtain 9.52 hours.

Then divide 9.52 by 12, thus obtaining 0.79 hours. This was the length of each diurnal planetary hour on that day, for Lisbon's latitude. Convert this value back to hours and minutes: 0.79 hours correspond to 47.6 minutes.

*Following the same principle:*

> 1 h — 60m
>
> 0.79 h — **b**          **b** = (0.79 x 60)/1 = 47.6m

It is therefore 47.6 minutes, whose decimal may be converted to seconds: 0.6 minutes is equal to 36 seconds.

*If one minute correspond to 60 seconds, then:*

> 1 m — 60s
>
> 0.6 m — **c**          **c** = (0.6 x 60)/1 = 36s

Therefore, each planetary hour had the duration of **47 minutes e 36 seconds.**

| Hour | Begins at |
|------|-----------|
| 1st | 07h 55m |
| 2nd | 08h 42m 36s |
| 3rd | 09h 30m 11s |
| 4th | 10h 17m 46s |
| 5th | 11h 05m 21s |
| 6th | 11h 52m 56s |
| 7th | 12h 40m 31s |
| 8th | 13h 28m 06s |
| 9th | 14h 15m 41s |
| 10th | 15h 03m 16s |
| 11th | 15h 50m 51s |
| 12th | 16h 37m 26s |
| **end** | **17h 26m 00s** |

**Figure 5. Calculation Example: Determining the Diurnal Hours**

| Hour | Begins at | Ruler |
|------|-----------|-------|
| 1st | 07h 55m | ☉ |
| 2nd | 08h 42m 36s | ♀ |
| 3rd | 09h 30m 11s | ☿ |
| 4th | 10h 17m 46s | ☽ |
| 5th | 11h 05m 21s | ♄ |
| 6th | 11h 52m 56s | ♃ |
| 7th | 12h 40m 31s | ♂ |
| 8th | 13h 28m 06s | ☉ |
| 9th | 14h 15m 41s | ♀ |
| 10th | 15h 03m 16s | ☿ |
| 11th | 15h 50m 51s | ☽ |
| 12th | 16h 37m 26s | ♄ |
| **end** | **17h 26m 00s** | |

**Figure 6. Calculation Example: Attributing the Diurnal Hours Rulers**

| Hour | Begins at | Ruler |
|------|-----------|-------|
| 13th | 07h 55m | ☉ |
| 14th | 08h 42m 36s | ♀ |
| 15th | 09h 30m 11s | ☿ |
| 16th | 10h 17m 46s | ☽ |
| 17th | 11h 05m 21s | ♄ |
| 18th | 11h 52m 56s | ♃ |
| 19th | 12h 40m 31s | ♂ |
| 20th | 13h 28m 06s | ☉ |
| 21st | 14h 15m 41s | ♀ |
| 22nd | 15h 03m 16s | ☿ |
| 23rd | 15h 50m 51s | ☽ |
| 24th | 16h 37m 26s | ♄ |
| end | 17h 26m 00s | |

**Figure 7. Calculation Example: Determining and Attributing the Nocturnal Hours Rulers**

From this value, we can calculate all the diurnal planetary hours for that day. To determine the beginning of the second hour, merely add 47 minutes and 36 seconds to the sunrise hour; to obtain the beginning of the third hour, one simply adds another 47 minutes and 36 seconds to the beginning of the second hour, and so on.

Now determine the planetary ruler for each hour. January 1, 2006 occurred on a Sunday, the day ruled by the Sun. Therefore, the Sun is also the ruler of the first hour. The rulers of the remaining hours follow the Chaldean order as shown in Figure 6.

A similar method is used to obtain the nocturnal hours. The length of the whole night is calculated by subtracting the sunset hour from the hour of sunrise on the next day from. As we did with the diurnal hours, we have to divide that value by 12 to obtain the length of each nocturnal hour. This value is then added to the moment of sunset, and each hour thereafter, to determine the beginning of each nocturnal planetary hour.

For example, for January 1, 2006, we would consider the hour of sunset (17h 26m) and the hour of sunrise the next day, January 2 (7h 55m, the same as the day before). To subtract 17h 26m (or 5:26 PM in military time) from 7h 55m (7h 55m – 17h 26m) it is necessary to first add 24 hours to the sunrise hour; therefore, 7h 55m + 24h 00m = 31h 55m.

Now calculate the total length of the night: 31h 55m – 17h 26m = 14h 29m. Then we convert the 29 minutes to a decimal, thus obtaining 0.48 hours, which are then added to the 14 hours. The result is 14.48 hours, which now have to be divided by 12, to obtain the duration of each nocturnal planetary hour. The result is 1.21 hours, which correspond to 1 hour 12 minutes and 25 seconds.

Now follow the same procedure as for the diurnal hours to determine the start of each hour; the Chaldean sequence is picked up at the same point where it had previously left off (see Figure 7).

The first hour of the night is ruled by Jupiter, therefore, this planet is the nocturnal ruler.

# Practical Application

The planetary hours are used to determine the quality of a given moment in time. They are mainly used in horary astrology and in astrological elections. In mundane and natal astrology their application is more limited. In a nativity, the day and hour rulers are used to assess the essential qualities of the native by combining the qualities of these planetary rulers to the overall delineation.

In horary astrology they are used to determine the validity of the question. If in a given horary chart the ruler of the planetary hour has no affinity with the ruler of the Ascendant, or has no prominence in the chart whatsoever, it suggests that the question was inadequately expressed or that it doesn't make sense. It is however, in astrological elections that the planetary hours are more widely applied, assisting in the selection of the most suitable moment.

## General Meanings of the Planetary Hours

The hours ruled by Saturn are always appropriate for deep thought, the organization of ideas, and the performance of tasks that require patience and discipline. They can represent somewhat depressing moments due to the melancholic nature of the planet. In practical terms, they also indicate good moments for initiating agricultural activities and for making plans against one's enemies. They are not appropriate for the start of any kind of treatment, for taking medication, nor for speaking to the authorities; they are also inappropriate for any type of construction, as well as the formation of partnerships or marriages.

The hours ruled by Jupiter are propitious for any kind of venture or endeavor. They are the ideal moments for the expansion of one's horizons and for increasing inspiration. They are temperate and serene hours, favorable for any exchange or matters related to money, as well as for business, travel, medical treatments, construction, and sowing. They also indicate good moments to attend to matters of peace and agreements, friendship, and government.

The hours ruled by Mars are moments of action, conquest, and beginnings. They are therefore good for initiating a treatment or for taking medication. They favor all kinds of work involving fire.

Tasks requiring assertiveness and competition are the most appropriate at these moments, but it is necessary to be cautious of misunderstandings and conflicts. They do not favor negotiations or travel, and those things that are also inappropriate for the Saturn hours.

During the hours ruled by the Sun, it is appropriate to engage in activities related to energy and leadership. They are favorable for the initiation of public actions which require visibility. They are therefore beneficial moments for speaking to the powerful. The Sun's planetary hours are neutral for other matters, namely for business, associations, marriages, and construction.

The moments ruled by Venus are appropriate for activities related to harmony, beauty, pleasure, social contacts, and relationships. They are the most indicated moments for buying jewelry and all manner of adornments, leisure activities, and all activities commonly attributed to women, such as embellishments. They are also excellent for marriages and partnerships, as well as for speaking to superiors and to women in general. Due to their joyful and careless nature, they are not appropriate for activities demanding great seriousness and effort.

Mercury hours are good for communication as well as for signing documents. They are appropriate for study, writing, teaching, and learning in general. They are likewise indicated for business transactions, commerce, and all manner of exchanges and connections, and favor all requests, including prayers and marriage proposals. They are also good for treatments and travel, particularly business travel.

The hours of the Moon favor all so-called domestic activities, particularly the acquisition and handling of food. They are propitious for all activities requiring imagination (from the invention of useful products, to less recommended activities such as fraud and treason). They are also beneficial for enterprises requiring swiftness, but unfavorable to the ones demanding stability.

## Combining Planetary Days and Hours

The significations of the ruler of the day and the ruler of the hour must be combined to achieve a more comprehensive understanding of the chart. The ruler of the day offers a general signification, while the ruler of the hour describes the actions of that moment. Because it extends for a longer period, the day ruler's signification is more broad; the qualities given by hour rulers are more specific, and therefore more significant. For instance, on a Venus day (associated with pleasure and comfort), a Jupiter hour may be appropriate for relaxing, engaging in enjoyable activities, and conceding to some indulgences. On the same Venus day, a Saturn hour may represent a more melancholic and reflexive moment, which can tone down the animation of a party, or the reunion of friends.

On a Moon day, which is generally somewhat agitated, the Mars hour can trigger misunderstandings and weaknesses, although it can also be a good time for making an appeal to a cause. On the same day, the Mercury hour can favor contacts and all manner of communication. On a Jupiter day (favorable for any kind of endeavor), the Sun hour is best suited for making a request to a superior. On the other hand, on that same day the Mars hour would be better suited for bold actions that demand physical courage (for instance, engaging in extreme sports). A Venus hour on a Mars day can add a strong erotic/passionate tone to the dynamic environment of the day. The reverse combination, a Mars hour on a Venus day, can indicate a moment of competition or perhaps jealousy that arises unexpectedly in a pleasant and cordial environment.

*Note that all these significations should be combined with the condition of the ruling planet at that particular moment in order to obtain a more detailed interpretation.* The condition of the planet is obviously determined by its essential dignity, angularity, speed, and the aspects it forms.

For example, to choose a favorable moment for a declaration of love, consider a Venus day and hour. Venus days are Fridays, and the Venus hours on Friday are the first (right after sunrise) and the eighth (in the afternoon, around 2:30 p.m).

There are, however, other factors to be taken into consideration. First of all, it is crucial that Venus be in a good condition at the chosen date. It should be as strong and as dignified as possible because any debility of Venus will affect the hours it rules. It is also important to ascertain the condition of the other significators of the matter, in this case the Ascendant and its ruler (signifying the person who declares his or her love) and the Descendant and its ruler (the person to whom the declaration is made); any planets placed in the first or in the seventh houses will also be relevant to this matter.

Let us now suppose that the declaration had to be made in the week of April 26-May 2, 1998. In that week, Friday (day of Venus) falls on May 1. The ephemeris for that day shows Venus is greatly dignified in Pisces, where it has exaltation and triplicity. The day is therefore favorable for Venus-ruled activities.

Now it is necessary to choose, within the hours of Venus, the most appropriate moment. The first hour begins at 6h44, exactly at sunrise, and ends at 7h52. In practical terms, it is far too early for this type of contact and it is also not very favorable from an astrological point of view. So this leaves us with the second hour of Venus, which begins at 14h42 and runs to 15h50 (or 2:42 p.m. to 3:50 p.m.). Within this time frame, the chart for 15h40 is chosen for the following reasons:

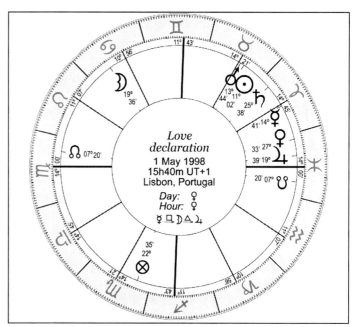

**Figure 8. Elective Chart for a Love Declaration**

- Besides being dignified, Venus is angular in the seventh house of relationships; it is also conjunct Jupiter, equally dignified in Pisces, and ruling the seventh house.
- The Ascendant is at 14° Virgo 00′, where Venus has triplicity, term and face, thus reinforcing its power over the matter.
- The Moon, the significator of the action, has several favorable placements: it is dignified in Cancer, posited in the eleventh house of hopes and, more importantly, it makes a translation of light between the two main significators: it separates from the square to Mercury, ruler of the Ascendant, and applies to the trine to Jupiter, ruler of the seventh house.
- Mercury is in its own term, thus acquiring some strength, and compensating for the debility due to its conjunction to the eight house cusp (which suggests some anxiety and fear)
- The selection of this particular time avoids a conjunction of the North Node to the Ascendant (always a source of disturbance) and therefore could not have been earlier. It could not have been much later either, because the Moon would have perfected and surpassed the trine to Jupiter, thus cancelling the translation of light and beginning to apply to the square of Saturn, an extremely unfavourable aspect.

As another example, consider the presentation of an important project to the boss. This presentation must take place in the first week of April 2003. A favorable day would be Thursday, ruled by Jupiter, a benefic planet. In that week, Thursday falls on the 3rd. By consulting the ephemeris for that day, notice that Jupiter is in Leo, where it has triplicity; it is therefore a good place to start.

Now the task is to select a favorable time within normal working hours. The hour of the Sun is favorable for speaking to people in authority and for the presentation of ideas that require visibility (the Sun is the luminary, so it brings light to everything it touches). The nature of the Sun also combines easily with the nature of Jupiter, and the power of the former is moderated by the natural temperance of the latter. On this day, the Sun is exalted in Aries, which is also very favorable. Besides, the two planets are in trine, thus reinforcing and supporting their mutual qualities.

The only hour of the Sun that falls within normal working hours is the second, between 8h29 and 9h32. The hour of 9h30 is chosen as the more adequate moment, for the following reasons:

- The Sun, ruler of the hour, is posited in the eleventh house of friends and allies, a favorable position.

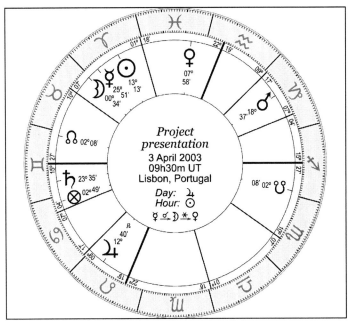

**Figure 9. Elective Chart for Presenting a Project**

- Jupiter, ruler of the day, is in the third house of communication, trining the Sun, its dispositor.
- Saturn, ruler of the Midheaven (and thus significator of the boss and the career) is in the first house, suggesting the boss's interest in the project.
- Mercury, ruler of the Ascendant (and significator of the native) is in the eleventh house and forms a sextile to Saturn, which it also disposits; the native has therefore some influence over the boss (as Mercury disposits Saturn) because there is good will (sextile) between them.
- The Moon, also well-posited in the eleventh and in exaltation, separates from the conjunction of Mercury and applies to the sextile of Venus; this translation of light connects the native (Mercury) to a promising career (Venus exalted in the tenth house of career and authority).

In both these examples of electional charts, the planetary rulers of the day and hour combine with the essential and accidental dignities and with the aspectual dynamics.

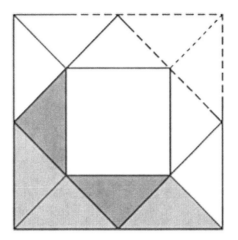

# *Astrological Chart Calculations*

This appendix includes basic instructions for calculating an astrological chart (see the bibliography for books with instructions on more complicated calculations).

In order to erect an astrological chart the following data are needed:
- Date and time of the event (of the birth, of the question, etc.)
- Geographical longitude and latitude of the location (where the event occurs)

Longitudes and latitudes, including their time zones, can be obtained from a good atlas (*ACS American* or *International Atlases* are typically used for this purpose), or databases available on the Internet.

## Materials

An ephemeris is needed in order to erect an astrological chart. This book lists the daily positions of the planets as well as the sidereal time, and the majority contain the positions of the planets and sidereal time for 00:00 hours Universal Time at the Prime Meridian (Greenwich, England).

A tables of houses (*The Michelsen Book of Tables*) is used to calculate the house cusps, and each is specific to a particular house system. These tables show the cusps for the tenth, eleventh, twelfth, first, second, and third houses for a particular sidereal hour and latitude. As of the date of publication, there is no known table in print for Alchabitius houses. For this reason, the examples presented here were not calculated using this house system (used in all other charts in this book), but by using Regiomontanus houses, another traditional house system. Currently, the most popular systems (and therefore the easiest tables to find) are Placidus and Koch.

## Calculations

There are two parts involved in erecting an astrological chart. In the first part the 12 house cusps are calculated in order to establish the framework within which the planets will operate. Only after this is complete are the planetary positions determined.

## Part I. Calculating the House Cusps

A. Converting Birth Time to Universal Time (UT or GMT)

1. Expressing AM and PM in 24-hour format: To start, convert a.m. or p.m. time to a 24-hour format (known in the US as "military" time and used to express time internationally). This is done by adding 12 hours to any PM birth time after 1:00 p.m. Thus, 12:43 p.m. in 24-hour format would be expressed 12:43, while 2:29 p.m. would be expressed 14:29 in 24-hour format.

2. Convert the hour of the birth to Universal Time: (this is equivalent to the old Greenwich Mean Time or GMT) To do this, look up the time zone of the birth. If the birth occurs at an eastern longitude (that is, east of the Prime Meridian at Greenwich), subtract that time zone from the birth time. If the birth occurs at a western longitude (west of the Prime Meridian at Greenwich), add the time zone to the birth time.

Note: Ensure that the time zone is adjusted for Daylight Savings Time, if it was in effect at that time. If the US Atlas shows Daylight Savings Time in effect (DST is also known internationally as Summer Time), subtract an hour from the birth time to make the adjustment to Universal Time. It is not necessary to do this if you use the *ACS International Atlas* because it is organized differently and already includes Summer Time adjustments.

B. Obtaining the Mean Solar Hour

1.Calculate the Longitude-Time Equivalent (LTE):Multiply the longitude of the location by 4 in order to convert it to time.

> ### *The Reason for the Adjustment*
>
> The adjustment known as the LTE is made because it takes 4 minutes for Earth to rotate 1 degree on its axis. Thus, this is a conversion of the distance into time from the place of birth to the Greenwich Meridian.
>
> 24 hours = 1440 minutes
> 1440 minutes divided by $360°$ = 4 minutes per degree

2. If the birth place is east longitude, add the LTE to the Universal Time (obtained in A.2 above) and if the birth place is West longitude, subtract the result from the Universal Time. The result is the **Mean Solar Hour**.

C. Calculating the Local Sidereal Time (LST)

1. Sidereal Time for 0:00 hours: Consult the ephemeris and look up the sidereal hour at Greenwich for 0:00 hours on the birth or event date.

> Important: Remember that you are looking up the date *corresponding to your Universal Time*, not to your local time. If the birth or event occurs close to midnight and the adjustments to Universal Time placed it in the previous day, use the new birth date for this step. The same is true if your Universal Time advances the birth to the following date.

Longitude Correction: Divide the longitude by $15°$ and then multiply the result by 10 seconds. This makes a 10 second correction for every $15°$ of longitude. This value is subtracted from the sidereal time if the longitude is east, and added to it, if the longitude is west.

---

*The Reason for the Correction*

The time it takes the Sun to cross a specific place on earth (the Greenwich Meridian, for example) is not the same as the time it takes a specific star (like 0 Aries) to cross that same location. This is because the earth is not only rotating on its axis but is also orbiting the Sun. Thus, by the time the earth has made a 24-hour rotation it has also moved a tiny bit in its orbit. More specifically, a 24-hour sidereal "day" is really about 3 minutes and 56 seconds *shorter* than a 24-hour solar day. If we reduce the day to hours, we find that one hour of sidereal time is 9.86 seconds shorter than a solar hour. Thus, in order to convert solar time to "star" time, we must make this correction, which we've rounded up to 10 seconds.

---

2. Mean Solar Hour Correction: Take the Mean Solar Hour (obtained in B.2) and also correct it by adding 10 seconds for each hour of solar time. Thus, if the birth time were 11:45, multiply 11.75 (the decimal format of 11:45) by 10 seconds and add this value to the Mean Solar Hour.

3. Add the corrected Mean Solar Hour (obtained in C.2) to the corrected Sidereal Time (obtained in C.1). The result is the **Local Sidereal Time**. With this figure, then consult the tables of houses for the latitude of the birth or event to obtain the house cusps.

If the houses are calculated for the northern hemisphere and the latitude of the chart is for the southern hemisphere, simply add 12 hours to the local sidereal time and switch the signs in the table for their opposites.

## Part II. Calculating the Longitude of the Planets

Consult the ephemeris for the date of the event. Note the positions of the planets for midnight prior to the Universal Time of the event. Note the positions of the planets for midnight of the next day and calculate the difference. This value is **the daily motion of the planets**.

**Note**: the daily motion will be a negative number if the planet is retrograde.

Take the Universal Time of the birth and the daily motion of the planets and calculate how far it moved on the birth date by using a simple proportion and cross-multiplying. Thus, if the planet covered "X" degrees in 24 hours (1 day), then from midnight of the previous night until the birth hour (using Universal Time) it will have covered "Y" degrees. Mathematically this would be expressed as follows:

$$\frac{\text{Daily motion X  Universal Time}}{24 \text{ hours}} = \text{distance covered at birth}$$

Add this distance to the positions of the planets for midnight of the day prior to the birth. This will give you **the radical positions of the planets**.

Note: It is necessary to covert the degrees, minutes, and seconds, as well as the hours, minutes, and seconds to decimal format before adding them. To do this, keep these equivalencies in mind:

60 seconds = 1 minute
60 minutes = 1 hour or 1 degree
360 degrees = 0 degrees

The zodiacal longitudes can be converted to absolute longitude as follows:

| 00° | ♈ | = | 0° |
|---|---|---|---|
| 00° | ♉ | = | 30° |
| 00° | ♊ | = | 60° |
| 00° | ♋ | = | 90° |
| 00° | ♌ | = | 120° |
| 00° | ♍ | = | 150° |
| 00° | ♎ | = | 180° |
| 00° | ♏ | = | 210° |
| 00° | ♐ | = | 240° |
| 00° | ♑ | = | 270° |
| 00° | ♒ | = | 300° |
| 00° | ♓ | = | 330° |

## Chart Calculation Examples

*Example 1*
Consider a child born November 17, 2005 at 1:10 AM in Lisbon, Portugal. The data:

Date: 11-17-2005
Hour: 1:10 PM
Location: Lisbon, latitude 38°N43′ and longitude 09°W08′

*House Cusp Calculation*

A. Convert birth time to Universal Time:

The official clock time is 1h 10m and Daylight Savings time was not in effect at this time of the year, which means no adjustment is needed. The time zone for Lisbon, Portugal is the same as Greenwich Mean Time, or Universal Time, or UT +0. Thus, 1h 10m of Lisbon time corresponds exactly with 1h 10m of UT.

B. Obtaining the Mean Solar Hour

When the longitude of Lisbon (09°W08′) is mltiplied by 4, the difference in time is 00h 36m 32s (each degree corresponds to 4 minutes of time).

Since Lisbon is located to the west of the Greenwich Meridian, this value must be subtracted from the UT of birth to obtain the Mean Solar Hour.

1h 10m 00s − 00h 36m 32s = 00h 33m 28s
Thus, the Mean Solar Hour is: **00h 33m 28s**

C. Calculating the Local Sidereal Time

The sidereal hour for Greenwich at 00 hours on November 17, 2005 is 3h 44m 36s.

Now make a correction to the sidereal hour of 10 seconds for every 15° of longitude: Lisbon is at 09°08′, so the correction is approximately 6s (note that 10 seconds per 15° = .67s per degree).

Since Lisbon is west longitude, these 6 seconds must be added to the sidereal time:

3h 44m 36s + 6s = 3h 44m 42s

Therefore, the corrected sidereal time is **3h 44m 42s**

The same correction must now be made to the Mean Solar Hour of the birth (0h 37m 28s) by adding the same 10 seconds for each hour. This also results in approximately 6 seconds.

0h 33m 28s + 6s = 0h 33m 34s

Therefore, the corrected Mean Solar Hour is **0h 33m 34s**

Now add the corrected Sidereal Time to the corrected Mean Solar Hour to obtain the Local Sidereal Time for the birth:

3h 44m 42s + 0h 33m 34s = 4h 18m 16s

**The result is a Local Sidereal Time for the birth of 4h 18m 16s.**

Using this figure, look up the birth latitude of 38°N43′ (or the closest latitude) in the tables of houses to obtain the house cusps. Consulting a Regiomontanus tables of houses for the latitude 38° (the closest latitude in the table) and using the two closest sidereal hours—4h 12m and 4h 24m—the result is the following values for the cusps:

For 4h 12m (38° latitude):

| | |
|---|---|
| Midheaven | 04°57′ Gemini |
| Eleventh house | 12°00′ Cancer |
| Twelfth house | 13°00′ Leo |
| Ascendant | 08°05′ Virgo |
| Second house | 03°00′ Libra |
| Third house | 00°00′ Scorpio |

For 4h 24m:

| | |
|---|---|
| Midheaven | 07°47′ Gemini |
| Eleventh house | 14°00′ Cancer |
| Twelfth house | 15°00′ Leo |
| Ascendant | 10°30′ Virgo |
| Second house | 05°00′ Libra |
| Third house | 03°00′ Scorpio |

Each of these lists provides approximate values. However, by calculating more precisely for latitude 38°N43′ and for 4h 18m, the result is:

| | |
|---|---|
| Midheaven | 06°26′ Gemini |
| Eleventh house | 13°08′ Cancer |
| Twelfth house | 14°03′ Leo |
| Ascendant | 09°29′ Virgo |
| Second house | 03°50′ Libra |
| Third house | 01°48′ Scorpio |

Now draw the chart with the degrees and house cusps placed in the circle (use a zodiacal ruler on the outside for ease of planet placement later). Or, the information can be presented in a square chart.

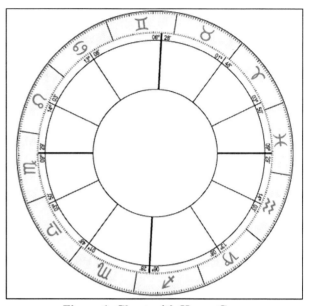

**Figure 1. Chart with House Cups**

### Calculation of the Planetary Positions

To calculate the position of the Moon, look in the ephemeris for the Moon's position at midnight prior to the date of birth (November 17) and at midnight after the date of birth (November 18):

Position at 00h of the birth date: 16°31′ Gemini
Position at 00h of the next day: 19°32′ Gemini

Next, take the difference between both positions in order to find how far the Moon has moved in 24 hours:

19°32′ - 16°31′ = 13°01′

Therefore, the Moon moved 13°01′ in 24 hours.

Now calculate how far the Moon moved until the moment of birth. To do that, set up a simple proportion and cross-multiply: if in 24h the Moon moved 13°01′ then in 1h 10m it moved "X". It is better to convert the values to decimal format in order to do the calculation:

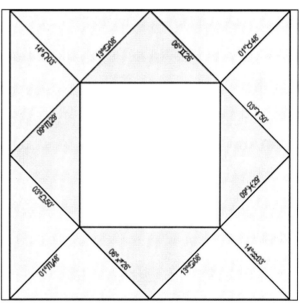

**Figure 2. Square Chart with House Cusps**

$$13°01′ = 13.0167°$$
$$1h\ 10m = 1,1667h$$

$$\frac{13.0167°\ X\ 1.1667\ h}{24h} = 0.6328°$$

Converting back to degrees and minutes, the result is: 00°38′. This is the number of degrees that the Moon moved from 00h UT until the moment of birth.

Now add this value to the position of the Moon given in the ephemeris (for 00h UT) in order to get its position at the hour of the birth: 06°31′ + 00°38′= 07°09′. **Therefore, the Moon at the hour of birth was 07° Gemini 09′.**

Now calculate the position of Mercury. Consult the ephemeris and locate the positions for midnight on the birth date and on the following date.

Position at 00h of the birth date: 10°20′ Sagittarius
Position at 00h of the next day: 09°47′ Sagittarius

Note that Mercury is moving backward in Sagittarius, which means it is in retrograde motion. Subtracting the difference, the result is:

09°47′ - 10°20′ = 00°33′

The motion is negative, which means Mercury moved backward 00°33′ in 24 hours. Now set up a simple proportion and cross-multiply in order to find out how far it has retreated in 1h 20m:

1h 10m = 1.1667h

$$\frac{33' \times 1.1667h}{24h} = 1.6042'$$

That is, Mercury moved approximately 00°02′. By removing this amount to the midnight position, its position at the hour of birth is:

10°20′ - 00°02′ = 10°18′

**Mercury is located at 10° Sagittarius 18′.**

Repeat the above procedure for the remaining planets, paying special attention to any retrograde planets. When the planets move very slowly (which is the case with Saturn and the Nodes) the calculations can quickly be estimated.

In order to facilitate these calculations, collect all of the data in a table:

| Figure 3. Planetary Positions, Example 1 | | | | | | | | |
|---|---|---|---|---|---|---|---|---|
| *Planet* | ☽ | ☿ | ♀ | ☉ | ♂ | ♃ | ♄ | ☊ |
| *Position at 0h prior to birth date* | 06°31′ Gemini | 10°20′ Sagittarius | 11°01′ Capricorn | 24°44′ Scorpio | 11°50′ Taurus | 04°43′ Scorpio | 11°17′ Leo | 11°23′ Aries |
| *Position at 0h after birth date* | 19°32′ Gemini | 09°47′ Sagittarius | 11°55′ Capricorn | 25°45′ Scorpio | 11°32′ Taurus | 04°56′ Scorpio | 11°18′ Leo | 11°20′ Aries |
| *Motion in 24h* | +13°01′ | -00°33′ | +00°54′ | +01°01′ | -00°18′ | +00°13′ | +00°01′ | -00°03′ |
| *Motion until the moment of birth* | +00°38′ | -00°02′ | +00°02′ | +00°03′ | -00′45″ | +00′30″ | +00′30″ | - 0′08″ |
| *Planet's position in the chart* | 07°09′ Gemini | 10°18′ Sagittarius | 11°03′ Capricorn | 24°47′ Scorpio | 11°49′ Taurus | 04°43′ Scorpio | 11°17′ Leo | 11°23′ Aries |

Note that the position of the South Node is exactly opposite the North Node: 11°23′ Capricorn.

Now position the planets in the chart using the zodiacal ruler on the wheel as a guide. Place the glyph for the planet, its degrees and minutes, and an indicator of retrograde motion when this applies. At the center of each chart we place the name of the native (or of the event), the birth information, and some astrological notes, such as the ruler of the day/night, the planetary hour ruler, and the planet (and aspect) to which the Moon next applies.

The Part of Fortune is calculated according to the method already outlined in Chapter XIII, while the planetary hours are determined according to the instructions in Appendix 6, The Planetary Hours.

In a square chart, the placement of the planets is somewhat different. In this kind of diagram, the planets are adjoined to the house cusp that contains the same sign as the planet. In this example, note that the Sun and Jupiter, both located in Scorpio, are on the third house cusp, which is positioned at 09°07′ of the same sign.

From the motion of the planets that were just calculated, it is immediately easy to tell the speed of the planets (see Chapter V).

In a list or grid next to the chart the aspects can be noted, along with their applications or separations and whether they are dexter or sinister. They can also be diagrammed within the center of the chart, as was explained in Chapter VIII, but the data would have to be noted somewhere else.

To determine the prenatal lunation, look once more in the ephemeris for the last lunation just prior to November 17, 2005. In this example, the prenatal lunation was a Full Moon on November 16, 2005 at 23° Taurus 46′.

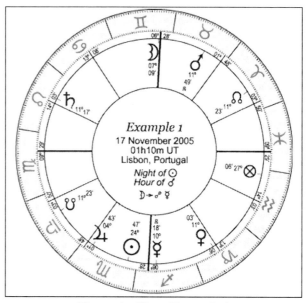

**Figure 4. Chart Example 1**

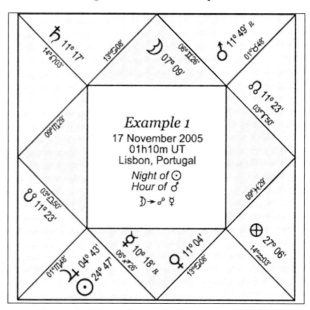

**Figure 5. Chart Example 1, Square Version**

*Example 2*

Now consider a horary chart erected for September 1, 2005, at 3:33 PM in Lisbon, Portugal (the same chart used in Chapter XIV, "How will the championship unfold?").

The data are:
**Date**: 09-01-2005
**Hour**: 3:33 p.m.
**Location**: Lisbon, Portugal, latitude 38°N43′ and longitude 09°W08′

*House Cusp Calculation*

A. Convert birth time to Universal Time

The official hour, when converted to military time, is 15h 33m. At this time of the year, Daylight Savings Time (UT +1) was in effect. Thus, in this case, subtract 1 hour from the clock time in order to get the hour at the meridian:

15h 33m – 01h 00m = 14h 33m (hour at the meridian)

As in the prior case, the official meridian of Lisbon is the same as Greenwich, which corresponds to UT+0. Thus, the Universal Time for the question is: **14h 33m**.

B. Mean Solar Hour Calculation

Multiply the longitude of Lisbon (09°W08′) by 4 to obtain the temporal difference: 0h 36m 32s. Since Lisbon is located west of the Greenwich Meridian, this value is subtracted from the UT of the question to obtain the Mean Solar Hour.

14h 33m 00s – 00h 36m 32s = 13h 56m 28s

Thus, the Mean Solar Hour of birth is: **13h 56m 28s**.

C. Local Sidereal Time Calculation

The Sidereal Time for Greenwich at 00h of September 1, 2005 was 22h 41h 02s. The result, when corrected 10s per 15° of longitude to the Sidereal Time, is:

09°08′ implies a correction of approximately 6 seconds
(10s for each 15° = .67 seconds per degree)

Since the latitude is west, these 6 seconds are added to the Sidereal Time:

22h 41m 02s + 6s = 22h 41m 08s

**Therefore, the corrected Sidereal Time is: 22h 41m 08s.**

If the same correction of 10 seconds per mean solar hour (13h 56m 28s) is calculated, the result is:

13h 45m 28s+ 140s = 13h 58m 48s

**Thus, the corrected Mean Solar Hour is: 13h 58m 48s**

Now add the corrected Sidereal Time to the corrected Mean Solar Hour to get the Local Sidereal Time:

22h 41m 08s + 13h 58m 48s = 36h 39m 56s

**The Local Sidereal Time is: 13h 58m 48s.**

Use this figure to consult the Regiomontanus tables of houses and find an entry for 12h 36m for the latitude 38°:

| | |
|---|---|
| Midheaven | 09°48′ Libra |
| Eleventh house | 05°00′ Scorpio |
| Twelfth house | 27° Scorpio |
| Ascendant | 20°23′ Sagittarius |
| Second house | 22°00′ Capricorn |
| Third house | 04°00′ Pisces |

Then interpolate from these cusps (and from those for the next sidereal hour) to get the following more precise house cusps:

| | |
|---|---|
| Midheaven | 10°51′ Libra |
| Eleventh house | 06°41′ Scorpio |
| Twelfth house | 27°51′ Scorpio |
| Ascendant | 20°46′ Sagittarius |
| Second house | 22°14′ Capricorn |
| Third house | 04°01′ Pisces |

*Planetary Position Calculation*

In order to calculate the planetary positions, use a table to collect the information, as in the previous example:

| Figure 6. Planetary Positions, Example 2 | | | | | | | | |
|---|---|---|---|---|---|---|---|---|
| *Planet* | ☽ | ☿ | ♀ | ☉ | ♂ | ♃ | ♄ | ☊ |
| *Position at 0h prior to birth date* | 08°16′ Leo | 23°22′ Leo | 17°33′ Libra | 08°39′ Virgo | 17°07′ Taurus | 18°30′ Scorpio | 05°50′ Leo | 15°27′ Aries |
| *Position at 0h after birth date* | 20°07′ Leo | 25°05′ Leo | 18°43′ Libra | 09°37′ Virgo | 17°29′ Taurus | 18°42′ Scorpio | 05°57′ Leo | 15°24′ Aries |
| *Motion in 24h* | +11°51′ | +01°43′ | +01°10′ | +00°58′ | +00°22′ | +00°12′ | +00°07′ | +00°03′ |
| *Motion until the moment of birth* | +07°11′ | +00°41′ | +00°42′ | +00°36′ | +00°20′ | +00°07′ | +00°04′ | +00°02′ |
| *Planet's position in the chart* | 15°27′ Leo | 24°24′ Leo | 18°15′ Libra | 09°15′ Virgo | 17°20′ Taurus | 18°37′ Scorpio | 05°54′ Leo | 15°25′ Aries |

Now calculate the position of the Moon in this horary chart, including the seconds.

Position at 00h of the event date: 08°15′59″ Leo
Position at 00h of the next day: 20°07′09″ Leo

Take the difference between both positions in order to get the Moon's motion in 24 hours:

20°07′09″- 08°15′59″ = 11°51′10″

**Therefore, the Moon moved 11°51′10″ in 24 hours.**

To calculate how far the Moon moved until the birth hour of the question, set up a simple proportion and cross-multiply: if in 24 hours the Moon moved 11°51′10″, then in 14h 33m it will have moved "X". Converting the values to decimal format, the result is:

11°51′10″ = 11.8528°
14h 33m = 14.55h

$$\frac{11.8528° \times 14.55h}{24h} = 7.1857°$$

When converted back to degrees and minutes, the result is: 07°11′09″, or the number of degrees and minutes that the Moon moved from 00 UT to the hour of the question. Now add this figure to the position of the Moon at midnight (its ephemeris listing) to obtain its position at the moment of the question:

08°15′59″ + 07°11′09″ = 15°27′08″

**The Moon was therefore, at 15°27′08″ of Leo.**

For the remaining planets, repeat the procedure (in the ephemeris, the only positions that include seconds are those for the Sun and Moon).

After completing the calculations for the cusps and planetary positions, we can diagram them in the round chart, or a square chart.

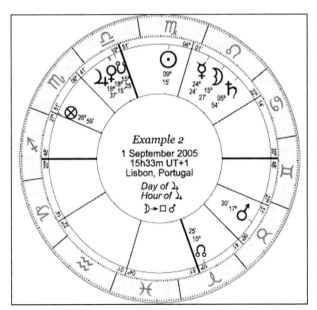

**Figure 7. Chart Example 2**

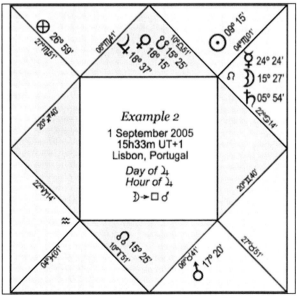

**Figure 8. Chart Example 2, Square Version**

## Technical Bibliography

Santoni, Francis. *The New International Ephemeris.1900-2050*. Paris, Auréas Editions, 1996.

*Tables des Maison Placidus Lat.0°-66°,* Saint Michele de Boulogne, Editions St. Michele, 1994.

*Regiomontanus Table of Houses*, Issaquah, WA, USA, JustUS Associates, ed.

Shanks, Thomas G., *The International Atlas*, San Diego, CA, ACS Publications, 1997.

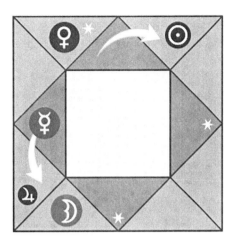

*Addendum*
# Basic Astrological Delineation

This work would not be complete without a brief introduction of astrological delineation. Therefore, we've outlined here two basic approaches that will allow the student to apply the material covered in this book in a structured manner.

## Temperament

The study of temperament constitutes an important key to an understanding of the natal chart. It reveals the underlying characteristics of an individual (physical and behavioral traits, psychological, and metabolic predispositions) that condition his or her actions and choices. Temperament is, therefore, the framework that comprises the totality of dynamics in the chart as a whole (for a complete treatment on the temperaments see Chapter II).

In every individual four temperamental types exist—choleric, sanguine, melancholic, and phlegmatic—although present in varying amounts. In some cases, one of the temperament types clearly predominates. In others we find a combination of the two more dominant types. In still other cases, it is difficult to detect a predominance of any one of the types. Every human being has a unique mixture of temperamental types that compose his or her *constitution*: a combination of behaviors, motivations, and dynamics that are natural to that individual and that, in broad terms, characterize him or her.

The tradition supplies us with formulas to determine the individual temperament from the main factors of the natal chart. This assessment is traditionally derived from three fundamental factors: the Ascendant, Moon, and Sun. The Ascendant is without a doubt the main factor in this equation as it defines the actual individual; the Moon is next in importance because it is co-significator of the motivations and dynamics in the nativity; and, lastly, the Sun contributes the general "tone" given by the season into which the individual was born.

In practice, temperament is assessed by scoring the classical qualities predominant in these three points. These qualities associated with every astrological factor are shown in Figure 1.

## Scoring Individual Temperament

Using a table in order to facilitate this assessment we can create a list of each of the qualities present in the three fundamental points mentioned. In the case of the Ascendant and the Moon, aside from their own inherent qualities, consider other factors that are associated with them. Thus, consider the qualities of the following factors:

1. Ascendant
   - Its sign
   - The sign of its ruling planet
   - The nature of the planets in the first house
   - The signs of any planets making aspects to the Ascendant (any aspect)
2. Moon
   - The phase of the Moon
   - The sign where the Moon is located
   - The nature of the planets conjoined with the Moon
   - The sign of any planets making aspects to the Moon (any aspect)
3. Sun
   - The qualities of the annual season represented by the Sun's sign

| Sign | | Qualities |
|------|------|-----------|
| ♈ | Aries | Hot + Dry |
| ♉ | Taurus | Cold + Dry |
| ♊ | Gemini | Hot + Moist |
| ♋ | Cancer | Cold + Moist |
| ♌ | Leo | Hot + Dry |
| ♍ | Virgo | Cold + Dry |
| ♎ | Libra | Hot + Moist |
| ♏ | Scorpio | Cold + Moist |
| ♐ | Sagittarius | Hot + Dry |
| ♑ | Capricorn | Cold + Dry |
| ♒ | Aquarius | Hot + Moist |
| ♓ | Pisces | Cold + Moist |
| ☊ | North Node | Hot + Moist |
| ☋ | South Node | Cold + Dry |

| Planet | | Qualities |
|--------|------|-----------|
| ♄ | Saturn | Cold + Dry |
| ♃ | Jupiter | Hot + Moist |
| ♂ | Mars | Hot + Dry |
| ☉ | Sun | *Spring:* Hot + Moist / *Summer:* Hot + Dry / *Autumn:* Cold + Dry / *Winter:* Cold + Moist |
| ♀ | Venus | Hot + Moist |
| ☿ | Mercury | Slightly Cold and Dry |
| ☽ | Moon | *1st Quarter:* Hot + Moist / *2nd Quarter:* Hot + Dry / *3rd Quarter:* Cold + Dry / *4th Quarter:* Cold + Moist |

**Figure 1. Qualities of the Signs, Planets and Lunar Nodes**

> Note: The spring signs (Aries, Taurus, and Gemini), are hot and moist; the summer signs (Cancer, Leo, and Virgo) are hot and dry; the autumn signs (Libra, Scorpion, and Sagittarius) are cold and dry; the winter signs (Capricorn, Aquarius and Pisces) are cold and moist.

## Important

- If the Moon aspects the Ascendant, add the qualities of the phase of the Moon rather than those for the Moon's sign. The only time when the qualities of the Moon are to be counted is for the actual Moon (in that case, they are counted twice: by phase and by sign).
- If the Sun aspects the Ascendant or the Moon, add the qualities for the corresponding season of the year, not those for the Sun's sign (in this case, the qualities for the Sun's sign are not considered).
- For planets in aspect to the Ascendant or the Moon (opposition, trine, square, or sextile) count the qualities of the signs where they are located. But for the conjunctions, count the qualities corresponding to the intrinsic nature of the planet itself. If the aspecting planet happens to be the Sun or the Moon, then consider the Sun's season and the Moon's phase.
- In this system, preference is given to aspects in sign and/or to those that are tighter, since they have a more marked contribution to temperament.

Following is an example using the chart of Friedrich Nietzsche:

1. Ascendant
   - Scorpio, a water sign, cold and moist

- Ascendant Ruler: Mars in Virgo (earth), cold and dry
- In the first house: 1st Quarter Moon, hot and moist
- In the first house: the North Node (nodal quality), hot and moist
- A sextile of Mars in Virgo, cold and dry
- Trine of Jupiter in Pisces, cold and moist

2. Moon
    - First Quarter, hot and moist
    - Located in Sagittarius, hot and dry
    - Conjunct the North Node (nodal quality), hot and moist
    - Square of Venus in Virgo, cold and dry
    - Sextile of Saturn in Aquarius, hot and moist
    - Sextile of Mercury in Libra, hot and moist
3. Sun
    - Autumn sign (Libra), cold and dry

The scoring is easier when the considerations are placed in a table, as in Figure 2.

The scoring results in a predominance of a sanguine temperament (hot and moist) with a melancholic sub-tone (cold and dry). The moist quality, which is characterized by adaptability and versatility, predominates (see Chapter II for a thorough description of the sanguine temperament combined with the melancholic). The life of this philosopher was marked by his mental vivacity, characteristically sanguine. From early on he exhibited exceptional intellectual capabilities, and at age 23 was nominated to chair a position in philology in Basel and shortly thereafter received a doctorate due to his exceptional work—without passing any exam. The melancholic sub-tone adds a strong introverted component to his intellectual capacity, giving him greater depth and rigor.

| | | Hot | Cold | Moist | Dry | Temperament |
|---|---|---|---|---|---|---|
| **Rising Sign** | ♏ | | Cold | Moist | | *Phlegmatic* |
| **Sign of Ascendant Ruler** | ♂♍ | | Cold | | Dry | *Melancholic* |
| **Qualities of Planets in 1st House** | ☽ (1st Quarter) | Hot | | Moist | | *Sanguine* |
| **Sign of planets in aspect with Ascendant** | ✶♂♍ | | Cold | | Dry | *Melancholic* |
| | △♃♓ | | Cold | Moist | | *Phlegmatic* |
| **Moon's phase** | 1st Quarter | Hot | | Moist | | *Sanguine* |
| **Moon's sign** | ♐ | Hot | | | Dry | *Choleric* |
| **Qualities of planets conjunct the Moon** | ☊ | Hot | | Moist | | *Sanguine* |
| **Sign of planets in aspect to the Moon** | □♀♍ | | Cold | | Dry | *Melancholic* |
| | ✶♄♒ | Hot | | Moist | | *Sanguine* |
| | ✶☿♎ | Hot | | Moist | | *Sanguine* |
| **Season of the year** | Autumn (☉ in ♎) | | Cold | | Dry | *Melancholic* |
| | **Total:** | **6** | 5 | **8** | 5 | |

**Sanguine: 5** Choleric: 1 **Melancholic: 4** Phlegmatic: 2

**Figure 2. Temperament Assessment for Friedrich Nietzsche**

This compound temperament frames the broader interpretation of the chart, allowing for a greater understanding of its dynamic elements. For example, the Moon in Sagittarius in the first house indicates sensibility, mutability, and enthusiasm, and tends to manifest for the most part within the sphere of ideas because of the overarching framework given by the sanguine-melancholic chart. Also, the strong tension indicated in the opposition of Jupiter to Mars and Mercury was channeled into intellectual endeavors and ideas with rigidity, perseverance, and pragmatism because of this same sanguine-melancholic combination. In contrast, in the chart of a choleric type, these same planetary combinations might have pointed toward more physical action and direct expression, while that of a phlegmatic type would have tended more toward emotional expression. Temperament is, therefore, a kind of background upon which the chart patterns are cast.

The sanguine-melancholic combination also presents some negative aspects. Under ordinary circumstances, these undesired traits might normally be found within manageable limits, but in this case they were taken to extremes. The sanguine tendency toward inconstancy and dispersion, mixed by the depressive nature of the Melancholic type, led to an under-compensation of sorts. After an acute delusional phase where Nietzsche proclaimed himself a genius, he fell into a type of stupor that lasted until the end of his days; the last 11 years of his life were spent in a semi-vegetative state under the care of his family.

Note that this mental under-compensation is inherent in Nietzsche's dynamic nature; it was not caused by the combination of temperaments. In this case, the combination sanguine-melancholic served merely to frame a latent problem, allowing it to manifest through the mental plane. If Nietzsche had had another temperament, his mental under-compensation might have manifested in some other way; if he were a choleric type, perhaps by extreme rage, if a phlegmatic type, perhaps by a tendency toward excessive emotional followed by periods of apathy.

We encounter a very different combination in the chart of the Portuguese poet Florbela Espanca.[46]

1. Ascendant
   - Libra, an air sign, hot and moist
   - Ascendant ruler, Venus in Sagittarius (fire), hot and dry
   - Saturn in the first house (planet's quality), cold and dry
   - A sextile of Venus in Sagittarius, hot and dry
   - A sextile of the Sun in Sagittarius (Autumn), cold and dry
   - Opposition of the Moon in 2nd Quarter, hot and dry

2. Moon
   - Second Quarter, hot and dry
   - Located in Aries, hot and dry
   - Conjunct Mars (planet's quality), hot and dry
   - Trine of Venus in Sagittarius, hot and dry
   - Trine of Sun in Sagittarius (Autumn), cold and dry

3. Sun
   - Autumn sign (Sagittarius), cold and dry

The results are shown in Figure 3.

| | | Hot | Cold | Moist | Dry | Temperament |
|---|---|---|---|---|---|---|
| Rising Sign | ♎ | Hot | | Moist | | Sanguine |
| Sign of Ascendant Ruler | ♀ ♐ | Hot | | | Dry | Choleric |
| Qualities of Planets in 1st House | ♄ | | Cold | | Dry | Melancholic |
| Sign of planets in aspect with Ascendant | ⚹ ♀ ♐ | Hot | | | Dry | Choleric |
| | ⚹ ☉ (Autumn) | | Cold | | Dry | Melancholic |
| | ☍ ☽ (2nd Quarter) | Hot | | | Dry | Choleric |
| Moon's phase | 2nd Quarter | Hot | | | Dry | Choleric |
| Moon's sign | ♈ | Hot | | | Dry | Choleric |
| Qualities of planets conjunct the Moon | ♂ | Hot | | | Dry | Choleric |
| Sign of planets in aspect to the Moon | △ ♀ ♐ | Hot | | | Dry | Choleric |
| | △ ☉ (Autumn) | | Cold | | Dry | Melancholic |
| Season of the year | Autumn (☉ in ♐) | | Cold | | Dry | Melancholic |
| Total: | | 8 | 4 | 1 | 11 | |

Sanguine: 1     Choleric: 7     Melancholic: 4     Phlegmatic: 0

**Figure 3. Temperament Assessment for Florbela Espanca**

---

[46]Florbela Espanca was a well-known Portuguese poet who died at the age of 36 in 1930. She was a precursor of the feminist movement in Portugal as her writings are known for their erotic and feminist qualities.

There is in this example a clear predominance of a choleric temperament (hot and dry) that corresponds with an enthusiastic, active, determined, and courageous character that is easily evidenced in Florbela's life and poetry. Also present in her turbulent personal life are the more negative aspects of this temperament, notably her impatience, emotional excess, and lack of receptivity. Her poetry also reflects this choleric backdrop, which produces an exuberant expression of the personality and large emotional outbursts. Florbela was an enterprising, strong-willed, and industrious woman; she was the first woman in her country to attend high school and university. Her refusal to accommodate herself to an unhappy marriage may be connected to this temperament—by nature very active (hot) and inflexible (dry).

Notwithstanding the marked predominance of the choleric temperament in this chart, there are other important indicators that should not go ignored. The most important is the position of Saturn in the first house, which gives her a melancholic tone. This indication is reinforced by the conjunction of a fixed star of the nature of Mercury and Saturn (Seginus, in the constellation Boötes) to the Ascendant. Furthermore, Florbela was born in the autumn, a melancholic season. Although these indicators do not nullify her choleric temperament, they add a melancholic nucleus which emerges from time to time.

As can be seen, an analysis of temperament must always be accompanied by a careful examination of the natal chart. Only in this way can we obtain a complete and detailed image of the personality being studied.

> As has been mentioned elsewhere in this book, one should not randomly count up factors, but rather look at the natal map. Only a direct understanding, based upon the full chart, allows one to translate the numerical (quantitative) indicators into the qualitative.

### Considerations About the Assessment of Temperament

The method described is largely based upon the work of William Lilly, one of the few authors who presents a system of scoring supported by a practical chart example. In our scoring we've omitted two considerations included by this author: the qualities of the sign of the Moon's dispositor, and those of the sign of the Lord of the Nativity (the planet with the highest score in the table presented in Chapter XIV).

Some authors take into consideration the effect of orientality and occidentality on the qualities of the planets. These are the rules usually followed for the qualities of the planets according to orientality and occidentality:

| Planet | Oriental | Occidental |
|---|---|---|
| ♄ Saturn | Cold + Moist | Dry |
| ♃ Jupiter | Hot + Moist | Moist |
| ♂ Mars | Hot + Dry | Dry |
| ♀ Venus | Hot + Moist | Moist |
| ☿ Mercury | Hot | Dry |

These attributions, which are intended to refine the scoring of the temperament for each planet, are in our opinion too complex for beginners. On the other hand, not all authors use them, and their omission does not significantly alter the final result of the weighing. Some modern astrologers disagree with Lilly's temperament method and have put forth their own. In any case, all the proposed variants are based upon the same three factors—the Sun, Moon and Ascendant—differing only in the weight they assign to each one.

# Personal Motivations

### The Ascendant and Its Ruler

Aside from the study of temperamental constitution, there are other essential factors to take into consideration when examining a natal chart. One of the most important is the examination of the ruler of the Ascendant and its condition. Since the Ascendant represents the individual, its ruler gives an indication of the underlying motivations, choices, and orientation of the individual. This motivating force is always present in his or her decisions, although they may not always be obvious to the individual.

There are three fundamental criteria to take into account in this study: 1) the nature of the ruling planet, 2) its position by sign, and 3) its position by house. The nature of the ruling planet indicates the manner in which the individual expresses his or her personal motivation. Logically, the manner of expression and the general attitude of the individual are strongly connected with the planet that represents that individual (ruler of the Ascendant). Thus, if the ruler of the Ascendant is Saturn, there is a sober, refrained, and cautious attitude. Jupiter suggests an attitude that is more comfortable, optimistic, and confident. Mars implies an intense, conquering attitude that can become imposing and, in the extreme, bellicose. The Sun expresses itself in a naturally authoritative, self-assertive, and dominant manner. Venus indicates a sociable, conciliatory manner oriented toward comfort. Mercury represents a laid-back, versatile, and diversified expression. Lastly, the Moon as ruler of the Ascendant conveys a fickle, albeit very adaptable, attitude that attempts to mold itself in the most diverse situations in order to realize its motives.

The sign position of the Ascendant ruler adds its characteristics (element and mode) to the nature of the planet. Thus, a fire sign gives the ruling planet an active expression; an air sign an interactive and social expression; a water sign, a more reflective and emotional expression; and an earth sign, a more pragmatic expression. The cardinal signs indicate active and agitated styles, the fixed signs reflect a preoccupation with security and continuity, and the mutable signs indicate a diverse, oscillating (between change and security) style. The element and mode of expression combine with the nature of the planet, either reinforcing or attenuating its basic expression. Lastly, the house where the ruling planet is located indicates the area of life where the native attempts to realize his motivations (the meanings of the twelve houses are outlined in Chapter VII).

In addition to these three fundamental factors, it is also necessary to consider the aspects formed by the ruler of the Ascendant and its essential and accidental condition in the chart. The planets that aspect the ruler (particularly by conjunction) depict situations that affect (aiding or impeding) the expression of the personal motivation, while the essential and accidental conditions indicate the quality and force, respectively, that the planet possesses in order to realize the motivation it represents.

In summary, the factors to consider in relation to the ruler of the Ascendant are:
- The nature of the planet
- Its sign position
- Its house position
- Its aspects
- Its dignities and debilities

## Practice Examples

*Case 1*

Nietzsche's chart has a Scorpio Ascendant, ruled by Mars in Virgo in the tenth house. The personal motivation of this philosopher is, therefore, expressed in an aggressive, intense, and bellicose manner (Mars), through actions that are concrete, practical, and diverse (Virgo, earth, mutable), and oriented toward public recognition and the realization of his career (tenth house).

The position of Mars scores 5 essential dignity points, which signals its elevated capacity for action and self-fulfillment. It is in its own triplicity in Virgo, which grants it great acceptance, and in its own terms, which grants it the ability to produce. In addition, it is oriental of the Sun, which allows it to have a more direct and frontal expression.

Also, Mars makes various aspects, of which the conjunction to Mercury is the most salient. Through this conjunction, Mercury brings its influence to the personal motivation of this chart, adding to Mars' expression a curious and intellectual facet that may at times be argumentative. The conjunction also indicates a connection between the personal motivation and the areas of life represented by Mercury. The career (tenth house) and relationships (co-ruler of the seventh house) therefore become extremely important to Nietzsche's personal sense of fulfillment. Another Mars aspect that needs to be highlighted is the opposition to Jupiter, indicator of a certain antagonism inherent in Nietzsche's nature. Jupiter is co-ruler of the Ascendant (it rules Sagittarius, intercepted in the first house), and its opposition to the ruler of the Ascendant represents an internal schism in his personal motivations. Because it is also the ruler of the fourth house, it indicates a separation between the individual and his family. As we've already described, Nietzsche was characterized by the intensity with which he expressed his ideas, even when he tried to acquire the public recognition which he so longed for. Also well known was the contrast between his self-proclaimed atheism and the extreme religiosity of his traditionally Lutheran family.

*Case 2*

Florbela Espanca's chart has Venus, ruler of the Ascendant, in Sagittarius in the third house. Therefore, there is a personal motivation focused on communication, learning, and all forms of exchange (third house) expressed in a dynamic, diverse manner (Sagittarius, fire, mutable), and very focused on aesthetics and harmony (Venus). Venus is peregrine in this degree of Sagittarius and is out of *hayz* (that is, out of its natural sect condition), which suggests an underlying dissatisfaction.

The conjunction with the Sun is particularly relevant in this chart because of its combust condition (covered in Chapter X). The matters represented by the Sun (eleventh house: friends, hopes, projects) dominate the personal motivation and were significant in the life of this poet. The trine of the Moon with Mars in the seventh house is a motivator for relationship matters. Relationships become especially important because Venus, significator of Florbela's motives, applies by trine to Mars, ruler of the seventh house and significator of relationships (she actively searches out others). The trine from the Moon, ruler of the Midheaven, brings a desire for success and recognition to the personal motivation. The life of Florbela was characterized by a large contrast between her romantic, entrancing poetry and her challenging marital life (she had three marriages, all very unhappy).

*Case 3*

Jim Morrison's chart has Saturn, ruler of the Ascendant, in Gemini in the fifth house. This placement points to a personal motivation oriented toward leisure and the search for pleasure (fifth house), but expressed in a "heavy" (Saturn) manner, yet with a strong intellectual and versatile streak (Gemini, air, mutable). Through the band *The Doors,* Morrison found a natural form of expression in music and poetry (fifth house themes), yet even his more playful compositions denote a touch of melancholy and disillusionment (Saturn).

Saturn, ruler of the Ascendant, is in its own triplicity, fast, and oriental of the Sun, which gives potency and power to Morrison's capacity to realize his motives. On the other hand, it is retrograde, which indicates hesitation in his personal choices.

There is also a personal internal conflict because Saturn is opposite Mercury, which is the actual ruler of the fifth house and the dispositor of Saturn. This configuration indicates a powerful gamble on his friendships and hopes (eleventh house), with grand expectations (Mercury receives Saturn); but these friends and hopes are often viewed as antagonistic (opposition) to the native himself (Saturn). Seen another way, this opposition also indicates controversial ideas (Mercury) and ideals (the eleventh house) that end up being prejudicial to the native (Saturn).

The fact that Saturn rules not only the first but also the twelfth indicates on the one hand a powerful need for isolation, but also a tendency for self-sabotage, which will manifest primarily via the fifth house where Saturn is located. It was the excess of "pleasures" (drugs) which led Morrison to a premature death at age 27. This situation is reinforced by Mercury, ruler of the fifth house (pleasures), also ruling the eighth house (death) and opposition Saturn (significator of Morrison himself).

| | | Hot | Cold | Moist | Dry | Temperament |
|---|---|---|---|---|---|---|
| Rising Sign | ♒ | Hot | | Moist | | *Sanguine* |
| Sign of Ascendant Ruler | ♄ ♊ | Hot | | Moist | | *Sanguine* |
| Qualities of Planets in 1st House | ☋ | | Cold | | Dry | *Melancholic* |
| Sign of planets in aspect with Ascendant | △♂♊ | Hot | | Moist | | *Sanguine* |
| | ✱☉ (Autumn) | | Cold | | Dry | *Melancholic* |
| | □☽ (2nd Quarter) | Hot | | | Dry | *Choleric* |
| Moon's phase | 2nd Quarter | Hot | | | Dry | *Choleric* |
| Moon's sign | ♉ | | Cold | | Dry | *Melancholic* |
| Qualities of planets conjunct the Moon | (none) | - | - | - | - | - |
| Sign of planets in aspect to the Moon | ☍♀♏ | | Cold | Moist | | *Phlegmatic* |
| | △☿♑ | | Cold | | Dry | *Melancholic* |
| Season of the year | Autumn (☉ in ♐) | | Cold | | Dry | *Melancholic* |
| | Total: | 5 | **6** | 4 | **7** | |

Sanguine: 3 Choleric: 2 **Melancholic: 5** Phlegmatic: 1

**Figure 4. Assessment of Jim Morrison's Temperament**

Everything described here operates within the larger context of a predominantly melancholic temperament. The dry quality predominates, indicating a focused and extremely determined attitude. This combination indicates an attitude that is inflexible to exterior influences and that cultivates individualism and seclusion, all of which reinforce the tendencies shown by the ruler of the Ascendant. In his life and in his works, Morrison's aversion to authority, to group think, and to conservativism are all notorious.

*Case 4*

Edgar Allan Poe's chart is an example of an Ascendant ruler in a fairly debilitated condition. Mars, ruler of the Scorpio Ascendant, is in the twelfth house in Libra, its sign of detriment. The twelfth house indicates a powerful need for isolation and limiting situations that are not under the control of the individual. In reality, Poe did have a difficult start to his life: he was only two when his father abandoned the family, and the next year his mother died of tuberculosis, which forced him to live with an adoptive family. From early on he displayed great emotional fragility.

The essential debility of Mars (in detriment and peregrine) suggests that his attempts at personal fulfillment through self-assertion (Mars) had a tendency to degenerate into misunderstandings and

| | | Hot | Cold | Moist | Dry | Temperament |
|---|---|---|---|---|---|---|
| **Rising Sign** | ♏ | | Cold | Moist | | Phlegmatic |
| **Sign of Ascendant Ruler** | ♂♎ | Hot | | Moist | | Sanguine |
| **Qualities of Planets in 1st House** | ♄ | | Cold | | Dry | Melancholic |
| | ☋ | Hot | | Moist | | Sanguine |
| **Sign of planets in aspect with Ascendant** | △♀♓ | | Cold | Moist | | Phlegmatic |
| | △♃♓ | | Cold | Moist | | Phlegmatic |
| | △☽ (1ˢᵗ Quarter) | Hot | | Moist | | Sanguine |
| **Moon's phase** | 1ˢᵗ Quarter | Hot | | Moist | | Sanguine |
| **Moon's sign** | ♓ | | Cold | Moist | | Phlegmatic |
| **Qualities of planets conjunct the Moon** | ♀ | Hot | | Moist | | Sanguine |
| | ♃ | Hot | | Moist | | Sanguine |
| **Sign of planets in aspect to the Moon** | □♄♐ | Hot | | | Dry | Choleric |
| **Season of the year** | Winter (☉ in ♑) | | Cold | Moist | | Phlegmatic |
| | **Total:** | 7 | 6 | 11 | 2 | |

Sanguine: 6    Choleric: 1    Melancholic: 1    Phlegmatic: 5

**Figure 5. Assessment of Poe's Temperament**

conflicts (characteristic of a debilitated Mars). This difficulty in personal fulfillment led him to auto-destructive behaviors, including the abuse of alcohol, heroin, and opium.

The twelfth house also indicates a certain conformity and general lack of motivation, which tends to hinder any attempt at overcoming obstacles. Many times, it is the actual individual that places himself into such situations, and in fact, Poe made several choices (such as leaving the university and the military academy) which had a negative impact on his future.

Mars receives a square from the Sun, which because it is ruler of the Midheaven, adds to the personal motivation the need for success and recognition. It is, however, a square, which in combination with Mars' debility, indicates a powerful dissatisfaction. On top of this, the aspect is separating (the Sun is moving away from Mars), which indicates a distancing between the individual and his goals. Another relevant factor is the conjunction between Mars to the antiscion of the Moon and Venus (in Pisces, conjunct on the cusp of the fifth house), which brings to the personal motivation a need for pleasure and a marked auto-indulgence.

The scoring of Poe's temperament reveals an oscillation between the sanguine and phlegmatic types, with a clear predominance of the moist quality. This constitution, markedly receptive, frames everything we've previously said within the context of extreme sensitivity and permissiveness, suggestive of an addictive personality.

**The First Step . . .**

In closing, the study of temperamental constitution and motivation, constitutes only the first step in the delineation of a natal chart. To obtain a complete and detailed picture of an individual's whole potential, it is necessary to systematically apply the collection of methods that compose the system of traditional delineation. Once the individual's potential is understood, it is possible to determine the periods in life when those potentials will manifest. This determination is an important aspect of astrology: **prediction**.

In traditional predictive astrology, specific techniques are used that indicate **how** and **when** this potential will be activated. Among the principal predictive techniques are directions, planetary periods, returns, and transits. **Directions** involve directing a planet to the place of another planet (or to a position that aspects another planet), thus activating the potential of the planet touched. This motion is ruled by a symbolic time during which the most notable techniques are primary directions, which equate a degree of ascensional time to a year of the life, and profections, which equate a month of the life to 2° 30′ in the zodiac (or 30° for a year). **Planetary periods** divide the life of an individual into temporal segments, each one under the rulership of a particular planet. Of these, note the Firdaria and the Ages of Man (the latter covered at the end of Chapter IV). **Returns** or revolutions, as they are called in the traditional literature, make up the study of the moment when a planet returns to its own natal position. The most commonly used in the tradition are solar returns, which offer a whole year's perspective, and lunar returns, which examine a month's period. **Transits** result from the interaction of the natal chart with the position of the planets at a given moment in time; these serve as complimentary to the aforementioned techniques.

The remaining branches of astrology also possess their own delineation techniques. In horary, there are specific rules for each type of question posed, and in mundane astrology, there are specific delineations for eclipses, annual ingresses, planetary cycles, etc. Nevertheless, the rules for delineation and prediction are another level of study, whose complexity, specialization, and scale are beyond the scope of this textbook. They will however, be covered in future works.

# Final Thoughts

If you have read this book from the beginning and studied its content, you now possess the basics to understand astrology. At this point you have acquired a structured vision of the astrological principles. This is the first and most important step in its study—a full understanding of the laws and rules that underly the art. We leave you with the framework of the art, the starting point for further studies on your journey through the universe of astrology.

Today, the preservation and recovery of the astrological tradition is a vanguard activity. Thanks to the work produced by dedicated researchers, we can finally drink from the most ancient sources without having to filter it through modern concepts or dilute it with ideas from other areas. The legacy of the ancient astrologers is capable of reaching us today. We can finally receive the testament of that incredibly long lineage of astrologers, who, over the course of centuries, have deciphered the meaning of the stars and planets and who compiled that knowledge in priceless works. In order to receive that patrimony, only one thing is asked of us: that we are worthy of the gift, that we honor it, and preserve it.

**The best way to honor astrology is to study it.**

*Helena Avelar and Luis Ribeiro*
*Students of Astrology*

# Annotated Bibliography

When one studies a new subject, invariably the question most frequently asked is: Which books do we start with? A diligent student always begins by acquiring a quality bibliography that contains accurate and coherent information that can be verified in practice. The objectives from the onset are to be able to organize one's thoughts, clarify confusions, and establish solid foundations that will be further developed in the future.

Nevertheless, those who are currently introduced to the world of astrology with the intent of learning it, are faced with an avalanche of books, schools, teachers and courses, many of which offer an abundant amount of information that is often disorganized and contradictory.

In this bibliography we offer some suggestions for a few reference works. We do not propose to outline an exhaustive list of all of the works that are representative of the astrological tradition, since nothing is more confusing to a new student than an overly long bibliography.

**Reference Works**

The following books are those we believe best represent the astrological tradition, and which, as such, can offer students invaluable information on their astrological path. All of them have served as sources for the current handbook.

*Christian Astrology* by William Lilly. Originally published in 1647, this work is still one of the principal sources for the student of the astrological tradition. Strongly versed in the tradition, William Lilly wrote a very comprehensive manual (in three volumes) covering both natal and horary astrology. His book became one of the main sources of information about the practice of astrology in its time since it explains the techniques and their application in an instructional manner with plenty of examples. William Lilly, *Christian Astrology,* Exeter, Regulus Publishing Co. Ltd, 1985.

*Tetrabiblos* by Claudius Ptolemy. This is an astrological classic and probably the most widely cited in the history of the art. It is one of the most important and influential works in the field of astrology. Although it is not a practical work, as are the other works referenced here, it is without a doubt, indispensable for any serious student of astrology. In addition, it is also a wonderful source of information because its approach to basic astrological principles became the canon of astrology. Claudius Ptolemy, *Tetrabiblos*, Loeb Classical Library, 1940.

*The Book of Reasons* by Abraham Ibn Ezra. This is a compilation of medieval astrological thought, still rich in Arabic influences. The first volume contains excellent references about the nature of the planets, signs, and houses, and a glossary of common astrological terms. The second volume contains a summary of the main rules for the practice of astrology, covering all branches: natal, horary, mundane, electional and medical. A very useful work, it offers the student a vast panorama of practical medieval astrology. Abraham Ibn Ezra, *The Book of Reasons*, Brill Academic Publishers, 2007. Translation and commentary by Shlomo Sela.

*El Libro Conpilado en Los Iudizios de las Estrellas* by Ali ben Ragel. Written at the end of the 11th century, this work is a collection of the Arabic-Medieval tradition and is one of the most important works for the rules and astrological aphorisms in all of the branches of astrology. It is an aggregate of various interpretative perspectives, which makes it a bit difficult to read. But it is one of the most valuable and complete sources for the tradition. *Ali ben Ragel, El Libro Conpilado en Los Iudizios de las Estrellas, Barcelona, Ediciones Indigo. 1997.* This edition is in Spanish. There is no current English translation available at this time.

*The Book of the Instruction in the Elements of the Art of Astrology* by Abu-Alraihan Al-Biruni. As its name indicates, this book contains the basics and principal technical definitions needed for the practice of astrology. It is more theoretical than practical, but contains valuable information to clarify certain ambiguities in the art. It is recommended for more advanced students. Abu-Alraihan Al-Biruni, *The Book of the Instruction in the Elements of the Art of Astrology,* Luzac & Co., London, 1934. Translation by R. Ramsay Wright.

*Carmen Astrologicum* by Dorotheus of Sidon. One of the oldest known works on astrology, the work of Dorotheus is the source for much of the subsequent western astrological tradition. It is not recommended for beginners, since it presents an approach that is very characteristic of the Hellenistic era, which may confuse beginners. It is nevertheless, an important source in the library of the more advanced student. Dorotheus of Sidon, *Carmen Astrologicum*, K.G. Saur Verlag GmbH, Munich, Germany, 1976. Translation by David Pingree. In 2005, Astrology Classics Publishers reprinted a copy of Pingree's translation of Dorotheus, which also contains a translated foreword by Dorian Greenbaum.

*Matheseos Libri VIII* by Firmicus Maternus. A classic of the astrological tradition which includes an array of practical instructions for natal astrology, which encompass interpretation, ethics, and the practice of astrology. It is among the most extensive works known from the Hellenistic era (c. 355). *Matheseos Libri VIII* by Firmicus Maternus, Noyes Press, Park Ridge, NJ, 1975. Translated by Jean Rhys Bram. Astrology Classics Publishers also reprinted a copy of this translation in 2005.

## Other Works of Interest

Abraham, Ibn-Ezra, *The Beginning of Wisdom*, Notts, Ascella Publications, 1939.
Abu Ali Al-Kayyat, *The Judgment of Nativities, T*empe, AZ, American Federation of Astrologers, 1988.
Antonius de Mutulmo, *On the Judgment of Nativities*, Berkeley Springs, WV, The Golden Hind Press, 1995.
Claudius Dariot, *Judgment of the Stars*, Notts, Ascella Publications, 1583.
Guido Bonatti, *Liber Astronomiae*, Berkeley Springs, WV, The Golden Hind Press, 1994.
Guido Bonatti, *On the Arabic Parts*, London, New Library, 2002.
Jean-Baptiste Morin, *Astrologia Gallica, T*empe, AZ, American Federation of Astrologers, 1994.
Johannes Schoener, *Oposculum Astrologicum,* Berkeley Springs, WV, The Golden Hind Press, 1994.
John Partridge, *Opus Reformatorum*, Notts, Ascella Publications, 1693.
Messahallah and Ibn Ezra, *Textos Astrólogicos Medievales*, Madrid, Editorial Barath, 1981.
Placidus de Titis, *Primum Mobile*, Institute for the Study of Cycles in World Affairs, 1983.
Vettius Valens, *Anthology*, Berkeley Springs, WV, The Golden Hind Press, 1994.

## Contemporary Works of Interest

*History of Horoscopic Astrology* by James Holden. This excellent reference book offers a deep vision into the practice of astrology throughout history. The author divides the history of astrology into various phases from the Mesopotamian period to the current times. He studies the particularities of each age and presents short biographies of its major authors and practitioners. James H. Holden, *History of Horoscopic Astrology,* Tempe AZ, American Federation of Astrologers, Inc. 1996.

*Fixed Stars and Constellations in Astrology*, by Vivian E. Robson. A valuable source of information about the fixed stars and their use in astrological interpretation. Published in 1923, this work lists most stars and their respective traditional characteristics and is to this day the major reference for this topic. The student should hold some reservations with regard to the interpretations of Simmonite, Alvidas and other modern authors, whose opinions are debatable. Vivian E. Robson, *Fixed Stars and Constellations in Astrology*, London, Ascella Publications, 2001.

*Uranus, Neptune and Pluto: an Investigation into the Sources of their Symbolism*, by Sue Ward. A notable investigation published online, where the author explores the origins and development of the symbolism attributed to the modern planets. A work that questions many of the presuppositions associated with the interpretation of these planets. Recommended to all students of astrology. Sue Ward, *Uranus, Neptune and Pluto: an Investigation into the Sources of their Symbolism, London, 2002.*

*The Real Astrology* by John Frawley. An irreverent book where the modern practice of astrology is questioned and compared with traditional approaches. John Frawley, *The Real Astrology*, London, Apprentice Books, 2001.

A special reference is made to all of the works of Robert E. Zoller, whose efforts to translate the work of Guido Bonatti and to restore the traditional system has served as the basis for much of today's work in the field.

# Chart Data

All of the charts presented and studied in this book were calculated using the Alcabitius house system, the mean lunar node, and the tropical zodiac. Only the charts in Appendix 7, Astrological Chart Calculations, use the Regiomontanus house system.

Chart 1: Nativity of Friedrich Nietsche, October 15, 1844, 10:00 AM LMT; Rocken, Germany (Lat: 51°N15', Long: 12°E08'). Source: The biography, "The Young Nietsche" according to Astrodatabank.

Chart 2: Nativity of Agatha Christie, September 15, 1890, 04:00 AM GMT; Torquay, England (Lat: 50°N28', Long: 03°W30'). Source: the native herself, according to Astrodatabank.

Chart 3: Nativity of Florbela Espanca, December 8, 1894, 02:00 AM, (Lisbon Meridian); Vila Viçosa, Portugal (Lat: 38°N47', Long: 08°W13'). Source: The biography, *Florbela Espanca*, by Agustina Bessa Luiz.

Chart 4: Nativity of Karl Marx, May 5, 1818, 02:00 AM LMT; Trier, Germany (Lat: 49°N45', Long: 06°E38'). Source: Birth Certificate, according to Astrodatabank.

Chart 5: Nativity of King Sebastian, January 20, 1554, 07:18 AM, LMT; Lisbon, Portugal (Lat: 38°N43', Long: 09°W08'). Source: coeval horoscope calculated by the court cosmographer, João Baptista Lavanha. Also corroborated by other Iberian astrologers of the time and by historical accounts of the birth.

Chart 6: Nativity of Johannes Kepler, January 6, 1572, 02:37 PM, LMT; Weill der Stadt, Germany (Lat: 48°N45', Long: 08°E52'). Source: the native, in his book *Harmonics*, *Book IV*.

Chart 7: Nativity of Edgar Allen Poe, January 19, 1809, 01:30 AM, LMT; Boston, MA, USA, (Lat: 42°N21', Long: 71°W03'). Source: approximate birth time from a biography, according to Astrodatabank.

Chart 8: Nativity of Jim Morrison, December 8, 1943, 11:55 AM, EWT (UT-4h); Melbourne, FL, USA, (Lat: 28°N04', Long: 80°W36'). Source: Birth Certificate, according to Astrodatabank.

Chart 9: Nativity of Princess Maria, June 8, 1521, 07:00 PM, LMT, Lisbon, Portugal, (Lat: 38°N43', Long: 09°W08'). Source: *Historia Geneológica da Casa Real Portuguesa e Relações de Pêro de Alcáçova Carneiro*

Chart 10: Horary Chart: "Is the Computer Motherboard Broken?", December 30, 2004, 07:14 PM, GMT, Lisbon, Portugal (Lat: 38°N43', Long: 09°W08'). Source: authors' files

Chart 11: Horary Chart: "How will the championship unfold?", September 1, 2005, 03:33 PM, GMT, Lisbon, Portugal (Lat: 38°N43', Long: 09°W08'). Source: authors' files

Chart 12: Horary Chart: "Is this house a good buy?", October 29, 2003, 01:05 PM, GMT, Lisbon, Portugal (Lat: 38°N43', Long: 09°W08'). Source: authors' files

Example 1: Nativity of a Child, November 17, 2005, 01:10 AM GMT, Lisbon, Portugal (Lat: 38°N43', Long: 09°W08'). Source: the parents